Developing Societies in a Changing World

Developing Societies in a Changing World

First Edition

Michael Skladany and Rongjun Sun

Cleveland State University

Bassim Hamadeh, CEO and Publisher
Michelle Piehl, Senior Project Editor
Christian Berk, Production Editor
Jess Estrella, Senior Graphic Designer
Stephanie Kohl, Licensing Coordinator
Natalie Piccotti, Director of Marketing
Kassie Graves, Vice President of Editorial
Jamie Giganti, Director of Academic Publishing

Printed in the United States of America.

Contents

Preface

The **Global South**, the **developing world**, and the **Third World** are all terms commonly used to describe significant parts of modern world organization. Our mass media, for example, often fails to account for these parts of the world in relation to what is referred to as the **West**, the **Global North**, or the **developed world**. To overcome this gap, our guiding theme throughout this book is to illustrate the so-called developing world in its relationship to the Western, developed world. In other words, we cannot begin to explain how our world has come to manifest its current organizational form by leaving out Western postindustrial societies and their vast influence in shaping a range of developing societies, or vice versa. Our world is a globalized one that is much more interconnected and interdependent than ever before. In this book, we take up the challenge of developing a more complete understanding of our world and the environment that shapes it.

In this book, the dynamic shape and ever-changing form of our world and environment resonates through the concept of **development**. Development is a **transformative process** that originates from collective behavior. Development is made manifest by various collective entities that act in unity or discord with each other and the environment. The nation-state, global institutions, social groups, and to a lesser degree, individuals, are all global and local actors. In keeping within the overriding context of sociology, we explore development from our disciplinary standpoint. In the broadest sense we can state that development is a "step-by-step evolutionary process, influenced by exogenous circumstances combined with endogenous unfolding. ... It is the confrontation between imperfect human beings and an imperfect world" (Heim et al. 1986, 107). We note that this process is, in practice, a nonlinear one, in which development overlaps with other human dimensions and produces cohesion, contradiction, paradoxes, and oftentimes dilemmas. Specifically, this process has unfolded, more or less, under a capitalist framework, although we note that counterefforts have appeared at historical intervals on the world stage. Above all, the title of this book refers to the dynamic, active pace of social change that influences the ever-changing shape and form of both local and global world capitalist organization. Indeed, this is a daunting task for both the authors and readers of this text. Our intentions are therefore twofold:

First, to provide a concise, readable introductory textbook on the developing world. All too often, textbooks on developing societies or globalization assume a familiarity with economics, sociology, world affairs, geography, political science, anthropology, and so on. Furthermore, concerted study of developing societies typically begins with graduate studies or at the advanced undergraduate course level. Our goal is to avoid these obstacles and hit the ground running in a manner that resonates with students' own everyday experiences. Hence, it is necessary for the student to make the necessary connections—theoretical, conceptual, and applied—with due diligence! These connections are not mysterious, mystical, or painfully abstract. These connections are ubiquitous and derive from our everyday life. For example, from what and where are your clothing, electronics, and food sourced? Who makes it? What goes into the process of getting it to you? How much do you pay and why?

Second, we augment our presentation with key concepts, theoretical frames, examples, case studies, illustrations, figures, and tables. We further emphasize that *we are all actors in both the localized and globalized world.* Locating who we are in rapidly changing societies requires foremost a spirit of adventure, a sense of inquisitiveness, a fostering of intellectual capacities, and the drive to master highly complex material. At the same time, we have made every effort to write a readable text without sacrificing intellectual integrity.

Since this book serves as an introductory text on this subject, we have structured the materials in a straightforward manner. After laying out the basic concepts and empirical findings regarding developed and developing countries in the first two chapters, we attempt to present explanations in two broad perspectives in the following four chapters. One is to explore possible contributing factors from *within* developing countries themselves, describing the challenges and constraints faced by people in those societies. This is termed by some the "South explanation" (Baker 2013), and it is introduced in chapters one and five. But our focal explanation, as suggested by the title of this book, is about developing countries' dynamic relations with developed countries in the past and present. In other words, the outcomes we observe today about the underdevelopment of developing countries are examined in historical and global contexts. This perspective is termed by some the "West explanation" (Baker 2013), and it is further discussed in chapters one, three, four, and six.

We are fully aware that the development process is very complex and the study of it is dynamic. Even the term **developing countries** has been recently called into question. But the complexity of the subject should not forbid a focused presentation of the materials nor distract attention from the big picture. To this end, we offer the following reminders to the readers:

First, we are all involved in the dynamic and ongoing concept and processes of development, regardless of our individual location and status associated with place and country of origin. The overly simplistic observation that some societies are more "developed" than others carries with it a number of central assumptions that are fundamentally flawed. It is very important therefore to avoid inherently **ethnocentric** assumptions about "us" and "them." We advise seeing our world in a more holistic, compelling, and human manner. Hence, practicing **cultural**

relativism—understanding a particular culture or situation in and on its own terms—is essential for a more full comprehension of developing societies in a changing world. In a way, the content and cases presented in this book are best approached as puzzles, narratives, or even mysteries regarding who and what we are becoming as human beings. In other words, we all have stories to tell, share, and understand.

Second, all societies are changing in untold and multifaceted ways. Our world exhibits tremendous social, economic, and environmental integration against the vast backdrop of human diversity, culture, collective action, and organizational makeup. In other words, we live in a world metaphorically characterized by multidirectional, colorful, ever-changing **mosaics**. While concepts such as the Third World or the Global North/South provide us with rudimentary organizational frameworks, we will explore the overlapping reach of these concepts, where we encounter and engage with seemingly contradictory phenomena. For example, why does a so-called "developing country" exhibit great levels of social stratification, poverty, and inequality? Conversely, why does a "developed country" exhibit wealth, inequality, poverty, and conflict? Finally, we cannot forget the local in looking only at the global. Both places intersect and reveal a more compelling and nuanced reading of the dynamics of human development—past, present, and into the future.

ORGANIZATION OF THE BOOK

The book consists of nine chapters that are grouped as follows. Chapters one and two examine the concept of development. In **Chapter 1**, we first frame and then define what constitutes official forms of modern development by tracing its Cold War origins and then comparing differences between developed and developing countries. We then define three different economic sectors that characterize the organization of developed and developing economies. We illustrate where developing countries are located. Finally, we introduce two perspectives, that of the Global North and the Global South, to shed some light on the underdevelopment of developing countries. **Chapter 2** builds on the guiding concept of development in terms of quantitative measurements by multilateral agencies and governments. Our focus on the measurement of development pertains to quantified economic output and outcomes. We further introduce the United Nations (UN)–sponsored Human Development Index and assess the UN's progress toward their Millennium Development Goals over the period of 2000–2015. We then discuss the turn toward sustainable development (2016–2030). Finally, we conclude with some criticisms of these measures and introduce the more subjective concept of Gross Human Happiness.

Chapters 3 to 6 provide a chronological sequence of capitalist world development. We intend to build a chronological history behind the concepts, figures, and measures discussed in chapters 1 and 2. In **Chapter 3**, we examine how the origin of capitalism was the engine that drove European powers to seek out resources and slave labor in Asia, Africa, and Latin America. We begin by reexamining national holidays; upon critical reflection, we surmise that these holidays are much more than merely festive celebrations. The origin of national holidays can be traced to colonial times, and they consistently display a distinct set of power relations. We then identify four critically important changes that led to the establishment of capitalism: the transformation of common property into private property, the concept of surplus labor value, and the capitalist mode of production. The result of these changes, the fourth change in human economic organization created a society and world that requires perpetual economic growth. We then examine two case studies from the US colonial era involving relations with Indigenous Peoples and early colonialists. Another important feature during the colonial era was the development of the plantation model of development. We trace the origin of the plantation up to the present, notably in the Caribbean and parts of South America. The need for perpetual economic growth led to the colonialization of Africa and how the attendant emergence of the slave trade was critically important for wealth accumulation in Europe and North America conclude the chapter.

Chapter 4 examines the postcolonial era. The postcolonial era (1945–1990) witnessed widespread decolonialization in Asia, Africa, and Latin America. The result was the establishment of over 100 nation-states, a conflict-prone ideological divide called the Cold War, and the creation of global institutions. With the overthrow and withdrawal of former colonial powers, over 100 new nation-states embarked on plans to modernize their economies and institutions. We first examine global governance through creation of multilateral agencies such as the UN, the World Bank, the International Monetary Fund, and the World Trade Organization. Second, we define the social contract, the authority, and the distribution of power that compose the foundation of the modern nation-state. We then present two mixed economic development strategies commonly adopted by the new nation-states: import substitution and light manufacturing by invitation. These strategies resulted in a global shift of industrial production to select developing countries, the rise of transnational corporations, and the growth of world cities in developing countries. We use Thailand as a case study of state-sanctioned rural development, which occurred beginning in the 1970s and peaked in the late 1980s. The tracing and eventual dominance of neoliberalism closely parallel efforts to promote earlier state-generated economic growth. In assessing the broad outcome of the postcolonial era, we can see that building modern nation-states and economies produced mixed results and in many instances produced developmental paradoxes and dilemmas. Lastly, we will illustrate a common outcome of postcolonial development, the middle-income trap.

Chapter 5 concerns the modernization project and complements and runs parallel to chapter 4. Modernity is a multidimensional concept. On one hand, modernity entails comprehensive macroeconomic processes that are transformative in terms of a society's economy, technology use, and cultural practices. On the other hand, modernity also operates on a micro level that includes and alters community, family, and individual outlooks and life orientation. The effect of both processes—modernization—becomes simultaneously manifest in *both* macro and micro settings. Understanding modernity requires a grasp of both dimensions, the aggregate macro level of the nation-state or region and micro-level impacts on the community, family, and even individual. In this chapter, we begin by introducing the concept of modernity, followed by modernization theory. Second, we will examine major obstacles to modernization faced by developing countries. These obstacles include shortcomings in terms of physical, human, and social capital. We further examine the prevalence of corruption as an obstacle to modernization. Finally, we turn to two examples in which these conditions deteriorated into genocide by examining the cases of Cambodia and Rwanda.

Chapter 6, introduces the concept of globalization, its history, and how it became deeply entrenched in our everyday lives. We briefly review what makes globalization possible politically, technologically, and economically, shedding light on why globalization has become so powerful. We discuss the far-reaching impacts globalization has had in both positive and negative terms. The chapter features references to the impacts of globalization on a number of countries. We then call attention to multipolar globalization, a new and recent restructuring of the global economic order. Examples derived from China, with reference to the "One Belt One Road" initiative, and increased development involvement in Africa provide evidence that a reshuffling of the economic order and a new and more volatile organization of the world is imminent. In conclusion, we discuss the rise of global inequality, one of the world's most pressing social problems.

Chapter 7 presents the general gap between the developing and developed world in population, not only in size but in growth potential and age structure as well. These different population profiles underscore different challenges faced by societies in the demand for social services, including public education, health care, labor force, and employment opportunities. We provide a brief description of the world population, its geographic distribution, history, major transitions, and the prospect for growth in the future. Meanwhile, we will introduce some basic concepts in demographic studies. We then illustrate the complexity of the relationship between developing and developed countries and highlight the paradoxical coexistence of both a divide and convergence in the global demographic process.

Chapter 8 focuses on the environment and culture against a backdrop of global capitalist development. The environment, or the **biosphere** (the sum total of all life-sustaining ecosystems), provides humans with their sustenance. Our interaction with and outlook on the environment is greatly influenced by our **culture**—our worldview consisting of our values and beliefs and the material objects that comprise the substance of our lives. Western capitalism is driven by an outlook that views the environment as a commodity that we express **dominion** over, the idea that nature was put here for our use. In Western capitalism, there is a sharp division between nature and society. Not all cultural groups hold this view of dominion over the natural world, but strong similarities prevail within those regions of the world that embody a capitalist framework.

This chapter examines the relationship between the environment and the culture of capitalism. All too often the environment is seen and experienced as an abstract, distant realm removed from our everyday lives. We start with the reader assessing their own **ecological footprint**—an estimated total of the resources used to sustain one's current lifestyle. Through our consumptive activities, such as our daily transportation, housing, food, and the services we make use of, we can see that we do in fact utilize more than the Earth can sustainably produce to support our lifestyles. In the first section, we provide a simple link that calculates the number of Earths required to support us. Second, we draw attention to what may be the most critical environmental issue of the twenty-first century—**climate change**. Climate change also overlaps across a wide array of other global social and economic issues (Klein 2014). These issues include but are not limited to trade relations, (multipolar) globalization, development, migration, agriculture, the environmental movement, and the well-being of countless communities.

Finally, we examine **commodity chains**, the processes by which the natural world is transformed into the material objects that make up our everyday lives and, in part, our capitalist culture. We use three commodity chain examples to illustrate their complexity and how understanding the links between a commodity's production and consumption allows us to envision a way to better manage the destructive impacts our seemingly innocent lifestyles have on our environment. We start by examining our local and global food systems, using the examples of beef (meat consumption), salmon, and shrimp (seafood consumption). Understanding of our food system is an area that is not well known to consumers. We then look at electronics, with an emphasis on cell phones and other electronic commodity chains. Finally, we conclude by acknowledging the changes that seem to be on the horizon in terms of our relation to the environment and culture.

Chapter 9 addresses global social change. We begin by revisiting the concept of development and present an alternative definition of development. With major development agencies dropping the terms *developing* and *developed* to categorize countries, we raise the question of whether or not we have entered a "postdevelopment" world. We then turn to a review of social movements and their systemic and antisystemic origins. Three major global arenas are then identified as the loci of major global social change: sustainability, gender inequality, and the middle classes. Examples derived from the Climate Justice Movement, Women's Movement, and the importance and relevance of the middle classes in terms of social change illustrate the three arenas.

We conclude this book on a personal note to the reader regarding the citizen-activist and the development worker.

REFERENCES

Baker, Andy. *Shaping the Developing World: The West, the South, and the Natural World.* Washington, DC: Sage Publishing, 2013.

Heim, Franz G., Bantorn Ondam, Jitti Mongolnchaiarunya, and Akin Rabibhadana. *How to Develop the Small Farming Sector.* Bangkok: Thammasat University, 1986.

Klein, Naomi. *This Changes Everything: Capitalism vs. the Climate.* New York: Simon & Schuster, 2014.

CHAPTER ONE

Development and the Developing World

INTRODUCTION

The multifaceted concept of development guides this book. We first define what constitutes development, beginning with its Cold War origins. We then chart development's evolution beginning from the Cold War era up to the Globalization/Neoliberal period. We draw attention to the differences between developed and developing countries, and we examine three different economic sectors to characterize the economic organization of developed and developing economies. A map illustrates where developing countries are located. Finally, we introduce two perspectives that broadly account for underdevelopment and then envision the future of development.

OVERVIEW AND FRAMING OF THE CONCEPT OF DEVELOPMENT

Development is a **transformative process.** The Cambridge English Dictionary defines development as "the process in which someone or something grows or changes and becomes more advanced" (Cambridge English Dictionary 2019). Development encompasses a broad number of changes under way in a society. These changes occur over time in the economic, social, political, and cultural spheres. In a fundamental sense, development refers to a progression from basic to more complex and modern levels of productivity and efficiency. This progression is initiated by functioning social organizations and institutions. The intended result of development is human betterment, made variously manifest by economic growth, material abundance, and expanding human freedoms, among a multitude of other salient measures, as illustrated in chapter 2. To planners and policy makers, for example, earlier forms of development were primarily about how developing countries transitioned from agrarian to modern industrial societies, using the Western experience as a guide and model. For governments and aid agencies, development is about adopting a capitalist economy, building markets, engaging in export-oriented free trade, establishing and enforcing laws that protect private property and enterprises, and embracing values such as freedom, competition, and creativity. Over time, the meaning of *human development* has changed from a narrow focus on economic growth to a broader tapping into full human potential.

In this book we define development as "the organized intervention in collective affairs according to a standard of improvement" (Pieterse 2010, 3). Development as an intervention can be framed by four interrelated dimensions: theory, policy, organization, and application. Figure 1.1 below visualizes these interrelated dimensions:

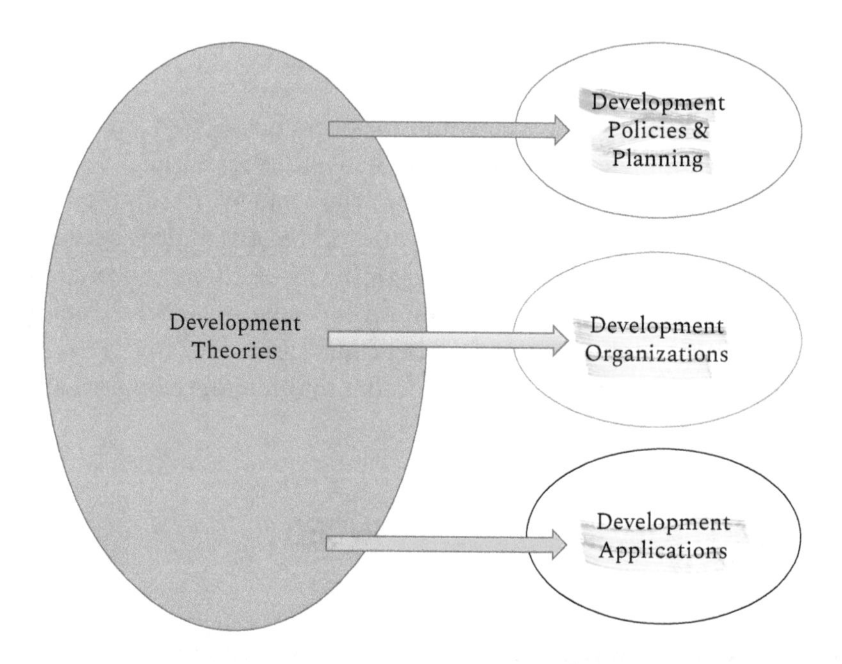

FIGURE 1.1 Interrelated Dimensions of Development (adapted from Pieterse).

Development theory refers to formal knowledge that focuses on why, how, what, and where development occurs. Development theory and knowledge borrows from other social science disciplines, primarily economics, history, sociology, anthropology, geography, and political science, and builds upon past theories, reflections, data, and observations in an abstract sense. Development knowledge emerges in an evolutionary manner. In other words, development theories are never totally discarded but grow from previous positions conditioned by specific historical, economic, social, cultural, and even religious contexts. Pieterse observes that development theory arose as a "reaction to the crises of progress" (1). Early development thinkers, such as the political economists David Ricardo, Thomas Malthus, Adam Smith, and Karl Marx, theorized on the disruptions and dislocation brought on by industrialization that initially began in Europe. These thinkers developed grand theories about how to explain and correct social and economic problems, thereby illuminating a pathway for improving society.

Development policies and planning refers to the institutional dimensions of development whereby specialists implement theory in an applied fashion. Policy, a determined course of action, and its attendant plans carry with them a worldview or **ideology** about what constitutes an improved society. In large measure, the goal of policy and planning is to **modernize society**. Over time, what it means to be modern has greatly changed, to include more pluralism and cultural adaptation to **modernities**. In contrast, earlier forms of development were largely imitative of the Western industrial model.

Closely intertwined with policy formulation and planning stages are **development organizations.** Over the past 70 years, the major development organization has largely been the nation-state. Other major development actors have been multilateral agencies such as the United Nations (UN), the World Bank, the International Monetary Fund (IMF), the World Trade Organization (WTO), and more recently, nongovernment organizations (NGOs), the private sector, and even local communities. As a result, there are numerous organizational actors in the field of development. It is notable to mention that Western institutional domination of the development field is becoming dislodged due to institutional growth occurring in developing regions of the world. The BRICS countries (Brazil, Russia, India, China, and South Africa), for example, now initiate development in other countries in accord with their own development objectives. As a result, the field of development is highly diverse and in great flux.

Finally, we call attention to **development applications,** which refers to projects, programs, and any activity intervening into collective affairs that seeks to improve human well-being and society at large. Building infrastructure, applying science and technology to industry, building up agriculture and fisheries, organizing farmers into cooperatives, instituting small-scale credit schemes for artisanal women's groups, introducing modern education, and providing science-based health care are just a few examples of the areas where development applications unfold. In each instance, the responsible development organization envisions an improvement over a previous condition or standard. As we see in chapter 4, as rural poverty in Thailand was considered a social and political problem, a range of Thai nation-state agencies attempted to alleviate this condition through poverty eradication programs and projects. In a sense, then, development applications are intended to bring about improvements that correspond with the standards and benefits of a modern society. It is important to note that these developmental applications do not unfold in a strict linear fashion but are historically influenced by economic, political, social, and cultural conditions and contexts at a given time.

AN EVOLUTIONARY OUTLINE OF SOME MAJOR DEVELOPMENT THEORIES

The modern form of development, or the **age of developmentalism**, begins in the aftermath of the Second World War (McMichael 2012). Europe was devastated, Asia was suffering from near-famine, and the United States ascended as a major international power. At his inauguration on January 20, 1949, President Harry S. Truman outlined a vision for the world that would take shape and become known as the modern form of development.

> The American people desire, and are determined to work for, a world in which all nations and all peoples are free to govern themselves as they see fit, and to achieve a decent and satisfying life. … In the pursuit of these aims, the United States and other like-minded nations find themselves directly opposed by a regime with contrary aims and a totally different concept of life.
>
> That regime adheres to a false philosophy which purports to offer freedom, security, and greater opportunity to mankind. … That false philosophy is communism. (Truman 1949).

Truman then proceeds to condemn communism due to its suspension of individual rights and propensity for oppression, totalitarianism, and war. Later in the inaugural address, Truman outlines a program ushering in the age of modern development:

> More than half the people of the world are living in conditions approaching misery. Their food is inadequate. They are victims of disease. Their economic life is primitive and stagnant. Their poverty is a handicap and a threat both to them and to more prosperous areas. … The United States is pre-eminent among nations in the development of industrial and scientific techniques. … I believe that we should make available to peace-loving peoples the benefits of our store of technical knowledge in order to help them realize their aspirations for a better life. And, in cooperation with other nations, we should foster capital investment in areas needing development.
>
> Our aim should be to help the free peoples of the world, through their own efforts, to produce more food, more clothing, more materials for housing, and more mechanical power to lighten their burdens. (Truman).

At the end of the Second World War, Truman envisioned a crisis in world betterment, stability, and peaceful order. He further implies world organization in the context of the **Cold War,** a global theater that pitted the **First World** capitalist countries, such as the United States and a rebuilding Western Europe, against the **Second World** communist countries, led by the Soviet Union and, later, China. In between these two dominant worlds were the poor and newly independent nations of the postcolonial era, the **Third World**. Both the First World and the Second World competed for influence in the developing regions of Asia, Africa, and Latin America. The United States and her allies were determined to prevent communism from spreading to the developing parts of the world, hence the *necessity* for modern development.

Modern development theories and applications take an evolutionary form of expression that builds upon previous efforts. Figure 1.2 below illustrates this evolutionary progression, noting the expanding emphasis on human development rather than the earlier focus on economic growth:

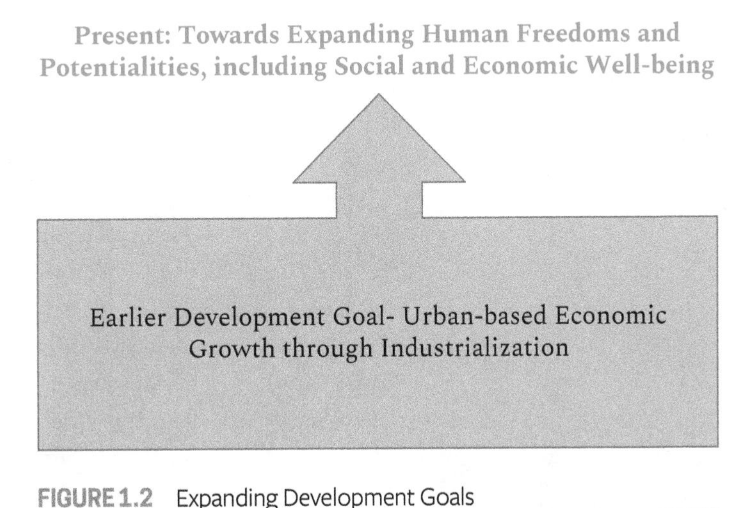

FIGURE 1.2 Expanding Development Goals

Modern development has taken a number of evolutionary forms: **modernization**, **dependency**, **alternative development**, **globalization/neoliberalism**, and more recently, **sustainable development**. These forms of development are presented in Table 1.1 below.

Modernization theory lies at the heart of President Truman's inauguration speech. Initially, the major means of establishing modernization was through **economic development.** Up to the present and despite significant variation, economic development remains the dominant form of development. **Economic development** refers to the stimulation of economic and social growth and is measured by the gross domestic product (GDP), the standard of living, and the ability of a country to build and maintain physical infrastructure. **GDP** is the monetary value of all finished goods and commodities produced annually within a country. GDP includes private and public

TABLE 1.1 *Forms of Modern Development*

DEVELOPMENT CATEGORY	PERIOD	MAIN ACTORS	COMMENTS
Modernization	1950s ->	Nation-States; Multilateral Agencies	Economic growth through urban-based industrialization - imitates the Western experience discussed in chapter 5
Dependency	1950s ->	Nation-States	Response to modernization core-periphery relations - development and underdevelopment as different sides of the same coin discussed in chapter 3
Alternative Development	1980s ->	NGOs	Self-reliance - focus on basic human needs and the poor - small-scale applications; features endogenous over exogenous change discussed in chapter 9
Neoliberalism/Globalization	1990 ->	Multilateral Agencies; Private Sector; Nation-States	Time/space compression - rise of transnational corporations (TNCs) - state withdrawal from economic management and deregulation - market solutions for economic, social and political problems discussed in chapters 4 and 6
Sustainable Development	2016 ->	Multilateral Agencies; NGOs; Nation-States	The new UN development agenda (2016–2030) - development that meets the needs of the current generation without compromising the needs of future generations to meet their own needs - considers climate change, renewable energy and resource limitations - integrates environmental protection and economic growth; discussed in chapter 9

Source: Adapted from Pieterse (2010), Potter et al. (2018)

consumption of goods. Examined in chapter 2, **standard of living** is an aggregate measure that entails income per person, life expectancy, education, health, poverty rate, and access to goods and services. The standard of living equates with quality of life. Lastly, infrastructure constitutes the basic physical and organizational structures and facilities, such as schools, hospitals, roads, and power lines, needed for the operation of a society or enterprise.

Closely related to economic development is **interventionist development** or **project-based development.** Interventionist development is a focused and directed process by which government agencies organize and implement projects and programs to help develop the underdeveloped. Interventionist development is a top-down form of development, because those with authority, power, or expertise tend to be the initiators. A more detailed examination of modernization and its economic emphasis on growth is given in chapter 5.

Modernization, with its emphasis on linear economic growth modeled on the Western experience, produced unsatisfactory results (Pieterse 2010). A rebuke to this method, inspired by the writings of Karl Marx, came to be known as **dependency theory**, which originated in Latin America and then spread throughout the Third World. Dependency proponents argued that modernization and imitating Western economic development fundamentally resulted in unequal relations between **core** capitalist countries (such as the United States and Western Europe) and **peripheral** ones (the Third World during the Cold War). Unequal exchange, going back to the colonial era, perpetrated widespread poverty and inequality. The relationship between the core and periphery was an uneven and highly exploitative one. In essence, **social surplus**, the net production over and beyond subsistence consumption needs, generated great wealth in the core countries and left isolated pockets of conspicuous consumption in largely urban areas in the peripheral countries. In rural peripheral regions of the Global South, extreme poverty was a ubiquitous condition of everyday life (Potter et al. 2018, 119). In other words, development and underdevelopment are opposite faces of the same coin. One condition (development) reinforces the other (underdevelopment), and vice versa. Dependency theorists and practitioners advocated a way out by erecting trade barriers (**protectionism**) and reigning in footloose transnational corporations (TNCs), along with promoting regional trade relations and stimulating local production and development (ibid.). Chapter 3 provides a case study of colonial Africa that illustrates dependency theory.

Both modernization and dependency theory are only partial, because both fall back on **economic determinism** to explain and formulate development. Both were top-down approaches, initiated by nation-state or international agencies. Beneficiaries of these efforts were simply passive recipients. Potter et al. go so far as to state that by the late 1970s, top-down development thinking reached a recognizable impasse. Persistent poverty and a host of social and economic problems remained in the wake of earlier top-down development efforts. **Alternative Development** was the response and emphasized a bottom-up, **endogenous**, rather than **exogenously** imposed, development scheme, thinking, and application. Unlike with top-down approaches, the beneficiaries of development became active participants in the process. NGOs were instrumental in partnering with local communities by addressing basic human needs and fostering self-reliance on the part of development participants. Local contexts that included environmental concerns, gender inequality, poverty alleviation, and sustainable livelihoods were at the forefront of alternative development applications (Potter et al.). In sum, grassroots development and indigenous knowledge lie at the core of alternative development. As put by Potter et al.:

> Communities, often in the rural areas in the [Global] South, frequently rely on their indigenous technical knowledge, particularly with respect to issues such as land management, farming and resource use. Such approaches often have lower levels of environmental impacts and are more sustainable than [exogenous] introduced methods of farming and resource use. (127)

The 1980s witnessed rapid NGO formation and initiatives, both on an international and local level. Chapter 9 provides a more detailed exposition of alternative development.

Globalization and the **Neoliberal Turn** can be traced back to earlier global relations. Throughout the colonial and the postcolonial eras, international trade occurred between countries in Europe and Asia. Contemporary globalization, however, exhibits distinct features that set this development formation apart from previous historical antecedents. As Potter et al. comment, contemporary globalization brings forth three components that were less prominent in earlier eras: (1) **time-space convergence**, (2) the rise of **transnational corporations**, and (3) **consumption convergence**, coupled with **production divergence**. Beginning in the 1990s, the intensification of economic, social, cultural, and political relations have become inextricably bound up with each other in relatively consequential ways. As a result, time and space have become condensed as global communications and transport immediately bring together diverse populations who previously did not interact with each other. Twenty-four-hour news cycles, the internet, and new electronic technologies have given rise to both time and space becoming much more concentrated, with the result that North America, for example, is much closer in a relative sense to East Asia. Other regions, such as Sub-Saharan Africa, have become more distant to North America in a relative sense. Likewise, as chapter 6 demonstrates, international economic relations between different regions of the world are more tied together, with downturns in one region affecting other distant regions, for example.

Another key component of contemporary globalization has been the removal of trade barriers and the global spread of TNCs into regions of the world that offer favorable incentives for foreign investment, cheap labor, modern infrastructure, and a relatively docile (read: nonunionized) labor force of semi-skilled workers. In other words, production sites have diverged by **outsourcing** and **offshoring** to key locations throughout the world. As manufacturing jobs left the established Northern industrial parts of the world, a select number of mainly East Asian countries were able to develop what Pieterse (2010) refers to as "sustainable industry," which has stimulated rapid economic growth and rises in the standard of living in these select regions of the world. TNCs have become dominant developmental actors in this phase of contemporary globalization as Northern economies have stagnated and become much more service-oriented in their overall economic profile and activities. A major consequence of this global shift has been the rise of new "mega cities" in the Global South, with global consumption now converging around middle-class preferences and tastes in terms of automobiles, housing, clothing, food, and other commodities.

The development ideology at the core of contemporary globalization, briefly outlined in the above section, is traceable to **neoliberalism**, the driving force behind world development from the 1980s up to the present. Neoliberalism, like globalization, has older antecedents that can be traced back to English political economist Adam Smith's 1776 *Wealth of Nations.* Smith advocated free markets unhindered by governmental regulation. In contrast, John Maynard Keynes argued that government should play a role in economic management due to drastic unemployment during the Great Depression of the 1930s. This view was later eschewed by the rise of neoliberals, who espoused the utopian promise of the free market and withdrawal of government in economic management. The ascent of neoliberalism came to the forefront and was crystallized by the elections of Margaret Thatcher and Ronald Reagan in Great Britain and the United States, respectively, in the 1980s. Coupled with the dismantling of the "welfare state" in Great Britain and the United States and the adoption of neoliberalism by multilateral aid agencies such as the World Bank, the WTO, and the IMF (**The Washington Consensus**), the promotion of free markets and deregulation spurred a number of far-reaching changes in the world development field in the 1990s. Neoliberalism clearly emerged as the new dominant development model. Neoliberalism has also been called **neomodernization** and further draws from earlier modernization theory.

In sum, neoliberalism established the primacy of the unencumbered market to produce developmental gains and advancement. Neoliberal advocates argued that governmental interference in markets gave rise to inefficient allocation of resources and dampened economic growth. Governments deregulated economic activities that spurred the privatization of services that once fell under governmental domain. This movement occurred in a number of formerly government-managed economic sectors, such as education, health care, energy, labor, and communications. The entrepreneurial private sector and TNCs greatly benefited. In chapter

8, an interesting market-based solution to climate change is discussed in some detail. Coupled with contemporary globalization, the neoliberal development era stimulated unprecedented movement of people, unrestricted free trade, and the bypassing of significant portions of the world, leading to political, economic, and human crises. In short, cracks have appeared in the neoliberal position. When markets do in fact fail, ironically, government is called upon to rectify the situation, as evidenced by the bailout in the United States of Wall Street, automakers, and banks in response to the 2007 fiscal crisis that led to a major global economic recession, particularly in the Global North, where economic growth remains slow. Major scandals, military conflicts, and social unrest were common during this recent era (Pieterse 2010). Chapters 4 and 6 further examine neoliberalism and globalization in greater depth.

The recent Globalization/Neoliberalism model has run into a number of intractable problems caused by what Pieterse refers to as excessive deregulation of economic activities. Unregulated economic development led to problems known as **externalities**. An externality is a cost of production that is not internalized in the production process. In other words the cost is simply passed on to wider society. A good example would be air and water pollution. Who pays for it? Does the producer pay for air and water pollution? Typically society bears the costs of pollution that are passed on to it by the polluter. This failure to internalize externalities is at an unprecedented global crisis level in the case of climate change, covered in chapters 8 and 9. As a result, development thinking has shifted to sustainable development to address this pending calamity.

Sustainable Development, then, is a development idea that has arrived. The seeds of this form of development are traceable to the environmental movement of the 1960s, alternative development in the 1980s, and ubiquitous land, water, and air pollution problems that go hand and hand with modern development. **Sustainable development** is defined as development that meets the needs of current generations without compromising the ability of future generations to meet their needs and aspirations. Sustainable development attempts to balance economic development with environmental protection. There is, however, a notable tradeoff between economic development and protecting the environment. Since both of these variables cannot be maximized at the same time, some entities may practice **greenwashing**—giving lip service and making ineffectual gestures that do little to ensure a clean and sustainable environment.

The observant reader will further notice that in this review of development theories, the environment is given little attention outside of the alternative development model. The result is that we have exceeded our biocapacity to sustain ourselves, producing a **development paradox**, which is defined as "the universalization of U.S.-style high mass consumption economy [that] would require several planet Earths" (McMichael 2012, 11). In global terms, we consume 1.5 Earths, over 50 percent of the earth's capacity to support us. Clearly this pattern is not sustainable, and chapter 8 allows the reader to calculate the number of earths required to sustain their current lifestyle. Moreover, attention to the relationship between environmental quality and poverty demonstrates that they are closely intertwined with each other. This inverse relationship shows that the world's poor are impacted more negatively by environmental degradation than the world's wealthy population. In sum, the sustainability turn in development thinking has arrived with one of the most ambitious agendas in the history of development.

In 2015, the UN announced 17 sustainable development goals that will strongly influence the trajectory of world development for the period of 2016–2030. (United Nations 2015) These goals link sustainable human needs to environmental integrity at all levels of society and apply to both the Global North and Global South. The cost of this program is estimated to be two to three trillion USD annually, a sum that may be difficult to generate due to reluctance on the part of wealthier nations and an overall lack of political will to do so (Potter et al. 2018, 34). Early evidence shows this to be the case for mitigating climate change. Chapters 2, 8, and 9 further detail these sustainable development initiatives.

A CONCISE OVERVIEW OF THE DEVELOPING WORLD

In sum, developing countries are generally defined in reference to **developed countries.** Developed countries have completed the industrial process, resulting in high economic output and make use of advanced technology. They have political and social institutions that are relatively stable and accountable. Citizens enjoy relatively high living standards and well-protected basic human rights. **Developing countries**, in contrast, show shortcomings in one or more of these areas. They are at the beginning or at an incomplete stage of industrialization, with low economic output, and make use of relatively simple technology. Developing countries often exhibit less stable political and social institutions, where citizens more or less suffer from low living standards and inadequate human rights. In short, while developed countries are synonymous with rich countries, developing countries refer to poor countries that have difficulty in meeting the basic needs of their citizens. Although they are considered underdeveloped, this does not mean that these countries have not developed at all. All societies are a product of hundreds or even thousands of years of history, be it through geographic or demographic expansion, migration, or wars. The reason for developing countries to be viewed as underdeveloped is that, in comparison to the industrialized, developed countries, they are quantitatively behind in industrialization, productivity, mass consumption, and an array of living standard indicators.

The Third World

In the modern era of development, the term **developing countries** was closely related to another term, the **Third World**. This term was coined by French scholar Alfred Sauvy in 1952 in a published article, "Three Worlds, One Planet," in *The Observer* (*L'Observateur*), a community newspaper (Solarz 2012). While no longer in current use, originally the term **Third World** referred to countries that gained independence from colonial rule after the Second World War. The Third World was distinct from the **First World**, the Western nations led by the United States, and the **Second World**, the Eastern Bloc led by the former Soviet Union. There was a clear divide between the two dominant camps in their ideologies and economic systems. Whereas the First World embraced capitalism and liberal democracy and was driven by the market economy, the Second World embraced communism and adopted centrally planned economies. The historical period in which these two Worlds competed for prominence (1945–1989) is often labeled as the **Cold War.**

Third World countries, newly independent from colonial rule, aspired to become a third force or block of nations that would have an independent voice on the world stage. They sought to distinguish themselves from both dominant world blocs to claim significance, importance, and equality. They did not want to join either Moscow or Washington. The nonalignment movement, initiated by these countries, underscored such political aspirations. The Afro-Asian Conference in Bandung, Indonesia, in 1955 marked a milestone of the movement, where 29 countries from Africa and Asia participated. In the declaration of the conference, all forms of colonialism or external interventions were condemned, while some colonies were still struggling to win independence, and cooperation among nations was promoted.

According to Regis Debray, however, a contemporary French Philosopher, the solidarity among Third World countries is from outside rather than from within (Debray 1977). They face the same political opponent (imperialism) and the same economic exploiter (the industrialized West). Other than that, there is not much commonality underlying the unity. As a matter of fact, this diverse set of countries varied in historical experience, cultural heritage, economic patterns, and political and religious forms. What made them identify with each other was their common colonial history and its legacy—underdevelopment in economic and social affairs. Gradually, the original political connotation of the term **Third World** has faded, giving way to socioeconomic measures becoming synonymous with the term adopted in this book, **developing countries**.

There are a few other world organizational terms used almost interchangeably with **developing countries** in academia and mass media. These terms include **less developed countries, underdeveloped countries** as opposed to **developed countries**, and the **Global South** as opposed to the **Global North**. Each term has its validity and drawbacks. Critics argue that the term **less developed** or **underdeveloped countries** implies **eurocentric** imposed inferiority status upon certain countries in comparison to developed country standards. Less developed or underdeveloped status assumes only one linear developmental model to follow, the one taken by Western developed countries. More recently, the term Global South reflects the fact that most of the developing countries are geographically located in the southern hemisphere of the planet relative to the developed countries, such as South versus North America, Africa versus Europe, and Asia versus Russia. But Australia and New Zealand are exceptions to this divide. Both are in the category of developed countries and located south of the equator. The term developing countries, meanwhile, may leave a false impression that all these countries are undergoing progress or developing, which is not the case. The progress in some developing countries has been stagnant, and in some cases, the situation may even worsen due to conflict, war, disease epidemics, natural disasters, or other events. In this book, we adopt the term **developing countries**, because by various quantitative measures, the majority of these countries exhibit partial socio-economic development. These terms and measures are brought out in chapter 2.

Diversity Among the Developing Countries

Some scholars reject the term **developing countries** and other interchangeable variants on the grounds that they are too general to take into account the great diversity among these countries. When more than 150 countries are lumped together in one category, it inevitably masks huge differences in culture, historical heritage, religion, lifestyle, and development circumstance. Oil-exporting Arab countries in the Middle East are certainly different from many countries in South Asia, where agriculture is the primary production sector. How much, for example, do Brazil and Malawi have in common? The former is a newly industrialized powerhouse in South America by the Atlantic Ocean. It has well-developed agricultural, mining, manufacturing, and service sectors, with an average annual income equal to the world average of more than $15,000. More than 80 percent of its population lives in cities. The latter is landlocked in Eastern Africa, one of the world's poorest, with an average annual income of $250. Its economy is predominantly agricultural, with about 80 percent of the population living in rural areas. Yet both of these are considered developing countries. To partly overcome this overgeneralization, we have created some subcategories to draw further distinctions.

One subcategory of developing countries is **Newly Industrialized Countries (NICs)**, which are in transition from agricultural to industrial economies. NICs actively participate in global export trade and have achieved relatively higher economic growth by world standards. China, India, Indonesia, Malaysia, the Philippines, Thailand, and Turkey in Asia; Brazil and Mexico in South America; and South Africa in Africa are all examples of NICs. These countries have a relatively dynamic economy with millions joining the rank of the middle class, exhibiting a lifestyle similar to their counterparts in developed countries. The emergence of these nations is a major contributing factor to the overall reduction in world poverty. While some also put

Argentina, Chile, South Korea, and Singapore on the list, others view South Korea and Singapore as developed countries.

Overall, some developing countries are being left behind, where the economy is either stagnant or even going backwards. The UN classifies 48 countries as the **Least Developed Countries (LDCs)**. These countries are the most economically vulnerable, have the lowest average income, and fare the poorest in an array of socioeconomic indicators. The citizens of LDCs face great challenges in meeting basic needs. Of the 48 LDCs, 33 of them are in Africa, such as Ethiopia, Mali, Niger, and Somalia; 14 are in Asia, such as Afghanistan, Bangladesh, Nepal, and Yemen; and one is in the Caribbean, Haiti (United Nations 2012). In these countries, significant portions of the population continue to struggle with meeting basic human needs and represent a group that lies at the core of the UN sustainable development initiative, which aims to end poverty and hunger, for example, along with provide access to improved services, environments, and livelihoods, thereby expanding upon human potential.

Economic Sectors

In a fundamental sense, a nation's economic development level can be gauged by the composition of economic sectors. There are four major sectors, which are categorized on the basis of their economic organization and direct involvement with natural resources. The **primary sector** of the economy concerns itself with production and extraction of raw materials from the earth, including agriculture, forestry, fishing, and mining, along with production of food, wood, coal, and iron. The **secondary sector** involves the processing or transformation of raw materials into finished goods. All manufacturing and construction activities are in this sector, including steel, auto, clothing, and energy production; chemical and material manufacturing; and construction of housing and ships. The **tertiary sector** is the service industry, which supplies services or support to the general population and business. It is a mixed-bag of a large variety of economic activities, spanning vastly in terms of both intellectual sophistication entailed and level of compensation. Retail, entertainment, transportation, restaurant work, banking, health care, education, and government administration are all in this category. A further distinction entails a difference in intellectual complexity. The **quaternary sector** refers to those knowledge-based activities that occur in the fields of culture, health, education, and research, among others.

Developed countries, which have completed industrialization, are distinguished by postindustrial economies, where the tertiary sector provides high value-added services and products. The share of the economy from the primary and secondary sectors is rather small. For example, in the United States, the tertiary or service sector contributes about 80 percent to the US economy, including health care, retailing, business services, and education. The secondary sector, composed of manufacturing and construction, contributes about 12 percent, while only 2 percent is from the primary sector, including agriculture, forestry, fishing, hunting, and mining.

In contrast, since developing countries, to a varying degree, are only in the process of industrialization, the primary and secondary sectors tend to be a lot bigger. The secondary sector, manufacturing in particular, has been dominant in China's economy. It remained the biggest sector until 2013, when it was surpassed by the tertiary sector for the first time, and both contributed 45 percent to the national economy, whereas the primary sector contributed 10 percent, which is a lot higher than that of the US. At the same time, more than a quarter of the national GDP of Ghana, a country in western Africa, was from the primary sector. An examination of the economic sectors of a given country allows us to illuminate a general development profile in comparison with other countries.

Where Are the Developing Countries?

In practice, the distinction between developed and developing countries is not clear-cut, as the classification of countries into these two categories follows convention. We adopt the convention implemented by the UN Statistics Division, which designates all 40 European countries as developed countries, plus the United States and Canada in North America, Australia and New Zealand in Oceania, and Japan in Asia. The rest of the world belongs to developing countries. Following this convention, Figure 1.3 shows a world map of how developing countries are geographically distributed. It is clear that developing countries are mainly in Asia, Africa, and Latin America. Of the 210 sovereign countries, 160 are developing countries, or

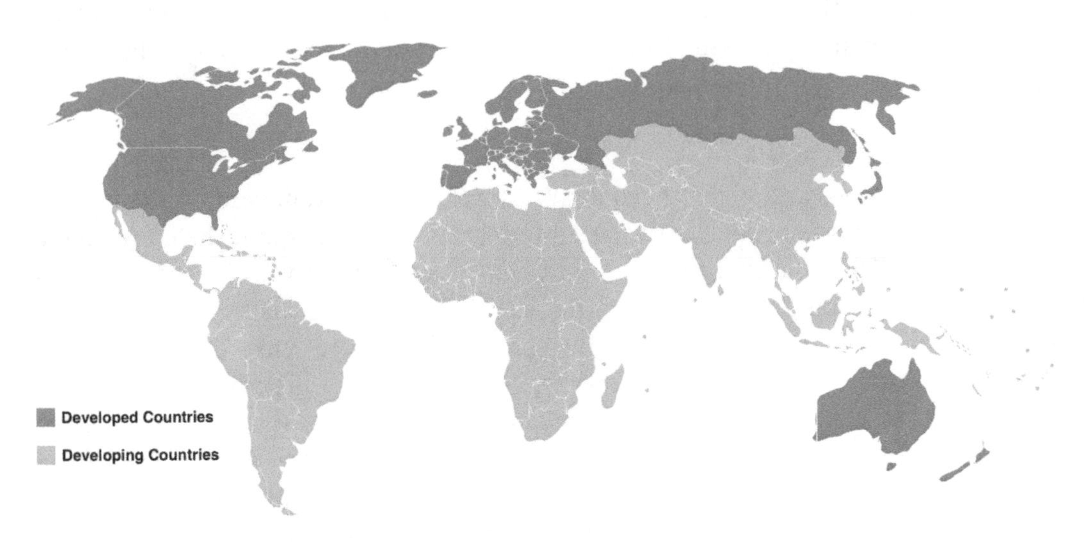

FIGURE 1.3 World Map of Developed and Developing Countries. Drawn based on the definition of the UN Statistics Division.

76 percent of all the countries, while 50, or 24 percent, are developed countries. Furthermore, not only are developing countries the majority of countries in the world, they are also the host of a majority of the human population. Demographically, of the 7.4 billion global population in 2015, roughly 6.2 billion resided in developing countries, or 84 percent of the world population. Only 1.2 billion, or 16 percent, resided in developed countries. The world's two most populous countries, China and India, together accounting for 37 percent of the world's population, are both considered developing countries in Asia.

Another convention in classification is simply to regard all member countries of the Organization for Economic Cooperation and Development (OECD) as developed countries. It currently has 34 members, 25 from Europe; the United States and Canada in North America; Australia and New Zealand in Oceania; Japan, South Korea, and Turkey in Asia; and Mexico and Chile in Latin America. But this classification is not as commonly adopted as the UN's convention.

Explaining the Underdevelopment of Developing Countries

The major purpose of this book is twofold: (1) to draw a generalized picture of the current state of developing countries and its gap with developed countries and (2) to shed light on the underlying forces that shape such disparity. Development draws interest from a variety of disciplines, such as economics, political science, sociology, history, anthropology, geography, and so on. We intend to illustrate in this book explanations as to why certain countries are poor and others are rich. A preliminary way to look at the question of poverty and prosperity is to identify internal obstacles within a given country that effectively block the attainment of higher modern standards of living. Another way to look at this condition is to seek answers from their relationship with the developed world. Following from the earlier overview of development theory, we can group these ideas into the North and South perspectives.

The North Perspective

The first perspective, the Northern (or Western), evaluated developing countries against the standards of developed ones. Modernization theory and the more recent Globalization/Neoliberal framework embody this perspective. Since developing countries lag behind developed countries, the question is how is the former different from the latter? Or, more explicitly, what has happened with the former? The seeds of prosperity or poverty were sown hundreds or thousands of years ago, wisely or unwisely, by the people in different societies. In these historical contexts, often powerful people made choices that influenced their development pathway. Influential factors could be cultural heritage, religion, environmental or demographic pressure, or simply accident. The Northern development perspective, articulated by **modernization theory** and later **globalization/neoliberal theory**, proposes that the main reason for developing countries' falling behind is that they have encountered significant obstacles that impede development, such as lack of natural resources, civil unrest, war, rapid population growth, and so on. What we observe today is a consequence of past choices and actions. The Northern perspective thus seeks answers from *within* developing countries themselves and holds up the Western model of development as the standard to follow. Since most of the developing countries are geographically located in the southern hemisphere, the Northern perspective identifies reasons from *within* the developing countries and from the natural world (Baker 2014). Modernization and globalization/neoliberalism then offer developing countries a means to overcome these physical, social, and economic constraints under the tutelage of developed countries.

The South Perspective

The second perspective argues that the underdevelopment of developing countries results from unequal relations with developed countries. This view equates with the **dependency** and **alternative theories of development**. This perspective views the world as interconnected in that different countries and regions impact each other. The South perspective rejects the basic thesis of modernization theory, and the current disparity between the rich and poor countries is assumed to have failed from following the Western industrial experience. Accordingly, the Southern perspective explains underdevelopment (and development) as a product of history, and not just the history of the developing countries. Rich and poor countries have not been on separate development paths; instead, there have been unequal interactions between them, often exploitative ones, as seen in chapter 3. As a result, poor countries were greatly influenced and shaped by rich ones. It is not true that developing countries were isolated or trapped in a primordial state of underdevelopment. They did change, but these changes were unfairly imposed upon them by the powerful, rich countries. This is reflected in the title of a book written by dependency theorist Walter Rodney, a Caribbean historian, *How Europe Underdeveloped Africa* (Rodney 1972). In sum, the South perspective seeks answers from examining the relationships *between* the developing and developed countries. Alternative development responds to the conditions of underdevelopment.

Development Futures

What does the future hold for the field of development? Against the oscillating backdrop of human crises, human potential, and the human condition, a number of salient trends sketch possible development futures. Above all, the field of development will exhibit greater pluralism moving forward. Various combinations of globalism, neoliberalism, alternative, and dependency responses will inform development policies encapsulated by the global push toward sustainable development. Each country and region will fine-tune development priorities and policies to align with specific requirements. There is clearly no one-size-fits-all linear model of development, as was the case in modernization theory. Development theorist and scholar Jan Nederveen Pieterse (2010) does however, identify three future trajectories as:

> Newly industrializing countries in the global south have become important drivers of the world economy; the agency of development shifts from metropolitan centres to developing countries; and the pendulum shifts from markets to states. (203)

Over the past two decades, deregulated US capitalism has lurched from one crisis to the next. As economic growth stagnates in the Global North, developing countries no longer feel required to succumb to Global North hegemony and its institutions that previously defined developmental relations. Developing countries are no longer the sweatshops for American consumer goods. They have broken from the Northern development establishment by instituting south-south trade, regional economic cooperation, technological upgrading, new development institution building, and robust investment in research and development. While American consumers are saddled with debt and stagnant northern economies grow only at a rate of 1 to 2 percent per annum, a number of developing countries exhibit higher growth rates of at least 6 percent per annum. Pieterse calls this largely Asian-driven model "sustainable industrialization." Thus, development dynamics have begun to shift to the Global South moving forward. Chapter 6 explores this recent development configuration as multipolar globalization.

Ecological integrity and sustainable development aside, the main driver in the new south-south development formation has been the reemergence of the **development state.** In developing countries, the state never fully receded, as development was always a priority matter. Emboldened by the economic and political crises in the Global North, the development state has more aggressively intervened in economic management throughout the Global South. It is not a mere soundbite when President Paul Kagame of Rwanda states that he envisions his country becoming the "Singapore of Africa" (*The Economist* 2012). A caveat is in order here, however. Rwanda, China, Thailand, the Arab Emirates, and Latin American states are not democratically constituted, and future crises clearly lie on their horizons. Pieterse cautions:

> It is tempting to applaud the arrival of emerging societies and to view it as an emancipation of sorts because we are at a historic juncture, yet their arrival, so far, also implies an extension and institutionalization of present patterns, rather than a transformation. Emerging markets meet with applause because they become an annex of world capitalism, rather than transforming its compulsions. As ratings record the growth of the middle classes in China, India and Latin America, workers and peasants are absent from such accounts. (211)

Politically, economic growth leads to regional power and cultural standing in the world hierarchy. Notably, a wide number of developing countries have achieved significant economic growth but by nondemocratic means. Moving forward, the old development crises of poverty, inequality, ecological sustainability, energy, migration, citizenship, and human rights remain festering and volatile under these largely autocratic states.

Finally, Pieterse remarks that "the development industry is not as important as it thinks; its self-importance is part of the problem" (216). He anticipates the long-standing but perhaps ultimately ineffective decline of previous development cooperation between the Global North and South. A startling example shows that remittances from migrants to their countries of origin amounted to at least USD 300 billion in 2007 alone, dwarfing the sum total of all international foreign aid (Pieterse, 216). Yet where can we find a coherent, sensible development policy on international migration? Developmental actors haven't produced one as we head into an increasingly pluralized arena of transformative change. Whether we call this development as conventionally formulated or something radically and structurally different remains to be seen.

CONCLUSION

In this chapter, we introduced the concept of development, its origins in the Cold War period, and some formal definitions of how the concept evolved and is envisioned by development actors up to the present. As this chapter demonstrates, modern development exhibits great flux and variation. We can state that development is evolutionary in nature and is influenced by economic, social, cultural, religious, and especially political crises and contexts. Development is not a strict scientific field but rather a **political** one. Some comparative characteristics of developed and developing countries introduced the concept of economic sectors. We found that the majority of developing countries are located in the southern hemisphere, with the developed countries predominantly found in the northern one. Two encompassing perspectives were introduced to group earlier development theories together. The North perspective focusses on internal obstacles to development within a country's overall makeup, and the South perspective examines obstacles resulting from a country's relationships with other countries. Both perspectives attempt to address the question: why underdevelopment? Finally, we identified some new configurations that will influence the direction of development.

REFERENCES

Baker, Andy. *Shaping the Developing World: The West, the South, and the Natural World*. Thousand Oaks, CA: Sage Publishing, 2014.

Cambridge English Dictionary. "Development." http://dictionary.cambridge.org/us/dictionary/english/development?q=Development, 2019.

Debray, Regis. *Revolution in the Revolution? Armed Struggle and Political Struggle in Latin America*. New York: Grove Press, 1967.
McMichael, Phillip. *Development and Social Change: A Global Perspective*, 5th ed. Los Angeles: Sage Publishing, 2012.
Pieterse, Jan Nederveen. *Development Theory*, 2nd ed. Los Angeles: Sage Publishing, 2010.
Potter, Robert, Tony Binns, Jennifer A. Elliot, Etiene Nel, and David W. Smith. *Geographies of Development: An Introduction to Development Studies*, 4th ed. New York: Routledge, 2018.
Rodney, Walter. *How Europe Underdeveloped Africa*. London: Bogle-L'Ouverture Publications, 1972.
Solarz, Marcin W. " 'Third World': The 60th Anniversary of a Concept that Changed History." *Third World Quarterly* 31, no. 9 (October 2012): 1561–73.
The Economist. "Africa's Singapore?" February 25, 2012. https://www.economist.com/business/2012/02/25/africas-singapore.
Truman, Harry S. Inaugural Address. January 20, 1949. https://www.trumanlibrary.org/whistlestop/50yrarchive/inagural20jan1949.htm.
United Nations. "Country Classification." UN English. 2012. http://www.un.org/en/development/desa/policy/wesp/wesp_current/2012country_class.pdf.
United Nations. "Sustainable Development Goals." UN English. 2015. https://sustainabledevelopment.un.org/?menu=1300.

Figure Credits

CHAPTER TWO

Measuring Development

INTRODUCTION

In the previous chapter, we introduced the guiding concept and some characteristics of development. In this chapter, we closely examine the ways development is quantified and measured by multilateral agencies and governments. We first present the measurement of development pertaining to quantified economic output and outcomes. We then introduce measures of development as desirable outcomes, including the Millennium Development Goals, Human Development Index, and Sustainable Development Goals. Finally, we conclude with some criticisms of these measure and introduce the concept of Gross Human Happiness.

DEVELOPMENT AS ECONOMIC OUTPUT: THE CONCEPTUAL CONTENT

According to this perspective, development is viewed as a transformative process that refers to progression from lower to higher levels of economic productivity. The success of this change manifests in measurable economic growth and higher incomes, which is believed to be able to solve many other economic and social problems. Along this line, **development** has become synonymous with **consumption** and **commercialization** (putting items up for sale) of either tangible or intangible materials and products, labor, and even the environment (McMichael 2009).

Income Indicators

The most commonly used indicator of a nation's economic condition is income. Three income-related measures will be introduced here: Gross National

Income (GNI), GNI per capita, and GNI per capita in Purchasing Power Parity (PPP). In this book, we use GNI to measure the total income of a country. It is generally the total value of all products and services plus taxes within a country and net income from abroad. You may have heard other terms such as **GDP (Gross Domestic Product)** and **GNP (Gross National Product)**. They are more or less similar, although there are distinctions between them. According to the World Bank (2019a), the following ten countries had the highest GNI in trillions of dollars (USD) in the world in 2017: the United States (19.87), China (12.20), Japan (5.04), Germany (3.77), France (2.65), United Kingdom (2.59), India (2.57) Brazil (2.02), Italy (1.95), and Canada (1.63). Among these top ten countries, three of them are developing countries: China, Brazil, and India. On the one hand, it is somewhat surprising to see three developing countries make the top-ten list. On the other hand, it is understandable, considering the size of their population. All three countries have relatively large populations, especially China and India. This means that as we compare income between countries, we have to take the size of population into account.

The GNI per capita, the average gross national income per person, is a good measure of a country's economic strengths and the general standard of living enjoyed by its citizens. It tends to be related to other socioeconomic factors such as well-being of the people, access to services, and health outcomes. The world distribution of GNI per capita is highly uneven. There is a huge gap between the richest and poorest countries. Table 2.1 lists side-by-side the top ten and bottom ten countries or territories in GNI per capita with the most recent data from the World Bank (2019b). For

TABLE 2.1 ***The Top- and Bottom-Ten Countries in GNI per Capita (USD)***

TOP TEN COUNTRIES	GNI PER CAPITA	BOTTOM TEN COUNTRIES	GNI PER CAPITA
Liechtenstein	116,300	Eritrea	520
Bermuda	106,140	Sierra Leone	510
Switzerland	81,130	Congo, Dem. Republic	460
Isle of Man	79,910	Mozambique	420
Norway	76,160	Madagascar	400
Macao SAR, China	72,050	South Sudan	390
Luxembourg	70,790	Central African Republic	390
Channel Islands	65,430	Niger	360
Qatar	60,510	Malawi	320
Iceland	60,500	Burundi	280

Data source: World Bank 2019b.

the top ten richest, their average income is above US$60,000, although most of them have small populations. In stark contrast, for the ten at the bottom, their average income is just over or below US$500, and all of them are located in Sub-Saharan Africa. When we compare GNI per capita of the highest, Liechtenstein (US$116,300), with that of the lowest, Burundi (US$280), the former is 414 times higher than the latter.

Shedding further light on the diversity among world countries, the World Bank classifies countries into four categories by GNI per capita:

- 79 high income economies, largely overlapped with developed countries and with a GNI per capita of US$12,056 or more;
- 56 upper-middle income economies, with a GNI per capita between US$12,055 and US$3,896;
- 47 lower-middle income economies, with a GNI per capita between US$3,895 and US$996; and
- 34 low income economies, with a GNI per capita of $995 or less.

Table 2.2 lists a few examples within each category.

TABLE 2.2 ***Selected Countries by Income Level in 2017***

HIGH INCOME COUNTRIES	GNI PER CAPITA (USD)	GNI PPP PER CAPITA (INT. DOLLARS)
Norway	76,160	64,760
United States	59,160	61,120
Portugal	19,930	31,840
UPPER-MIDDLE INCOME COUNTRIES		
China	8,690	16,800
Brazil	8,610	15,270
South Africa	5,430	13,120
LOWER-MIDDLE INCOME COUNTRIES		
Egypt	3,010	11,380
Vietnam	2,160	6,460
India	1,790	6,950
LOW INCOME COUNTRIES		
Nepal	800	2,730
Rwanda	720	2,000
Burundi	280	730

Data source: World Bank 2019b, 2019c.

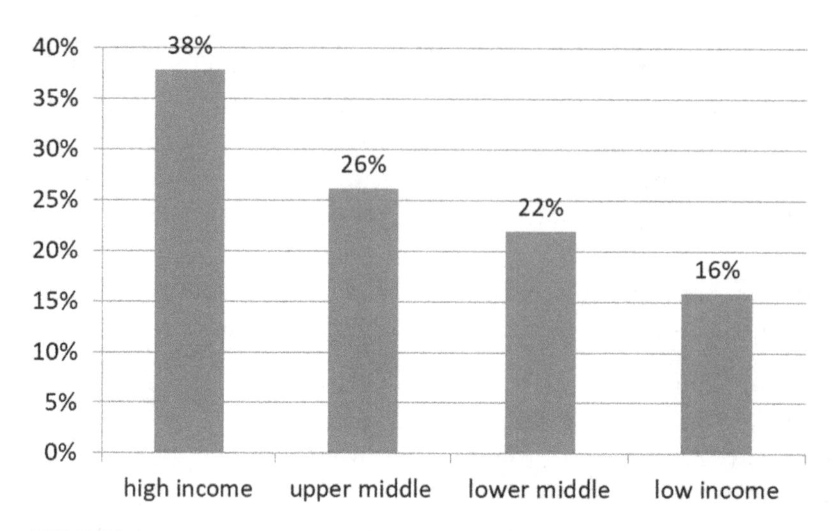

FIGURE 2.1 World Distribution of the Number of Countries by Income Level

Figures 2.1 and 2.2 show a contrast in the distribution of these four income groups by the number of countries and size of population of each category. While Figure 2.1 seems to show that the largest category is high income countries, with nearly 40 percent of all the countries falling in this category, Figure 2.2 gives a more accurate description, in which the majority of the human population lives in the two middle categories. High income countries account for only 16 percent, or one in six, of the global population. Upper- and lower-middle income countries together host over three-quarters of the global population, with China and India falling in these two categories, respectively. Only 10 percent of the global population lives in

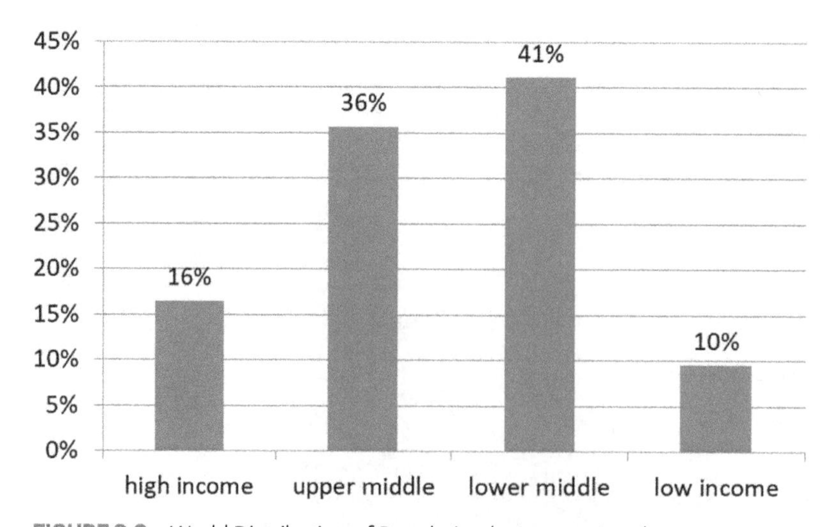

FIGURE 2.2 World Distribution of Population by Income Level

low income countries. It is the highest or lowest category that tends to get the media's attention to illustrate the phenomenal gap between the rich and poor, while stories of what is happening in the middle, where the majority of humanity is, tend to get lost.

GNI per capita is usually expressed in US dollars, in accordance with the exchange rate of a national currency. Strictly speaking, it is called **nominal GNI per capita** (not the real one), because it still has its shortcomings for at least the following two reasons. First, it does not take inflation into account. Even within the same national currency, value usually depreciates over time. Five dollars could buy one week's grocery for an American family during the Great Depression in the 1930s. What can you get with five dollars today? Second, it does not take into account the cost of living in international comparisons. A dollar can go a lot further in a poor country. Two hundred and fifty dollars will not be enough for paying a month's rent for a one-bedroom apartment in the US, but it is the annual income for an average citizen in Malawi! One way to address this issue is the **Purchasing Power Parity (PPP) conversion**, which assesses the real power of different currencies by purchasing the same kind of products or services, such as buying a dozen eggs or getting a haircut, across different economies. By applying this conversion factor, one can convert a country's nominal GNI per capita into its real term as measured by its purchasing power. This is called GNI PPP per capita. It provides a better comparison of average income or consumption between economies, as shown in Table 2.2.

BOX 2.1 UNDERSTANDING THE RATIONALE OF PPP

The Economist compares the prices of a McDonald's Big Mac across the world to gauge the purchasing power of different countries. Since the ingredients and preparation of hamburgers are generally standardized, a Big Mac should carry similar consumption value. According to Statista, a German statistics service firm, in 2015 the price of a Big Mac was US$6.82 in Switzerland, US$4.79 in the United States, and US$3.11 in Mexico. That means the purchasing power of $6.82 in Switzerland is equivalent to that of $4.79 in the U.S. and $3.11 in Mexico. Note that all the currencies are already converted to US dollars. The fact that they are different is due exactly to their different purchasing power within their societies. To gauge such a difference, we can calculate a ratio of **relative purchasing power** of these currencies. For example, let's calculate the ratio of the relative purchasing power of the currency of Switzerland against that of the US.

Purchasing power ratio of Switzerland to US = $6.82 / $4.79 = 1.42

This means that when buying a Big Mac, you will need to spend US$1.42 in Switzerland to get what you purchase for every one dollar you spend in the US. It is simply saying things are more expensive in Switzerland than in the US, or that money is worth relatively less in Switzerland. By the same token, we can calculate the ratio of purchasing power in Mexico to that of the US.

Purchasing power ratio of Mexico to US = $3.11 / $4.79 = 0.65

In this case, when buying a Big Mac, you need to spend just 65 cents (in US currency) in Mexico to get what you purchase for every dollar you spend in the US. In simple terms, things are cheaper in Mexico than in the US, or money worth relatively more in Mexico.

If we assume all other products and services in these three countries follow the same pattern of purchasing power, we can use these ratios to convert nominal income per capita into **income PPP per capita**. According to the World Bank in 2014, GNI per capita for Switzerland, the US, and Mexico were US$90,670, US$55,200, and US$9,860, respectively. As done above, if we use purchasing power in the US as the benchmark, we can use the ratios obtained above to calculate the GNI PPP per capita for Switzerland and Mexico (GNI PPP per capita is expressed in **international dollars**):

GNI PPP per capita for Switzerland = US$90,670 / 1.42 = $63,850

GNI PPP per capita for Mexico = US$9,860 / 0.65 = $15,170

Now, the income gaps between Switzerland and the US, and between the US and Mexico, both get narrower when purchasing power is taken into account. The average income is not as high as it seems in Switzerland, nor as low as it seems in Mexico. GNI PPP per capita is a more accurate measure of standard of living in different societies. Of course, in this exercise we made a strong assumption that all products and services in these three countries follow the same pattern of purchasing power of a Big Mac, which cannot be necessarily true. For instance, gasoline in Mexico is more expensive than in the US. In practice, the PPP conversion is more complex because it has to take many more products and services into account. Here, we use the Big Mac example to illustrate the basic rationale of PPP adjustment.

Here is an exercise for the reader. If the price of a Big Mac is US$5.13 in Sweden and US$3.17 in Thailand and their nominal GNI per capita is US$61,600 and US$5,370 respectively, can you calculate GNI PPP per capita for these two countries, assuming all other products and services follow the same pattern of purchasing power as that of a Big Mac?

Since the cost of living is lower in developing countries, GNI PPP per capita tends to be higher than nominal GPI per capita, as in the case of Mexico shown in Box 2.1. Thus, it somewhat narrows the gap in income per capita between developed and developing countries. However, as statistics show, a significant gap remains. According to the Population Reference Bureau (2018), developed countries had an average GNI PPP per capita of $43,409 in 2017. In contrast, developing countries had an average of $11,445 in the same year, and the least developed countries had an average of only $2,723. The world average was $16,101. The last column in Table 2.2 gives the GNI PPP per capita for each of the selected countries (GNI PPP per capita is expressed in international dollars). It is true that the income per capita for lower income countries gets bumped up quite substantially, but the gap between rich and poor countries remains highly unequal.

This section shows a clear ranking order in average income among all the nations. Overall, developing countries lag considerably behind developed countries. While the gulf between the richest and poorest countries is extreme and often brought to light in the public sphere, what is less well known is what lies in the middle income strata, where the majority of the global population lives.

A CRITICAL NOTE

As illustrated in chapter 1, this characterization of development overemphasizes the importance of following the Western model of modernization, which features the centrality of the market economy. Critics claim that the Western model overlooks the ultimate objective of the development process. In short, they ask, what is the goal of economic growth or modernity? Or, is economic growth or higher income in and of itself the endpoint? Hamilton (2004) argues that human beings have fallen victim to economic growth, which fosters empty materialism, erodes social relations, and degrades the natural environment. A life of riches seems achievable only through a rich life. It is relatively easier to tell which countries are richer and which are poorer, but countries with similar average incomes can differ substantially in the **quality of life**, such as in health and working conditions, educational and employment opportunities, access to safe drinking water and clean air, and public safety, among other variables.

Japan has one of the highest incomes per capita in the world, higher than that of Australia. As one comparative study showed, however, its **standard of living** is not necessarily higher than that of the latter (Castles 1992). Tokyo and three other major Japanese cities were compared with Sydney; because of the much higher population density, Japanese city residents have much less access to private and public spaces. While the average size of dwellings in Japan is about half the size of those in Australia, the disparity in access to public open spaces is even more striking, with a ratio of 1 to 16 (250 hectares versus 4,000 hectares per million of population). The ratio of public playing fields between the two countries is also 1 to 16. And behind Japan's higher income comes a price of longer working hours: Sydney residents on average worked 35 hours a week, while their Japanese counterparts worked 47 average hours per week. Putting all this information together, can you tell which country enjoys a higher living standard? Or, given a choice, where would you want to live, between the two? Is higher income always the better choice?

DEVELOPMENT AS OUTCOMES OF DESIRABLE TARGETS: THE CONCEPTUAL CONTENT

As explored in chapter 1, development theories and policies have expanded into a broad range of goals. When development is focused only on establishing a capitalist society and on economic growth, the ultimate goal, which should be improving human well-being in the short and long term, goes missing. Otherwise, what is the point of earning more income, when people's lives become more miserable? Therefore, improving citizens' well-being, or human development, should be the final goal of any economic strategy. As articulated by the United Nations (UN), when it comes to the relationship between human development and economic growth, the former is the end, whereas the latter is the means (United Nations 1996). This vision is fully expressed in the annual **Human Development Report** published by the UN Development Program (UNDP). The focus on human well-being is clearly highlighted in its first report, produced in 1990, with the following opening lines:

> This Report is about people—and about how development enlarges their choices. It is about more than GNP growth, more than income and wealth and more than producing commodities and accumulating capital. ... People are the real wealth of a nation. The basic objective of development is to create an enabling environment for people to enjoy long, healthy and creative lives. This may appear to be a simple truth. But it is often forgotten in the immediate concern with the accumulation of commodities and financial wealth. (United Nations 1990)

Although economic growth increases a nation's wealth and boosts its potential for reducing poverty, it does not necessarily result in progress in human development. For example, Equatorial Guinea, a country in middle Africa, has an average income at least three times higher than the African average, but its life expectancy is below the African average (Kaneda 2015). On the west coast of Africa, with a population of 1.2 million in 2015, Equatorial Guinea has become one of Sub-Saharan Africa's biggest oil producers and fastest growing economies since the mid-1990s. But the benefits of the oil boom are not shared by the majority of the population, most of whom are still in poverty. According to UNICEF (2008), less than half of the nation's population has access to safe water. About one child out of five die before the age of five, often from diarrhea, cholera or other diseases linked to poor water quality. Thus, it is critical to incorporate human well-being outcomes into the concept of development.

It is in this spirit that the eight **Millennium Development Goals** (**MDGs**) articulated by the UN are commonly used as benchmarks to assess the level of development. The MDGs were established following the Millennium Summit of the UN in 2000. They were approved by all the 189 UN member countries. Specific targets and dates were set for each goal. The eight goals are: to eradicate extreme poverty and hunger; to achieve universal primary education; to promote gender equality; to reduce child mortality; to improve maternal health; to combat HIV/AIDS, malaria, and other diseases; to ensure environmental sustainability; and to develop a global partnership for development. In this chapter, we examine four of the eight goals.

TARGETED OUTCOME INDICATORS

The 2015 Millennium Development Goals Report issued by the UN offers the most recent assessment of how developing countries fare in these basic measures mentioned above. Here we focus on four indicators in the following discussion: poverty and hunger, education, health (including child mortality, HIV/AIDS, and other diseases) and gender equality. We then introduce a comprehensive measure of well-being, the **Human Development Index**.

Poverty and Hunger

Living in **extreme poverty** is defined by the UN as living on less than US$1.25 a day, which seems unthinkable to many in developed countries. The MDG target set by the UN in 1990 was to reduce the proportion of people living in extreme poverty by half by 2015. The goal was reached in 2010. The proportion of extreme poor has plummeted in developing countries from 47 percent in 1990 to 14 percent in 2015. Meanwhile, the proportion of undernourished people in developing countries has fallen from 23.3 percent in 1990–1992 to 12.9 percent in 2014–2016. Virtually all developing regions had met the target at varying paces except Sub-Saharan Africa. The world's two most populous countries, China and India, played a crucial role in the global reduction in poverty. Figure 2.3 below shows the trend in selected regions. Extreme poverty was mainly concentrated in Asia and Africa in 1990. Since then, Asia has

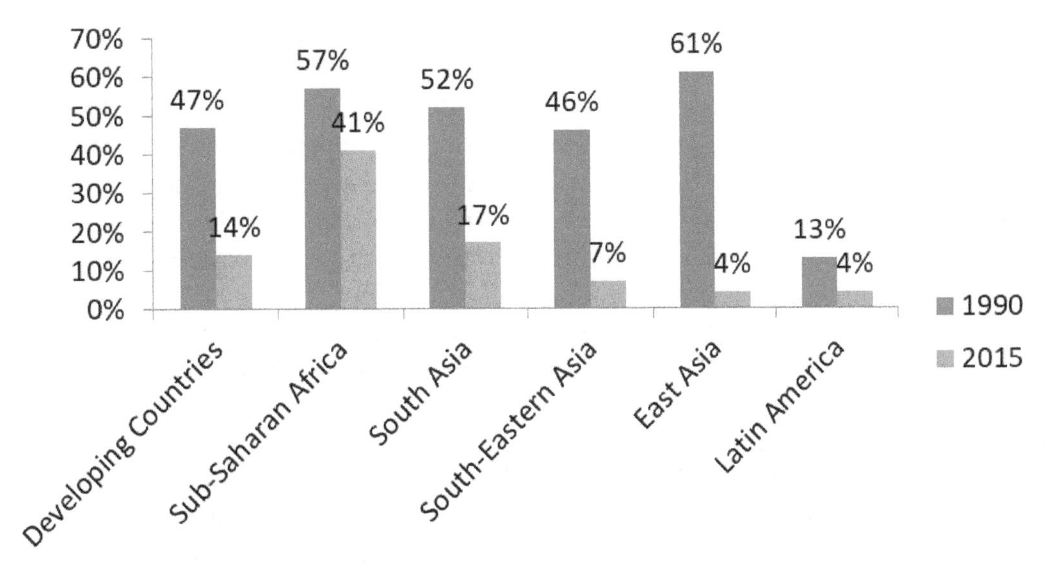

FIGURE 2.3 Proportion of People Living on Less than US$1.25 a Day, 1990 and 2015

made great strides in lowering poverty rates. East Asia, where China is located; South Asia, where India is; and South-Eastern Asia witnessed an impressive decline in poverty. The change in Latin America is less dramatic because it was relatively low to start with. Sub-Saharan Africa's poverty rate did not fall as fast. As of 2015, there was still more than 40 percent of the population living in extreme poverty in this region.

Although the MDG target of cutting the rate of extreme poverty by half has been met for developing countries as a whole, the world is still far from eradicating it, along with hunger. In 2015, about 825 million people still lived in extreme poverty and 800 million still suffered from hunger. Over 160 million children under age five experience developmental problems, such as stunting, due to lack of food. Over 90 million children under age five—one in seven children worldwide—remain underweight. Underweight children are at greater risk of dying from infections and suffering impaired cognitive ability. Two regions—South Asia and Sub-Saharan Africa—account for nearly 90 percent of all underweight children in the world. Although the percentage of underweight children has fallen in both regions since 1990, the number of underweight children has actually risen in Sub-Saharan Africa due to the region's rapid population growth. In sum, in the past two decades, progress in eliminating extreme poverty has been substantial but uneven. It is largely an Asian success story. More than 10 percent of humanity has not yet escaped from its grip.

Education

Education, defined as the acquired skills and knowledge that individuals can utilize to create economic or social values, is an important aspect of human capital. It is at the heart of improving individuals' lives. Well-educated individuals are empowered by their knowledge and competencies and enjoy more economic opportunities. They tend to be productive and to make informed decisions about lifestyle and well-being. It is estimated that every additional year of schooling provides an individual with a 10-percent increase in annual earnings (Psacharopoulos and Patrinos 2002). Education also plays a significant role in the development of a society. Investments in education are usually rewarded with great returns. A more educated population provides a larger number of skilled workers and nurtures greater ability to utilize advanced technology, which in turn brings about higher productivity and economic growth. There are also immeasurable social benefits, such as a more open and stable society, more public health benefits to children and women's health, and control of diseases.

There is a clear gap between the developed and developing countries in average educational attainment of citizens. Figure 2.4 shows the trend of average years of schooling of population aged 15 and over by region from 1950 to 2010. There are clearly three sets of parallel lines, with developed countries at the top forming its own group; Latin America, East Asia, and the Pacific Islands in the middle; and South Asia and Sub-Saharan Africa at the bottom. As of 2010, the average years of

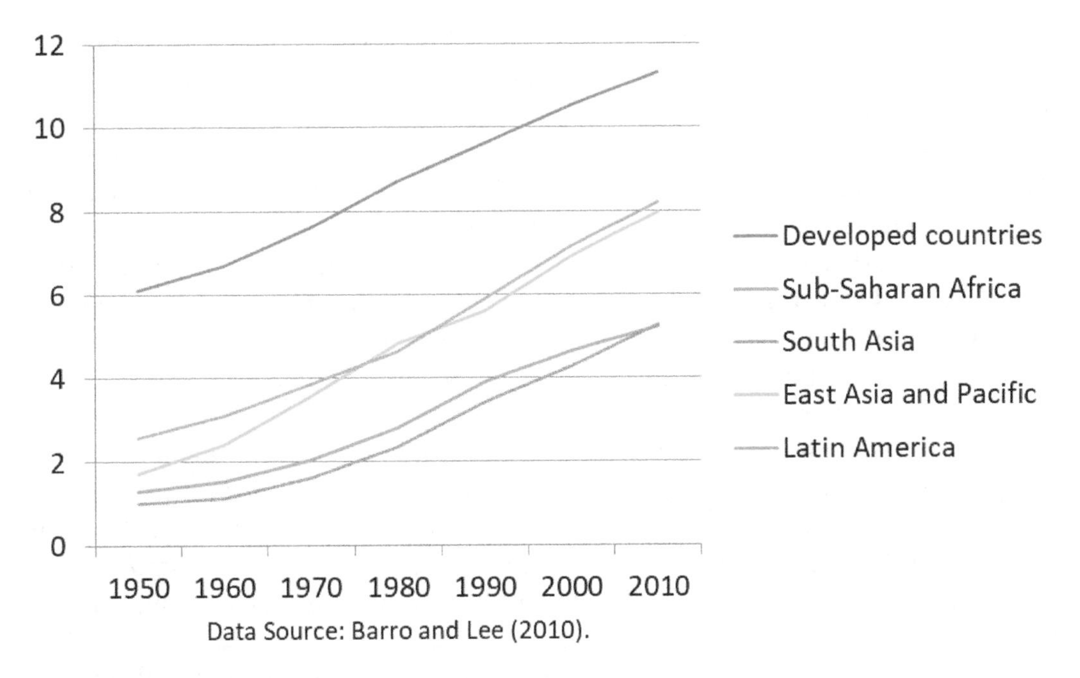

FIGURE 2.4 Trend of Average Years of Schooling of Population Age 15 and Over by Region

schooling for these three groups was about 11, 8, and 5 years, respectively. The chart conveys two messages. First, all regions, rich and poor, have made strides in education over the past six decades. Second, the initial gap between regions has persisted 60 years later. The source of such disparity becomes more revealing when the overall comparison is broken down by educational level: primary, and secondary, or higher levels of education.

Achieving universal primary education—that all children would be able to complete primary schooling by 2015—is the second goal of the MDGs. Although it has not been fully reached, considerable progress has been made in expanding primary education in developing countries since 1990. According to the UN, **universal enrollment** is attained by passing a threshold of at least 97 percent. By this benchmark, all developed countries have basically achieved universal primary education, with 96 percent in 2015. It was 91 percent for developing countries as a whole, where only East Asia (97%) and North Africa (99%) passed the threshold, and South Asia (95%) and South-East Asia (94%) closely approached it. Although Sub-Saharan Africa has the lowest primary education enrollment rate, it registered the largest increase among developing regions, from 52 percent in 1990 to 80 percent in 2015. However, obstacles for further improvement remain challenging, including rapid growth of the primary-school-age children (an 86 percent increase between 1990 and 2015), poverty, conflicts, and other emergencies.

As the gap in providing primary education is quickly narrowing between regions, the gap at the next level—secondary education—remains. While the mandate of primary education is to teach fundamental skills, such as literacy and numeracy, the mandate of secondary or higher education is to provide students with the skills that they need to become productive citizens. While secondary education has more direct impact on productivity, it also costs more to operate and requires more investment. Larger gaps at this level are evident between regions, as shown in Figure 2.5. **Secondary School Enrollment Ratio** is the number of students enrolled in secondary schools per 100 of the secondary-school-age population. The ratio can be over 100, because enrolled students can be underage or overage. To facilitate the following description, we assume that the number of underage or overage students is minimal, and thus treat the ratio roughly the same as the proportion of enrollment. Virtually every child of appropriate ages in developed countries is enrolled in a secondary school. The enrollment ratio is 100 out of 100 for both boys and girls. Note that this is about enrollment, not graduation. Among developing countries, East Asia and Latin America take the lead, with the enrollment ratio at or over 90 per 100, followed by South-East Asia at 78. South Asia and Sub-Saharan Africa not only lag behind (in the 60s and 40s, respectively) but are also the regions where girls are less likely to go to secondary school than boys.

The number of children being enrolled in schools is just one aspect of the state of education. Its quality is equally if not more of a concern in many developing countries,

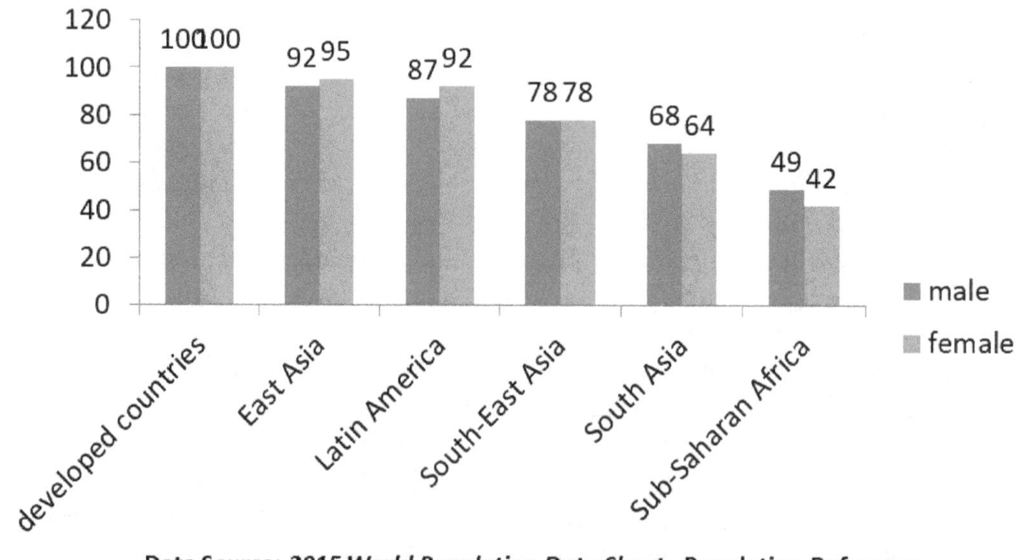

FIGURE 2.5 Secondary School Enrollment Ratio by Gender

where going to school does not necessarily mean actual learning. Many children who are in school do not acquire basic skills, including literacy and numeracy. For example, in some Sub-Saharan African countries, children with five years of education have a 40 percent chance of being illiterate (Brookings Institute 2011). In Ghana, only 50 percent of children complete grade 5, and of those, less than half can comprehend a simple paragraph (Epstein and Yuthas 2012). In Pakistan, only half of the population can read; about 50 million adults are illiterate. In one of the poorest regions, the literacy rate for rural women is below 10 percent. Of the children who are enrolled in school, 30 percent will drop out by grade 5. Only one-third of Pakistani children receive a secondary education (Winthrop and Graff, 2010). Among the things that are responsible for such poor outcomes are insufficient infrastructure at schools, poor quality of teaching, limited supply of competent teachers, and political instability in some areas.

In one province of Pakistan, for example, there are 1,000 schools that do not have any physical building at all. In some schools where there are classrooms, fewer than half of them have desks for the children. Many countries cannot build schools or hire teachers fast enough to keep up with growing student-age populations. While it is challenging to find competent teachers, the lack of basic working standard and governance is another problem. One study reported a large number of "ghost schools" in Pakistan, which were dysfunctional or existed on paper only. In two provinces, 25,000 teachers from more than 1,000 such schools were found on payroll but never showed up to work (Winthrop and Graff 2010). In some rural schools in India, a quarter of teachers were absent. In some African countries, teachers in public schools are absent 15–25 percent of the time (*The Economist* August 2015).

When parents see that their children are not getting any education from public schools due to unmotivated teachers or poor-quality facilities, they often pull their children out of school, or they have to find alternatives. ls are one option to fill in the gap. Private schools in developed countries usually bring to mind the image of elite schools and high expenses. Private-school students account for only 10 percent of total primary school enrollment in rich countries. But many private schools in developing countries are low-cost, run by entrepreneurs in poor areas. In Lagos, Nigeria's economic capital, for example, the average fees are about US$35 per semester, and it can be even lower in other areas. In 2010, there were approximately one million private schools in developing countries (*The Economist* August 2015).

Recently, some scholars argue that it is in the interest of developing countries to shift the curriculum from the content mastery model to a school-for-life model (Epstein and Yuthas 2012). Currently, in developing countries,

> Educational programs typically adopt traditional Western models of education, with an emphasis on math, science, language, and social studies. These programs allocate scarce resources to topics like Greek mythology, prime numbers,

> or tectonic plate movement—topics that may provide intellectual stimulation, but have little relevance in the lives of impoverished children.

High scores on academic tests may not be a sound return on the scarce resources invested in the youth. Instead, education should aim to help children develop skills and attitudes that they can directly apply to their lives and use to lift themselves out of poverty. Therefore,

> We fervently believe that what students in impoverished regions need are not more academic skills, but rather life skills that enable them to improve their financial prospects and well-being. These include financial literacy and entrepreneurial skills; health maintenance and management skills; and administrative capabilities, such as teamwork, problem solving, and project management. ... Students learn and practice workplace skills and attitudes like delegation, negotiation, collaboration, and planning—opportunities that are rarely available to them outside their families. (Epstein and Yuthas)

Some of the practical knowledge is as simple as boiling water before drinking and using bed nets to prevent malaria. This shift of focus from performing well on standardized tests to applying practical skills to real life issues may suit the context of many developing countries. Whether it proves fruitful remains to be seen.

Health

Health is the most fundamental aspect of human capital. It is the most basic element of well-being. Without health nothing can be achieved. The following measures point to a substantial gap in health between the developed and developing countries.

Life expectancy, the average number of years an individual in a population is expected to live, calculated at birth, is a common benchmark of a population's well-being. Developing countries, on average, are about 10 years behind developed countries. In 2014, life expectancy for males and females in developing countries was 68 and 72, respectively. It was 76 and 82 for developed countries (Kaneda 2015). There were regional differences within the developing world, as well. Life expectancy for males and females in Africa (58, 61) and South Asia (66, 70) was far below the average of developing countries, whereas East Asia (74, 79) and Latin America (72, 78) led the pack and were approaching parity with developed countries.

Infant mortality rate, the number of deaths per 1,000 live births by the first birthday, or under-five children's mortality rate, the number of deaths per 1,000 live births by the fifth birthday, is another important measure of a country's health care quality. Figure 2.6 depicts an encouraging downward trend in under-five child mortality rate, which has fallen, remarkably, by half in virtually all regions around the world between 1990 and 2015, with a decline of under-five child deaths from 12.7 million in 1990 to

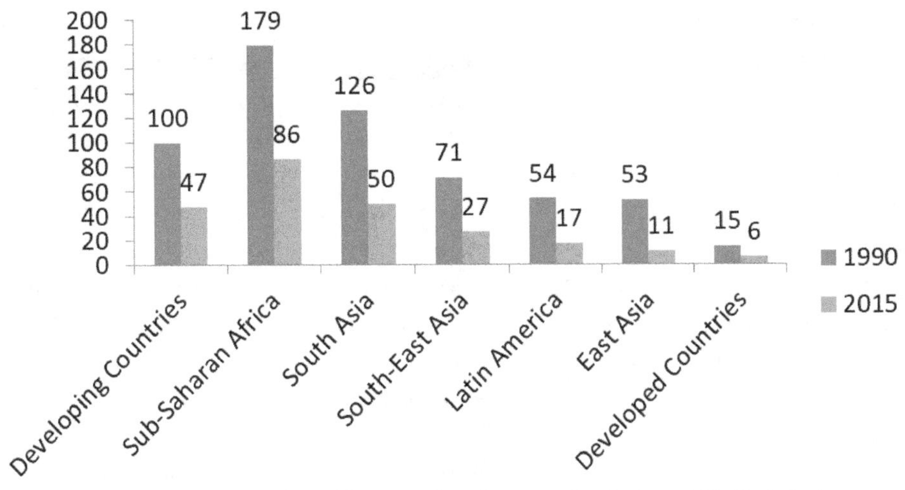

FIGURE 2.6 Under-Five Child Mortality Rate (per 1,000), 1990 and 2015

about 6 million in 2015. This dramatic decline is hailed by the UN as one of the most significant achievements in human history.

Although progress in developing countries has been impressive, the gap between the developed and developing world remains striking. In 2015, 47 out of 1,000 children under age 5 died in developing countries, whereas it was only 6 out of 1,000 in developed countries. A similar pattern emerged among developing countries as in life expectancy. Sub-Saharan Africa had the highest child mortality rate, 86 per 1,000, followed by South Asia, 50 per 1,000. Both regions were above the average of developing countries. East Asia and Latin America registered the lowest levels.

Sub-Saharan Africa has the world's highest child mortality rate but has experienced the largest absolute decline in the past two decades. It still faces the sternest challenge down the road, because this region will see a continuing expansion of its young population over the next decades. Unless progress is made to accelerate decline in child mortality rate, the number of under-five deaths may actually be on the rise in the near future. Currently, about 16,000 children under five die every day. Of the annual total of 6 million deaths, 3 million take place in Sub-Saharan Africa and 1.8 million in South Asia. Most of the deaths are from preventable causes, such as pneumonia, diarrhea, and malaria. And the fact that a number of low income countries, such as Bangladesh and Ethiopia, have significantly cut their under-five mortality rates suggests that further improvement in saving children's lives is possible without huge input of extra resources.

The discrepancy in health outcomes between countries largely reflects the fact that countries are in different stages of **epidemiological transition**, which encompasses shifts in three aspects of death patterns: falling mortality from high to low levels, delay of the age of death, and change in causes of death (Ratzan, Filerman, and LeSar, 2000). According to a simpler version of the transition, most of human history fell into the pretransition stage, marked by high death rates resulting from famine and other unfavorable conditions. Hunger and infectious or communicable diseases were primarily the direct causes of death. With the rise of living standards, access to clean drinking water, provision of public health measures, and the introduction of modern medical technologies, the death rates started to fall, especially at younger ages. The main causes of death shifted to noncommunicable or degenerative diseases, which tend to occur at older ages. The discrepancy in the level of mortality is shown in the aforementioned comparison of life expectancy and child mortality.

The second aspect of the transition, delaying age of death, is shown in Figure 2.7. In its assessment of global burden of disease, the World Health Organization (WHO) displays a sharp contrast in the age profile of death between Africa and the world's high income countries (WHO 2008). Of the three age groups, most death—46 percent—occurs in Africa within the youngest age group, 0–14, followed by the middle and oldest age groups, 34 and 20 percent, respectively. In high income countries, however, the deaths that occur in the 0–14 range are virtually negligible, only 1 percent. Most death is concentrated in the oldest age group, with 84 percent happening

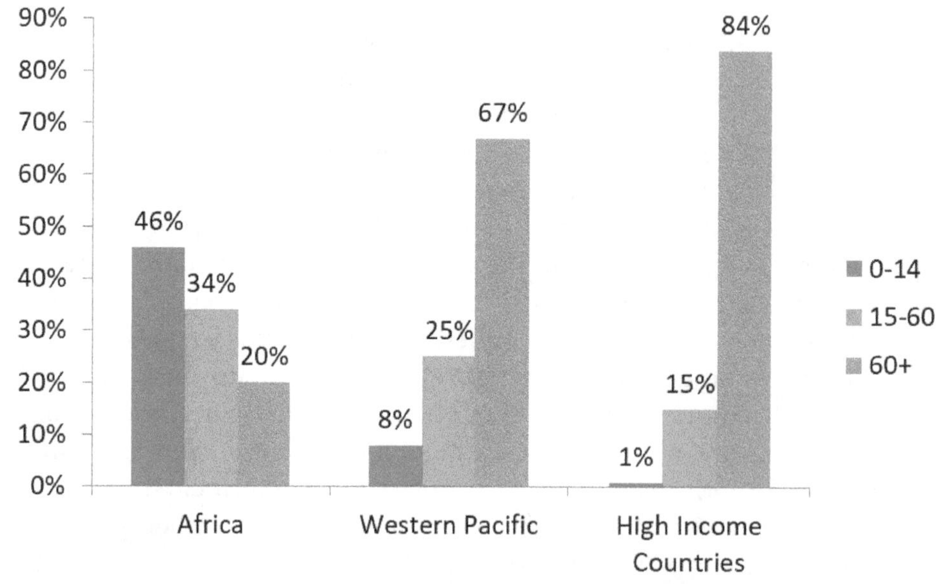

FIGURE 2.7 Distribution of Age of Death

after age 60. Western Pacific countries, including parts of East and South-East Asia, and Pacific islands, such as China, Malaysia, and Fiji, lie in between. Their age profile looks similar to high income countries, but more deaths occur at younger ages.

The shift in causes of death marks the third aspect of the transition. Figure 2.8 below shows variation in the causes of death in developing (low and middle income) countries and developed (high income) countries. In low income countries, which have not or have only recently started the transition, the dominant causes are communicable or infectious diseases, such as diarrhea, measles, malaria, and HIV/AIDS, which account for more than 60 percent of all deaths.

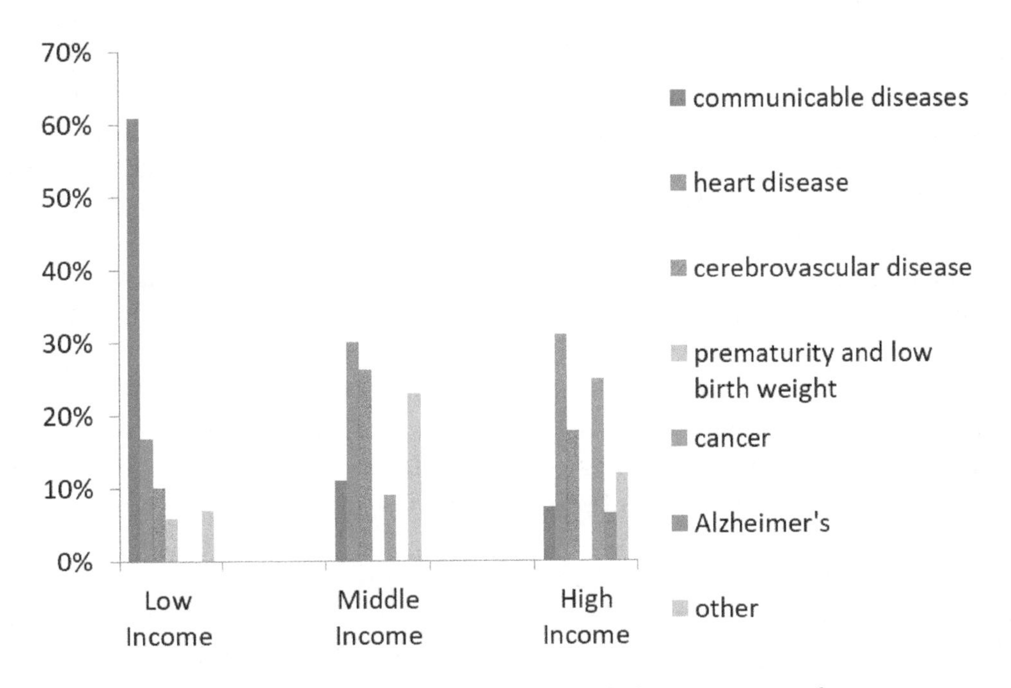

FIGURE 2.8 Shares of Ten Leading Causes of Death

AIDS, or **acquired immunodeficiency syndrome**, caused by the **human immunodeficiency virus (HIV)**, is ranked the fourth leading cause of death in low income countries. HIV weakens the body's immune system and renders it no longer able to fight infection. Many patients eventually die from other infectious diseases such as pneumonia and tuberculosis. The AIDS epidemic is one of the most destructive health crises in human history. Its burden is disproportionately borne by poor, developing countries. Worldwide, about 1 percent of adults carries the HIV virus. Two regions stand out above this world average: Sub-Saharan Africa (6.1%) and the Caribbean (1.6%) (UNAIDS 2006; United Nations 2015). In Swaziland, a country in southern

Africa, more than one-third of the adults are infected with HIV (Lamptey, Johnson, and Khan 2006). The surge of AIDS reversed gains in life expectancy in many countries in Africa. Lesotho used to have a life expectancy of nearly 60 years in the late 1990s, but its life expectancy plunged to 34 years between 2005 and 2010; it has just recovered to 44 years in 2015 (Ashford 2006; Kaneda 2015).

HIV/AIDS leaves its devastating footprint on many aspects of societies. In individual families, adults lose their spouses and children lose their parents. As more parents die from AIDS, the number of orphans starts to rise. More than 10 million children were orphaned by AIDS in Sub-Saharan Africa (Lamptey, Johnson, and Khan 2006), and they were then susceptible to hunger, abuse, exploitation, and child trafficking, which in turn increases the risk of being infected themselves with HIV. Business suffers from a loss of workers, absenteeism, low productivity, and rising costs of health care benefits. The treatment of HIV/AIDS patients also poses great challenges to the already strained health care systems in developing countries, where the most basic needs of the general population have hardly been met. In Uganda, for example, more than half of hospital beds were occupied by adult patients with HIV/AIDS.

Women in developing countries bear more of the brunt of HIV/AIDS than men, accounting for about three-fifths of adults living with HIV (Ashford 2006). In Sub-Saharan Africa, women between ages 15 and 24 are three times more likely to be infected with HIV than their male counterparts (Lamptey, Johnson, and Khan 2006). Poverty drives some women into commercial sex. In a male dominant culture, women's dependent or subordinate status exposes them to unprotected sex even within marriage. In India, many new infections happened to married women whose husbands engaged in extramarital sex.

The good news is that the number of new HIV infections has been in a fall since 2000, from 3.5 million to 2.1 million, roughly a 40 percent reduction (United Nations 2015). There are also success stories in fighting against HIV/AIDS in developing countries. The case of Brazil demonstrates the effectiveness of national commitment in this battle. In Latin America, one-third of the HIV-infected used to live in Brazil. As a response, the Brazilian government mandated free **Antiretroviral Therapy** (**ART**) for all AIDS patients covered by national insurance, which was a costly and bold move for a developing country. The result was equally impressive: more than 170,000 HIV-positive Brazilians received this treatment, and the national HIV/AIDS death rate was cut in half. In another case, Cambodia, a country in South-East Asia, tries to block the major channel of HIV transmission, the sex industry. It launched a prevention program to enforce complete condom use among commercial sex workers. New HIV infections dropped by two-thirds between 2005 and 2013 (Lamptey, Johnson, and Khan 2006; UNAIDS 2014).

More obstacles, however, both social and economic, must be overcome for further and sustainable progress. For example, the number of people with HIV/AIDS nearly doubled in the Middle East and North Africa between 2003 and 2005. This region's conservative culture was believed to play an important role in this surge (Roudi-Fahimi 2007). The social norms forbid extramarital sex and stigmatize and discriminate HIV-positive persons, who are perceived as a shame or disgrace to their families and communities. A study in Egypt found that only one-quarter of women surveyed would be willing to take care of an HIV-positive family member. As a result, avoidance of testing and counseling, cover up, and denial are prevalent, which makes it harder to detect and prevent the spread of the virus.

The financial burden of HIV/AIDS treatment is another factor to consider. ART significantly suppresses the HIV virus, stops the progression of the AIDS disease, and reduces HIV transmission. It is estimated to have averted 7.6 million deaths from AIDS between 1995 and 2013 (United Nations 2015). By 2014, over 13 million people living with HIV in the world were receiving ART, a great increase from just 800,000 in 2003. Meanwhile, only 36 percent of the 31 million people living with HIV in developing countries were receiving ART in 2013. One major barrier is the high cost of the treatment, which can be hundreds of dollars per patient per year even at generic prices (Granich et al. 2012), which is beyond the reach of many patients in developing countries.

The recent outbreak of Ebola in West Africa, mainly in Guinea, Liberia, and Sierra Leone, which started in March 2014 and was declared ended in December 2015, is another example of developing countries' vulnerability to infectious diseases. According to the WHO, the Ebola virus is spread through human contact and can cause an acute, serious illness. The average death rate for infected patients is around 50 percent. It can be as high as 90-percent fatal. As of late May 2015, there were over 27,000 confirmed or suspected cases and over 11,000 deaths worldwide (United Nations 2015).

The outbreak has affected many other aspects of development in this region: it had a total fiscal impact of over US$500 million, or 5 percent of combined GDP in 2014, and an output loss of more than 12 percent of GDP in 2015. In addition, the region suffers from declined agricultural production, reduced wages, and reduced foreign investment. About 5 million children could not go to schools, which were closed for months. Health care facilities were overwhelmed by Ebola cases and were unable to deliver other services. Meanwhile, the public shunned health services for fear of contagion. There was a nearly 40-percent decline in children under five seeking malaria treatment in Sierra Leone between May and September in 2014. As recently as 2018, there was another Ebola outbreak in the Democratic Republic of the Congo, located in central and southern Africa, where close to 600 cases were identified, including 54 health care workers. About 60 percent of them had died at the time of reporting (WHO 2018). This adds a further burden to the country's health care system, which is still fighting other epidemics, such as cholera and malaria.

In contrast, the major causes of death of middle income developing countries and developed or high income countries look alike, although there is still some difference. Communicable diseases play a minor role for both groups: only 11 percent for middle income countries and 7 percent for high income countries, respectively. Heart disease and cerebrovascular disease together account for about half of all deaths (56% and 49%, respectively). Cancer, which is virtually negligible in low income countries, is the second leading cause of death in high income countries (25%) and the fourth in middle income countries (9%). Alzheimer's disease, which is the fifth leading cause of death in high income countries (7%), is not yet among the top ten leading causes for all developing countries. All the diseases mentioned above fall in the category of noncommunicable diseases, and most of them are degenerative diseases, which result from a long-term deterioration of tissues or organs and usually occur in old ages.

The similarity in causes of death between middle income and high income countries suggests a peculiar challenge faced by some developing countries: while a portion of their population is still hassled by health conditions related to poverty, such as malnutrition and infectious diseases, others are burdened by diseases associated with wealth, such as diabetes and heart disease. For developing countries as a whole, there are already more people dying from strokes and heart attacks than infectious diseases. "The poor are dying more and more like the rich" (Lomborg 2015). Mexico is a case in point. Deaths from noncommunicable diseases swelled from under 50 percent to 75 percent of all deaths between 1980 and 2009. For all developing countries, it is projected that degenerative conditions, such as diabetes, depression, heart disease, and cancer, will rise from 40 percent of the health burden in 1998 to nearly 75 percent in 2020 (Levine 2004).

Challenges notwithstanding, the improvement in the general population's health in developing countries has been impressive. There has been encouraging progress on a number of fronts. According to the WHO, the number of polio cases has been reduced by over 99 percent since 1988, from more than 350,000 cases to just about 350 reported cases in 2014, because of wide adoption of the polio vaccine, which given multiple times can protect a child for life. The UN estimates that the global malaria incidence rate has fallen by more than a third and the mortality rate by more than half, which is equivalent to a reduction of 6.2 million deaths caused by malaria between 2000 and 2015. The tuberculosis mortality rate was cut by almost half between 1990 and 2013. Thirty-seven million lives were saved from tuberculosis by prevention and treatment. As more children worldwide receive measles-containing vaccines, up from 73 percent in 2000 to 84 percent in 2013, more than 15 million deaths were prevented in the same period of time (United Nations 2015).

Furthermore, some of the progress was achieved without huge financial investment. Health interventions have succeeded in poor developing countries. In Sub-Saharan Africa, by learning to filter water, families have reduced the prevalence of guinea worm disease by 99 percent (Levine 2004). In Bangladesh, women learned how to use **oral rehydration therapy (ORT)**, providing kids with a mixed water and salt-and-sugar solution, to prevent them dying from diarrheal disease. The same method was introduced in

Egypt as well, where infant diarrheal deaths were reduced by 82 percent between 1982 and 1987. Insecticide-treated mosquito nets were proven to be effective in preventing malaria, and more than 900 million nets were delivered to Sub-Saharan Africa between 2004 and 2014. The cost to control river blindness in Sub-Saharan Africa is less than US$1 per person, and 60,000 cases were prevented between 1974 and 2002.

Health status and patterns of diseases seem to form a continuum, with poverty-related diseases on one end and those that come with economic development and modernity on the other. From the perspective of the epidemiological transition, many developing countries in Asia and Latin America are catching up with developed countries. Their mortality level, age profile of death, causes of death, and the pattern of risk factors are becoming close to those of developed countries, while some regions, especially Sub-Saharan Africa, still have improvement to make.

BOX 2.2 GENDER INEQUALITY AND EMPOWERMENT OF WOMEN

According to the UN's Millennium Development Goals Report in 2015, substantial progress has been made in promoting gender equality in developing countries, although significant challenges remain to be addressed in many aspects.

In educational attainment, gender disparity has narrowed substantially at all levels since 2000. The greatest improvements have been made in primary education, where gender parity has been achieved. Southern Asia has made the most substantial progress, where the **gender parity index**—the ratio of number of girls enrolled in schools to corresponding number of boys—had increased from 0.74 in 1990 to 1.03 in 2015, followed by North Africa, Sub-Saharan Africa, and Western Asia. Gender disparity in primary education remains the highest in Sub-Saharan Africa, where the gender parity index was 0.93 in 2012. Gender disparity overall remains more apparent at the secondary or tertiary level. While Central Asia, Eastern Asia, Northern Africa, South-Eastern Asia and Southern Asia had achieved gender parity in secondary education in 2015, girls in Sub-Saharan Africa and Western Asia remained at a disadvantage, and in Latin America, boys are at a disadvantage. In Sub-Saharan Africa, for example, the gender parity index was 0.61 in 2011. Gender disparity at the tertiary level is even more striking.

Obstacles that prevent girls from going to school include poverty, a lack of sanitation facilities, violence against girls, child marriage, and teen pregnancy. Various actions are taken to address these problems. For example, a UNICEF-sponsored program in Somalia provided scholarships to girls that helped pay for tuition, school supplies, and other expenses. The World Bank helped Yemen recruit and train female teachers and provided cash transfers to parents who allowed girls to go to school. UNESCO partnered with Procter & Gamble Company to support teachers in commitment to providing literacy and life skills to girls. In Brazil, a website and smart phone app provide information to women and girls to tackle violence. They help women find the closest police station, women's center, medical center, and other psychological and legal support.

Women's share of paid employment has continued to grow. The proportion of women employed outside the agriculture sector had increased from 35 percent in 1990 to 41 percent in 2015. However, women remain at a disadvantage in the labor market. Their participation in the labor force remains especially low in Northern Africa, Southern Asia, and Western Asia, where the ratio of women to men in the labor force ranges from 1:4 to 1:3. Barriers to women's employment include household responsibilities and cultural constraints.

Women are also more likely to live in poverty than men. Women earn 24 percent less than men globally. A study examining wealth assets found that women are more likely to live in poverty in 41 out of 75 countries with data, and particularly, widows and single mothers were at a greater risk of falling into poverty. In Latin America, despite declining poverty rates for the whole region, the ratio of women to men in poor households increased from 108 women for every 100 men in 1997 to 117 women for every 100 men in 2012. Factors that contribute to women's heightened vulnerability to poverty include unequal access to paid work, lower earnings and benefits, lack of financial security and social protection, and limited access to assets, such as land and property. Some measures are taken to address these issues. For example, in Rwanda, UN Women, a UN organization dedicated to gender equality and the empowerment of women, launched programs to train women in budgeting skills and business decision-making.

Women are gaining ground in the world's parliaments, although their representation is still far below gender parity. In 2012, women constituted 20 percent of parliament members globally, much of which was boosted by quota systems. In countries with legislated quotas, women took 24 percent of parliamentary seats, but only 12 percent in countries without quotas. Chapter 9 provides more discussion on gender inequality and women's movements globally.

SUSTAINABLE DEVELOPMENT AGENDA (2016–2030)

Most of the MDGs were largely met by 2015. Building on the success of the MDGs and keeping in mind the need of a new development agenda in the future, about 200 member states of the UN in 2015 reached consensus on the new agenda, "Transforming our World: The 2030 Agenda for Sustainable Development," which outlined a plan for the next 15 years with 17 specific **sustainable development goals** (**SDGs**). These goals were approved by world leaders at a UN summit in September 2015 and officially came into effect in 2016 (United Nations 2015).

According to the UN, **sustainable development** is development that meets the needs of the present without compromising the ability of future generations to meet their own needs. There are three interconnected and core elements: economic growth, social inclusion, and environmental protection. One major aim is to end all forms of poverty in the world.

In comparison to the MDGs, which included eight goals with 21 targets, the SDGs delineate 17 goals with 169 targets (United Nations 2018). See Table 2.3 for a discussion of these goals.

TABLE 2.3 2016–2030 SDGs

GOAL	WHAT IT LOOKS LIKE
1) No Poverty	ending extreme poverty in all its forms by 2030
2) Zero Hunger	ending hunger, achieving food security and improved nutrition, and promoting sustainable agriculture
3) Good Health and Well-Being	ensuring healthy lives and promoting well-being for all people at all ages
4) Quality Education	ensuring inclusive and equitable quality education and promoting lifelong learning opportunities for all
5) Gender Equality	achieving gender equality and empowering all women and girls
6) Clean Water and Sanitation	ensuring availability and sustainable management of water and sanitation for all
7) Affordable Clean Energy	ensuring access to affordable, reliable, sustainable, and modern energy for all
8) Decent Work and Economic Growth	promoting sustained, inclusive, and sustainable economic growth; full and productive employment; and decent work for all
9) Industry, Innovation, and Infrastructure	building resilient infrastructure, promoting inclusive and sustainable industrialization, and fostering innovation
10) Reduced Inequalities	reducing inequality within and among countries
11) Sustainable Cities and Communities	making cities and human settlements inclusive, safe, resilient, and sustainable
12) Responsible Consumption and Production	ensuring sustainable consumption and production patterns
13) Climate Action	taking urgent action to combat climate change and its impacts
14) Life Below Water	conserving and sustainably using the oceans, seas, and marine resources for sustainable development
15) Life and Land	protecting, restoring, and promoting sustainable use of terrestrial ecosystems; sustainably managing forests; combating desertification; and halting and reversing land degradation and biodiversity loss
16) Peace, Justice, and Strong Institutions	promoting peaceful and inclusive societies, providing access to justice for all, and building effective, accountable, and inclusive institutions at all levels
17) Partnership for the Goals	strengthening the means of implementing and revitalizing the global partnership for sustainable development

While MDGs only targeted developing countries, SDGs apply to all countries, poor and rich. World leaders recognize that ending poverty, fighting inequalities, and maintaining environmental protection must involve coordinating all countries and people to work together and to ensure that no one is left behind. The SDGs have drawn concerns and criticism for their too broad goals and formidable cost. The SDGs are expected to be more costly than the MDGs. While estimates vary, total investment needs in developing countries could cost in the order of \$3.3 to \$4.5 trillion (USD) per in-state spending, investment, and aid to meet the SDGs. Total investment need in economic infrastructure, including power, transport, telecommunications, and water and sanitation, is projected to rise to between \$1.6 and \$2.5 trillion annually over the period 2015–2030. There is an annual investment gap of between \$1.9 and \$3.1 trillion (UNCTAD 2014). Much of the additional amount needs to come from the private sector and external financing, such as development aid from developed countries, especially for low income countries (Council on Foreign Relations 2015).

Speaking in New York in 2014, former UK Prime Minister David Cameron said there were too many goals to communicate effectively. "There's a real danger they will end up sitting on a bookshelf, gathering dust," he said (Renwick 2015). Bjorn Lomborg, the head of the Copenhagen Consensus, argued that some of the SDGs' absolutist targets, such as ending malnutrition, HIV, malaria, and tuberculosis, are "unrealistic and uneconomical" and argued that focusing on fewer targets could produce better results (Lomborg 2014). The process of seeking to consult as widely as possible has resulted in "something for everyone." Some developing countries equated more goals with possibly more aid (Renwick 2015). There is still a divide between rich and poor countries. For example, "there is no consensus on how to tackle climate change and most countries are demanding that others, not they, should make sacrifices to strengthen the global economic system" (*The Economist* March 2015).

THE HUMAN DEVELOPMENT INDEX (HDI)

The **Human Development Index** (**HDI**), constructed by the UN in the 1990s, is a composite of three different indicators: GNI PPP per capita, life expectancy at birth, and education as measured by school enrollment and adult literacy. Apparently, it is superior to any individual component alone. It offers a more comprehensive assessment of people's well-being. It is about not only income but also stock in human capital. As discussed earlier, while some countries have found new sources of wealth, such as oil, the surge in national income does not necessarily benefit everyone, and it is not always translated into better well-being of the entire population. HDI, in some ways, corrects such potential bias. It has been adopted by the UN as an important measure of progress.

Figure 2.9 shows the mean of HDI in several developing regions and developed countries in 1980 and 2013 based on the information from the UN Development Program

(2014). There is not much surprise in the distribution of HDI across regions. The developed countries with an average HDI of 0.890 in 2013 were considerably ahead of the developing regions, among which Latin America took the lead with an average of 0.740, followed by East Asia, 0.703. While the Arab States were in the middle (0.682), South Asia and Sub-Saharan Africa were at the bottom at 0.588 and 0.502, respectively.

Figure 2.9 also shows the trend in HDI since 1980. All regions advance with no exception, though the pace of progress is uneven. South Asia and East Asia registered the largest improvement, with the index enlarged by more than half, followed by the Arab States and Sub-Saharan Africa. The two highest HDI groups on this chart, Latin America and developed countries, achieved the lowest advance, understandably, because they started off at higher levels in the first place.

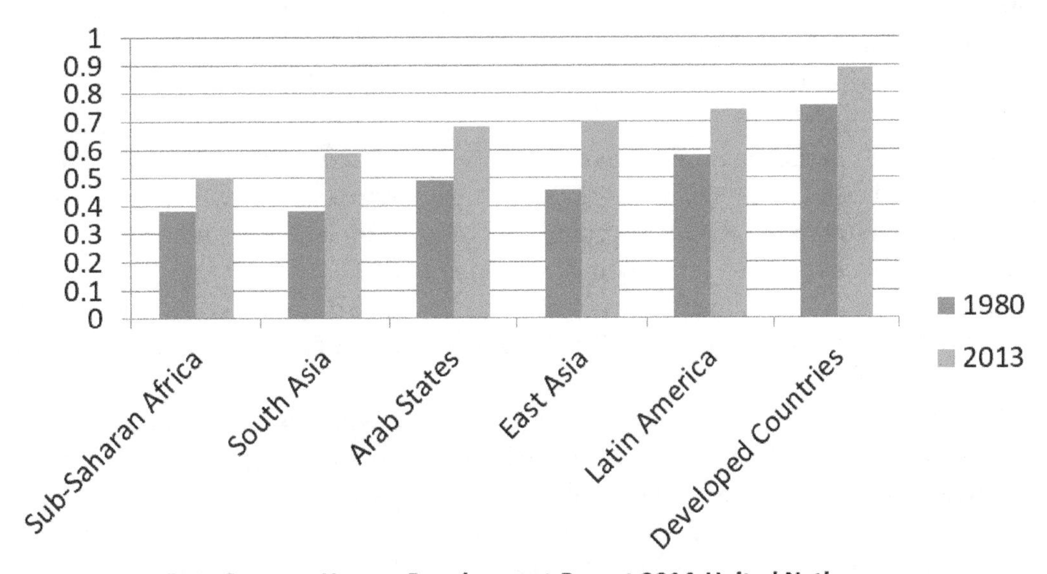

FIGURE 2.9 Human Development Index (HDI) in 1980 and 2013

The UN divides countries into four groups according to the HDI. Most of the countries in the **very high human development** group (HDI > 0.8)—49 of them—are developed countries, with some exceptions, such as Qatar, Chile, and Argentina. Of the 53 **high human development** countries (0.7 < HDI < 0.8), some of them are developed countries in Europe (like Romania), some developing countries from Latin America (like Mexico), and Asia (like Thailand). Most of the 42 **medium human development** countries (0.55 < HDI < 0.7) are from Asia (like India) and Africa (like Egypt). Finally, 43 countries fall in the category of **low human development** (HDI < 0.55). They are largely the least developed countries introduced above, mostly in Sub-Saharan Africa (like Sudan) and South Asia (like Nepal).

TABLE 2.4 ***HDI and Its Three Components of Selected Developing Countries in 2013***

	HDI RANK	HDI	GNI/CAPITA	LIFE EXPECTANCY	MEAN YEARS OF SCHOOLING
QATAR	31	0.851	$119,029	78.4	9.1
SAUDI ARABIA	34	0.836	$52,109	75.5	8.7
CUBA	44	0.815	$19,844	79.3	10.2
KUWAIT	46	0.814	$85,820	74.3	7.2

Data Source: Human Development Report 2014, UN Development Program.

Of course, the ranking of each country is not unchangeable. There has been movement of countries between human development groups since 1990, and 141 countries can be tracked. What is impressive is the upward mobility of the countries at the lower levels of the ladder. "Of the 47 countries in the low human development group in 1990, 16 are now in the medium group and 1 is in the high group (China), and of the 45 countries in the medium human development group in 1990, 29 are now in the high human development group and 3 (Argentina, Croatia and Saudi Arabia) are in the very high human development group" (UN Development Program 2014).

Since HDI is determined not by income alone but also by health and education, it is possible that some countries perform better in human development than others even though their income is lower. Table 2.4 compares four developing countries in HDI and its three components.

All of these four developing countries are in the very high human development category. What looks unordinary is Cuba, which is ranked number 44 globally, right above Kuwait and not far from Qatar and Saudi Arabia. Cuba's average income is about one-sixth of Qatar's, two-fifths of Saudi Arabia's, and a quarter of Kuwait's. Yet it stands close to these far richer peers in human development. The reason comes from the last two columns of the table. Cuba does better in life expectancy and average years of schooling of its population than all the other three. It is a result of strong investments in rural health and education, which directly benefited the general population.

Overall, lower human development groups continue to converge with the higher levels, although progress has slowed since 2008, thanks to the global financial crisis (UN Development Program 2014).

CRITICISM OF DEVELOPMENT AS OUTCOMES OF DESIRABLE TARGETS

One criticism to this approach is that it tends to be limited to measurable aspects of well-being, such as educational attainment and health. The qualitative dimension is left out, such as sense of security, life satisfaction, happiness, and spirituality. Some also argue that the objectives put forward by the UN or other international agencies may not be shared by all societies. It implies a kind of universality of a set of values or practices that are supposed to transcend particular cultural and historical heritage. The French parliament passed an act in 2010 to ban wearing face-coverings, such as masks and veils, in public places. The underlying rationale is that face-coverings hinder personal identification and thus pose a security risk, and they create hindrance for face-to-face communication in the society. To some, it also symbolizes suppression of women, which is in conflict with modern values of freedom and equality. The law imposes fines on those who are directly in violation and more severe terms on those who force others to wear face-coverings. Those who oppose the law argue that wearing face-coverings is part of Muslim cultural heritage, and many Muslim women wear them out of their faith and not of their husband's will. When there is a conflict like this, the question is who gets to decide winners and losers. Where does the legitimacy of judging come from? At the end of the day, is it a matter of power? Because of these concerns, some view development as a project imposed on developing countries by developed ones. One attempt to add a subjective dimension to development is the introduction of the concept of **happiness**.

GROSS NATIONAL HAPPINESS (GNH)

When it comes to the well-being or quality of life, measuring what one has, such as their income, property, education, or physical health, seems inadequate. In modern times, **happiness** seemingly can only be found in what one possesses. Psychological studies have shown, however, that what matters is how individuals feel about their life. The cliché "Money cannot buy happiness" is to the point. The rich enjoy financial freedom (buy what they want) and temporal freedom (do what they want), but they have their fair share of concerns. In a study of wealthy individuals who have a net worth of $25 million or more in the United States, these individuals were found to be anxious about the development of their children (their character, motivation, friendship, and achievement), their relationships, and fears of isolation. In addition, they face a common dilemma of how to best use their time and resources. As one wealthy person said, "You can just buy so much stuff, and when you get to the point where you can just buy so much stuff, now what are you going to do?" (Novotney 2012). In another study analyzing more than 450,000 responses to a Gallup survey, researchers found that although emotional well-being (i.e., experiences of joy, stress, sadness, anger, and affection) rises with income, it reaches a ceiling at an annual income of $75,000 in the United States. Health, care-giving, and loneliness are stronger predictors of daily emotions than income. The bottom line is higher income does not always bring more happiness (Kahneman and Deaton 2010).

The term **Gross National Happiness (GNH)** was first coined by Bhutan's fourth King, Jigme Singye Wangchuck, who received part of his education from the West, in 1972. Instead of pursuing a Western development model, which was focused on economic growth, or **Gross National Income (GNI)**, the King declared the happiness of the people to be more important and that national policies should be geared toward improving the well-being or general happiness of the citizens. Development should be more than merely satisfying material demand. Spiritual and material development should occur side by side to complement each other. GNH was put forward in the wake of this movement. Over time, this term has evolved into a multidimensional concept, which covers nine domains (psychological well-being, time use, health, good governance, education, community vitality, cultural diversity, ecological resilience, and living standard) measured by 33 indicators (Ura et al. 2012), all of which are listed in Table 2.5.

TABLE 2.5 ***Specific Domains and Indicators of GNH***

DOMAIN	INDICATOR	DOMAIN	INDICATOR
Psychological Well-Being	Life Satisfaction	Time Use	Work
	Positive Emotions		Sleep
	Negative Emotions		
Health	Self-Reported Health	Good Governance	Political Participation
	Healthy Days		Services
	Disability		Government Performance
	Mental Health		
Education	Literacy		
	Fundamental Schooling		
	Rights		
	Knowledge	Community Vitality	Donation
	Value		Safety
Cultural Diversity	Skills in Arts and Crafts		Leadership
	Cultural Participation		Family
	Native Language Speaking	Ecological Resilience	Wildlife
	Etiquette		Urban Issues
Living Standard	Income per Capita		Environmental Responsibility
	Assets		
	Housing		Ecological Issues

Source: Ura et al.

In addition, one distinctive feature of GNH is its going beyond self-orientation. It not only concerns the well-being of individuals themselves but also involves responsibility for others and harmony with nature. This point was well elucidated by Jigme Thinley, the first elected Prime Minister of Bhutan, in 2008:

> We have now clearly distinguished the "happiness" ... in GNH from the fleeting, pleasurable "feel good" moods so often associated with that term. We know that true abiding happiness cannot exist while others suffer, and comes only from serving others, living in harmony with nature, and realizing our innate wisdom and the true and brilliant nature of our own minds. (Ura et al.)

CONCLUSION

In conclusion, we can put forth the claim that there is no one method of development. We suggest that it is more fruitful to examine the problem of human development, and with this in mind, a broader, more open way of thinking about this human endeavor becomes evident. Clearly the MDGs have achieved some positive results in the areas of poverty reduction, education, and health. At the same time, the example of the Newly Industrialized Countries (NICs) discussed earlier are equally impressive and cannot simply be ignored either. Yet poverty and its consequences remain entrenched in a number of regions of the world. So the jury remains out. Problems arise, however, when we begin thinking that every country needs to follow the Western model of necessity. If human development is, as the UN put it, "much more than the rise or fall of national incomes" and is rather more about "expanding the choices people have to lead lives that they value," then building upon and expanding human capacities and capabilities in terms of good health, decent living standards and civic participation becomes the ultimate goal of development (UN Development Program 2001, 23).

By no means is this a perfect measure of development. However, it does point to a unique perspective, which takes into account the subjective or spiritual aspect of development. Even further, it raises a fundamental question about the definition of development itself. Is there supposed to be a universal standard that applies to all societies or cultures? And who gets to define it?

REFERENCES

Ashford, Lori S. "How HIV and AIDS Affect Populations." *Bridge*. Population Reference Bureau, 2006.

Brookings Institute. "A Global Compact on Learning: Taking Action on Education in Developing Countries." Washington, DC: Center for Universal Education at Brookings, 2011.

Castles, Ian. "Living Standards in Sydney and Japanese Cities: A Comparison." In *The Australian Economy in the Japanese Mirror*, edited by Kyoko Sheridan. Brisbane: University of Queensland Press, 1992.

Epstein, Mark J., and Kristi Yuthas. "Redefining Education in the Developing World." *Stanford Social Innovation Review* 10, no. 1 (Winter 2012): https://ssir.org/articles/entry/redefining_education_in_the_developing_world

Granich, Reuben, James G. Kahn, Rod Bennett, Charles B. Holmes, Navneet Garg, Celicia Serenata, Miriam Lewis Sabin, Carla Makhlouf-Obermeyer, Christina De Filippo Mack, Phoebe Williams, Louisa Jones, Caoimhe Smyth, Kerry A. Kutch, Lo Ying-Ru, Marco Vitoria, Yves Souteyrand, Siobhan Crowley, Eline L. Korenromp, Brian G. Williams. "Expanding ART for Treatment and Prevention of HIV in South Africa: Estimated Cost and Cost-Effectiveness 2011–2050." *PLoS ONE* 7, no. 2 (February 2012): https://journals.plos.org/plosone/article?id=10.1371/journal.pone.0030216

Hamilton, Clive. *Growth Fetish.* Sterling, Virginia: Pluto Press, 2004.

Kahneman, Daniel, and Angus Deaton. 2010. "High income improves evaluation of life but not emotional well-being." *Proceedings of the National Academy of Sciences* 107, no. 38 (September 2010): 16489–93.

Kaneda, Toshiko, and Kristen Bietsch., "2015 World Population Data Sheet." Washington, DC: Population Reference Bureau, 2015.

Lamptey, Peter R., Jami L. Johnson, and Marya Khan. 2006. "The Global Challenge of HIV and AIDS." *Population Bulletin* 61, no. 1 (March 2006): 1–24.

Levine, Ruth. "Millions Saved: Proven Successes in Global Health." *CGD Brief*, 3, no. 3 (October 2004): 1–7.

Lomborg, Bjorn. "Setting the Right Global Goals." *Eco-Business.* May 21, 2014. https://www.eco-business.com/opinion/setting-right-global-goals.

Lomborg, Bjorn. "The Spread of Western Disease: The Poor Are Dying More and More Like the Rich." *The Guardian.* March 2, 2015. https://www.theguardian.com/global/2015/mar/02/stroke-heart-disease-attack-cancer-developing-countries.

McMichael, Philip. "Contemporary Contradictions of the Global Development Project: Geopolitics, Global Ecology and the 'Development Climate.'" *Third World Quarterly* 30, no. 1 (January 2009): 247–62.

Novotney, Amy. "Money Can't Buy Happiness." *Monitor on Psychology* 43, no. 7 (July/August 2012): 24.

Population Reference Bureau (PRB). *2018 World Population Data Sheet.* Washington, DC: Population Reference Bureau, 2018.

Psacharopoulos, George, and Harry Anthony Patrinos. "Returns to Investment in Education: A Further Update." Policy Research Working Paper WPS2881. Washington, DC: The World Bank, 2002.

Ratzan, Scott C., Gary L. Filerman, and John W. LeSar. "Attaining Global Health: Challenges and Opportunities." *Population Bulletin*, 55, no. 1 (April): 1–48.

Renwick, Danielle. "Backgrounder: Sustainable Development Goals." Council on Foreign Relations, 2015.

Roudi-Fahimi, Farzaneh. "Time to Intervene: Preventing the Srpead of HIV/AIDS in the Middle East and North Africa." MENA Policy Briefs. Washington DC: Population Reference Bureau, 2007.

The Economist. "Learning Unleashed: Low-Cost Private Schools." August 1, 2015. https://www.economist.com/briefing/2015/08/01/learning-unleashed.

The Economist. "Unsustainable Goals: Global Economic Development." March 26, 2015. https://www.economist.com/international/2015/03/26/unsustainable-goals.

UNAIDS. *2006 Report on the Global AIDS Epidemic.* 2006. http://www.data.unaids.org/pub/report/2006/2006_gr_en.pdf.

UNAIDS. "Cambodia Commits to Stopping New HIV Infections by 2020." December 9, 2014. http://www.unaids.org/en/resources/presscentre/featurestories/2014/december/20141208_cambodia.

UN Conference on Trade and Development (UNCTAD). *World Investment Report 2014: Investing in the SDGs: An Action Plan.* New York.

UN Development Program. *Human Development Report 2001,* New York: United Nations, 2001.

UN Development Program. *Human Development Report 2014.* New York: United Nations, 2014.

UNICEF. "Water and Sanitation Fit for the Children of Equatorial Guinea." February 29, 2008. https://www.unicef.org/infobycountry/equatorialguinea_43041.html.

United Nations. *Human Development Report 1990.* New York: Oxford University Press, 1990.

United Nations. *Human Development Report 1996.* New York: Oxford University Press, 1996.

United Nations. "Sustainable Development Goals." UN English. May 30, 2019. https://www.un.org/sustainabledevelopment/sustainable-development-goals/.

United Nations. *The Millennium Development Goals Report 2015.* New York: United Nations. 2015.

United Nations. *The Sustainable Development Goals Report 2018.* New York: United Nations, 2018.

Ura, Karma, Sabina Alkire, Tshoki Zangmo, and Karma Wangdi. *A Short Guide to Gross National Happiness Index.* Thimphu, Bhutan: The Centre for Bhutan Studies, 2012.

Winthrop, Rebecca, and Corinne Graff. *Beyond Madrasas: Assessing the Links Between Education and Militancy in Pakistan.* Washington, DC: Brookings Institution, 2010.

World Bank. 2019a. Accessed on May 30, 2019. https://data.worldbank.org/indicator/NY.GNP.MKTP.CD?most_recent_value_desc=true

World Bank. 2019b. Accessed on May 30, 2019. https://data.worldbank.org/indicator/ny.gnp.pcap.cd

World Bank. 2019c. Accessed on May 30, 2019. https://data.worldbank.org/indicator/ny.gnp.pcap.pp.cd

World Health Organization (WHO). *The Global Burden of Disease: 2004 Update.* Geneva: WHO Press, 2008.

World Health Organization (WHO). "Ebola Virus Disease—Democratic Republic of the Congo." *Disease Outbreak News.* WHO. December 28, 2018.

Figure Credits

Fig. 2.2: Data Source: The Millennium Development Goals Report 2015, United Nations.

CHAPTER THREE

The Advent of Colonialism

INTRODUCTION

Chapters 3 through 6 chronicle capitalist world development. As discussed in chapter 1, of the two perspectives explaining the underdevelopment of developing countries, the South Perspective views the developing countries as immensely impacted by developed countries in the past and present. Colonialism begins this chronology. Chapter 4 examines the postcolonial era in a manner that draws parallels with modernization in chapter 5. Chapter 6 frames globalization and ends with the emergence of multipolar globalization, the current trajectory of global economic and political world order.

As a means of introduction, we begin by reexamining **national holidays**. We present holidays as a living history that can partially be traced to colonial times. Holiday narratives also embody distinct power relations between **dominant** and **subaltern** (subordinate) social groups. We then outline four critically important changes that led to the establishment of capitalism: the transformation of common property into private property, the concept of surplus labor value, and the capitalist mode of production are the first three. The fourth factor, the result of these changes, creates a world that requires **perpetual growth**. Settler colonialism was a direct European political intervention. Settler European colonialism required a political-administrative presence in the colonized country to ensure reliable continuation of the highly profitable export of raw materials and people to fuel industrial development at home. We then examine two case studies from the internal US settler colonial era involving relations with Indigenous Peoples. Another important mode of production during the settler colonial era was the development of the plantation model. Here, we trace the history of the plantation from its origin up to the present, notably in the Caribbean and parts of South America. The colonizers' need for perpetual growth and new sources of raw industrial materials and slave labor both within colonies and abroad led to the colonialization of Africa, where concludes the chapter.

THE COLONIAL ROOTS OF HOLIDAYS

Every year, nation-states around the world celebrate their independence and other auspicious events in their histories. These holidays and the accompanying stories symbolize and reflect upon cherished values that lie at the center of a national identity. In the United States, we celebrate the Fourth of July, Thanksgiving, Veterans Day, and Columbus Day along with other officially recognized national markers that address "who we are and what we stand for." It is important to examine these narratives because they often reveal a colonial backdrop and a hidden structure of power relations. Who is powerful, right, and strong and who is subordinate, misguided, and weak is illuminated in these representations and foundational narratives.

In these narratives the storyteller is often the one who is dominant and holds power. Presented as historical fact, these narratives and their legitimacy are never really scrutinized for accuracy, inclusiveness, or context. The **subaltern group** (those who are subordinate) is generally ignored or sanitized in these stories in a way that fits the dominant view of the storyteller. Thanksgiving is a sharp example of this myth-making. Traced to colonial times, the story is told about the Pilgrims and the "Indians" coming together to share a feast. The event has never been factually substantiated. The "Thanksgiving Indians," who are the present day Wampanoag Tribe of Massachusetts, have their own narrative that is nothing like that which is celebrated in mainstream America. As discussed later in the chapter, the Wampanoag were subjected to oppressive colonial domination that led to their almost complete demise. Likewise, the "discovering" of America by Columbus was more of an accident than discovery, and the ascension of Columbus as a revered historical figure came later, when the United States adopted Greco-Roman forms of government. Along these same lines, Phil Deloria (1998) convincingly argues that the early patron saint of America was not Columbus but a Delaware Chief, Tammany, and colonialists organized secret societies to honor him. Columbus and Columbiana came only later to fit the new Greco-Roman sensibilities of building a nation-state. Yet who has ever heard of Chief Tammany?

The Fourth of July is yet another example of our colonial myth-making and celebration of these exercises in power. In contrast, the great African American abolitionist, Frederick Douglass (1817–1895) gave a speech on the 4th of July in 1852 from the standpoint of the subaltern—the slave:

> I am not included within the pale of this glorious anniversary! Your high independence only reveals the immeasurable distance between us. The blessings in which

> you this day rejoice are not enjoyed in common. The rich inheritance of justice, liberty, prosperity, and independence bequeathed by your fathers is shared by you, not by me. The sunlight that brought life and healing to you has brought stripes and death to me. This Fourth of July is yours, not mine. You may rejoice, I must mourn. To drag a man in fetters into the grand illuminated temple of liberty, and call upon him to join you in joyous anthems, were inhuman mockery and sacrilegious irony. Do you mean, citizens, to mock me, by asking me to speak today? If so, there is a parallel to your conduct. And let me warn you, that it is dangerous to copy the example of a nation (Babylon) whose crimes, towering up to heaven, were thrown down by the breath of the Almighty, burying that nation in irrecoverable ruin. (Douglass 1852)

Many of these dominant nation-state holiday narratives were shaped in a colonial context. We celebrate them today. Those in power tell the story and clearly demarcate who has power and who does not. These stories legitimate the capitalist nature of societal organization that began during the colonial period and led to the accumulation of great wealth. We now turn to an examination of the origins of capitalism, highlighting distinct features that in turn spurred the advent of colonialism.

THE ORIGINS OF CAPITALISM

Early capitalist development during the colonial period was a project of European nation-states. These states engaged in efforts to control other peripheral regions, territories, kingdoms, and nascent states in Africa, Latin America, Asia, and North America. Broadly, **imperialism** refers to any effort to control another state, region, or territory economically, militarily, and politically. A specific form of imperialism. defined as **settler colonialism** or **internal colonialism**, is the focus of this chapter. **Colonialism** entails the political control of another state, region, or territory.

Capitalism is a relatively recent historical phenomenon emerging in the 1600–1700s. There are four conditions essential to capitalism: the institutionalization of private property and the surplus value of labor are combined into the capitalist mode of production, leading to the necessity for perpetual growth.

First, **common property** is property held collectively by a select group of users. It entails rights of customary use by that user group. Common property arrangements exclude those outside the group. Users follow specific rules that allow for the sharing of benefits to be obtained by every user, no more and no less. This communal arrangement was widespread prior to the full development of capitalism and nation-states. The transformation of common property to private property became a necessary requirement for capitalist growth (see Figure 3.1).

FIGURE 3.1 The Transformation of Common Property into Private Property

Figure 3.1 above illustrates one of the key features in the establishment of capitalism—the **institutionalization of private property**. Meiksins Wood (2000) provides a detailed historical account of how this new property regime came to be. She states that capitalism *did not* originate in cities but rather first occurred in the British countryside—the origins of capitalism were agrarian. Britain, as early as the sixteenth century, was a relatively well-unified, centralized state. A village population had certain rights of access to open fields, such as agricultural areas divided into narrow strips for cultivation, and wastes, which were unproductive areas, such as marshes and rocky land to pasture animals, fish the waters, or collect firewood. Profit motives were tied to increasing the productivity of the land. Large landowners who strongly desired to remove impediments to profit and capital accumulation saw the common property system as an obstacle in doing so. For the stated purpose of making the land more productive, the British Parliament passed the Enclosure Acts, a series of acts passed primarily between 1750 and 1860. The land was consolidated, and much ended up in the hands of large landowners, who were usually politically connected. Many peasants lost their prior access to rural land. Hence the move was made to realign property rights from common to private rights. As put by Meiksins Wood (2000),

> Enclosure is often thought of as simply the privatization and fencing in of formerly common land, or of the "open fields" that characterized certain parts of the English countryside. But enclosure meant, more particularly, the extinction (with or without a physical fencing of land) of common and customary use-rights on which many people depended for their livelihood. (33)

As a result, rural peasants forced by economic necessity flocked to the industrializing cities of Britain, resulting in the early formation of an industrial society. Note that common property entails much more than a physical barrier, such as a fence. Common property also includes customary use rights by those who utilize the field. These use rights apply to all members of the group, no more and no less. Hence a farmer, for example, would not be permitted to decide to arbitrarily increase his herd size, because his decision violates customary use rights held by all user group members.

The second key condition of capitalist development involves the taking of surplus labor value by the capitalist in the form of paying to workers wages that are only a portion of the full value of the work (see Figure 3.2 below). Imagine peasants who work a common property field under the watchful eye of a feudal lord. While the peasant has direct control over the means of production, the tools and seed required to produce the crop, the lord takes part of the harvest as a means of tribute, taxes, and so on, in return offering the peasant protection from unwanted intruders. The peasant is exploited but does not lose access to the means of production. With the transformation of the commons into private property, the peasant loses access to the means of production and is forced to sell the only factor under his or her control—labor.

Under these conditions, the peasant was then forced to migrate to the growing industrial urban centers to find work. The peasant, now a laborer, receives a wage

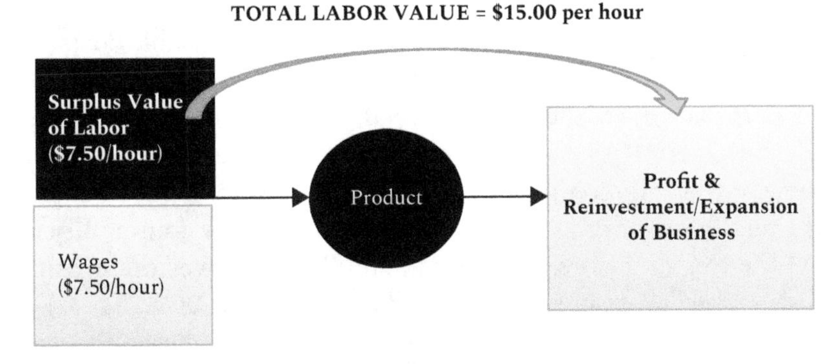

FIGURE 3.2 The Surplus Value of Labor

that represents *only partial value of the full value of that labor.* The full value of the worker's labor power is expropriated (taken away) by the owner of the factory. This surplus value of labor provides the capitalist a means to profit and accumulate capital and expand the business, as shown in Figure 3.2 above.

Private property and the taking of surplus labor value by the capitalist set into motion the following generalized equation that depicts the third factor, the capitalist mode of production, where

> I = **investment**, refers to the mobilizing of assets that can be used to create more wealth. Assets can be monies, stocks, bonds, loans, property, time, and effort. Capitalist entrepreneurs can aggregate these items in order to secure the raw materials and means of production in order to produce goods or commodities.
>
> RM = **raw materials**, unprocessed items that can be converted into goods and commodities. A good example of raw material is crude oil, which is then processed into fuel for cars. Another example would be wood used for the building of houses.
>
> MP = **means of production**, refers to the actual facilities and tools used for production. A factory, machines, and transport are all part of the means of production.
>
> CG = **commodity/good, the product or item produced and sold**
>
> La = **labor**, used to produce the commodity/good.
>
> Pr = profit, the net revenue after costs

Hence, adding the components of the above into the equation format below shows how commodity/goods and profit are produced in a capitalist society.

$$I + RM \dashrightarrow \frac{MP}{La} \dashrightarrow CG \dashrightarrow Pr$$

Producing a commodity/good involves both fixed and variable costs. **Fixed costs** refers to the nonfluctuating **operating expenses** of producing a commodity/good independent of the volume of the item produced. **Variable costs** can fluctuate depending on production quantities. Labor for example can increase or decrease depending on the volume of the commodity/good produced. The sum of the fixed and variable costs are the total costs of production. The total sales of the commodity is the **gross revenue**. Subtracting gross revenue from the total costs leaves the **profit** or a loss if the total costs exceed gross revenue (adapted from Robbins 2011, 34–37).

These first three factors, common property to private property, the surplus value of labor, and the mode of production, lead to a fourth factor: the need for capitalism to perpetually grow. Nation-state-bound capitalists quickly required more raw materials and labor than what their local environs could supply. With the harnessing of wind power for ocean travel, they began the search for overseas markets and new sources of raw materials, such as sugar, tea, coffee, spices, ivory, rubber, and gold, among many others, and other humans to produce and source the necessary goods. The question became where to look? And the answer was overseas, hence solidifying the rise and shaping of earlier forms of colonialism, illustrated by two examples in the next section.

SETTLER COLONIALISM AND INDIGENOUS PEOPLES IN THE UNITED STATES: A CASE OF INTERNAL COLONIALISM

Colonialism is a specific form of imperialism, a policy in which one nation-state dominates another state, territory, or region economically, politically, militarily, diplomatically, or culturally. Colonialism refers "to the period from the beginning of the sixteenth century onwards in which economic and political motivations fused together to give spatial expression to the accelerating of globalization of capitalism" (Potter et al. 2013, 51). The key to this definition is the political control established by one state (the colonizer) over another state, region, or territory (the colonized). The following two examples from North America focus on the early internal colonial relations between settler colonialists and Indigenous Peoples.

Conquest of Indigenous Peoples began with first contact by Europeans and continues up to the present. In the initial stages, contact with Europeans and colonial settlers generally involved mutually agreed on trade relations and sharing of territorial spaces. These market-based economic relations, however, favored Europeans and quickly became antagonistic due to geographical proximity and direct competition over access to land and resources. A good example involves the Wampanoag, an Indigenous group often associated with the United States holiday of Thanksgiving.

The Wampanoag

The Wampanoag inhabited what eventually became the Northeastern part of the United States (later Rhode Island and Massachusetts) for thousands of years (Weinstein-Farson 1989). First contact with Western explorers may have taken place as early as the 1500s, with the later establishment of the Plymouth Colony in the 1600s bringing the Wampanoag into much more proximate contact with the English settler colonialists. This early contact gave rise to the Thanksgiving story, in which the Wampanoag shared their corn, squash, and beans with the inhabitants of the colony at New Plymouth, saving them from starvation (Weinstein-Farson). Although highly romanticized and with no Wampanoag account or specific reference to this event by the Pilgrims themselves, we can assume that a measure of stability prevailed during these first encounters.

These early relations quickly deteriorated as increased settlement by British colonialists impinged upon Wampanoag territories, resulting in conflict. The Wampanoag were subject to encroachment by increasing numbers of colonial settlers into farming, fishing, and hunting territories and were also subjected to the colony's court system. Despite treaties established between the colonialists and the Wampanoag, tensions remained and led to King Philip's war from 1675 to 1676. The war left the Wampanoag decimated and confined to reservations or subordinate status in the New England region (Weinstein-Farson). As a result, the Wampanoag were forced to accommodate Western cultural influences. The Wampanoag were recently added as one of the 566 US federal government's recognized tribal entities. At present, about 1,500–2,000 Wampanoag carry on with restoring their traditional practices and preserving their rich cultural history. See Wamapanoag Tribe of Gay Head (2019) for a recent overview of some present day Wampanoag tribal government activities.

This brief case of the Wampanoag elicits a pattern consistent with the experiences of many other Indigenous groups in both the Global North and the Global South. When considering the idea of ethnocide, or the systematic destruction of a group's culture, there is a four-step process that is clearly illustrated by the plight of the Wampanoag. First, in order for the process of ethnocide to begin, the subordinate group must occupy a desired territory. The colonial settlers desired the resources controlled by the Wampanoag, which led to the second step of the process, **military intervention**. Despite treaties with the Europeans, the Wampanoag suffered huge losses in King Philip's war, which further weakened their society. The third step, **extension of government control**, is evident in the fact that this Indigenous group was subject to the colony's court system. The fourth and final step of ethnocide is the **destruction of indigenous culture**. The Wampanoag were dispersed after the war diminished their population and remained under the threat of more violence as they were forced to submit to Western cultural influences. In almost all instances of indigenous conquest and other colonial cases from Africa, Asia, and Latin America, violence and virulent racism were a common thread of colonial relations.

The Fur Trade

Cornell and Hartmann (1998) also provide an overview of early colonial—Indigenous relations during this period of North American history. An interesting observation regarding initial contact provided by Cornell and Hartmann explains that "when most Indians first encountered Europeans, they saw them simply as another variety of stranger—a people they had previously come across" (109). Unlike the Europeans, who viewed Native Americans as the exotic Other, Indigenous groups generally accepted the white men as equals, the same as any other people. This perception changed during the establishment of the fur trade. There was a high demand for fur clothing in Europe, and Indigenous groups residing away from the coast possessed the skills and access to fur-bearing populations of animals to produce these goods.

In exchange, Indigenous groups received European manufactured goods. Hence, the market was an intermediary institution that facilitated these voluntary modes of exchange (Cornell and Hartmann, 108–13).

As the demand for fur waned (along with the Indian labor essential for producing it), by the end of the eighteenth century, settler colonial expansion set its sights on land and natural resources (Cornell and Hartmann). Through treaties, military occupation, and the removal of Indigenous Peoples onto reservations, the United States marginalized Indigenous tribes. In some cases genocide occurred. For example, the slaughter of the American bison on the Great Plains led to the demise of tribes that inhabited that region (LaDuke 1999; Robbins 2011). Substituting industrial-scale beef cattle for Bison led to further ecological degradation of fragile grasslands. Indigenous groups throughout North America have proven, however, to be incredibly resilient to these onslaughts. With the emergence of Indigenous social movements in the late 1960s, we find measurable gains being attained by some tribes, even though conflict over oil and minerals with corporate and US governmental interests remains unabated.

THE PLANTATION SYSTEM

Another settler colonialist form of organization that emerged during the mercantile and industrial eras of capitalist development was the plantation system (see Table 3.1 below). The first plantations were established in the fifteenth century off the West African coast and then later by the Spanish in the Caribbean and South America and by the Portuguese in Brazil (Potter et al. 2013, 57–58). Indigenous Caribbean populations were subjected to genocide, and other populations in central and southern America were severely diminished, if not completely eliminated (Kiernan 2007). Dutch, English, and French colonialists during the mercantile period also established colonies in Asia and North America and supplanted the Spanish in the Caribbean. In this context, Potter et al. (2013, 102–06) introduce the plantation model of development, which tracks the growth of this organizational form predominantly in the Caribbean up to the modern era. Early plantations (1750–1832) involved an autonomous plantation connected to a town that served as a center for commerce and social control. The emancipation phase (1833–1949) was much like the first phase, except that peasant farmers occupied small plots close to the main plantation. These subsistence peasant producers also supplied the labor for the plantation. In the modern era (1950 onward), the integration of the plantation with industry, tourism, and urban outgrowth displays a highly uneven pattern of development. In many Caribbean countries, the urban—plantation connection is a dominant pattern that structures and concentrates wealth, power, and political control among the elites of a particular Caribbean nation.

In Europe, the growing demand for tea, tobacco, and especially sugar stimulated plantation production, which was undertaken by African slaves. As Mintz (1995) notes;

> In the case of the history of sugar in Britain, it was the servants of the imperial political and economic system that carved out the West Indies colonies and gave them governments; saw to the successful—immense and centuries-long—importation of enslaved Africans to the islands; bequeathed land wrested from the indigenes to the first settlers; financed and managed the ever-rising importation of tropical goods to Britain, including chocolate, coffee, cotton and tobacco as well as sugar, rum, molasses, tea and much else; and levied taxes at all levels of society to benefit its servants and the [colonial] state. (6)

The emergence of sugar and tea consumption in Britain itself reflects the transition from mercantile to industrial capitalism. In conjunction with this transformation, we find increased urbanization and the emergence of the British working class. As Mintz (1995, 4–5) speculates, the addition of sugar to other plantation imports such as coffee, tea, chocolate, and tobacco acted as a stimulant to ease one through the industrial working day. While once a luxury, sugar's increasing availability entered it into a wide array of food items. The distant plantations run by slave labor fueled this commodity's growth.

The above examples further suggest that colonialism has exhibited long periodic waves of growth, transformation, and expansion in the overall development of global capitalism. Table 3.1 below brings to light the expansive drive of capitalism and shows how colonialism took shape, overlapping and corresponding with different eras of capitalist development.

Table 3.1 above just begins to illustrate the enormous complexity of the colonial era and the formation of postcolonial relations, as will be described in chapter 4. For present purposes, three salient points stand out:

1. The continuing need for capitalism to grow.
2. The desire to maximize profit, whether through direct conquest by the colonizing power or by indirect means through host country intermediaries who worked on behalf of the colonizers.
3. The effects of the colonial era are embedded at the macro and micro levels in both developing and developed countries. At present, these lasting effects are currently evident in a number of global and local situations.

The establishment of colonies varied enormously across geographical space and time. For example, peak colonization occurred from roughly 1500 to 1800 in Latin America; 1600–1760 in North America; 1800–1945 in Asia; and 1880–1945 in Africa (Potter et. al. 2013, 57). Colonization tended to develop in terms of periodic waves and periods of stagnation that correspond with the eras illustrated in Table 3.1. For

TABLE 3.1 *A Partial Depiction of the Colonial Era (1400–Present)*

ERA	PERIOD	FEATURES
The Age of Discovery; Contact and Conquest	1400–1650	The beginning of international trade, brought on by Portuguese and Spanish advances in oceangoing merchant ships and navies. Followed by the Dutch, British, and French, these European powers made contact and established dominant trade relations with the peoples of coastal West Africa; Asia, especially India and China; Latin America; North America; and the Caribbean region. Plunder and decimation of Indigenous Peoples was common. These relations were highly profitable for the European nations.
Mercantile Capitalism	1650–1780s	The mercantile era of capitalism saw the intensification of trade and commerce. This era brought forth the rise of the plantation system in the Caribbean and South America and significant growth in the coastal West African slave trade that filled the demand for labor to produce plantation-based sugar, coffee, tea, and tobacco. Colonial powers administered and managed these systems through large monopolistic trading companies such as the French West India Company and the Dutch West India Company. The British Royal African Company traded in slaves as Liverpool and Bristol emerged as major slave-trading centers. The expansion of trade required direct European presence in the new colonies.
Industrial Capitalism	1780s–1920	This era can be characterized by greater volume and demand for manufactured goods. Raw materials were obtained from overseas colonies, especially in Africa and Asia. As an example of internal colonization, the United States became a power in its own right and proceeded to subdue Indigenous populations in the Eastern and Western portions of the country. The slave trade provided capitalists the ability to coerce further profits and expansion. As markets expanded, the demand for export commodities increased. A direct foreign presence was required to enforce these uneven trade relations. Agricultural crops for export were established to keep food prices low in the industrializing countries. The Berlin Conference of 1884 began the process of partitioning the continent of Africa into colonies among the European powers.
Late Colonialism	1920–1945	The colonial presence was intensified after the First World War. British, Dutch, and French migrants established themselves as economic, military, and political administrators in Asia (e.g., India, Vietnam, Cambodia) and parts of Africa (e.g., Rhodesia, Kenya). Other European migrants occupied prime agricultural lands, where they produced crops for export. Early independence and nationalist aspirations began during this era.

Source: Adapted from Potter et al. (2013) and Robbins (2011).

example, as capitalism transitioned from **mercantile** to **industrial capitalism**, the number of colonies declined. As industrial capitalism took hold in the late 1880s, a number of North American and European countries expanded colonial control over African and Asian countries, only to decline in the post–Second World War era to virtually none. However, as demonstrated in chapter 4, new forms of imperialist domination became prominent during the Cold War era and persist up to the present.

In summation, the expansion of global capitalism lies at the heart of explaining how forms of colonialism developed and became manifest. This development varied widely among the United States, Great Britain, and France, to mention a few colonizing powers. As Rodney (1972) notes, both colonizer and colonized must be accounted for when analyzing these historical frames. We will turn our attention to the African continent to clarify this complex moment in world capitalist development.

COLONIALISM IN AFRICA

The scope of colonialism is aptly summarized by Clapham (cited in Potter et al. 2013, 55), who observes that "the Americas [were] rich and easy to control; Asia [was] rich but difficult to control; and Africa, for the most part was poor and so [was] scarcely worth controlling." Difficulties in producing adequate revenue and managing colonial administrations and rebellions made the going for French, Dutch, and British colonialists very difficult in Asia. Africa was another case altogether.

Prior to European contact, we find an African continent that shows great diversity in terms of social organization, development, and commerce. For the most part, **communalism** prevailed in semisubsistence societies, with the extended family being the key unit in largely patriarchal or matrilineal forms of social organization (Rodney 1972). As summarized by Rodney, "most African societies before 1500 were in a transitional stage between the practice of agriculture (plus fishing and herding) in family communities and the practice of the same activities within states and societies comparable to feudalism" (38). Rodney further notes that prior to European contact:

> In Africa, there were few slaves and certainly no epoch of slavery. Most of the slaves were in Northern African and other [Islamic] societies, and in those instances a man and his family could have the same slave status for generations, within the overall feudal structure of society. Elsewhere in Africa, communal societies were introduced to the concept of owning alien human beings when they took captives in war. At first, those captives were in a very disadvantaged position, comparable to that of slaves, but very rapidly captives or their offspring became ordinary members of the society, because there was no scope for the perpetual exploitation of man by man in a context that was neither feudal or capitalist. (38)

African life was harsh, precarious, and short for the majority of Africans. These subsistence-based societies developed finely grained adaptations to their own environments in foraging, growing staple crops, and raising livestock. In these societies, there was little discernible class stratification, but a hierarchy did arise between the young and their elders and between already existing pastoralists, cultivators, and fishers. Contact with other social groups also accentuated differences between Africans. Trade in gold and salt was also an early precontact activity that led to wars and raids by those elite groups who attempted to control production as a form of social status and prestige.

African communal societies, small-scale foragers, fishers, pastoralists, and agriculturalists, were well adapted to particular environmental settings for subsistence needs. Other African societies exhibited stronger mercantile organization, with well-developed bronze, iron, copper, ivory, and gold production, among other items. International trade routes were also prevalent between coastal African societies and Europe, China, and India. The interior of Africa exhibited local and regional trade relations (Hochschild 2006).

Outside of feudal North Africa (e.g., Egypt) the vast majority of the African continent was at this time transitioning from communalism to feudal relations (Rodney 1972). Early kingdoms emerged in Ghana, Mali, and in the vast savanna and forest regions (Potter et al. 2013, 49). As Rodney (1972, 78) notes, African river canoes and bronze castings were of high quality, yet they didn't measure up to the European ships and cannons. When it came to the establishment of laws governing trade relations, Europe unequivocally made all legal decisions. Africans had no say whatsoever.

As early as the 1530s, the early European contact along the Western African coast set into motion the **Transatlantic Slave Trade**, which became more prominent during the colonization of the Caribbean and South American continent (Hochschild 2006). The demand was for plantation labor, and African slaves were the source of this labor.

The Transatlantic Slave Trade accelerated during the mercantile capitalist era, which brought the plantation system to the Caribbean, South America, and the southern United States in order to produce sugar, cotton, and other exportable commodities. Originally, gold was a priority for European traders, but this commodity, which formed the wealth value of the currency system, was limited to only a few small areas on the African continent. In addition, Senegal engaged with European traders in gum, Sierra Leone had camwood, and Mozambique supplied ivory, all favorable in European terms of trade (Rodney 1972). The notorious case of Congo (see Box 3.1) was a source of ivory and later rubber that fueled Belgian King Leopold's enormous personal fortune. Leopold's private colony was built on slave labor and enforced by the brutal *Force Publique,* consisting of Belgian officers and conscripted African soldiers, often Congolese (Hochschild 2006). There is no doubt, however, that the slave trade was Africa's major export. As Europeans colonized the Americas, there was a pressing need for labor; land was abundant and the Indigenous populations were susceptible to diseases such as small pox and to military might, which effectively acted as genocide. The allure of European commodities, while of generally inferior quality, was the incentive that induced African rulers to offer up people as slaves. As Rodney (1972) illustrates;

> Estaban Montejo, an African who ran away from a Cuban slave plantation in the nineteenth century, recalled that his people were enticed into slavery by the color red. He said:
>
> > It was the scarlet which did for the Africans; both the kings and the rest surrendered without a struggle. When the kings saw that the whites were taking out these scarlet handkerchiefs as if they were waving, they told the blacks, "Go on then, go and get a scarlet handkerchief," and the blacks were so excited by the scarlet they ran down to the ships like sheep and there they were captured.
>
> That version by one of the victims of slavery is very poetic. What it means is that some African rulers found European goods sufficiently desirable to hand over captives which they had taken in warfare. (79)

The Transatlantic Slave Trade corresponded with the existing political divisions evident in communal African societies. Differences between one ruler and another could easily be exploited. One Portuguese slave trader remarked that Guinea-Bissau was "a slave trader's paradise," as there were a multitude of different ethnic groups that could easily be turned against one and another (Rodney, 79). When African rulers attempted to resist the European slavers, they were quickly put down by military force, as the Europeans deployed superior weaponry such as cannons and guns.

King Leopold's Ghost (Hochschild 2006, see Box 3.1) reminds us that it is critical to recognize that the underdevelopment of Africa must be considered as cojoined with the development of Europe (Rodney). Figure 3.3 below illustrates trade during the era of mercantile capitalism. In sum, the trade in slaves and other commodities facilitated the expansion of capitalism from the mercantile to the industrial system and, most importantly, allowed both Western Europe and North America to accumulate great wealth.

The embodiment of clearly defined nation-states in Western Europe and the internal colonization of the United States greatly facilitated the growth of industry. Africa remained vulnerable during this period. European forces found willing allies in local chiefs and colonized elites who acted as go-betweens to facilitate the flow of raw materials, market development, and assistance with investments. Coupled with these African facilitators were Christian missionaries, colonial administrators, and traders, who were infused with the ideology of racism that was used as a means to justify and legitimate blatant exploitation of the African continent.

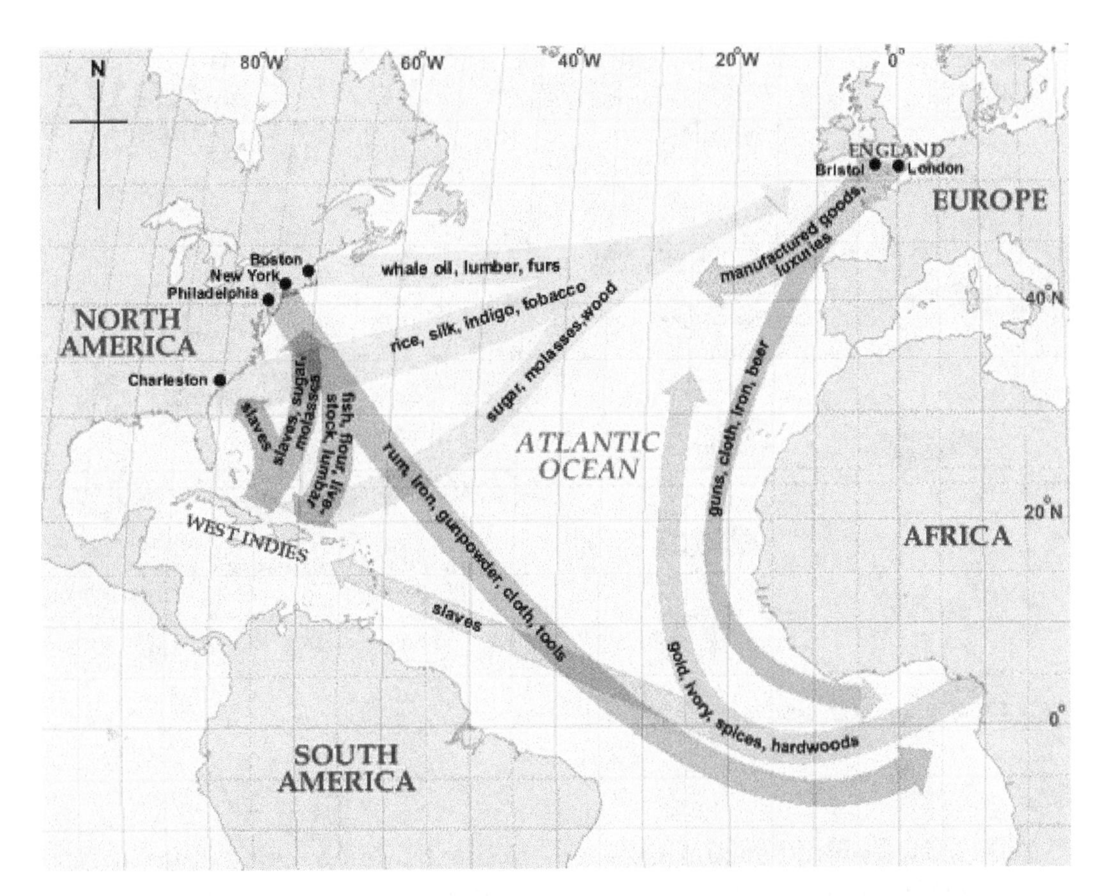

FIGURE 3.3 International Trade during the Mercantile Period of Capitalism

The Significance of Slavery

The Transatlantic slave trade established the means to create unsurpassed wealth in Europe and in the Americas (Emory University, 2019). Indeed, the development of the United States and underdevelopment of Sub-Saharan Africa at present largely rest upon the legacy of slavery (Rodney 1972). Enforced with virulent strains of institutional racism and superior and inferior hardening of a racialized social stratification ensured that the capitalist system continues to grow. Figure 3.4 below depicts the Transatlantic slave trade during the industrial era.

As can be seen from Figure 3.4, slavery was largely deployed in two primary-sector economies, agriculture and mining. The slave system suited the demand for labor at its most inhumane level. Slavery allowed the slave traders, merchants, trading companies, and plantation owners to accumulate enormous profit. This profit led to increased capital accumulation, leading in turn to the expansion of capitalist industries. As the plantation system gave way to industrialization, the need for slaves did not mesh with the demand for more skilled workers. It was not happenstance that the American South, for example, was the last region of the United States to industrialize.

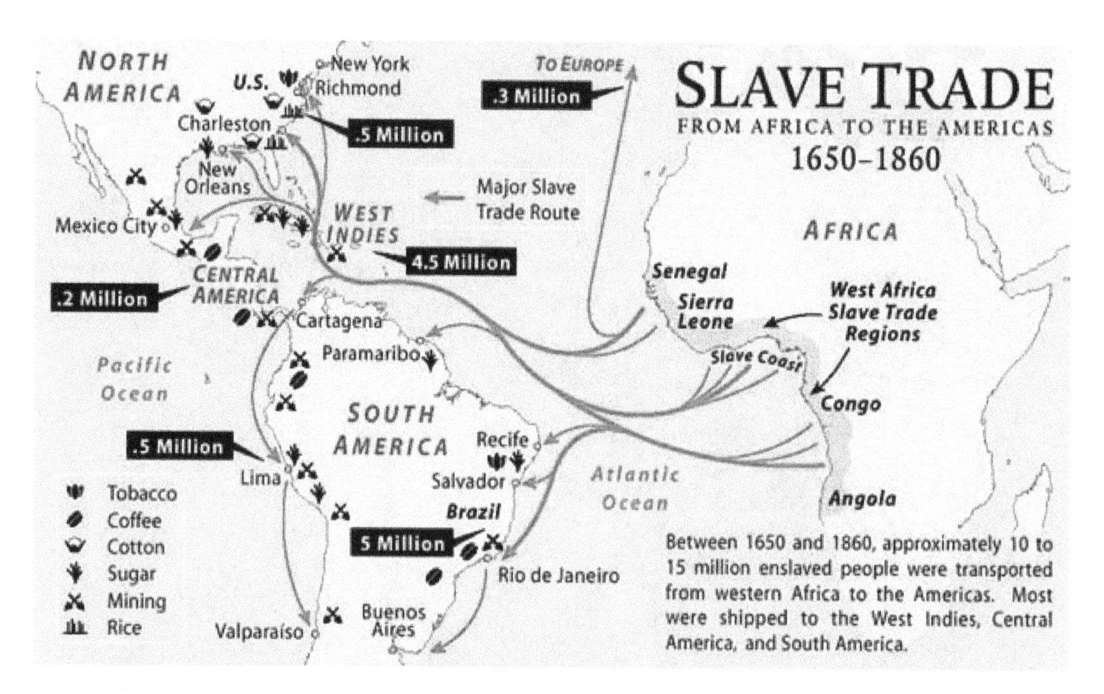

FIGURE 3.4 The African Slave Trade 1650–1860

The colonial advent found African societies maintaining their culture and traditions, but as Rodney (1972) points out, they lagged behind in a few key areas of technological-scientific advancement, which kept a better life out of reach for the majority. African states, territories, clans, and families were no match for the firepower brought forth by European capitalist nation-states. More importantly, Rodney remarks that while European forces faced difficulties in conquering the interior of Sub-Saharan Africa, in the final analysis it was the superiority of the capitalist mode of production, harnessing science and technology, that was the key driver in Europe's rise to global empire status.

The Partitioning of Africa

In the late colonial period, The Berlin Conference of 1884 convened Western European powers and began the division of Africa into formally administrated colonies as depicted in Figure 3.5. At this time the interior of Sub-Saharan Africa was finally penetrated, with Germany and Belgium gaining control over territories that later became Rwanda, Burundi, and Congo. Box 3.1 below examines the specific case of the Congo Free State under King Leopold II during the era of industrial colonialism (1865–1909).

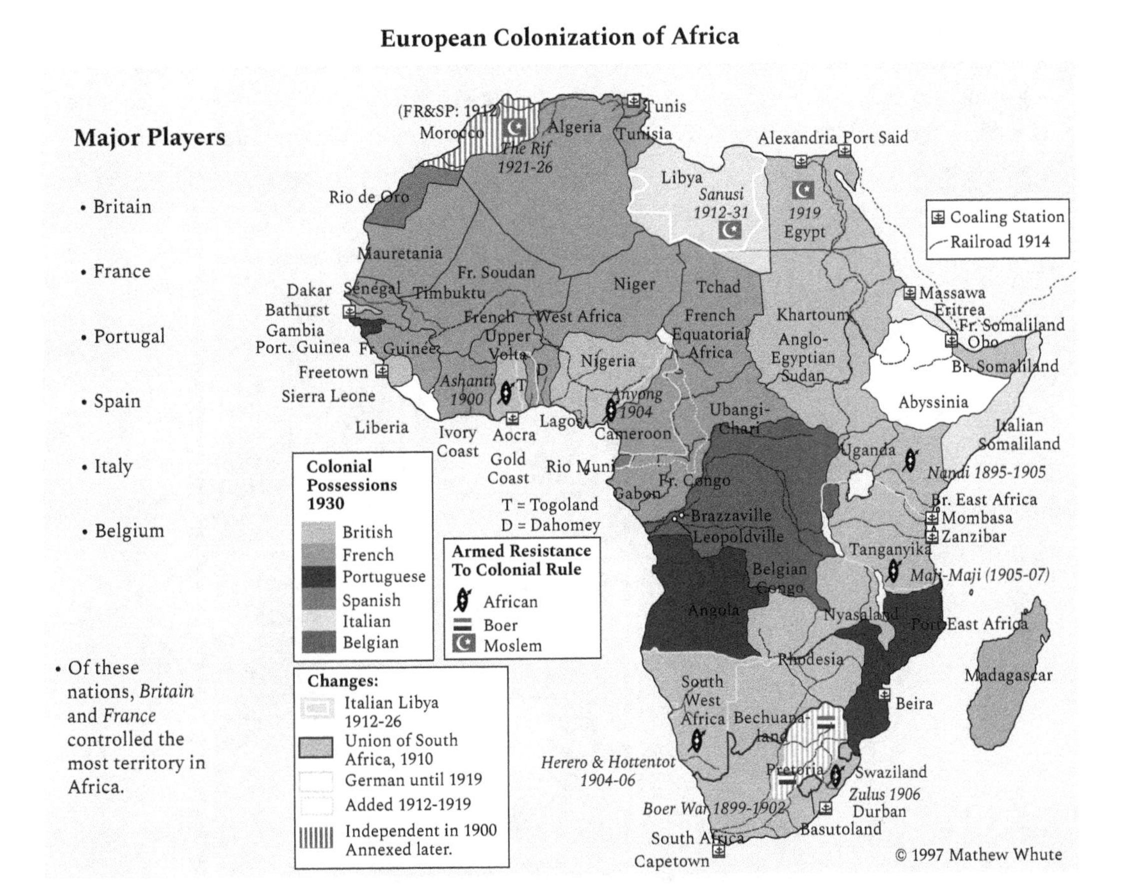

FIGURE 3.5 European Colonization of Africa

BOX 3.1 *KING LEOPOLD'S GHOST: A STORY OF GREED, TERROR AND HEROISM IN COLONIAL AFRICA* (HOCHSCHILD 2006)

During the reign of Belgium's King Leopold II (1865–1909), an estimated ten million Congolese, amounting to one half of the population, expired under a brutal colonial-imposed system of slavery, disease, starvation, and execution. In Belgium, Leopold, as the sovereign ruler of the Congo Free State, amassed a fortune of one-quarter of a billion dollars. The King's massive wealth was squandered on lavish palace buildings, one of the world's largest greenhouses, a grand African museum, monuments, and a number of luxury properties in the French Riviera. He also indulged his teenage wife, Caroline, in her penchant for fine clothing and jewelry. King Leopold undertook all of this in a Janus-faced manner. He justified his colony to the Belgian public, England, the United States, and

Germany in terms of humanitarianism and civilization. Leopold never once visited the Congo but shrewdly countered critics at home by aligning with other influential power brokers and manipulating media representations to fortify his duplicitous, profit-seeking mission. In the Congo Free State, one of the most infamous, most brutal, and least known cases of colonization unfolded under Leopold's reign of terror.

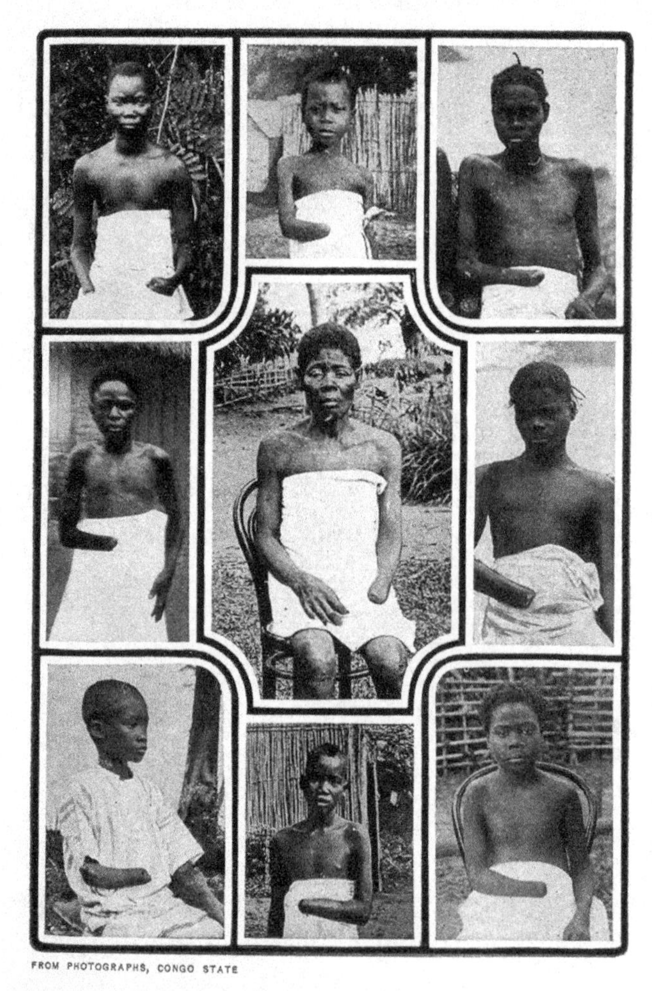

"The pictures get sneaked around everywhere."— *Page 40.*

FIGURE 3.6 Mutilated Children from Congo

In the remarkable and meticulously researched *King Leopold's Ghost*, Adam Hochschild uncovers, as Robert Harris states in the liner notes, "All the tension and drama that one would expect in a good novel." In an engaging and highly readable narrative, Hochschild chronicles Leopold's fascination with Africa and his obsession with creating his own personal colony that would above all enhance his personal wealth and status among fellow European royalty. Leopold accomplished this through a reign of terror that depended on slave labor for harvest of ivory and rubber. To enforce the harvest of naturally ocurring rubber in the jungles of Congo, Leopold's private army, the *Force Publique*, took Congolese women and children hostage and indeterminately held them in pitiful stockades until the men returned with their required quotas. Coming up short of one's quota resulted in a severe whipping and could result in death. Rubber harvesters received very little for their efforts. For the *Force Publique*, ammunition was precious, and soldiers were required to bring in the severed hand of those murdered as proof that the bullet hadn't gone to waste. If ammunition went missing or a soldier used it for hunting, they would procure the required number of hands from living human beings to account for the deficit. Slides of these Congolese amputees, presented by antislavery advocates, were featured in public presentations across the United States and Great Britain. These presentations, along with newspaper articles, were crucial in galvanizing oppostion to Leopold's practices in the Congo.

With much effort, determination, and media saavy, antislavery advocates were able to ultimately defeat Leopold, who turned the colony over to the Belgian government in 1908. Black American historian George Washington Williams and the first Black American missionary to work in the Congo, William Shepard, published scathing reports about the slave trade, the beatings, and the inhuman behavior of Leopold's colonial officers. Joseph Conrad, a British apprentice Congo River steamboat operator, penned the anti-imperialist classic, *Heart of Darkness*. Conrad largely drew fom his personal Congo experiences, and the central figure in the book, Kurtz, may have been based on Belgian *Force Publique* military officer, Leon Rom. Rom adorned his flower garden with severed Congolese heads on poles. He kept a gallows in front of his riverbank office. Edmund Dene Morel, a Liverpool shipping company clerk, and Roger Casement, an Irish career foreign service officer, were also instrumental in further galvanizing the overturning of Leopold's reign by mounting a landmark human rights campaign, one of the first of its kind. In 1908, Leopold, finally outmatched, ceded to mounting criticisms of his practices in the Congo and turned the colony over to the Belgian government in what became a lucrative exchange for him. Before the sale, however, Leopold incinerated all his colonial records, accounts, and files. Hochschild's story of King Leopold's colony has only been recently unearthed to inform a wider audience. In the afterword, he updates with the tragedy that has continued to unfold in the Congo, a matter that is taken up in chapters 5 and 8 of this book.

Other regions in Africa were also subjected to European intervention. The 160-kilometer-long Suez Canal was built in 1859 by Egyptian peasants specifically employed for that purpose. When it opened in 1869, the British began exerting indirect control of the canal by emplacement of garrisons along the way. The canal was considered vital to British interests. Surplus populations from Britain settled in Rhodesia (now Zimbabwe) and the highlands of Kenya, where they occupied prime agricultural lands and controlled vast quantities of it. Descendants of Dutch colonizers in South Africa likewise controlled prime agricultural lands. French populations occupied parts of Tunisia, Algeria, and Morocco. Technological advancement allowed British imperialist entrepreneur Cecil Rhodes to envision a railway linking Cairo in Egypt to Cape Town in South Africa (although the railway was never built). The European migrants to newly colonized African areas played prime roles in extending the colonial powers' grasp over productive forces abroad. African groups themselves would often play one European group against another, leading to the eventual demise of the initiator.

During the late colonialism era, after the First and Second World Wars, the rise of nationalistic movements in Cuba (Fidel Castro), Vietnam (Ho Chi Minh), and Kenya (Jomo Kenyatta) all launched armed struggles for national independence. Struggles for independence in the postcolonial period also saw the rise of corrupt and genocidal nationalistic dictators in Cambodia (Pol Pot—see chapter 5), Rwanda (Juvenal Habyarimana—see chapter 5), the Philippines (Ferdinand Marcos), Iran (Shah Mohammad Reza Pahlavi), and Sierra Leonne (Siaka Stevens). These dictators spurred a series of extended atrocities far beyond the bloody campaigns for national independence. In all cases, First World countries (United States, Great Britain, France) were opposed by Second World powers (China, Russia) in **proxy wars** that revealed significant military support for various opposition forces. A more detailed exposition of the post-Second World War era is taken up in the next chapter.

CONCLUSION

As we have conveyed in this chapter, the colonial era greatly contributed to both the development and the underdevelopment of our world. The privatization of property, the taking of surplus labor value, and the capitalist mode of production drove European, and later American, interests overseas in search of new sources of raw materials. The requirements of capitalist expansion and growth, capital accumulation, and wealth creation were further resolved through these rapacious endeavors. Africa proved to be the most vulnerable continent, and by 1884 the continent in its entirety was partitioned among European powers, who used its natural resources and especially its people to further the capitalist mode of production. As Rodney (1972) remarked, the capitalist mode of production was the source of European power that structured hegemonic relations between Europe and the rest of the world. The slave trade played a major role in contributing to accumulation of wealth in the colonizing country leading to a perpetual state of underdevelopment in vast parts of the world, especially Sub-Saharan Africa that fell under the yoke and terror of colonization.

REFERENCES

Conrad, Joseph. *Heart of Darkness: And, the Secret Sharer.* New York: Signet Classic. (1902) 1997.

Cornell, Stephen, and Douglas Hartmann. *Ethnicity and Race: Making Identities in a Changing World.* Thousand Oaks, CA: Pine Forge Press, 1998.

Douglass, Frederick. "The Hypocrisy of American Slavery." 1852. The History Place: Great Speeches Collection.

Deloria, Philip J. *Playing Indian*. New Haven, CT: Yale University Press, 1998.
Emory University. "The African Slave Trade." Slave Voyages. http://www.slavevoyages.org/assessment/intro-maps.
Hochschild, Adam. *King Leopold's Ghost: A Story of Greed, Terror, and Heroism in Colonial Africa*. London: Pan Books, 2006.
Kiernan, Ben. *Blood and Soil: A World History of Genocide and Extermination from Sparta to Darfur*. New Haven, CT: Yale University Press, 2007.
LaDuke, Winona. *All Our Relations: Native Struggles for Land and Life*. Boston: South End Press, 1999.
Meiksins Wood, Ellen. "The Agrarian Origins of Capitalism." In *Hungry for Profit: The Agribusiness Threat to Farmers, Food and the Environment*, edited by Fred Magdoff, John Bellamy Foster and Frederick. H. Buttel, 23–42. New York: Monthly Review Press, 2000.
Mintz, Sidney. "Food and Its Relationship to Concepts of Power." In *Food and Agrarian Orders in the World System*, by Philip McMichael. Westport, CT: Praeger Publishers, 1995.
Potter, Robert B., Tony Binns, Jennifer A. Elliott, and David Smith. *Geographies of Development: An Introduction to Development Studies*. 3rd ed. New York: Routledge, 2013.
Robbins, Richard H. *Global Problems in the Culture of Capitalism*. 5th ed. New York: Prentice Hall, 2011.
Rodney, Walter. *How Europe Underdeveloped Africa*. Washington, DC: Howard University Press, 1972.
Wampanoag Tribe of Gay Head (Aquinnah). "Tribal Council." Wampanoag Tribe. http://www.wampanoagtribe.net/Pages/Wampanoag_Council/Index.
Weinstein-Farson, Laurie. *The Wampanoag*. New York: Chelsea House Publishers, 1989.

Figure Credits

Fig. 3.1: Copyright © ian shiell (CC BY-SA 2.0) at https://commons.wikimedia.org/wiki/File:Private_property_-_geograph.org.uk_-_932141.jpg.

Fig. 3.3: Source: http://apworldhistory2012-2013.weebly.com/case-study23.html.

Fig. 3.4: Source: http://www.sahistory.org.za/topic/atlantic-slave-trade.

Fig. 3.5: Source: http://www.jamesriverarmory.com/index.php/buy/12481/.

CHAPTER FOUR

Postcolonialism

BUILDING NATION-STATES AND MODERN ECONOMIES

INTRODUCTION

The postcolonial era (1945–1990) still exerts significant influence on our present world. Notably, the creation of global institutions and the emergence of over one hundred new nation-states during a conflict-prone ideological divide called the Cold War continues to resonate. At the end of the Second World War, the world was confronted with innumerable global crises on a scale that no one nation-state could resolve. The response was global governance through creation of multilateral agencies such as the United Nations (UN), the World Bank, the International Monetary Fund (IMF) and the World Trade Organization (WTO). These multilateral agencies were designed to address and ensure global political and economic stability. Many new nation-states established the foundational blocks of statehood, including the social contract, authority, and the distribution of power. As we demonstrate in this chapter and the following, not all nation-states were successful in this endeavor.

New nation-states also had to build economies, and most adopted the mixed economy model early on. Two economic development strategies widely deployed by new nation-states were import substitution and light manufacturing by invitation. These strategies resulted in a global shift of industrial production to select developing countries. Coupled with an expanding role for transnational corporations (TNCs), growing world cities emerged in developing countries. The eventual dominance of neoliberalism closely paralleled efforts to generate economic growth through markets. In examining state-sanctioned development, we will highlight a Cold War case study of rural development in Thailand. In assessing the broad outcome of the postcolonial era, we find that the building of modern nation-states and economies produced mixed results. To conclude the chapter, we examine a common outcome of postcolonial development, the middle income trap.

DECOLONIALIZATION IN THE AFTERMATH OF THE SECOND WORLD WAR

The end of the Second World War ushered in global changes on a scale never witnessed before. The defining events of this era resulted in **decolonialization** throughout Asia and Africa and the building of over one hundred new nation-states throughout the world. For the most part, independence in Latin America was attained much earlier, before 1900, with the notable exception being Guyana in 1966 and Belize in 1981 (Potter et al. 2013, 56). The Caribbean region nation-states gained independence in the 1960s and 1970s. Decolonialization in Africa and Asia came about in the 1950s and 1960s and was often characterized by internecine national and civil wars. This characterization applies, for example, to former French colonies in Vietnam, Laos, Cambodia, and Algeria. Central to these conflicts was the Cold War divide between the First and Second Worlds.

The postcolonial era sparked strong nationalist movements worldwide. In India, for example, the Indian National Congress, founded in 1885, played a strong role in agitating for independence. Nationalist groups, led by Mahatma Ghandi, raised the stakes for a continuing colonial presence to remain, and India achieved independence in 1947. The Indian National Congress facilitated an interim government, leading to Jawaharlal Nehru's becoming Prime Minister of an independent India.

In another instance, Belgium granted Congo independence in 1960. The first democratically elected Prime Minister, Patrice Lumumba, advocated a complete break from Congo's European colonial past. At the time, Congo had fewer than 30 college graduates and no professional civil servants capable of running a government. The armed forces consisted of remnants of the *Force Publique*, which was composed of expatriate Belgian officers and conscripted Congolese soldiers. The US Central Intelligence Agency (CIA) was also active in the country. In the early 1960s, Cold War tensions between the First and Second Worlds were tense, and when Lumumba aligned with the Soviet Union, the United States government and entrenched Belgian, British, and American mining interests acted, and Lumumba was subsequently "eliminated" by President Eisenhower. The CIA worked with Joseph Mobutu, a Congolese colonel from the old *Force Publique* who arranged for Lumumba's kidnapping and execution. Mobutu then became the President of Zaire (the new name for Congo), and his dictatorial rule lasted until 1997 (see chapter 5). Without a functioning government, Mobutu amassed great personal wealth and, like King Leopold, ran the country as his personal fiefdom (Hochschild 2006).

Conflicts such as these were widespread in the postcolonial era. By 1955, the United States assumed the lead in the Cold War in preventing communist takeovers in Third World countries. South-East Asia was one major theater. United States involvement in Vietnam began in 1955 and accelerated in support of South Vietnam, with over 550,000 American soldiers based in the country by 1968. The US intervention lasted until 1973, and communist North Vietnam gained control of South Vietnam in 1975. In a "sideshow" to the Vietnam conflict, the communist Khmer Rouge waged civil war against the US-backed Lon Nol regime in Cambodia from 1970–1975. Upon achieving victory in April of 1975, the Khmer Rouge began their tragic and total reconstruction of the country in "Year Zero" (see chapter 5). French-educated intellectuals made up the Khmer Rouge leadership, and only a few have been recently sentenced to life imprisonment for genocide and crimes against humanity.

In the wake of these conflicts, one strategy that was eventually taken up by the former colonial powers was based on the realization that former colonies could be incorporated into the global capitalist economy without the need to directly administer them. Newly independent nations were highly dependent on advanced technology, sufficient capital, and modern expertise made available to them either through official aid or bilateral military, diplomatic, political, and economic relations. The United States extended its newly minted influence in this manner by adopting an imperialist stance toward former colonies in other regions of the world (Potter et al. 2013, 70–71).

The Creation of Multilateral Agencies

At the end of the Second World War, the world confronted problems on a scale that no one nation could effectively resolve. The 1930s Great Depression, the devastation of Europe, the emergence of the Cold War, and astute poverty in many recently independent nation-states called for collective address. Emerging as a super power after the Second World War, the United States initiated and dominated the establishment of a number of postwar international institutions, such as the UN, and their rules (Kelleher and Klein 2009). The UN is the world's largest major institution in maintaining peace, security, and people's well-being. Its key agency, the Security Council, has the right to determine whether a peacekeeping operation should be deployed, with possible military intervention in the case of conflicts, including genocide. Of the council's 15 member states, five are permanent and have veto power to prevent the passage of any resolution: the United States, the United Kingdom, France, Russia, and China. The other ten seats are elected by all the UN member states every two years. The UN also works with member nations in the areas of development and poverty eradication, promoting democracy, human rights, and sustainable development (Potter et al. 2013).

The IMF and the World Bank were created by the UN during the Monetary and Financial Conference held at Bretton Woods, New Hampshire, in 1944. It was attended by delegates from 44 Allied nations. The immediate focus of these institutions was to finance postwar efforts in reconstructing the European economy and to prevent future worldwide economic depressions (Stiglitz 2003). Their general functions were to (1) restore national finances and international trade, (2) fund Third World countries in developing infrastructure, and (3) promote Third World exports to enable those countries to purchase imports from the First World (McMichael 2012). The IMF largely serves the first function by providing credit to countries in need to stabilize their national currency, and the World Bank serves the last two functions by providing loans to states for infrastructure projects such as building roads, railways, and dams. From their inception, these institutions have been largely controlled by Western powers through a quota system, in which the voting power of a member country corresponds to its economic standing in the world. The United States appoints the president of the World Bank.

The **General Agreement on Tariffs and Trade (GATT)** was also set up after the Second World War. It was an international mechanism to promote international trade by encouraging member states to lower or remove trade barriers such as tariffs or quotas. It was later replaced in 1995 by the WTO, which has a broader agenda and greater power in enforcement (Kelleher and Klein 2009). The WTO's major functions, among others, include administering WTO trade agreements, monitoring national trade policies, and addressing trade disputes (WTO 2018). The United States is the only country that has veto power in IMF decisions.

Critics of these institutions claim they represent the economic agenda of Western powers and commercial interests of multinational corporations. There is a concern that the IMF has become solely a champion of market fundamentalism. Free markets are advocated by the IMF as the orthodox solution to problems in developing countries (Stiglitz 2003). Funds are provided on the basis of certain conditions that have to be met by the borrower in return for assistance. Typically, the IMF will require the receiving country to implement **structural adjustment polices (SAPs)**, such as raising taxes and cutting government spending that disproportionally impacts the poor and vulnerable. The immediate effects of these austerity measures lead to high unemployment and fewer public services. In addition, because of the lack of safety nets in many developing countries, putting IMF recommendations into practice may leave more people in poverty and bring about social unrest, violence, and increased crime. These social costs tend to be overlooked. The IMF leans toward a one-size-fits-all approach, which in many cases is not well suited to a country's particular circumstance. IMF policies have been seen to exacerbate the economic turmoil in Thailand and Indonesia during the Asian financial crisis in 1997 and to contribute to the economic collapse in Argentina in 2001 (Stiglitz).

Recent examples of IMF austerity programs with earlier precedents can be seen in the cases of Tunisia and Egypt. Tunisia lies in North Africa, bordering the Mediterranean Sea, with a population of over 11 million. The country is known for its role in sparking the Arab Spring in 2010, a movement upending authoritarian governments in the Arab world. It was triggered by the suicide of a street vendor in protest of government corruption and poor living conditions. In the end, the former Tunisian president, Ben Ali, was ousted. But a better life did not arrive for many Tunisians, even years after the movement. In 2016, the country received a US$2.9 billion loan from the IMF, which urged the government to balance its budget. As a result, in 2018 new policies were undertaken that included raising taxes on basic goods such as gasoline and food. Meanwhile, the unemployment rate of young people reached 35 percent, even higher than its 29 percent in 2010 (Malsin and Morajea 2018). A new round of protests erupted in at least 10 cities and towns in January 2018. More social and economic opportunities for unemployed young people were central to these protests and were met by violent police suppression and an unyielding authoritative state apparatus (McMichael 2012, 224–28).

Egypt, also in North Africa, and the Arab world's most populous nation, was facing a similar predicament. After the IMF's approval of a US$12 billion loan in 2016, the Egyptian government agreed to economic reforms, including allowing its currency to trade freely, creating a value-added tax that increases government revenue, and reducing subsidies on energy and food. These measures, argued the IMF, were necessary in order to restore confidence in the Egyptian government and attract foreign investment. As a result, the Egyptian pound lost nearly half of its value. People's incomes were worthless, and savings were wiped out. The price of gasoline rose over 30 percent. Subsidies to electricity were gradually taken away (Hadid 2016). Food prices soared. Poorer Egyptians felt the pain of these changes the most. The price of rice had gone up so much that many families had to alter their eating habits and to rely on government-subsidized bread, which had become the staple food for all three meals. More than 80 million people were entitled to five loaves a day at the subsidized price. The government bread program was allowed to stay because it was viewed as crucial to prevent the spread of hunger and possible social unrest. A lesson was learned in 1977, when riots arose across Egypt as the government scrapped food subsidies to meet the conditions set by the IMF and World Bank for loans (Saleh 2017). These two recent examples from Tunisia and Egypt illustrate long-term disruptions by multilateral agencies such as the IMF and World Bank. They also demonstrate the shortcomings of the Global North dominant neoliberal agenda, which will be discussed in chapter 6.

The New Nation-States

Modern **nation-states** are the foundation of global capitalism. As the organizing principle of the modern world, nation-states exhibit a number of key features that make up their overall composition. First, a **nation** can be briefly defined as a collective entity that shares a relatively common culture, language, and identity. **Ethnicity** often plays a core role in the functioning of a nation, but not always, as nationhood can supersede ethnic claims. An ethnic group shares a distinct language, history, culture, and most importantly, a collective identity. **Ethnic groups** are distinguished from the mainstream members of a given society. Moreover, a nation-state can consist of many different ethnic groups. In conjunction with the concept of a nation is the **state**. A state is a geographically bounded area that is a politically constituted form of social organization. States are also **sovereign**; they consist of a set of sanctioned institutions that claim supreme power and forbid interventions from outside forces.

The fundamental relationship between the nation-state and its citizen population is through the **social contract**, the institutionalization of a series of entitlements and rights for citizens, who in turn legitimate the nation-state as the ultimate source of power (Robbins 2011).

State Authority and Power

The nation-state embeds and structures its authority and power in countless ways. The social contract represents the rights and entitlements of citizens in exchange for the state to act as the ultimate source of authority and power. Legitimating this relationship involves implicit agreements and consent on the part of both parties. When the state uses force, it must be justified and legitimate in accordance with codified laws. Entitlements and obligations by the state must be acted upon. Likewise, citizens are required to act in a civil manner and address grievances through properly identified channels, such as courts, contracts, or legal processes. In other words, the sovereign nation-state establishes a **totality** over a bounded geographical area through political institutions and organizations. Transitioning to state-sanctioned authority and power is *not* a seamless process. Since the majority of nation-states have been only recently established, since the end of the Second World War (142 new nation-states), conflict can erupt between citizen populations and the authoritative political class. Sovereignty can also be challenged and violated. In a number of cases, the nation-state can collapse and be considered a **failed state** or disintegrate in relation to other states and become a **rogue state**. With corporate power on the rise, some argue that the nation-state has taken on a secondary role in support of facilitating corporate aims and profit. State-sanctioned modern development began at the end of the Second World War. One of the first tasks for nation-states was to create conditions for economic growth and development.

EARLY POSTCOLONIAL APPROACHES TO ECONOMIC DEVELOPMENT

Nationalism, the sense of a collective national identity, was an early priority and mobilizing tool for new nation-states. Against the heightened backdrop of the Cold War, newly formed nation-states attempted to maintain independence or aligned with either capitalist or socialist blocs. Wars of liberation, suppression of dissent, institution building, and economic development all earmarked the era (see Table 4.1). At this time, there were two opposing currents featured, one in which state intervention into economic affairs was prominent, known as **the mixed model of the economy**, and another in which free market ideology, or **neoliberalism** ascended, fully emerging in the late 1980s. Many developing countries combined both models. With the fall of communism, neoliberalism became the new global economic orthodoxy.

The Mixed Model of the Economy

What is the best way to build an economy? This question confronted nation-states and economic policy makers throughout the postcolonial era. The subsequent policies pursued rested upon the balance between the role of the government and marketplace. Nation-states differed in their views and adopted opposing policies. Some countries firmly believed that the government or state could best manage the economy; only the nation-state had the capacity and capability to follow sound economic principles, eliminate unnecessary waste, and make sure that the economy would benefit the people, not the rich elite or special interests. Other policy makers were convinced that the marketplace, not the government, works better for the economy. The market ensures efficiency and competition and encourages innovation. According to Adam Smith, one of the founding fathers of modern capitalism, the mere pursuit of self-interest by individuals will in the end bring goods to the entire society in the most efficient and low-cost manner possible. Governments have put these tenets into practice, adopting economic policies one way or another as prompted by the conditions and circumstances of the national and world economy and politics. Over time, the majority of countries adopted the neoliberal market-based economic model, and the nation-state more or less receded from direct management of the economy.

Many newly independent Third World nation-states looked to more advanced economies, either the First World, led by the United States, or the Second World, led by the Soviet Union and later China, for guidance in order to develop their economies. Three forces were thought to be responsible for the rise of the role of the state in the postwar economy in the West (Yergin and Stanislaw 1998). First, the lingering phantom of the **Great Depression**, in which the failure of the market resulted in rampant bankruptcy, mass unemployment, widespread hunger, and deep despair; people lost confidence in what the capitalist system could deliver. Second, the pressing reconstruction of Europe posed an enormous undertaking, and results had to be quickly accomplished. The private sector, tarnished by its failure during the Great Depression, was believed unsuitable for such an effort. The state, instead, was counted on to restore the economy and deliver employment, thereby raising social and economic well-being. Third, the resilience of the Soviet Union during the war and its prestige after the war lent credit to the **centrally planned economy**, in which the government ran the economy, promising to eradicate inequality.

John Maynard Keynes (1883–1946), a British economist, stood out as an influential figure in promoting the idea of state intervention and managed capitalism. In his *The General Theory of Employment, Interest and Money*, published in 1936, he argued for the necessity of state government to step in with pubic investment to create jobs and to actively manage the economy. His theory became the orthodoxy of the time and dominated economic policies in the West (Stiglitz 2003). Taking lessons from the economic depression, the newly elected postwar government in Great Britain adopted a **mixed economy** model, in which the government played a major role in managing the economy, supplemented by a private sector and implementing an expansive welfare state. Many economic sectors were owned or operated by the state. For example, gas in Britain was monopolized by the state-run British Gas. Similarly, oil, coal, steel, airline, telephone, and other businesses were also under state control, and the government appointed a board to govern the corporations. The British mixed economic model became the new norm of the world economy, in which the state managed the economy and solved social and economic problems. The mixed economy model was subsequently adopted by countries in both the developed and developing worlds. For example, nationalization of the economy occurred in postwar France, where the state held major stakes in banking, electricity, coal, and some other industries. In the three decades after the Second World War, the mixed economy model was dominant. In the United States, instead of taking direct ownership of modern enterprises, the state exerted control through a series of regulations.

The mixed economy model became the global model. Most developing countries faced a daunting task of nation-building after gaining independence from colonial powers. They were eager to build a solid national economy of their own and to catch up with the developed West. New nation-states, however, were desperately lacking capital investment. Roads, power plants, and schools needed to be built. As a result, multilateral aid agencies such as the UN and the World Bank, along with bilateral aid agencies such as the United States Agency for International Development (USAID) and Overseas Development Assistance (ODA) in the United Kingdom, became major international actors in the developing world. These agencies provided developmental assistance to nation-states for a myriad of projects over a wide range of sectors, including agriculture, fisheries, industrialization, and infrastructure (Potter et al. 2013). As a result, nation-state governments, shored up by international aid, were thought to be the only reliable source for quickly and effectively solving development problems. These efforts focused predominantly on urban areas (Potter et al.).

India provides an example. Jawaharlal Nehru (1889–1964), India's first prime minister after independence from British rule in 1947, led India by installing mixed economy policies. He envisioned reserving the best aspects of both the Western market economy and the Soviet socialist model. A robust private sector would keep India's economy vibrant. At the same time, a strong public sector would tightly control the core of the economy, such as the auto, power, and chemical industries. The Soviet style of central planning and five-year plans seemed appealing and was adopted by India during this time.

Until the late 1970s, the mixed economy model was prevalent, but this dominant economic model was in many places dysfunctional. State-run enterprises became monopolies insulated from competition and as a result became inefficient and underperforming, less responsive to market signals and consumer demands. Because of state monopolies, state-owned enterprises performed poorly and incurred losses, which eventually had to be shouldered by tax payers. There were growing doubts about the competence of the government in managing the economy. As a result, there was a renewed appreciation for the marketplace. Hence, the roles of the government and market shifted to **free market economic policies**. For example, Britain's mixed economy model began to fail and put renewed emphasis on the need for enterprise and individual initiative, unencumbered by governmental interference in economic affairs. As British politician Keith Joseph declared, "What Britain needs is more millionaires and more bankrupts" (Yergin and Stanislaw 1998, 103). Socialism could only lead to poverty and decline. It was time to reverse the postwar trend of centrally managed economies in the Second World and state intervention in economic affairs in the First World. The problem was not that the government did too little but that it did too much. As Keith Joseph summed it up, "We are over-governed, over-spent, over-taxed, over-borrowed and over-manned" (Yergin and Stanislaw, 102). In sum, the government should get out of the business of doing business. Subsequently, by the end of the 1970s the **market economy** began to take center stage in economic policies. Public dissatisfaction with the poor performance of the mixed model and an ideological shift in economic thinking in the West brought about radical changes in Western governments. The two most conspicuous events were the coming to power of Margaret Thatcher in Britain and that of Ronald Reagan in the United States. They brought on a sea change and set in motion a new era of world economic and political transformation—the rise of neoliberalism.

Import Substitution Industrialization and Light Manufacturing by Invitation

Early approaches to economic development featured urban industrial development. Two such strategies were **import substitution industrialization** and **light manufacturing industrialization by invitation** (Potter et al. 2013, 145–47). Import substitution industrialization was an attempt by new nation-states to become self-sufficient in manufacturing goods, reversing dependency on foreign imports. Import substitution development was focused on relatively easy-to-produce commodities where there was already domestic demand, such as textiles, drinks, cigarettes, and food items. The majority of developing countries undertook this strategy, but few were able to progress to more advanced industrial development. Taiwan and India were notable exceptions. These two countries were able to overcome capital, infrastructural, and investment obstacles. In a number of cases, foreign competition worked against the majority of developing countries' ability to advance in terms of manufacturing complexity and output.

Import Substitution in Latin America

Import substitution industrialization (ISI) was an attempt by developing countries, especially in Latin America, to protect domestic production sectors from external competition and to reduce dependency on foreign products. For example,

ISI featured in the Brazilian economy from the 1930s until the end of the 1980s (Levy-Orlik 2009). It was intended to promote domestic development and self-sufficiency through the creation of an internal market. It was one form of state intervention into the economy through an array of policies, such as nationalization, subsidization of key industries, increased taxation, quotas, and high trade tariffs on imports (Street and James 1982).

Argentina, another country in Latin America, adopted the ISI policy from 1945 to 1976 (Casaburi 1998). In light of the country's infant industry base, unable to compete with advanced industrialized countries and in jeopardy of collapse, President Juan Perón implemented a series of measures right after the Second World War, including setting import quotas, raising tariffs, and directing banks to finance crucial domestic industries, such as petrochemicals, steel, and machinery. As a result, while the industrial sector claimed more share of the national output, from 21.6 percent between 1930 and 1939 to 24.2 percent between 1940 and 1949, the share of agricultural sector output declined. The industry sector further expanded between 1964 and 1974 with a 7-percent annual growth rate. Meanwhile, the state government subsidized the export of industrial products. The share of industrial goods increased from virtually nonexistent in 1965 to 20 percent one decade later (Bisang, Burachik, and Katz 1995, cited by Casaburi 1998).

By the mid-1970s, however, the ISI model became unsustainable in Argentina. Since it was mainly driven by government protectionist policies to insulate domestic industries from external competition, there was a lack of competitiveness in the internal market. Industries were overprotected. They relied heavily on government subsidies and had less incentive to be more efficient. For example, Nofal (1989) estimated that for every dollar of earnings from the export of passenger cars, the state had to subsidize 80 cents. Argentina's ISI experience was not unique. It was quite common in other countries in Latin America (Casaburi 1998). Regardless of its success or failure, we want to point out that the ISI model is one experiment initiated by developing countries in an attempt to become economically independent.

Likewise, **light manufacturing and industrialization by invitation** was designed to draw foreign investment to developing countries through offering incentives to establish branch plants and **free trade zones** (**FTZs**) in developing countries. There are well over 1,000 FTZs in the world today. A good example of light manufacturing and industrialization by invitation applies to the Mexican maquiladoras, or "sister" US plants established in Mexico within close proximity to the US border. Clothing, automotive parts, furniture, and electronics are outsourced to sister plants from US manufacturers, thereby allowing transnational corporations (TNCs) a means to reduce labor costs while employing over half a million Mexicans in 2,000 facilities as of the early 1990s (Potter et al. 2013, 147). The maquiladoras play an important role in Mexico's economy, but present concerns regarding the US role in the North American Free Trade Agreement (NAFTA), immigration policy, rising labor costs, and competing FTZs in China, South-East Asia, and Central America create considerable uncertainty as to the long-term economic stability of the maquiladoras.

Three discernible results from the industrialization efforts that began in the post–Second World War era are evident: the **global shift**, the **rise of TNCs**, and the emergence of **mega** or **world cities.** Globally, the manufacturing map has significantly changed, with China becoming the world's leading manufacturing country at 23 percent of the global total. The United States led the world in manufacturing output since 1871 but recently declined from 26 percent in 2005 to 17 percent as of 2013 (MAPI, 2019). Moreover, other recently industrialized nations are ascending in the world manufacturing order, such as South Korea (5th), Brazil (9th), India (11th), Mexico (12th), and Indonesia (13th). The **global shift** is uneven, with some regions able to attract more investment in industry than others. The availability of low-cost labor, financial incentives, favorable tax breaks, a nonunionized labor force, transport, and other infrastructural arrangements are also necessary to attract foreign businesses. While manufacturing is still dominated by North America, Japan, and Europe, countries such as Brazil and Mexico, along with the rapidly industrializing Asian countries of Hong Kong, Indonesia, Malaysia, Singapore, South Korea, and Taiwan, are areas of the world where manufacturing is increasingly concentrated (Potter et al. 2013, 149). Over the last 10 years, China and India have emerged as global manufacturing centers. In contrast, Africa as a whole has demonstrated little, and in some cases declining, industrial growth during the postcolonial era (Potter et al.). Due to expansive global production scales, consumption has become increasingly homogenized worldwide.

The **global shift** of industrial production to select developing countries has been spurred by **TNCs**. From the postcolonial era up to the present, powerful corporations have been the key catalyst in restructuring the world economy. Only since the end of the Second World War have the majority of TNCs become involved in manufacturing. Potter et al. (152) note that by 2005, foreign investment and production "was driven by more than 70,000 parent company TNCs with over 700,000 foreign affiliates." They further note that "TNCs account for approximately two thirds of world exports in goods and services." Other developed countries are the major recipients of foreign investment, with 19–41 percent of total investment directed to developing countries over the period of 1994–2005. Foreign direct investment in developing countries remains highly uneven and is concentrated in South-East Asia, Mexico, and parts of South America. In Africa, only South Africa demonstrates measurable foreign direct investment. The Ford Motor Company provides an example of global TNC expansion. From 1970 to 2000, Ford expanded from 65 to over 270 majority-owned foreign affiliates. Developed countries were host to the majority of these affiliates, but by 2000, China, India, Pakistan, Indonesia, Brazil, and Argentina also had Ford Motor Company affiliates (Potter et al., 156).

Coupled with the global shift and the expansion of TNCs has been the growth of **world cities**. In the postcolonial era, expansive urban centers such as Bangkok,

Tokyo, Hong Kong, Singapore, Taipei, Shanghai, Mexico City, Rio de Janeiro, and Johannesburg came to complement New York, London, and Paris, creating a global network where capital, finance, transportation, communications, manufacturing, and services stimulated the growth and concentration of a truly global economic order and functioning (Potter et al., 179). Rapid urban growth places enormous strain on urban planning and governments in the developing world. Governments must provide (and maintain) infrastructure and services to accommodate growing urban populations. As economic drivers, urban growth areas place governments in a two-fold dilemma. On one hand, urban areas can induce innovation, thereby stimulating economic growth for the country as a whole. Whether these innovations reach the more isolated parts of the country is highly questionable. On the other hand, decentralizing growth away from primary urban areas can lead to more regional equity but can depress overall economic growth. The historical track record clearly favors the first approach and often produces a dual economy, one based in the city and the other evident in the countryside (Potter et al.).

THE ASCENT OF NEOLIBERALISM

In Britain, Margaret Thatcher's Conservative Party came to power in 1979 and brought waves of privatization throughout the economy. The Thatcherite government withdrew its ownership from British Petroleum, North Sea oil and gas, Cable & Wireless, British Steel, British Coal, and British Rail. By the early 1990s, about two-thirds of state-run enterprises had been privatized. The economy started to move forward and become more competitive. The unemployment rate turned lower than that of the European continent. Looking back, Thatcher concluded, "Socialism was the flavor of the time for a long time. We in this country had an experiment in socialism. … Now they understand that freedom and enterprise under law is better than massive government control over industry and people. New Labour has an understanding of what socialism was and how it doesn't work, that somehow you have to create wealth before redistribution. Socialism started with redistribution before wealth" (Yergin and Stanislaw 1998, 123–24). In the US, Ronald Reagan claimed that "government is the problem." The government serves the economy best by getting out of the way of businesses. There should be less planning, less regulation, more unconstrained market forces, and more economic freedom. Following the new doctrine, governments around the world embarked on the same endeavors to sell off previously nationalized companies and turn them into private enterprises.

Faith in the marketplace became the new economic orthodoxy and led multinational agencies such as the IMF and World Bank to adopt market liberalism as conditions for loans to developing countries. Bilateral agencies followed suit. By the 1980s and 1990s, world economic thinking was dominated by the doctrine of the free market economy, which was articulated by the **Washington Consensus**, a meeting consisting of US-based institutions such as the IMF, the United States Treasury, and the World Bank, that set global economic policies aimed at limiting the role of the government, promoting deregulation, privatization, and trade liberalization (Pettinger, 2019). Fiscal austerity, privatization, and liberalization were the three pillars (Stiglitz 2003). Simply put, the state should withdraw from economic sectors that belong to the market. The role of the government is not to run the economy but to serve it and ensure fair competition. As Thatcher summarized, the state should perform the following serving functions: to keep finances sound, to enforce rule of law, and to provide defense, education, and a safety net (Yergin and Stanislaw 1998).

One illustration of the dominance of such an idea is the embrace of the market even by political parties on the left in many Western countries. Tony Blair, who was a candidate of the Labour Party in the UK and took office as prime minister in 1997, declared that the era of state intervention was over and the economy should be best left to the private sector. The government should invest in education and create human capital to make citizens more capable and competitive in a world economy. The role of the government is not as an economic manager but as a guard to ensure opportunities and equality. Blair dismantled the welfare state and believed that individuals should bear more responsibilities. Overall, developing countries adopted neoliberal policies to manage their economies.

The Washington Consensus has been challenged on both scholarly and empirical grounds. One concern for developing countries in adopting rapid market liberalization is that the infant industries in developing countries are usually not ready to compete with corporations in developed countries. Both the earlier import substitution and light manufacturing by invitation strategies demonstrate these shortcomings in most cases. When the developing countries open up their market, their industries are at a great disadvantage and are likely to fall victim to foreign competition. Since sound social safety nets are not in place in many developing countries, adopting economic liberalization polices usually results in massive unemployment and even more poverty and inequality, making development less sustainable (Stiglitz 2003). What happened to Russia and Eastern Europe during the 1990s was a case in point. Taking advice from the IMF and the West, many Eastern European countries after the fall of communism privatized their economy and opened up their market virtually overnight. Instead of the anticipated economic prosperity, hyperinflation crippled these countries' economies. Inflation in Ukraine at one point ballooned to over 3,000 percent. Russia's economic output fell by one-third, and its population lost four years of life expectancy between 1990 and 2000 (Stiglitz 2003).

More recently, the Asian fiscal crisis, the 2008 global recession, and the Obama stimulus package have illustrated a need for state intervention, casting doubts on the neoliberal model. The debate on economic development is not over yet. At present, the difference is that developing countries will not merely passively follow the policies of the West. The rise of China, India, and many other developing countries has changed the landscape of the world economy. Their voices will have a more fundamental impact, and they have injected new perspectives and policies that challenge the unadulterated neoliberalism led by the Global North. As will be discussed in chapter 6, the world economy has become increasingly integrated, and the rise of multipolar globalization has become the economic driver of the world's economy and represents a significant departure from North-directed neoliberalism in political and economic terms in the foreseeable future (Pieterse 2018).

POSTCOLONIAL STATE-SANCTIONED DEVELOPMENT

The end of the Second World War brought forth a dramatically new form of world organization. Europe was devastated, Asia was threatened with famine, and colonies around the world sought independence. The Cold War became the context in which newly formed nation-states sanctioned development and conflict and violence unfolded. McMichael (2012, xvi–xvii) provides a timeline of modern development that corresponds to two major eras in modern development: **developmentalism** (1945–1985) and **globalism** (1985–present). Table 4.1 below provides a brief list of key changes and events that ushered in modern development from 1945 to 1985.

The table below lists a few indicators that facilitated modern state-led development. The world changed dramatically at the end of the Second World War. The Marshall Plan was instituted by the United States to help rebuild a ravaged Europe. The horrors of the Holocaust instigated a global resolve to never allow for the rise of

TABLE 4.1 *Indicators During the Age of Modern Developmentalism: 1945–1985*

CHANGE/EVENT	DESCRIPTION	EXAMPLE COUNTRIES
World Organization: the Three Worlds	**Onset of the Cold War**	
First World	Capitalist Countries	United States, United Kingdom, France, Canada, Australia
Second World	Communist/Socialist Countries	Soviet Union, China, Cuba, North Korea
Third World	Ex-Colonies, Newly Independent Countries in Asia, Latin America, and Africa	Sierra Leone, Kenya, India, Rwanda, Cambodia, Vietnam, Laos, Indonesia, Argentina, Nicaragua, Guatemala

CHANGE/EVENT	DESCRIPTION	EXAMPLE COUNTRIES
Economic Policies	**Building a National Economy**	
	Import Substitution	Throughout the Third World
	Light Manufacturing and Industrialization by Invitation	Select Third World countries (e.g., Taiwan, Hong Kong, Singapore, South Korea, Japan)
	Mixed Economy	Throughout the Third World
	Neoliberalism	United States and England, spreading to the rest of the world
Social Goals	**Pacifying the Countryside and Cities**	
Rural Development	Land reform; community development; agricultural modernization; irrigation, markets, roads, and water storage projects	Throughout the Third World
Urban Development	State institution building; housing, roads, electrification; water; services; private sector	Throughout the Third World
Nationalism	Extending state control of territory; homogenizing language; education and identity	Throughout the Third World
Wars of Liberation	Overthrowing monarchies, colonialists; waging war for national independence	Vietnam, Cambodia, Laos, Burma, Cuba, Angola, Mozambique
Multilateral Agencies	**Toward Global Integration and Governance**	
United Nations (UN)	Global political organization, human rights, development, poverty alleviation	All member nations excluding the Second World
World Bank	Developmental loans, economic development policy	All developing countries except those in the Second World bloc
International Monetary Fund (IMF)	Developmental loans, fiscal management, debt servicing, austerity programs	All developing countries except those in the Second World bloc

Source: Adapted from McMichael (2012).

genocidal regimes through the aegis of the UN (this proved ultimately ineffective). Realizing the growing threat of communism in Asia, Latin America, and Africa, President Harry S. Truman set forth a vision in 1949 whereby US science and technology would come to the aid of underdeveloped countries mired in poverty, lifting them to improvements in socioeconomic well-being by eradicating disease, hunger, and illiteracy (see chapter 1). As hostilities between the United States and the Soviet Union increased, the Cold War became the defining feature of this era. Mao Zedong's communist revolution in China further intensified Western fears of a coming communist world. South-East Asia was the violent focal point where First and Second World countries engaged in proxy wars, contributing much to the region's instability. Castro's revolution in Cuba provided a blueprint for overthrowing colonial capitalist regimes. With the threat of nuclear war intensifying hostilities between the superpowers, a new organization of the world, the **Three Worlds**, came into being.

The Cold War was played out in all the major geopolitical regions of the world. The **First World**, led by the United States, consisted of industrialized, capitalist countries. The **Second World**, led by the Soviet Union and later China, consisted of communist and socialist countries. State-led central planning was the vehicle for develop ment in these countries. The **Third World** consisted of the vast majority of recently established nation-states who had thrown off the yoke of European colonialism. As the ascendant world power, the United States, along with her allies, engaged in a fierce and hostile conflict with the Soviet Union and China for **hegemony** over these recently established nation-states in Asia, Latin America, and Africa. South-East Asia is an illustrative and turbulent example. The United States adhered to the **domino theory** to justify containment of the communist movement in the region. The theory extrapolated that if a divided Vietnam were to fall under complete communist control, then Laos, Cambodia, Thailand, Malaysia, and Singapore would fall next, like dominoes in a line. Armed struggles in Vietnam and Laos and Cambodia subsequently led to communist regimes, including the genocidal Khmer Rouge regime in Cambodia. Thailand remained a frontline capitalist nation-state while Singapore became championed as a modern development success story.

While the terminology of the Three Worlds, and specifically "Third World," is outdated, it *does* depict world organization between 1945 and 1985. Outside of direct armed conflict, a number of First World allied developing countries undertook campaigns to improve the social and economic well-being of impoverished rural populations. These populations were vulnerable to communist influence and represented a significant threat to fledging capitalist societies. Perhaps the primary social goal during this period was to win the hearts and minds of the rural populace. Often, rural communities were neglected by the political classes who resided in the larger urban areas. Because of this, rural populations were vulnerable to communist influences, and a number of rural-based insurgency movements challenged the recently established nation-state apparatus, as well as its efforts to solidify bureaucratic control over the rest of the country. Hence, **rural development** became a stratagem that attempted to lift the rural population, often poor subsistence peasants, into modernization. Land reform, especially in Latin America, community development, agricultural modernization, irrigation, and other water storage projects were designed to thwart communist influence and discontent in the overwhelming rural areas of the Third World nations. For example, the **Green Revolution**, under the auspices of the UN Food and Agriculture Organization, introduced high-yielding cereal crops into underdeveloped agricultural regions of the Third World. Crops like rice, maize, and wheat all required attendant "packages" of fertilizers, irrigation, and pesticides. Only a small minority of rural farmers had access to irrigated water and credit for the required inputs. As a result, rural society became even more stratified (Cleaver 1973).

The nation-states also intensified their efforts in urban areas by consolidating power and authority in capital cities that were fast becoming **world cities**. Influx from rural areas often led to acute shortages in housing and basic human services. As a result, new world cities contained extensive slum areas where recent rural migrants erected inadequate shelter and lived in squalid poverty. Emerging institutions such as the police, finance, and public services all added an unstable sense of social order amidst the relentless expansion of infrastructure. Pollution and poverty were exacerbated, and the poor bore the brunt of the burden. An emerging private sector sought out opportunities to grow and expand and became a powerful economic force of its own.

The goal of both urban and rural development was in essence solidifying **nationalism**. In rural areas, roads reached some regions, and mass transportation in the cities facilitated travel and access to markets and employment sites. The nation-state homogenized language through education, and as societies became more industrialized, the need for a more educated workforce was apparent. At the same time, opportunities bypassed those living in the hinterlands, and the stratified nature of social classes became an often insurmountable barrier to achieving upward social mobility for rural populations. New nation-states exerted substantial effort nonetheless to instill national identity, causing citizens to align with the nation-state and its leaders. Obstacles to this sense of identity, such as monarchies, remnants of colonial regimes, and so on, were partially replaced with more modern civil constitutional forms of political organization. This included elections, the formation of political parties, and institutional address of grievances by courts. Overall, results were partial in many instances, as the case of Thailand shows below.

On a global level, multilateral aid agencies established in the wake of the Second World War at the Bretton Woods Conference guided nation-state development within a context of modernization. Nation-states borrowed money for development efforts, and a number of them quickly accumulated substantial debt to these lending institutions. The near-universal default of debtor nation-states led to the ascension of multilateral aid agencies as prime shapers of neoliberal state-sanctioned economic development policies, in specific countries as well as globally. This chain of events led to the emergence of a new period in world development that is called **globalization** (see chapter 6). The next section will examine the case of Thailand and some of the major efforts to consolidate the control over its geographical boundaries through rural development projects.

The Case of Thailand (1945–1985)

Thailand provides an interesting Cold War example that draws parallels to a number of other developing nation-states. In particular, Thailand was considered strategic by First World powers due to its neighboring Cambodia and Laos having aligned with communist China and the Soviet Union during the Cold War era. As a frontline nation-state, Thailand's uneven path toward modernization illustrates how complex the task actually is. Residual forms of precapitalist social relations, such as patron-client, permeate the society, as the country was largely agrarian during this period. The development of an overarching modern nation-state set of institutions has never completely eclipsed these earlier precapitalist forms of social organization. Because of this, conflict and violence intensified throughout the era. Thailand's efforts to modernize are also filled with paradoxes. In a number of situations, we witness the past also competing with or complicating the present ordering of the society and culture.

The Kingdom of Thailand is located in South-East Asia, as seen below in Figure 4.1, and has been in existence for approximately 2,559 years as marked by the Buddhist Era calendar. The Thai are a distinct Asian ethnic group with their own language, culture, and customs. A monarchy has prevailed throughout the country's existence. One monarch, King Mongkut, or Rama IV (1851–1868), is generally acknowledged as the first ruler who began efforts to modernize the Kingdom. In 1932, royal power was partially replaced by a group of military officers, and the country embarked on a long and uneven journey toward democracy, modernization, and integration with the rest of the world. With entry into the Western-dominated world, Thailand, which means "Land of the Free," became vulnerable to outside influences. Although Thailand was never a colony, both the British and the Japanese during the Second World War established significant domination over Thailand. With the United States and her allies victorious in the Second World War, South-East Asia became a flashpoint for the conflict and violence that characterized the Cold War. While Thailand maintained her independence from foreign powers, the Cold War was played out in neighboring Cambodia, Laos, and Vietnam. Thailand supported subsequent US warfare in these countries and domestically intensified efforts to address widespread rural poverty in more remote regions of the country.

In the post–Second World War era, Thailand's development, consistent with the mixed economy model, could be characterized as **state capitalism** with a policy of **economic**

nationalism (Charoensin-o-larn 1988). Import substitution through state enterprises and light manufacturing and industrialization by invitation was promoted. In hindsight, the overall direction was toward a free market economy. A World Bank mission to the country in 1959 advised that the Thai state "change its role from previous direct engagement in the economy to one of facilitating growth of private enterprises and industrial development" (Charoensin-o-larn, 4). This highly influential report redirected Thai development policy and administration toward the free market and private-sector development. The results over the following decades led to impressive economic development for the country as a whole while greatly increasing the stratification between urban and rural areas of the country. To overcome this disparity, **poverty eradication development** was focused in the rural areas, where impoverished villagers and regions were susceptible to communist influence. The next section will detail two case studies designed to address the problem of rural development during the Cold War era.

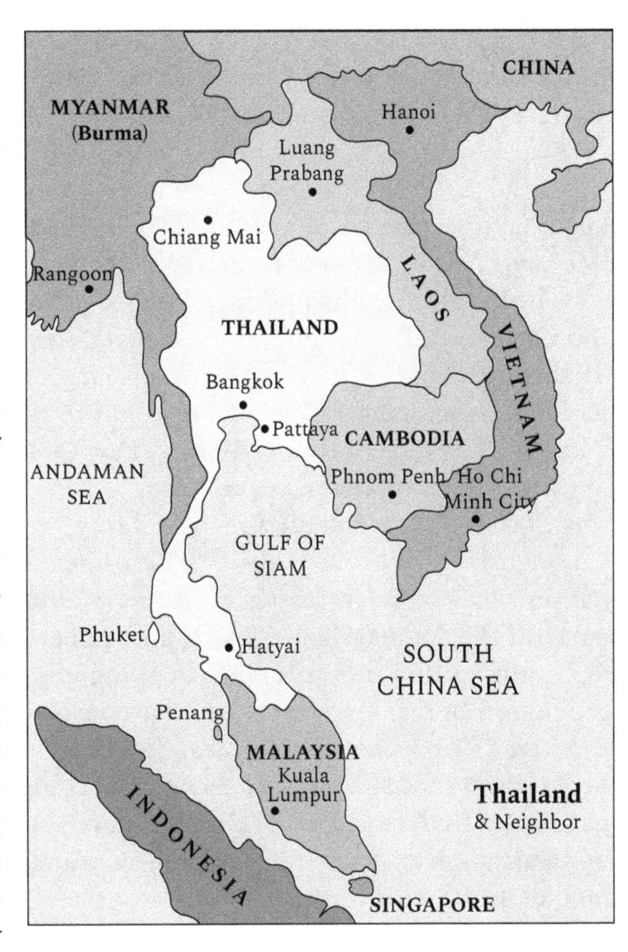

FIGURE 4.1 Thailand and South-East Asia

Accelerated Rural Development

Thailand aligned with the United States during the Cold War. As US involvement in the Vietnam War increased, Thailand permitted the US Air Force to establish a number of air bases in the impoverished northeast region of the country in order to bomb Vietnam, Cambodia, and Laos. In addition, the CIA sent Special Forces to work with various Indigenous groups on the northern border and in more remote, inaccessible regions of Laos to monitor activities in Mao's China and the movements of communist fighters in these areas (McCoy 1972). In October of 1973 and again in 1976, democratic-oriented Thai student protests were brutally suppressed by Thai Police and Royalist militias, leading to the students' fleeing the country and joining the ranks of the Communist Party of Thailand (CPT). The CPT, operating from bases inside the country and in Cambodia and Laos, engaged the Thai military in armed warfare. The northern part of the country, called the Golden Triangle, emerged as the world's major supplier of opium and heroin through collusion with Laotian, Thai, and South Vietnamese government officials. The United States experienced a major heroin epidemic as a result of GIs' returning home with significant addictions (McCoy). This situation is discussed in the next section below.

Within this turbulent political and economic context, conflicts and violence at the village, state, and international levels were unprecedented, and the capitalist Thai state fell into a crisis mode. Within this set of social parameters, **Accelerated Rural Development** (**ARD**) emerged out of the need for the Thai nation-state to adopt and implement **counterinsurgency** (**COIN**) campaigns to suppress the growing communist threat and pacify hostile and impoverished rural Thai villagers. In short, ARD was essentially a road-building agency of the Thai Ministry of Interior. Charoensin-o-larn (1988, 204–33) describes ARD as a comprehensive top-down, nationwide effort to extend state authority and order over remote, insurgent-prone parts of the countryside. These long-neglected impoverished areas were vital to maintaining US interests and to quelling discontent and increased violence from the forgotten rural populace. As Charoensin-o-larn states, "Simply put, the ARD program is a package of RD [rural development] projects that enables the state to penetrate into the Thai countryside more legitimately and effectively under the banners of COIN and RD" (205). The main thrust was rural road building, followed by an array of activities and income-generating schemes that included agribusiness, mobile health units, infrastructure improvements, and the formation of "cooperatives" that acted as COIN operations. Beginning in 1964 and then spreading throughout the rest of the country, ARD left behind a dubious legacy (the agency no longer exists).

ARD undertook a three-pronged approach: "Access, Assist, and Aggregate" (Charoensin-o-larn, 206). ARD roads provided the first step in opening up remote and isolated villages to the burgeoning Thai capitalist economy. Assisted efforts followed the initial infrastructure development, and ARD health teams, youth groups, and agriculture extension staff promoted income-generating opportunities in a number of areas, such as silk production and weaving, aquaculture, and the dispensing of medicine by a rural nurse team. Finally, once this development had taken root, the village was organized into farmer cooperatives to partake in loan programs and, more covertly, act as counterinsurgency vigilante-type groups. In practice, the ARD programs were disconnected and often never accomplished much else beside the road-building efforts (Charoensin-o-larn, 207). Road-building alone often exacerbated stratification in the villages, as proximity to the market favored those with land holdings nearest the road. Contractors and suppliers received the majority of payments, and corruption was rampant in the provincial ARD offices. In other words, ARD allowed the Thai state to exert control over its territory and suppress insurrection. Income disparity remained, however, as a major social problem.

Underlying the ARD effort was a sense of hostility, alienation, and resentment between villagers and government officials. Charoensin-o-larn observed the behavior government officials displayed to villagers. They were often arrogant and acted entitled regarding the language spoken, and they demanded food and alcohol when on work-related visits from the provincial center. In one case, he describes how one villager stabbed a government official to death for entering a villager's home in search of illegal alcohol. In areas where communist insurgents were active along the Thai-Cambodian or Laotian border, ARD equipment was destroyed. Conversely, Charoensin-o-larn discusses meetings between ARD officials and villagers at provincial centers. Here, villagers were vastly intimidated, as they spoke in local dialects rather than the official Thai language. He interprets this paradox as a residual effect of precapitalist social relations on the new rubric of modern, state-led development. He surmises that neither party was fully integrated or cognizant of modern democratic forms of communication and organization. Indeed, the acronym ARD was often jokingly retitled to mean "Gang of Wicked Men."

Rural Jobs Creation Program

While ARD accomplished little if anything in terms of alleviating poverty, the effort did extend the range of governmental social control over the countryside. The **Rural Jobs Creation Program (RJC)** by the Thai Government complemented ARD in that local leadership and class stratification were greatly strengthened (Charoeinsin-o-larn, 242–243). RJC attempted to address five rural development objectives:

1. Alleviate rural poverty by providing income for public works projects.
2. Lessen rural dry season migration to large urban areas.
3. Reduce income disparity in rural areas.
4. Increase agricultural production through infrastructure development, such as dams, ponds, and other water projects.
5. Most importantly, upgrade the efficiency of local village administration in carrying out these large projects.

Many urban-based Thai government officials, along with a number of prominent academics, held rather stereotypical views of the Thai peasantry. The rural Thai were characterized as simplistic and highly dependent and subservient to patron-client relations, a stereotype which has persisted up to the present (Charoensin-o-larn, 214). This impression of an impoverished rural peasant fit in well with top-down efforts by the Thai Government to alleviate poverty and, critically, serve its political objectives of consolidation, thereby paving the way for embedding capitalism throughout all sectors of the country. As a result, rural regions and populations were transformed from subsistence economies to market-based, capitalist ones. There was significant fall-out, however, with large numbers of rural residents migrating to the major cities.

After the annual rice harvest in the fall (mainly one crop of rain per annum fed the rice), villagers were envisioned as doing very little outside of their daily subsistence activities. However, during the dry season, from December to March, many of these rural inhabitants tend to other agricultural activities, crafts, hunting, gathering, and fishing. Young men and women often migrated to urban areas to work construction or in various service industries. RJC was designed to stem this flow through a direct transfer of funds from the Bangkok-based government to local village headmen (*phu yi ban*) and the more powerful *tambon* (a grouping of villages, one level up from the individual village) council chiefs, known as *kamnan*. Despite claims made that RJC addressed its stated objective, the long-term result was that the local *kamnan* and *phu yi ban* became powerful representatives of the state rather than the people they, served. Local contractors and merchants benefited greatly from this effort, as well (Charoeinsin-o-larn, 241). In particular, a few *kamnans* became godfather-like figures and came to control vast swaths of the country's burgeoning economic growth (Anderson 1990). In sum, both ARD and RJC were top-down rural development projects instituted by the Thai Government. While a variety of claims were made regarding the alleviation of rural poverty, little was achieved outside the consolidation of the Thai nation-state and the political rural elite. The next section examines another case study that occurred in Northern Thailand during the Cold War.

The Golden Triangle

We would be amiss not to briefly mention the entangled and compelling case of Indigenous groups that reside in the area known as the **Golden Triangle**, a rugged mountainous region that straddles Northern Thailand, Laos, and Eastern Myanmar (see Figure 4.2).

The ten indigenous groups that have occupied this region of South-East Asia have long been overwhelmingly considered the major political and economic impetus behind the international drug trade, specifically the production of opium, heroin, and more recently methamphetamine. A more accurate way to look at this scenario would indicate that Indigenous groups, such as the **Hmong**, **Karen**, **Lisu**, **Mien**, **Akha**, **Lahu**, **Lua**, **Thin**, and **Khamu**, have been used as pawns by geopolitical forces during the colonial era, the Cold War, and the present neoliberal, trade-oriented era. Practicing swidden agriculture, these groups traditionally subsisted on the growing of upland rice, depending on the altitude of a given settlement. The nation-states of the region, Thailand, Laos, and Myanmar, do not officially recognize these Indigenous groups, and as a result they remain marginalized up to the present.

In China and South-East Asia, British and French colonial administrations found opium to be a major source of revenue. As capitalist and communist forces clashed during the Cold War, a number of US clandestine operatives, initially assisted by

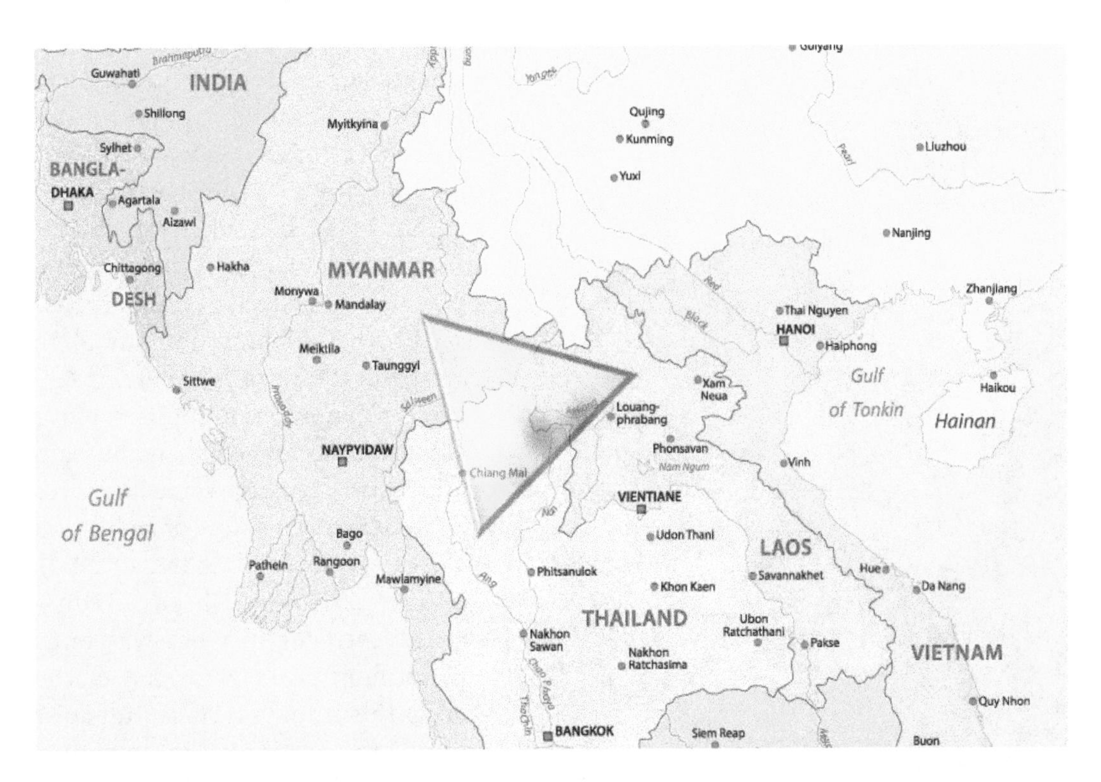

FIGURE 4.2 The Golden Triangle

Christian missionaries, were dropped into remote indigenous communities and trained villagers as militia to prevent what was rumored to be a Chinese communist invasion of South-East Asia (McCoy 1972). Indigenous militias further acted as bulwarks monitoring southern China and communist movements in Laos, Vietnam, Myanmar, and Thailand. As US dependency on the militias increased during the Vietnam War, Indigenous groups were encouraged, with tacit CIA support, to expand their poppy production. As a result, the Golden Triangle became the world's leading exporter of heroin, assisted further by corrupt military and political leaders of these South-East Asian nation-states (McCoy). As a heroin epidemic raged in the United States with the return of US soldiers from Vietnam, the US Drug Enforcement Agency stepped up efforts to suppress opium production at its source through alternative income-generating activities such as tourism and crop substitution programs. These programs have been somewhat successful to an extent, but the semiautonomous Shan states region in Eastern Myanmar remains the world's second-largest producer of opium (dwarfed, however, by Afghanistan's recent emergence).

In the current era of free trade, these Indigenous groups have been further incorporated into export economic activities such as tourism, handicrafts, and crop substitution programs, as the Golden Triangle region is about to embark on massive economic infrastructural development. Southern China seeks to utilize Thailand's

FIGURE 4.3 Northern Thai Hmong Mother and Daughter (Sarah Littlefield)

seaports along its well-developed eastern seaboard for export sites. Transportation of goods traverses through Laos or Myanmar to reach Thailand's well-developed export infrastructure. Some of these routes, especially in Eastern Myanmar, pass through the semiautonomous Shan states, and the situation remains volatile. As export commodities move south, customs and differing bureaucratic regimes at these trade junctures can hinder the free flow of goods and services (see Swe and Chambers 2011).

With additional Chinese industrial investment in what was once a prominent frontier region of the world, the impacts on Indigenous groups are anticipated to be significant (see Figure 4.3). The Mekong River is another global trade route, and deliberations between China and other South-East Asian countries are ongoing

In sum, the first case, ARD and RJC, shows how the Thai state was able to extend its political control over the rural countryside through rural development. The second case, the Golden Triangle, shows a much more nebulous outcome in which the Thai state was less effective in consolidating control over its territory due to a number of extenuating international, political, and economic circumstances.

OUTCOMES: THE MIDDLE INCOME TRAP

Since the end of the Second World War, the number of nation-states has grown from the original 51 UN members to 193 as of 2011. Table 4.2 below shows the increase.

These recently established countries all embarked on the road to modernization by increasing economic growth.

Early economic strategies to stimulate growth, such as import substitution, light manufacturing and industrialization by invitation, and the mixed economy model resulted in upward economic growth and rising living standards. In large measure, developing countries were able to make use of cheap labor to stimulate economic

TABLE 4.2 *The Growth of UN-Recognized Nations (1945–2011)*

YEAR	TOTAL NUMBER OF UN-RECOGNIZED NATION-STATES
1945	51 (original members)
1955	76
1965	117
1975	144
1984	159
1994	185
2011	193

Source: United Nations.

growth. In other cases, natural resources were exploited, contributing to economic advancement. With the global shift to manufacturing, a number of countries could not further develop more advanced industries. Consequently, wages stagnated, and when they did rise, other countries that offered even cheaper labor quickly fell in line to subsume the bulk of industrial development. Numerous countries faced the **middle income trap**, in which national income remained flat and stuck at about 30 percent of the US living standard (Pieterse 2108, 10; Kiel Institute for the World Economy, 2019).

According to a recent global economic symposium:

> The middle-income trap is the situation in which a country's growth slows after reaching middle-income levels. The transition to high-income levels then seemingly becomes unattainable. According to World Bank estimates, only 13 of 101 middle-income economies in 1960 had become high-income economies by 2008. This is an increasingly relevant phenomenon. The share of world population living in middle-income countries has risen dramatically over the last decades resulting from the rapid growth in Asian economies—particularly China and India. Empirical work suggests that the growth rate of per capita GDP typically slows substantially at incomes of between US$10,000 and US$15,000. Growth slowdowns can often be attributed to the disappearance of factors that generate high growth during an initial phase of rapid development. (Kiel Institute for the World Economy)

Figure 4.4 below illustrates three countries, the Republic of Korea, Brazil, and South Africa. Brazil and South Africa are examples of middle income trap countries. The Republic of Korea had gone beyond the middle income trap as of 1985. Development as measured in terms of GDP tends to initially grow, only to later

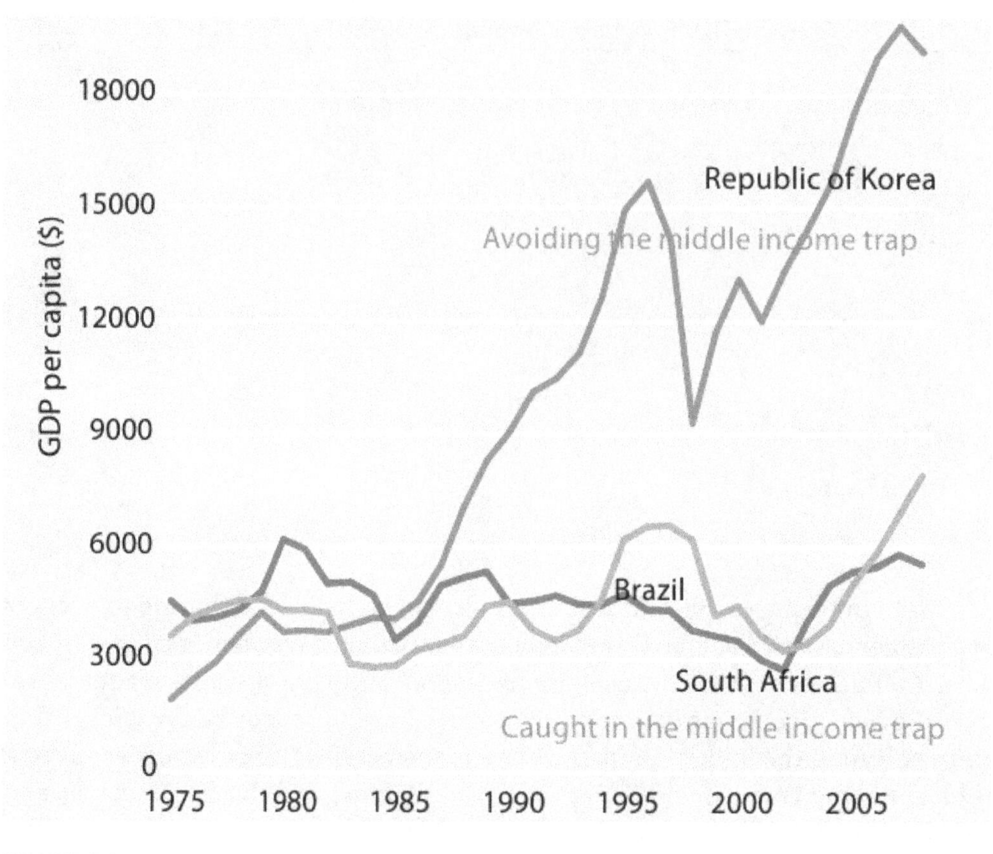

FIGURE 4.4 The Middle Income Trap in Selected Countries 1975–2005

level off. This is primarily due to an early **comparative advantage** that the majority of developing countries first exhibit. In particular, the exploitation of cheap labor and natural resources are at the basis of this initial growth surge. As the material standard of living increases, as do wages, the nation-state lags behind in terms of a more comprehensive consolidation of the institutions required to spur more growth and wealth accumulation. Middle income nation-states, for example, will require highly trained workers (college educated and beyond) to further develop an advanced wealth-generating economy. If, for example, education lags behind, then workers and the manufacturing sector fall back on simply copying and replicating what the Western nations and corporations discard. Western TNCs also seek advantages in terms of sourcing cheap labor and resources. They tend to leapfrog from country to country in pursuit of this advantage. Other innovative sectors, such as research, policing, military, courts, elections, and so on, are also necessary to further advance the modernization growth scheme. In other words, institutional development must also accompany sustained economic growth. We can surmise that many nation-states have only marginally achieved goals of sustained growth. A notable exception is China. Facing the middle income trap, the Chinese government has embarked on an economic policy of foreign investment, domestic demand-led growth, and strengthening economic relations in the region, given the US withdrawal (Pieterse 2018). The "One Belt One Road" initiative exemplifies the likelihood that China will not succumb to the middle income trap, given its high growth rates over the past three decades (see chapter 6).

CONCLUSION

The Postcolonial era was a period of great global change. The crucial Cold War divide acted as the basis for much conflict and far reaching social economic and political change. We depicted the establishment of global governance through the aegis of the UN, World Bank, IMF, and WTO. We introduced key political and economic features of the nation-state to show the establishment of state-based authority and power and early economic contexts and development strategies over the period 1945–1985. The era featured the mixed economy model and early economic development strategies of developing countries, along with the effects in terms of the global shift, rise of TNCs, and growth of world cities. The case of rural development in Thailand illustrates the nation-state's fundamental objective of building nationhood and promoting economic growth. We then traced the dominance of neoliberalism, which replaced the earlier mixed economy model. In conclusion, the middle income trap was a common outcome of these development efforts.

REFERENCES

Anderson, Benedict. "Murder and Progress in Modern Siam." *New Left Review* 181 (May/June 1990): 33–48.

Bisang, Roberto, Gustavo Burachik, and Jorge Katz (ed.). Hacia un nuevo modelo de organización industrial: el sector manufacturero argentino en los años 90. Santiago, Chile: Alianza Editorial, 1995.

Casaburi, Gabriel. Trade and Industrial Policies in Argentina since the 1960s. Buenos Aires: ECLAC, 1998.

Charoensin-o-larn, Chairat. "Understanding Postwar Reformism in Thailand: A Reinterpretation of Rural Development." PhD diss., University of Hawaii. Bangkok: DK Books, 1988.

Cleaver, Harry M., Jr. "The Contradictions of the Green Revolution." In *The Political Economy of Development and Underdevelopment*, edited by Charles K. Wilber. New York: Random House, 1973.

Hadid, Diaa. "Painful Steps Help Egypt Secure $12 Billion IMF Loan." *New York Times*. November 11, 2016.

Hochschild, Adam. *King Leopold's Ghost: A Story of Greed, Terror and Heroism in Colonial Africa*. London: Pan Books.

Kelleher, Ann, and Laura Klein. *Global Perspectives: A Handbook for Understanding Global Issues*. Upper Saddle River, NJ: Pearson Prentice Hall, 2009.

Keynes, John Maynard. *The General Theory of Employment, Interest and Money*. London: Palgrave McMillan, 1936.

Kiel Institute for the World Economy. "The Middle Income Trap." Global Economic Symposium. http://www.global-economic-symposium.org/knowledgebase/escaping-the-middle-income-trap.

Levy-Orlik, Noemi. "Protectionism and Industrialization: A Critical Assessment of the Latin American Industrialization Period." *Brazilian Journal of Political Economy* 29, no. 4 (October/December 2009), http://dx.doi.org/10.1590/S0101-31572009000400008.

Malsin, Jared, and Hassan Morajea. "Unrest Returns to Tunisia." *Wall Street Journal*. January 25, 2018.

Manufacturers Alliance for Productivity and Innovation (MAPI). "Leading Manufacturing Countries of the World." MAPI blog. https://www.mapi.net/blog/2015/09/china-solidifies-its-position-world%E2%80%99s-largest-manufacturer.

McCoy, Alfred W. *The Politics of Heroin: CIA Complicity in the Global Drug Trade*. Chicago: Lawrence Hill Books, 1972.

McMichael, Philip. *Development and Social Change, A Global Perspective*. 5th ed. Thousand Oaks, CA: Sage Publications, 2012.

Nofal, Maria Beatriz. *Absentee Entrepreneurship and the Dynamics of the Motor Vehicle Industry in Argentina*. New York: Praeger, 1989.

Pettinger, Tejvan. "Washington Consensus—definition and criticism." Economics Help. https://www.economicshelp.org/blog/7387/economics/washington-consensus-definition-and-criticism/.

Pieterse, Jan Nederveen. *Multipolar Globalization: Emerging Economies and Development*. New York: Routledge, 2018.

Potter, Robert B., Tony Binns, Jennifer A. Elliot, and David Smith. *Geographies of Development: An Introduction to Development Studies*. 3rd ed. Essex, UK: Pearson Education Limited, 2013.

Robbins, Richard H. *Global Problems and the Culture of Capitalism*. 5th ed. Upper Saddle River, NJ: Prentice Hall, 2011.

Saleh, Heba. "Egypt's Loan Conditions Leave Poor on the Bread Line." *Financial Times*. May 5, 2017.

Stiglitz, Joseph E. *Globalization and Its Discontents*. New York: W.W. Norton & Company, Inc., 2003.

Street, James H., and Dilmus D. James. 1982. "Institutionalism, Structuralism, and Dependency in Latin America." *Journal of Economic Issues* 16, no. 3 (September 1982), 673–89.

Swe, Thein, and Paul Chambers. *Cashing in Across the Golden Triangle: Thailand's Northern Border Trade with China, Laos, and Myanmar*. Chiang Mai, Thailand: Mekong Press, 2011.

United Nations. "Growth in United Nations Membership, 1945–Present." UN English. http://www.un.org/en/sections/member-states/growth-united-nations-membership-1945-present/index.html

Yergin, Daniel, and Joseph Stanislaw. *The Commanding Heights: The Battle for the World Economy*. New York: Simon & Schuster, 1998.

World Trade Organization (WTO). "Home." World Trade Organization. 2018. https://www.wto.org/en.

Figure Credits

Fig. 4.1: Source: http://www.aktaylor.com/asia/as_s_e.htm.

Fig. 4.2: Source: https://www.quantumbooks.com/other/politics-and-society/southeast-asia-drug-war-what-exactly-is-the-golden-triangle/.

Fig. 4.4: Source: http://blogs.lse.ac.uk/internationaldevelopment/2013/09/11/china-and-the-middle-income-trap-indiscriminate-tuna-fishing/.

CHAPTER FIVE

Modernization

PROSPERITY AND POVERTY

INTRODUCTION

Modernity is a multidimensional **metaconcept**. On one hand, modernity entails comprehensive macro socioeconomic processes that are transformative in terms of a society's economy, technology use, communications, and cultural practices. On the other hand, modernity also operates on a microlevel that also alters community, family, and individual outlooks. The **effects of modernization** are variable but become more or less manifest in *both* a macro and micro sense. Understanding modernity requires a grasp of both dimensions—the aggregate macro level of the nation-state or region and the microlevel impacts at the community, family, and even individual level. In this chapter, we will first introduce the concept of **modernity** and **modernization theory**. Second, we will examine major obstacles to modernization faced by developing countries. These obstacles include shortcomings due to the lack of physical, human, and social capital. Corruption is another serious constraint. We then turn to state-sanctioned violence and provide two cases of genocide, that of Cambodia (1975–1979) and Rwanda (1994). These factors demonstrate that modernization is a difficult and arduous project for countries to achieve.

MODERNIZATION DEFINED

Fundamentally, **modernization** refers to predominantly capitalist-driven economic, technological, media, and cultural change. Modernization centers on urbanized industrial growth, or what some scholars critically refer to as an "**urban bias**" (Potter et al. 2013). Modernizing changes tend to focus on cities, with spread effects reaching rural areas at a later time. Specific manifestations of these material changes occur over historical periods through shifting occupational changes in agriculture (from subsistence to commercial production involving mechanization and industrial inputs) and especially urban-based manufacturing (from artisanal to industrial production involving wage labor, large work forces, and intensive natural resource input). As a result, an economy diversifies from the primary sectors to include growing secondary and eventually tertiary sectors (see chapter 1). Populations become concentrated in cities as more economic and education opportunities and more services become available. Overall, life becomes more convenient. Accompanying the rural-to-urban shift are new forms of living amplified by mass transport, technology, livelihood patterns, and new vehicles of communication, such as the internet and mass media. Intertwined with this fundamental material form of modern transformative change are overriding nonmaterial factors, following Rigg (2007), which include the following:

- The use of rational, secular and "expert" knowledge, rather than religious knowledge, supported by national programs of education and widespread literacy
- The orientation of economic action in response to global demands and the market economy, rather than subsistence needs
- The acceptance of the political authority of the nation-state rather than the authority embodied in personal relationships; the growth of nationalism, national identity and a national consciousness; mass participation in politics
- The construction of identity through messages transmitted by the mass media, rather than by the ancestors through ritual. (59–60)

As Riggs aptly notes, modernization **doesn't necessarily equate with "Westernization"** but is

> shaped by the specific social and historical contexts in which it emerges. In other words, modernity is always contingent and therefore, always distinctive ... modernization tends to build on what has gone before, rather than [displacing the past all together]. So rather than rupture, modernization leads to social change that reworks, overwrites, and admittedly sometimes undermines, the patterns of the past. (61)

Perhaps it is more accurate to speak of **modernities**, as each country, region, and people adapts to modernization in a unique way, demonstrating that there is no singular definition of modernity. For example, citizens from the Middle East are modern but dissimilar to those who reside in Latin America. Each group, however, embodies its own particular version of modernity.

MODERNIZATION THEORY AND THE STAGES OF GROWTH

Scholars such as Black (1966) argue that the origin of the modern age can be traced back to the revival of Greek science in Western Europe in the twelfth century. Others such as Spengler (1966) claim that modernization beginning in the West did not occur until the late of eighteenth century in the wake of the industrial revolution. Only then did economic output in Western Europe surpass that from Asian countries such as China and Japan (Spengler 1966). As put by sociologist Shmuel N. Eisenstadt (1966):

> Historically, modernization is the process of change towards those types of social, economic, and political systems that have developed in Western Europe and North America from the seventeenth century to the nineteenth and have then spread to other European countries and in the nineteenth and twentieth centuries to the South American, Asian, and African continents. (1)

As initiated by President Harry S. Truman, modernization has been the major goal of world development since the mid-twentieth century (see chapter one). Appearing after the Second World War, **modernization theory** focused on the major conditions necessary for sustained economic growth and societal well-being. Modernization theory proposes that societies develop through a series of stages, from lower to higher, simple to complex, homogeneous to specialized forms of human organization, with each stage characterized by roughly distinctive economic, social, and cultural patterns. While a number of Global North societies are at the high end of modernization measures, contemporary Global South countries are still at variable phases of the modernization process. In a number of instances, traditional cultural practices, such as patron-client relations, can be intertwined alongside the high-end stage of mass consumption in various cultural, political, and social arenas.

In sum, modernization involves interrelated social, economic, political, and cultural processes that operate on large and small scales of human organization and activity. Modernization cannot take shape in the absence of capital investment, scientific and technological innovation, systematic education, nation-state building, sufficient foodstuffs, and intensive natural resource usage. Organizationally, modernization requires cultural orientations that favor political democracy, secularization, and free enterprise (Armer and Katsillis 2001). It is important to keep in mind that these factors often do not unfold in a strictly linear fashion, from one stage to the next, or from the traditional through to the high mass consumption stage.

As we will see, countries have undergone variable transitions and face innumerable obstacles in attaining modernity. In an extreme case, for example, which we detail later in this chapter, the Cambodian Khmer Rouge regime under Pol Pot (1975–1979) sought to renounce capitalist modernity altogether and return to a premodern peasant state. Everything modern was prohibited, including currency, personal possessions, markets, and families. Genocide was the result. In Zimbabwe, efforts to modernize from 1980 to 2000 led to rapid increases in per capita income and economic growth, some of the highest in Africa for this period. In 2000, however, the violent seizure of white-owned farms by President Robert Mugabe, currency instability, and hyperinflation led to deindustrialization and the dramatic shrinking of a once nascent industrial base. At present, 95 percent of Zimbabwe's workforce make their living in the informal economy (Onishi and Moyo 2017). Yet another example demonstrates that the Islamic State seeks to return to an earlier and harsher version of premodern society. As put by Wood (2015) in an insightful article, "What ISIS Really Wants";

> We can gather that their state rejects peace as a matter of principle; that it hungers for genocide; that its religious views make it constitutionally incapable of certain types of change, even if that change might ensure its survival; and that it considers itself a harbinger of—and headline player in—the imminent end of the world. ... much of what the group does looks nonsensical except in light of a sincere, carefully considered commitment to returning civilization to a seventh-century legal environment, and ultimately to bringing about the apocalypse.

Clearly, modern development **does not unfold in a linear fashion**. Societies can reject modernity all together. Some nation-states encounter significant obstacles to achieving modernization. Other countries respond to modernity on the basis of their own social, political, and economic standpoints.

Rostow's Five Stages of Modernization

In a theoretical sense, economist Walt W. Rostow (1960) proposed that modern economic development follows five stages from traditional to modern societies, consisting of (1) the traditional society; (2) the pre-takeoff stage; (3) the takeoff stage; (4) the drive to maturity stage; and (5) the age of high, mass consumption. The appeal of Rostow's modernization theory was that *any* country, regardless of its current status, could embark on the pathway to modernity. Modernization was also very much an anticommunist remedy for maintaining First World influence during the Cold War (Potter et al. 2013). Rostow (1960) titled his book *The Stages of Economic Growth: A Non-Communist Manifesto*. The next section begins with the initial stage of Rostow's modernization theory, that of the traditional society.

The Traditional Society

The entire world up to the seventeenth century could be characterized as a **traditional society**, including dynasties in China and the Middle East, the Mediterranean civilizations, and medieval Europe. A traditional economy is a subsistence-oriented one with little surplus produced beyond immediate survival needs. As Rostow remarks, however, traditional societies are not necessarily static,

> and it would not exclude increases in output. Acreage could be expanded; some ad hoc technical innovations, often highly productive innovations, could be introduced in trade, industry and agriculture; productivity could rise with, for example, the improvement of irrigation works or the discovery and diffusion of a new crop. (4)

In a general sense, science and technology are not applied in a comprehensive manner, and production reaches ceiling levels of output. For the majority of people, life is focused on meeting basic needs: food, clothing, and shelter. Family or the extended kin network is the basic unit of production. Economic activities are carried out in the family-community setting.

Daniel Lerner, an American scholar, studied a small village, Balgat, in Turkey, to illustrate the process of transition from a traditional to a modern society (Lerner 1958). Balgat lies about five miles south of Ankara, the national capital. It had been a traditional society until 1950. Lerner revealed the following features of a traditional society, summarized here in broad terms: Traditional societies emphasize social conformity rather than individualism. Individuals' behaviors are strictly regulated by religion, community codes, and sanctions, or what some critics refer to as the "tyranny of tradition." People follow directives from authorities. It was not uncommon for villagers in Lerner's study to ask the village chief what they were supposed to do if they had to go to the city. Obedience, loyalty, and bravery are valued. There was a strict hierarchy among the villagers, in which the village chief was unequivocally the leader, followed by the village elders. One's position in a society is inherited from earlier generations.

In a traditional society, life is often dictated by the agrarian seasons of the year. Change is perceived as shameful and condemned: "The traditional man is cut once and for all to a familiar pattern. The mold is the same for all men of the same age and rank" (Lerner, 133). There is little curiosity for the unfamiliar. People inherit their elders' points of view without question, an outlook called **fatalism,** in which one expects the same outcomes as one's parents and grandparents experienced. In a separate study of the development of Turkey, Morrison (1939) recorded the lives of farmers in the village of Alisar in the Kanak Su Basin of Central Anatolia in 1932, where things remained virtually unchanged from 3,000 years before. He found that the peasants of Alisar were concerned with the immediate circumstances of daily life. The past did not concern them whatsoever.

In a traditional society, one's life horizon is constricted to one's immediate world. In Lerner's study, one villager, when asked where he would like to live if he had to leave Turkey, responded that he would rather kill himself than leave the country. The villagers are largely cut off from the outside world, both physically (there was no paved road to the village) and mentally (people were not interested in leaving the village). There was no traffic passing through it. Villagers would travel to Ankara, the capital city, only once or twice in their entire lifetime. There was one radio in the village owned by the village chief, who allowing his fellow villagers to come to listen, would interpret the meaning of the content in the way he saw fit. Some villagers showed no interest in radio or newspapers at all because they were not interested in matters that did not immediately concern them. As put by a local resident, people just " 'stay in their holes all their life.' ... The traditional cares nothing, wants nothing, can do nothing about the world" (151).

Google Map Exercise

In reflecting on the above villages of Balgat and Alisar, Turkey, we can derive some insights regarding the process of modernization as contrasted with the accounts by Lerner (1958) and Morrison (1939) from Google Maps.

> **Directions:** go to Google Maps and type in "Balgat, Turkey." List key features that accurately portray the physical landscape of Balgat. Imagine what people do there for a living and how they live in this setting. Do the same for Alisar, Turkey.
>
> Has anything changed from the earlier characterizations of the traditional society by Lerner (1958) and Morrison (1939)?

Certainly from the mapping exercise, we can see tremendous change in Balgat. In Alisar, however, change is not that visibly evident. Clearly, more in-depth examination is required, but we can see specific modern changes in rural Alisar, such as all-weather roads and irrigation. One could suspect that within individual households, radios, plastic utensils, and clothing would indicate modern urban-based influences. This pattern has been repeated in many countries throughout the world (Potter et al. 2008).

In a traditional society, self-interest is taboo. Seeking money instead of the ways of God is profane. The young are supposed to care about the maintenance and well-being of their families and the community rather than themselves. These earlier accounts generally characterize traditional societies. It is important not to underestimate the pull and power of modernization, either in a national or individual sense. One powerful force that has significantly shaped modern outlooks is the amount of education one attains (Inkeles and Smith 1974). Furthermore, when we consider the growing reach of global economies and markets, we find that workers, farmers, and everyday citizens have become intertwined with events, patterns, and attitudes that originate from distant or more abstract sources (Rigg 2007). The results clearly demonstrate that humans are highly mobile, quick to adopt and respond to new social and economic opportunities in a way that can be defined in modern terms.

The Pre-Takeoff Stage

Led by Britain, Western Europe was the first region that entered the **pre-takeoff stage** in the late seventeenth and early eighteenth centuries, fueled by the application of science and technology to agriculture and industry (Rostow 1960). This is the eve of the economic takeoff stage, in which societies experience significant changes, one way or another, by putting together the components that stimulate economic development. These elements are called **preconditions for takeoff**. They require fundamental changes in production, way of life, and social structure. As

Rostow puts it, "The idea spreads not merely that is economic progress possible, but that economic progress is a necessary condition for some other purpose, judged to be good: be it national dignity, private profit, the general welfare, or a better life for the children" (6). Vital is the role of modern education and the political goal of establishing nationalism.

An important precondition for economic takeoff is building **social overhead capital**, or **physical capital**. The term **social** means that the products or services associated with this type of capital are available to everyone. **Overhead** means that they are not tightly linked to any particular production or business. This mainly refers to investment in a society's **infrastructure**. Because of this particular requirement, the government usually plays an eminent role in this realm (**interventionist development**). Examples of social overhead capital include the construction of roads, ports, power plants, banks, schools, and hospitals. To initiate this process, there has to be a shift in the economy from subsistence agriculture to profit-driven agricultural production for distant markets, both domestically and abroad. Urban-based manufacturing centers require significant investment, expertise, and infrastructure, with profits used for further investing and expansion. The scope of trade is expanded to national or even international settings.

In order to begin the transition to an industrial economy, which is accompanied by migration to urban centers, food production must be able to support growing urban populations. In addition to satisfying food consumption for urban populations, **agricultural surplus** is also needed for export to earn capital to support continuing industrial development. In the eighteenth century, the United States' major exports were wheat, corn, rice, and tobacco. These export earnings fueled industrial development. Finally, a skilled labor force is needed to fill manufacturing jobs. Formal education becomes necessary in this context.

In a traditional society, people are related to each other by kinship or geographic proximity. Their life interactions are limited to people they personally know on a face-to-face basis. In contrast, the transition to a modern society requires large-scale economic interdependence and a division of labor on the national level. People are no longer bound to their birth place. They leave home for new residencies, especially cities, looking for new opportunities. A new type of social bond emerges that revolves around what people do for each other in a manner that can satisfy personal needs even if they may be total strangers to each other.

In explaining these new social relationships, French sociologist Emile Durkheim (1858–1917) conceptualized two types of societies: mechanical and organic. In traditional societies, social relations are **mechanical**, in which individuals are tied by blood or consanguinity. Society is organized on the basis of the extended family, clan, or tribe. Individuals are homogeneous, performing the same kind of tasks and living in the same way. Society is segmental, composed of similar groups, whose members are like-minded. Solidarity is derived from common ancestors and collective responsibility. The relations that prevail in a modern urban society, however, are **organic**, characterized by an impersonal **division of labor. Individuals specialize in a particular occupation, often part of a whole production process** (e.g., a factory or automobile plant). This type of society, exhibited in cities, tends to be complex, large in scale, and primarily functional. The stability of the entire society depends on the coordination of individuals fulfilling their respective roles in the division of labor. As claimed by Durkheim,

> individuals are no longer grouped according to their relations of lineage, but according to the particular nature of the social activity to which they devote themselves. Their natural and necessary milieu is no longer that given by birth, but that given by occupation. It is no longer real or fictitious blood-ties which mark the place of each one, but the function which he fills. (cited in Giddens 1972, 143)

History shows that to achieve modernization, it is insufficient to simply improve economic performance by building roads, factories and schools, or even adopting new technologies. A case in point: when fishermen of Kakinada, India, were offered new nylon fishing nets, which were a technological improvement, less susceptible to breaking or tangling, one would expect a significant growth in fishing production and a boom in business. But something unexpected happened. With the new nets, more fish were caught within the same amount of time, certainly. But some fishermen stopped fishing once they had reached the same target as set in the past. For those who did catch more fish and make more money, the extra income was not invested in expanding business but used to buy alcohol. This case shows that technological change does not automatically lead to economic change. There also has to be a change in the mindset and in the culture's orientation. In another example, when the Industrial Revolution transformed Europe, including the northern shore of the Mediterranean, there was not much happening on the southern shore. It was not because people on the other side of the sea were unaware of it. As a matter of fact, they had fair exposure to it. It was simply because there was a lack of motivation to embrace and apply the new technologies (McClelland 1966).

In addition to the changes outlined above, there has to be a transformation of both one's mindset and the culture as a whole. These psychological changes include thoughts, values, and expectations. According to Max Weber (1864–1920), who is regarded as one of the founders of sociology, the **Protestant ethic laid the foundation for modernization in the West.** Calvinism complemented the modern mentality. On one hand, Calvinism holds to a doctrine of predestination, which means that an individual's fate or salvation is predetermined and can't be changed by one's faith or deeds. On the other hand, it acknowledges that goodness or personal achievement can be taken as a sign of salvation in the afterlife. Therefore, it contributes to defining an ethic of behavior that leads to economic success—"hard work, honesty, seriousness, the thrifty use of money and time" and "the making of a new man—rational, ordered, diligent, productive" (Landes 2000, 11–12). All these values complement the idea of striving for business success and capital accumulation.

In a secular sense, the development of modern attitudes is based on an urge to change traditional ways of life that no longer satisfy a people's new wants and outlooks. It is a new way of thinking, an impulse to do things better than what has been done before, more quickly, more efficiently, and with better results (McClelland 1966). A modern person no longer conceives of their fate as limited by their physical environment. One is no longer at the mercy of nature but rather exudes confidence in control over nature and the future. A core tenet of modernization is the application of science-based knowledge and skill to manipulate the environment to one's advantage (Rostow 1960). Modernization becomes self-sustaining only when modern ways of doing things are internalized in people's minds: the infusion of rationalist and positivist spirit, the notion of profit maximization, a vision of a better life, self-interest as a driving factor, and entrepreneurship with desire for business expansion. A person believes that they can control their own destiny. One's future is achieved by one's own determination and effort: "Men succeed or fail by the test of what they accomplish (not what they worship)" (Lerner 1958, 48).

The interdependent nature of a modern society calls for **nationalism**, in which individuals identify with each other on the basis of a common **national identity**. National affairs are no longer remote to individuals. Each person has a stake in the performance of the nation-state. The nation-state should also display an interest in the welfare and well-being of its citizens. Citizens see the connection between themselves and the larger world. In his study of Turkey, Lerner asked respondents to name the biggest problem to themselves and the biggest problem faced by the nation. While economic problems were mentioned most, the following table (Table 5.1), adapted from Lerner's study, shows a striking difference between the outlook of those in traditional and modern societies.

In Lerner's (1958) study, respondents were classified as traditional, modern, or in between (transitional), according to their exposure to media. The dramatic difference does not lie horizontally across the groups. Over half of all three groups identified

TABLE 5.1 *Percentage of Citizens Who Found Economic Issues to be the Biggest Problem Faced by Themselves and by the Nation in Turkey, 1958*

	TRADITIONAL	TRANSITIONAL	MODERN
FOR ONESELF	67%	59%	64%
FOR TURKEY	8%	21%	52%

Source: Adapted from Lerner, 143.

economic problems as the major challenge. Rather, it is the vertical difference, the connection/disconnection of one's personal problem with the state of the nation, that stands out. For those who held traditional points of view, only 8 percent mentioned the same problem at the national level. But for those who held modern views, over half of them saw the convergence of personal and national troubles, which was virtually absent for the traditionals. The transitionals, as implied by the name, are at an in-between stage in this regard.

Sociologist Alex Inkeles in the 1960s provided a portrait of a modern man with the following nine characteristics: (1) ready for new experience and open to change; (2) caring about issues beyond one's immediate environment and aware of diversity; (3) present- or future-oriented, punctual, and organized; (4) good at planning; (5) having a sense of efficacy (believing in one's ability to change his environment); (6) having a sense of control (believing the world is calculable); (7) respectful to others; (8) believing in science and technology; and (9) merit-oriented (Inkeles 1966).

There are two schools of thought about how a society becomes modern (Weiner 1966). While some scholars believe that the establishment of modern institutions, such as effective state, laws, banks, marketable land, education, communication, and transportation, is critical for building a modern society. Other scholars view the transformation of people's mindset or culture to be more important. It is fair to say that both are important elements for economic takeoff, and the latter can be a long and slow process. In his study of Turkey, Lerner decried the slow change in the villagers' mindset even after a road was built to connect the village with the outside world, like Ankara:

> The hatred sown by anti-colonialism is harvested in the rejection of every appearance of foreign tutelage. Wanted are modern institutions but not modern ideologies, modern power but not modern purposes, modern wealth but not modern wisdom, modern commodities but not modern cant. (Lerner 1958, 47)

Finally, dramatic economic and social changes at this stage have transformed families. Gradually, many of the functions of traditional families are replaced by social institutions. Economic activities, which previously were a major family function, gradually shift to larger, industrial sectors. Furthermore, the family training function is greatly weakened by education. The means through which individuals make their livelihood has also changed. Instead of relying on learning from their parents or ancestors the same trades and ways of life that have existed for centuries, people obtain their knowledge from professional educators in public schools, from the media, and from the larger world beyond their families. The willingness to become economically mobile ruptures traditional kinship ties, which used to serve as a support system for the young, old, and disabled. Nuclear families start to gain prominence over extended families. In place of family ties, nation-state-sponsored social welfare programs take hold.

The Takeoff Stage

The **takeoff stage** that Rostow (1960) labels as "the great watershed in the life of modern societies" (7) features radical, sustained, and self-reinforcing economic growth, usually spurred by a leading industry, such as textiles for Britain or railways for France, the United States, and Germany (Rostow 1960). The takeoff stage is accompanied by massive transformations of the economy and society. Whereas the traditional structure is modified incrementally during the pre-takeoff period, new values and especially institutions achieve a breakthrough during takeoff. The takeoff stage is triggered by a sharp stimulus, which can be a political revolution, such as the French and German revolutions in 1848 or Indian independence after the Second World War; technological innovation, such as the steam engine; or a favorable international business environment, such as the opening of British-French timber markets in the 1860s or the rise in export commodity prices in the nineteenth century that benefited the United States and Canada. This stage is built on the following three economic conditions: (1) a rise in productive investment; (2) the development of one or more manufacturing sectors; and (3) the considerable capacity to mobilize domestic savings and turn them into capital. The third condition means that income surplus is directed to further productive expansion rather than to wealth hoarding or luxury consumption (Rostow 1960).

The Drive to Maturity Stage

The **drive to maturity stage** is the period "when a society has effectively applied the range of (then) modern technology to the bulk of its resources" (Rostow 1960, 59). Rostow estimates the period from pre-takeoff to maturity to be between 40 and 60 years. In the United States, it was marked by emerging new industries, such as steel, ship building, chemicals, and modern machine instruments, at the beginning of the twentieth century. Although not everything is produced in a mature economy, anything *can* be produced. Technological constraints have been removed. Society has become one of perpetual economic growth. What to produce becomes a matter of economic choice or political priority. At this stage, not only are the economic sectors transformed but the composition of the workforce and working conditions change. The share of the workforce in agriculture steadily declines from 75 percent before takeoff to 40 percent by the end of takeoff, and further to 20 percent by maturity. Unskilled labor becomes professional, skilled, and semiskilled labor. At the same time, social movements to improve working conditions start to gain momentum, such as in the British Factory Acts and the American Progressive era. The Factory Acts were a series of labor laws passed by the United Kingdom to regulate working conditions of British industries. The early acts covered only the welfare of young children employed in textile mills. For example, the Health and Morals of Apprentices Act passed in 1802 applied to textile mills apprentices only and set the working hour limit to 12 per day. The law was gradually extended to women in 1844 and other industries from the 1860s onward. The 1878 Factory Act applied to all trades, banned child labor under age ten, and prohibited women from working more than 56 hours per week. On a similar path, the United States had adopted a series of progressive economic policies by 1916, such as the progressive income tax and the permission to form unions.

The Stage of High Mass Consumption

As a society develops beyond maturity, the emphasis shifts from production to consumption. At this stage, consumption transcends meeting basic needs such as food, clothing, and shelter and expands to durable goods and services. The United States is the first country that entered this stage, starting in the 1920s, symbolized by Henry Ford's assembly line. Automobiles topped the list of mass-consumption commodities. Between 1899 and 1937, the production of automobiles, a key and decisive factor in mass consumption, grew by more than 180 times; the consumption of cigarettes, milk, sugar, petroleum, and canned fruits and vegetables grew by about ten times. While the urban growth continued, the pace of suburbanization was even faster. In the 1920s, the American population grew by 16 percent, those living in urban centers by 22 percent, and those in the suburbs by an impressive 44 percent. Modern household appliances were found in more and more newly constructed single-family houses: radios and refrigerators, then followed by vacuum cleaners, washers, and televisions. Apparently, the era of mass consumption has by no means come to an end. After computers and smart phones, what is next? With material abundance at the final stage, Rostow (1960) was concerned about secular spiritual stagnation. He wondered if humanity can still find worthy outlets for collective human energies and talents or if it will just succumb to boredom. A Spanish historian vividly expressed such a sentiment hovering in the air of the West:

> All these countries enjoy two advantages which give them a certain prestige: the standard of living of their populations is relatively high; and their political life is undisturbed by any serious incidents. Internal peace and prosperity are such obvious benefits that other peoples contemplating them might perhaps let themselves be carried away by envy and admiration, ... The most striking of these is without doubt boredom. Well governed and well administered people are bored to death. (Madariaga 1958, 17)

Table 5.2 shows selected developed countries that have gone through all the stages. One takeaway message is that transitions in modernization are by no means linear. On the one hand, Britain had been the front runner up to the maturity stage, preceding the United States for half of a century (1850 vs. 1900). But it was the United States that first entered the stage of mass consumption, before the Second World War (WWII), while Europe fell relatively behind in the 1920s. The gap between the United States and Western Europe did not begin to narrow until after 1950. On the other hand, although it lagged the United States in mass consumption for some time in the

TABLE 5.2 ***Examples of Economic Growth Transitions***

	TAKEOFF	ECONOMIC MATURITY	MASS CONSUMPTION
GREAT BRITAIN	1783–1802	1850	after WWII
FRANCE	1830–1860	1910	after WWII
UNITED STATES	1843–1860	1900	before WWII
GERMANY	1850–1873	1910	after WWII
SWEDEN	1868–1890	1930	after WWII
JAPAN	1878–1900	1940	after WWII
CANADA	1896–1914	1950	after WWII

Source: Rostow 1960.

twentieth century, Western Europe made more rapid strides in building the welfare state due to stronger socialist ideals among industrial workers and intellectuals.

In general, developing countries exhibit a mix of stages, largely falling in the pre-takeoff or takeoff stages. Many are trapped in transition from the takeoff to maturity stage, where the former is characterized by focusing on a particular industry and the latter by developing a range of industries. Countries relying on a single industry are vulnerable to economic shocks. This is particularly notable in a number of Sub-Saharan African countries, such as Burundi, Congo, Malawi, Nigeria, Rwanda, and Zambia, among others (Potter et al. 2013, 347–9).

In Kitwe, an industrial town in Zambia, commodity prices used to boom with copper exports. The city was colored by shopping malls, brick homes, and private schools. Soaring prices of copper brought the rising middle class to Zambia and a conviction of many that they were already on the road to irreversible prosperity. The recent global economic slowdown, however, has revealed the fragility of its economy. Seventy percent of its exports rely on copper, of which the price has been cut by half in two years. The country's currency lost 47 percent of its value in 2015. Some 15,000 local workers were laid off, with more expected (McGroarty and Parkinson 2016). The economic downturn caught many Zambians off guard. Sales of durable goods, like refrigerators and televisions, are down. Subsidies to fight HIV and malaria have taken a hit. Crime and the number of suicides are rising. Meanwhile, international corporations have either reduced investment or cut their workforces. For example, Nestle laid off 15 percent of its employees in 21 African countries in June 2015.

Zambia's experience is far from unique. Many other countries in Africa and beyond suffer from the same predicament. Angola, Nigeria, South Africa, and Venezuela all face harsh challenges since global commodity prices of oil, gold, and platinum fell recently. The development in these countries has come to a halt. In this sense, the developing countries still have a relatively long way to go to catch up.

THE RELATIONSHIP BETWEEN STAGES OF DEVELOPMENT AND CULTURE

According to the modernization theory, societies go through a series of stages to develop from lower to higher levels in terms of technological complexity and economic output. Each stage is associated with a distinctive set of values and culture. As a result, one would expect to observe different values in societies at different development stages, and as societies transition from one stage to the next, new sets of values would replace the old ones. The question is, empirically, is this the case?

A study by sociologists Inglehart and Baker on modernization and cultural change sheds light on these interesting questions (Inglehart and Baker 2000). In the study, two particular dimensions of polarizing values are constructed: **traditional versus secular-rational** and **survival versus self-expression**. The study's authors asked questions that determined respondents' orientation within these dimensions and then plotted the answers against the country's gross national product (GNP) per capita (see Figure 5.1).

The traditional versus secular-rational dimension was measured by responses to the following five questions: whether the respondent agrees that (1) God is very important in respondent's life; (2) it is more important for a child to learn obedience and religious faith than independence and termination; (3) abortion is never justifiable; (4) respondent has a strong sense of national pride; and (5) respondent favors more respect for authority. **Positive answers to these questions amount to traditional values, whereas negative answers amount to secular-rational values.**

The survival versus self-expression dimension was measured by responses to the following five questions: whether the respondent agrees that (1) economic and physical security has a higher priority than self-expression and quality of life; (2) respondent is not very happy; (3) respondent has not signed and would not sign a petition; (4) homosexuality is never justifiable; and (5) one must be very careful about trusting people. **Positive answers to these questions indicate survival values, whereas negative answers indicate self-expression values.**

The study is based on three waves of the World Values Surveys from 1981 to 1998. Of the 65 countries examined, Inglehart and Baker divide them into nine cultural zones with distinctive traditional heritages, including Protestant Europe (e.g., Sweden, Germany, and Switzerland), Catholic Europe (e.g., Belgium, France, and Italy), English-Speaking (e.g., Great Britain, the United States, and Canada), Latin America (e.g., Mexico, Chile, and Brazil), Confucian (e.g., China, Japan, and South Korea), Baltic (e.g., Czechia, Latvia, and Estonia), Orthodox (e.g., Russia, Hungary, and Romania), South Asia (e.g., India, Philippines, and Pakistan), and Africa (e.g., South Africa, Nigeria, and Ghana). On top of this, some countries have the additional label of Ex-Communist countries (e.g., Russia, China, and Czechia).

The first analysis answers the question of whether countries at different development levels show different sets of values. In Figure 5.1, all 65 countries are placed on a two-dimensional chart, in which the horizontal axis, from the left to the right, transitions from survival to self-expression values and the vertical axis, from the bottom upward, transitions from traditional to secular-rational values. All high-income countries, with GNI per capita of US$15,000 or higher, are found to be clustered at the upper-right corner of the chart—the territory that embodied the strongest self-expression and secular-rational values or the weakest survival and traditional values. In stark contrast, all low-income countries, with GNP per capita of US$2,000 or lower, are found to be clustered at the lower-left corner of the chart—the territory that embodied the strongest survival and traditional values or the weakest self-expression and secular-rational values. The middle-income countries, with GNP per capita between US$2,000 and US$15,000, fall in the area between the two extreme clusters. Note that the high income countries cut across a number of cultural zones (Protestant, Catholic, English-Speaking, Confucian, and ex-Communist) and so do the low-income countries (Africa, South Asia, Orthodox, and Ex-Communist). It seems that the determinant factor of a country's prevailing set of values is its average national income, or development level, not its traditional heritage. The evidence so

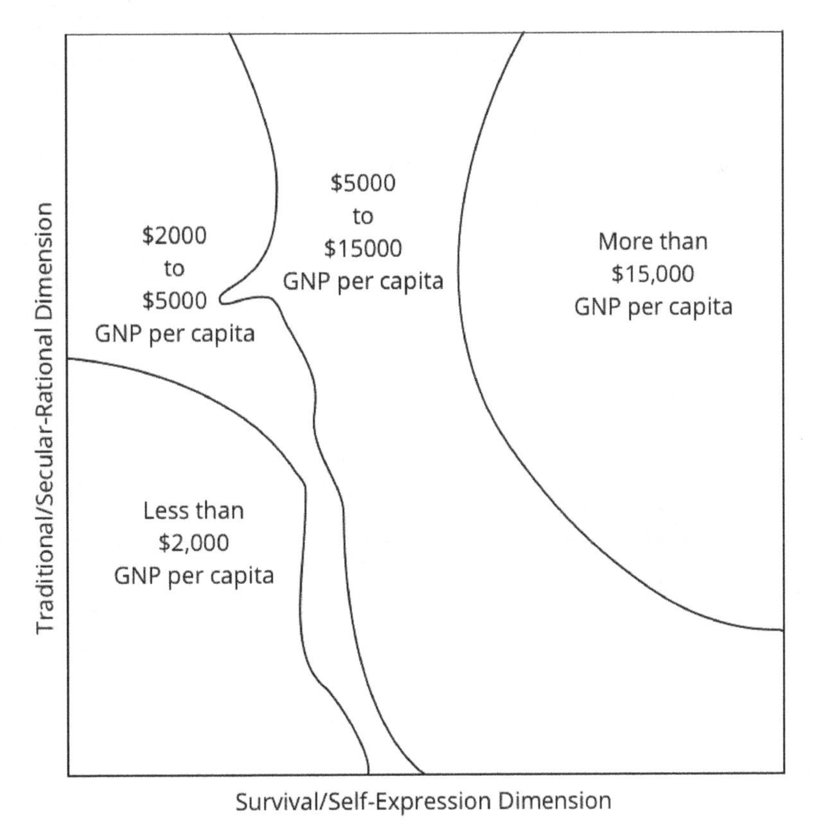

FIGURE 5.1 National Income and Social Values. Regenerated based on Inglehart and Baker, Figure 2.

far points to a clear message: "The value systems of rich countries differ systematically from those of poor countries" (Inglehart and Baker, 29).

In chapter 1, we introduced three economic sectors, the primary (mainly agricultural), secondary (mainly industrial), and tertiary (mainly service) sectors. Inglehart and Baker also investigated how the predominance of economic sectors, or the level of development, corresponds to changes in values. It is found that a higher percentage of the labor force in the industrial sector is correlated with stronger secular-rational values, and a higher percentage in the agricultural sector shows the opposite. A higher percentage in the service sector is found to be correlated with stronger self-expression values. Thus, there seems to be two sets of transitions in a clear parallel: the transition from an agricultural to industrial economy corresponds to a shift from traditional to secular-rational values, and the transition to a service economy nurtures self-expression values.

In terms of modern economic development and social values, do traditional heritages become totally irrelevant and quietly fade away? As it turns out, it is not that simple. In a separate analysis, Inglehart and Baker compared the relative contribution of economic development and traditional heritage in predicting traditional/secular-rational and survival/self-expression values, respectively. Economic development measured by GNP per capita, percentage of those employed in the industrial sector in 1980, and percentage enrolled in education, has a 42-percent predicting power for traditional/secular-rational values and 63-percent predicting power for survival/self-expression values. When cultural heritages are taken into account, the predicting power is augmented to 70 percent and 84 percent, respectively, as shown in Figure 5.2.

The final verdict is that although the impact of economic development on social values is substantial, a society's cultural heritage matters too. Even as a society

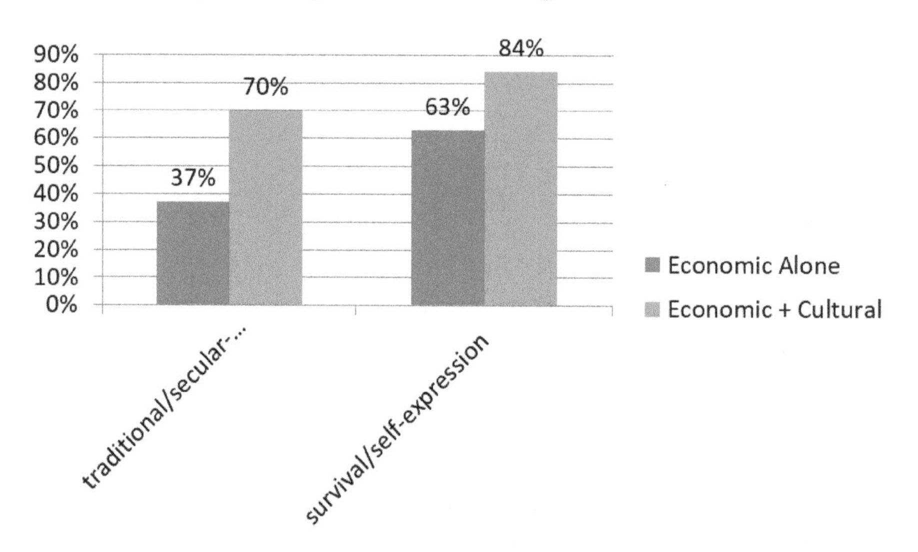

FIGURE 5.2 Contribution of Economic Development and Cultural Heritage in Predicting Social Values

undergoes economic development, its cultural heritage matters and influences the overall adaptation and trajectory of modernization.

MODERNIZATION AND UNDERDEVELOPMENT

Modernization theory asserts that underdevelopment can be attributed to constraints that originate from within developing countries. Constraints to modernization can include an unfavorable natural environment, the urban-rural divide, weak infrastructure development, poor education and health care, and ineffective governance. The following sections will focus on these constraints.

Natural Capital Constraints

There is no question that countries are unequally endowed with **natural capital**. Some countries benefit from fertile soils, some are rich in valuable minerals, some possess oil and gas within their territories, and some are endowed with long coastlines and natural ports. A country's historical context shows, however, that the relationship between a country's natural endowments and its development is quite complex. While the exploitation of natural capital can serve as the raw material base for economic takeoff, possessing natural capital has also proved to be a curse for some countries. Some countries with barely any natural capital, such as Japan, have achieved great success in modern development. In countries with abundant natural capital, foreign or elite ownership of natural resources can siphon off the profits and hinder development for the majority while enriching the owners (e.g., Equatorial Guinea). Overall, it is fair to say that both natural resource endowments and ownership play a critical role in a country's development.

Any extreme climate hinders development. A tropical climate, common to Global South countries, consists of a wet and dry season. A relatively short growing season dependent on the amount of rain and temperatures can greatly impact agricultural production for rice, maize, and wheat. In contrast, many African countries are situated in very hot, arid climates, prone to drought. It makes not only growing food but also building houses and roads very difficult. A tropical climate is also susceptible to cases of malaria and river blindness, among other diseases. Malaria is a disease caused by parasites that are transmitted to people through mosquitoes. As mentioned in chapter 2, it can be life-threatening. The rainy season in tropical countries provides favorable conditions for mosquitoes to thrive and transmit the disease. According to the World Health Organization, 15 countries—mainly in Sub-Saharan Africa, which is in a tropical climate—accounted for about 80 percent of malaria cases and deaths globally in 2015. With climate change and global warming occurring, the environmental vectors for the spread of malaria are expanding in areas where this disease was previously eradicated (see chapter 8).

Geography can also play an important role. Water transport is much less expensive than land transport. It is not a coincidence that most of the world's largest and most prosperous cities sit by seas, rivers, or lakes. In contrast, it is very hard for landlocked countries to actively engage in economic exchanges with the outside world or to attract investment. A World Bank study estimates that landlocked countries have only about 30 percent of the trade volume of coastal countries (Limão and Venables 1999). There are six countries in Africa and 12 in Asia (half of which are in Central Asia) that are landlocked. A new country, South Sudan, which gained independence from Sudan in 2011, is a landlocked country. Oil exports have to go through pipelines in Sudan to the Red Sea. The government of Sudan charges $25 a barrel for shipping the oil. When the global oil prices dropped to $30 a barrel, it was not worth continuing any production (Beaubien 2016).

Mountainous terrain is another deterrent for economic development. Most of the countries in Latin America, from Mexico through Central America and down to the end of the continent, are mountainous. This geographical barrier hinders investment and industrial development. In Bolivia, for example, only very high-value commodities, such as gold and silver, are exported, to overcome the high transport costs. Bolivia's mountainous and landlocked geography is believed to be an overriding factor of its chronic poverty (Sachs 2005). In conjunction with mountainous terrain, soil infertility can greatly constrain food production (Rosegrant et al. 2005). In Sub-Saharan Africa, more than 70 percent of arable land and 31 percent of pastureland suffers from degraded soil quality, such as erosion and nutrient deficiencies in nitrogen, phosphorus, and potassium. This condition is also prevalent in other parts of the Global South.

The Urban-Rural Divide

Another common phenomenon of underdevelopment pertains to the urban-rural divide. Urban areas and closely proximate **peri-urban** areas are typically the epicenter of modern development activities. The urban-rural divide refers to a sharp contrast between the cities and countryside in developing countries; cities host modern industrial and service sectors, whereas rural areas more or less remain residual and are dominated by a lagging agriculture sector. In the peri-urban areas, commercial agriculture, mixed with manufacturing and low-cost housing development, begins to occur on the outskirts surrounding the central city proper. Such a two-tier economic structure is called a **dual economy**. As a result, urban and peri-urban residents have much better access to health care and educational services and enjoy more employment opportunities and benefits.

According to the United Nations (UN), in developing countries worldwide, there is a clear urban advantage over rural areas in residents' well-being. While 87 percent of births are attended by skilled health personnel in urban areas, it is only 56 percent in rural areas. The percentage of people having access to piped drinking water is four-fifths versus one-third for urban and rural areas, respectively. The corresponding percentages of people covered by improved sanitation facilities are more than

80 percent and 50 percent, respectively. Children under age five in rural areas are about 1.7 times as likely to die as their urban peers (United Nations 2015). Youth in urban areas tend to stay in school longer. Of young people ages 15 to 24 in Chad, 21 percent of those in urban areas completed lower secondary school education, while only 2 percent of their rural counterparts did so. In Bhutan, the gap is 32 percent urban versus 11 percent rural (Population Reference Bureau 2015).

Early marriage occurs more often in rural areas and impacts a country's birth rate. The percentage of women age 20 to 24 who were married by age 18 was 49 percent in rural Ethiopia but only 22 percent in cities. Rural women also tend to have more children than their urban counterparts. In Ethiopia, women had 4.1 births on average in 2015, which concealed a significant divide between urban and rural areas, where the average was 2.6 and 5.5, respectively (Population Reference Bureau 2015). Such inequality stems from the unequal distribution of resources between urban and rural areas. For instance, health care services tend to be concentrated in urban areas, especially in major cities such as the nation's capital. More doctors and nurses work in urban areas than in rural areas, although the majority of the population resides in rural areas, where there is persistent shortage of health personnel. The motives for health workers' remaining in cities are plenty. In addition to higher income, nonfinancial draws include more training and career opportunities, higher quality of life, and better housing, infrastructure, and schools.

In sum, poverty is more rampant in rural areas. For example, 19 percent of the urban population in Angola was below the national poverty line in 2014 compared with 58 percent of its rural population. There was a similar urban-rural gap of 14 versus 26 percent in India (Population Reference Bureau 2015). Since the majority of the population of most developing countries lives in rural areas, where poverty is pervasive, living in poverty is the norm in the developing world. Out of 1 billion people in Africa, only 20 million met the middle-class criteria, which is a mere 2 percent of the continent's population (McGroarty and Parkinson 2016).

Capital Constraints to Modern Development

In addition to the less than optimal factors above that impact development, human or social constraints can also impede modern development. There are three types of capital under consideration: **physical capital**, **human capital**, and **social capital.** Much of the underdevelopment or poverty prevalent in developing countries can be attributed to shortcomings in each of these three types of capital.

Physical Capital Constraints

Physical capital refers to infrastructure, machinery, and equipment that are needed for production. At the very least, mobilizing physical capital combined with natural resources and wage labor constructs the foundation for modern development. We basically adopt the infrastructure designation and broadly define **physical capital** as all tangible hardware that is needed for modern economic development. In the view of the modernization theory, lack of physical capital is one of the bottlenecks that constrain modern development.

A case in point is that Africa's poor trade performance can be partially accounted for by poor infrastructure (Limão and Venables 1999). For example, a limited number of railways were built during the colonial era. These railways reflect the colonial objective of connecting natural resources such as mines to seaports for export to the colonizing power. Large areas that did not contribute to colonial enrichment were completely neglected and bypassed (Rodney 1972). At present, many rural households do not have access to clean drinking water, electricity, modern transportation, or communication services. In Sub-Saharan Africa, less than half the population has access to safe drinking water. Many women have to walk long distances in the predawn hours to fetch water, which may be neither safe nor adequate for their needs. In 2015, more than 600 million people worldwide used unsafe drinking water sources, such as unprotected wells, springs, and surface water, mainly in Sub-Saharan Africa and South Asia (United Nations 2015).

Over two-thirds of Africa's population lacks necessary sanitation services (Torero and Chowdhury 2005). Likewise,

> around 1.7 billion people in Asia and the Pacific have no access to modern sanitation. ... About 780 million people in the region still practice open defecation and 80% of wastewater is discharged with little or no treatment, resulting in pollution causing adult illness, long-term malnutrition, and exposure to diarrheal diseases, the second leading cause of infant and child deaths worldwide. (Asian Development Bank 2014)

Illnesses caused by water that has beem contaminated by human waste cost India more than US$50 billion a year. In India, having a toilet may carry political symbols. It may be regarded as setting a good example for others and even a necessary condition for running for public office. The northern state of Haryana passed a law requiring candidates for public office to have a toilet, on top of having no pending criminal charges and no unpaid electricity bills. It is estimated that "if all of India's 29 states adopted similar laws, more than 600 million people would be barred from holding office" (*Bloomberg Businessweek* 2015).

In parts of rural Sub-Saharan Africa, local roads can become impassable during the rainy season. Walking is the principal means of transportation for about 90 percent of rural residents in Burkina Faso, Uganda, and Zambia. Modern transportation remains elusive and hinders development in many parts of Africa. For example, it adds an extra cost of 30 to 80 percent in freight and insurance for imports to the Central African Republic and Chad and an extra 180 percent for coffee export to Europe from these two countries (Fishbein 2001; Torero and Chowdhury 2005). Unreliable and inadequate electricity supply is common. Only about 5 percent of Africa's rural residents have access to electricity. Over 95 percent of rural Africans depend on wood or cow dung for cooking, heat, and light. Refrigerated medicines cannot be stocked in clinics because of the lack of electricity. As put by Warrick (2015), "When it comes to electric power, Africa is still a continent in the dark. More than half of its 1.1 billion inhabitants lack access to electricity, and Africa's total generating capacity, from Cairo to Cape Town, is only 160 gigawatts, or about half as much as Japan, a country with one-tenth of its population."

Power shortages are certainly not only limited to Africa. Blackouts, for example, are common in India. When three of the country's five electricity grids failed in July 2012, more than 700 million people were affected across 20 of India's 29 states, including the nation's capital, New Delhi. As Pidd (2012) describes it:

> As engineers struggled for hours to fix the problem, hundreds of trains failed, leaving passengers stranded along thousands of miles of track from Kashmir in the north to Nagaland on the eastern border with Burma. Traffic lights went out, causing jams in New Delhi, Kolkata and other cities. Surgical operations were cancelled across the country, with nurses at one hospital just outside Delhi having to operate life-saving equipment manually when back-up generators failed. Elsewhere, electric crematoriums stopped operating, some with bodies left half burnt before wood was brought in to stoke the furnaces.

What is further overlooked is that many households do not have access to electricity at all. According to India's 2011 census,

> one-third of India's households do not even have electricity to power a light bulb. ... A large minority of those in the blackout zone have never been connected to any grid—just 16.4% of the 100 million people who live in the central-eastern state of Bihar have access to electricity. (Pidd)

As India's economy gains momentum, insufficient electricity supply becomes a barrier to its industrial growth and a problem to growing demand from its burgeoning middle class.

Human Capital Constraints

As discussed in chapter 2, two major components of human capital are health and knowledge. For a country to achieve **sustainable development**, it is critical to provide corresponding **human services** to nurture and maintain such capital: health care services and education. The following discussion is focused on the inadequate and constrained delivery of such services to impoverished populations.

Many developing countries fail to provide basic health services to their populations. Barriers to accessing health services tend to be on the supply side, such as low stocks and quantities of vital medicines, broken equipment, shortage and absenteeism of medical personnel, and inconvenient location. The recent Ebola crisis in Guinea, Liberia, and Sierra Leone showed the vulnerability of these countries' health services and their lack of capacity for a rapid and comprehensive response to public health outbreaks. The cost for building a 70-bed facility in Liberia is estimated to be US$170,000. The facility needs US$1 million monthly to keep it running. Operating costs include staff salaries, medical equipment and supplies, medications, medical clothing, waste management, and body disposal. A national health care service system consisting of a total of 100,000 beds would cost US$1–2 billion a month. That is much more than what a poor country can afford (*The Economist* 2014).

Because of limited tax revenue, health care financing is inadequate at the governmental level. This leads to a situation where most health care costs, as high as 80 percent, must be borne by individuals out of their own pockets. As a result, health care expenses can be catastrophic for poor families, and these health-related expenses have been identified as the most common cause of falling into poverty (Carr 2004). In this regard, providing primary health care is an effective strategy for lifting the health status of the general population. Its aim is to make basic health services available to the broad population, especially the poor and those living in rural areas. One common problem found in developing countries is that the lion's share of resources is directed toward advanced medical technologies and services in a few major hospitals located in the cities, while health facilities that provide services to a larger poor and rural population are understaffed and underfunded (Carr 2004).

The scarcity of facilities and qualified staff is just one part of the story. The lack of means of transportation to these facilities is another. In Ghana, for example, poor roads were cited as one of the main reasons for large rural populations' having limited access to health services. In a focus group study, one participant described the transportation situation in his area. As quoted in Atuoye et al. (2015), put it:

> From here to the compound, an individual can only go through a footpath. A car cannot use the road. There is also a big valley on the way and it is not passable during the raining season, from June to October. Those on foot and bicycle swim through but those on motorbike cannot pass. (333)

Likewise, free maternal health care has benefited women, but its impact is diminished by the absence of transportation. As a 46-year-old woman complained,

> These days, it is a joy to deliver in a hospital. You don't pay anything ..., it's absolutely free. This has motivated many of us to visit the hospital for delivery. But the problem is that there is no transport ... Here, the roads are so bad. You wonder whether government cares about us. Some of us are forced to deliver at home and that brings complications. (Atuoye et al., 333)

In the above quote, the mentioning of the role of government makes an important point: the provision of public health care not only directly benefits citizens by eliminating health hazards and improving their health but also reflects a social mentality, that is, the responsibility to care for each other's welfare. Such a mindset is a key ingredient for modernization (McClelland 1966).

As in health care services, the current challenges of education faced by developing countries are drawing a distinction between modernization *of* education and modernization *by* education. These two distinctions can be visualized as in Figure 5.3, below, forming a circle that links education and modernization in different ways; the former, A, weighs more on the route from modernization to education, and the latter, B, from education to modernization.

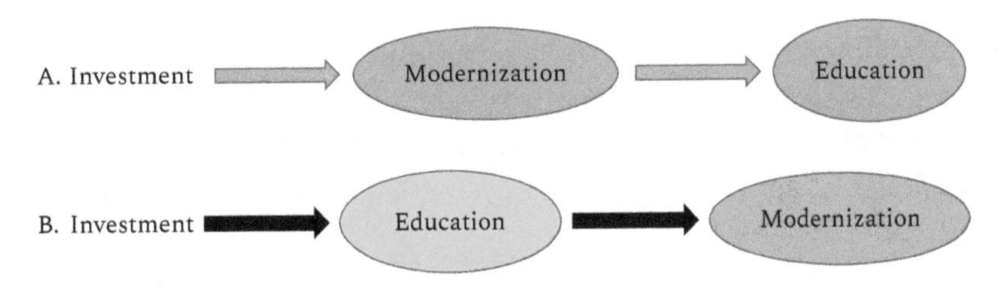

FIGURE 5.3 The Relationship Between Modernization and Education

For developing countries, a breakthrough is achieved when the latter route, B, is established, that is, when investment in education has born its fruit. As discussed earlier in chapter 2, when it comes to education, it is not just how many schools are built or how many students are enrolled that matters. The quality and content of education are equally important. Some warn that school learning is just part of the total education that is needed for modernization, which is built on more general skills, habits, and work ethics, such as technical know-how, business experience, and administrative skills, which may take generations to develop.

Africa's chronic food insecurity, to a certain degree, can be attributed to constraints in knowledge and access to more intensive farming techniques. Many farmers do not have access to more advanced technologies and new production practices, such as crop diversification, crop-management techniques, and fertilizer use (costs, how much to use, and where and how to apply it). These factors greatly limit farmers' ability to improve food production (Rosegrant et al. 2005).

Social Capital Constraints

While human capital concerns the status of health and education, whether developmental potential can bear fruit depends on whether there is a fertile social environment that nurtures it and makes it happen. The social environment in which individuals are situated points to another kind of capital—**social capital**. Social capital refers to "connections among individuals—social networks and the norms of reciprocity and trustworthiness that arise from them" (Putnam 2001, 19). Here we adopt a broader definition given by economist Michael Pettis (2014), where

> **social capital** is the set of institutions—including the legal framework, the financial system, the nature of corporate governance, political practices and traditions,

> educational and health levels, the structure of taxes, etc.—that determine the way individuals are given incentives to create value with the tools and infrastructure that they have. (emphasis added)

In other words, social capital is the environment and opportunities a society or state can offer to its citizens to grow, to reach their full potential as human beings. For example, the United States is said to be the "land of opportunities." People believe they have a fair shot to realize their potential as long as they put in the effort. Personal safety, the possibility of getting a business license, and fairness in competition and law enforcement are part and parcel of the everyday. In the United States, the social contract (the implicit agreement between a nation-state and its citizens concerning entitlements, authority, and guarantees) is taken for granted. The social contract in developing societies may be weak or not present. One of the most basic guarantees of the social contract is peace and stability.

The underlying causes of conflict and the absence of peace and stability are complex. One can trace the lack of peace and civil unrest back to the historical context of these societies. Colonialism and the postwar struggles for independence (see chapters 3 and 4) provide a wealth of explanatory content. In traditional societies, individuals' loyalty is rather restricted, usually to their family, extended kin, or a relatively small regional or ethnic group. There is physical and cultural distance among different tribes or villages. People are bound by common languages or dialects, customs, or religion. With a lack of national integration, diverse small societies are not drawn into one cohesive large national group. The map of Africa, for example, reflects colonial organization and not these traditional affinities and relationships. As a result, we find social coexistence comprised of "mosaic societies, made up of countless pieces, each neatly defined and separated from all the others. In many countries, indeed, men are set apart from each other by more than what binds them together" (Wriggins 1966). Many developing countries are composed of multiple racial or ethnic groups, which may have a long history of conflict and civil strife. After disparate groups are brought together as a country, old resentments persist. That is why, even nowadays from time to time, we witness repeated incidents of conflict, civil wars, and in extreme cases, genocide.

In large measure, the eruption of civil conflict can be related to underdevelopment. Underlying factors such as extreme social inequality, land scarcity and ownership, declines in market prices for major export commodities, (the lack of) job opportunities, and population pressure can contribute to often-violent clashes throughout the world. Statistically, low income countries are prone to civil conflicts. For a country at the middle of the national income spectrum, like Iran, the risk of experiencing civil conflict within five years is 7 to 11 percent. For a country at the bottom of the income distribution scale, such as Ghana or Uganda, the risk of insurgency is 15 to 18 percent (Graff and Winthrop 2010).

In the last 15 years of the twentieth century, Africa was plagued by at least 13 wars in Burundi, Congo, Ethiopia, Mozambique, Rwanda, Sierra Leone, and Sudan, among other countries. As a report shows,

> The economic costs of Africa's senseless wars and conflicts are incalculable. First and foremost is the wanton destruction they wreak. Infrastructure is reduced to rubble. Roads, bridges, communication equipment are bombed by combatants, houses and buildings destroyed. Second, the conflicts uproot people, forcing them to flee the general atmosphere of insecurity and war. Most of the refugees are women and children but women constitute about 80 percent of Africa's peasant farmers. Refugees fleeing conflict do not produce food crops. Thus, conflicts have a direct impact on Africa's agricultural production and partly explain why Africa, with all its rich natural endowments, cannot feed itself and imports 30 percent of its food needs. Third, conflicts create an "environment" inimical to development and deter investment. According to Algerian President Abdelaziz Bouteflika, Algeria's civil war that started in 1991 has killed 100,000 and caused $20 billion in economic losses. (Ayittey 1999, 1)

Later in this chapter, we briefly examine the "Great African War" of 1995–2005 that was centered in Eastern Congo and eventually involved 11 countries.

Corruption

Corruption, the seeking of private gain at public expense through illegal means, greatly impedes social development. Corruption erodes public trust in government agencies, hinders normal economic activities, and adds risk to investment and doing business. Although no society is immune from corruption, there are substantial differences in its level or extent among societies. Research shows that poorer countries suffer more from corruption. The incidence of corruption declines as national average income increases. This may be due to the fact that higher income reduces the motives to engage in corruption and the value gained from it while at the same time increasing the opportunity cost of potential penalties (Lipset and Lenz 2000).

The World Bank compiled data from a range of sources and created the Worldwide Governance Indicators, including that of corruption, for more than 200 countries and territories (Kaufmann, Kraay, and Mastruzzi 2009). Six measures of governance were quantified: (1) **Voice and Accountability**—"the extent to which a country's citizens are able to participate in selecting their government, as well as freedom of expression, freedom of association, and a free media"; (2) **Political Stability and Absence of Violence**—"the likelihood that the government will be destabilized or overthrown by unconstitutional or violent means, including politically-motivated violence and terrorism"; (3) **Government Effectiveness**—"the quality of public services, the quality of the civil service and the degree of its independence from political pressures, the quality of policy formulation and implementation, and the credibility of the government's commitment to such policies"; (4) **Regulatory Quality**—"the ability of the government to formulate and implement sound policies and regulations that permit and promote private sector development"; (5) **Rule of Law**—"the extent to which agents have confidence in and abide by the rules of society, and in particular the quality of contract enforcement, property rights, the police, and the courts, as well as the likelihood of crime and violence"; and (6) **Control of Corruption**—"the extent to which public power is exercised for private gain, including both petty and grand forms of corruption, as well as 'capture' of the state by elites and private interests" (6). Table 5.3 below summarizes the results:

TABLE 5.3 ***Countries with the Highest and Lowest Levels of Corruption and Government Effectiveness, 2014***

HIGHEST LEVEL OF CORRUPTION	LOWEST LEVEL OF GOVERNMENT EFFECTIVENESS
Equatorial Guinea	Somalia
Somalia	South Sudan
South Sudan	Haiti
Libya	Central African Republic
Yemen	Comoros
Syria	North Korea
Guinea Bissau	Libya
Angola	Eritrea
Sudan	Sudan
Zimbabwe	Democratic Republic of the Congo
Netherlands	Sweden
Liechtenstein	Denmark
Luxembourg	Norway
Singapore	Japan
Sweden	Netherlands
Finland	Hong Kong
Switzerland	New Zealand
Norway	Finland
Denmark	Switzerland
New Zealand	Singapore
LOWEST LEVEL OF CORRUPTION	HIGHEST LEVEL OF GOVERNMENT EFFECTIVENESS

Data source: World Bank.

Table 5.3 lists the top ten and bottom ten countries in both level of corruption and government effectiveness in 2014. All ten countries with the highest level of corruption are Global South countries: eight of them are in Africa and two are in the Middle East. Meanwhile, all the ten countries with the lowest level of corruption are in the Global North: eight of them are in Europe and two are in the Asia-Pacific region. The spectrum of government effectiveness is just the reverse: the poor developing countries score the lowest and wealthy developed countries score the highest. And there is some overlap between these two dimensions. Four out of the ten countries with the highest level of corruption are led by the least effective governments. Eight developed countries have both the least corruption and the most effective governments.

Corruption in Angola

The former Portuguese colony of Angola, located in Sub-Saharan Africa, offers an interesting case of corruption that is common to many recently established nation-states. With a population of 26 million and a per capita income of US$6,881 per annum, Angola has one of the highest income levels in all of Sub-Saharan Africa. Significant oil reserves and the end of a 27-year civil war preceded by a 13-year war against its former colonial ruler, Portugal, primed Angola to embark on the modernization project (Onishi 2017). Angola adopted a development model of "oil for infrastructure" and was able to parlay favorable export oil prices into Chinese loans. Outsourcing to Chinese construction contractors allowed Angola to modernize, with roads, railways, and "social housing" in the form of satellite towns on the outskirts of Luanda, the country's capital. The results from this modernization effort brought the rise of new skyscrapers, communications, and transport links that extended into Angola's interior. However, with the drop in global oil prices and corruption on the part of President Jose Eduardo dos Santos, the quality and maintenance of this infrastructure was poor. In order to obtain decent housing, an applicant must be connected to the ruling clique. The president's very own daughter has become Africa's first billionaire. On this account, monies (up to 35 percent of construction funds alone) are unaccounted for, leading to the conclusion that a state of **crony capitalism** exists in Angola, with the president's inner circle benefiting greatly from corruption. In one startling example, Odebrecht, a Brazilian construction company, has been charged with paying over US$50 million in bribes to Angolan officials. Odebrecht has been charged in US federal court with paying over US$800 million in bribes worldwide and agreed to pay US$4.5 billion to settle these cases (Onishi 2017). At present, Angola ranks 164th out of 176 countries in terms of corruption. As put by a former Angolan prime minister, "I'm no saint ... but I can't accept the vulgarization of corruption," thus revealing how common and widespread the practice is (Onishi 2017).

Corruption is not unique to developing countries. For example, British heritage has been identified with low levels of national corruption in British colonies because of its emphasis on following the rules rather than taking orders from authority (Lipset and Lenz 2000), but corruption during parliamentary elections was commonplace in nineteenth-century Britain. Three types of corruption were evident: **bribery** (a direct payment in cash or kind to the voter), **treating** (provision of free food and drink to voters), and **quid pro quo** arrangements (offering voters nominal jobs for their votes). Even though they were banned by law, these corrupt practices were still prevalent:

> The readiness with which candidates engaged in these practices is reflected (albeit imperfectly) by the fact that between 1832 and 1885 over 15 percent of election contests resulted in a petition (i.e., a legal action disputing the conduct of the election), the figure rising as high as 30 percent after the 1852 election. Only with the passage of the 1883 Corrupt and Illegal Practices Act did election petitions and corruption tail off. (Kam 2007, 2).

Corruption in Australia, one of 38 countries that signed the Convention on Combating Bribery, was brought to light when American and Canadian farmers accused the Australian Wheat Board of violating UN sanctions on Saddam Hussein's regime and paying millions of dollars to Iraqi officials as kickbacks and bribes for lucrative wheat sales to Iraq (*Whitton* 2007).

In broader terms, Robbins (2011) calls further attention to the inherent conflict and violence embedded in the functional nation-state apparatus. While order is maintained and a sense of collective national identity is embedded into the citizenry, the nation-state is more than capable of applying force to smash dissent and threats to the machinery of capitalist accumulation. The next section depicts the extreme potential result of this: genocide. A contrast between Rwanda (1994) and Cambodia (1977–1981) is intended to augment the above discussion on underdevelopment to further expose the underlying preconditions that give rise to genocide.

STATE-SANCTIONED VIOLENCE: GENOCIDE IN RWANDA AND CAMBODIA

It has been estimated that since 1917 over 200 million people have been murdered at the hands of their own nation-state (Robbins 2011). Expanding upon this point, Nagengast (1994) and Robbins (2011) state that "the modern nation-state is essentially an agent of genocide and ethnocide (the suppression and destruction of minority cultures)" (Robbins 106). Robbins explains,

> Given the glorification of the nation-state as a vehicle of modernization, unity and economic development, this statement [i.e., the above statement that the nation-state is essentially an agent of genocide and ethnocide] seems a harsh accusation. Yet there exists ample evidence that one of the ways states have sought to create

> nations is to eliminate or terrorize into submission those who refuse to assimilate or who demand recognition of their status as a distinct ethnic or national group. (106)

Two tragic examples from Rwanda and Cambodia strongly support this claim. Both Rwanda and Cambodia exhibit many differences in terms of ethnicity, ecology, occupation, and social organization. Cambodia is in South-East Asia, while Rwanda is located in central Africa. At the time of independence and up to the genocides, both Rwanda and Cambodia were largely poor agrarian countries. Their physical environments, however, are different. Rwanda is hilly and, in the northern part of the country, mountainous. In contrast, Cambodia is flatter, and the Mekong River dominates the central part of the country, with some mountains in the West and North along the Thai border.

Rwanda's ethnicities consist of the Hutu, Tutsi, and the Indigenous Twa. The dominant religion is Catholicism. At the time of the genocide, the Hutu comprised the majority of the population, with about 85 percent. The Tutsi were a distinct minority, estimated at 14 percent of the population. In contrast, Buddhist Cambodia is ethnically more diverse, consisting of Khmer, Vietnamese, Muslin Chan, and Chinese, along with a number of Indigenous groups in the northeast and along the Cambodia-Vietnam border. The rural population subsisted on rice-growing in Cambodia, and in Rwanda, rural occupations aggregated along ethnic lines. In Rwanda, the Tutsi were predominantly cattle herders, while the Hutu were farmers who grew beans and coffee as cash crops and also raised goats, which are a major source of meat, often reserved for special occasions. Both countries are former monarchies and colonies. Cambodia's monarchy-civil government was led by Prince Norodom Sihanouk, who played an intriguing political role up until the time of the Khmer Revolution. Rwanda's Tutsi monarchy was deposed earlier (Kiernan 2007). Cambodia was under harsh French colonial rule centered mostly in Phnom Penh. Rwanda was under the Germans and then the Belgians after the First World War. Both colonies experienced social and political changes with long-lasting effects. The social organization Cambodia and Rwanda draws comparisons as they both had only recently become independent nation-states, in 1953 and 1962, respectively. Both Rwanda and Cambodia were attempting to modernize and were caught between the transition from precapitalist forms of social organization and modern capitalism. Neither country emerged with a viable state apparatus. Instead, genocides of horrific proportions emerged, with lasting effects still evident.

Ben Kiernan is a historian who established the Genocide Studies Center at Yale University. Kiernan's major treatise, *Blood and Soil: A World History of Genocide and Extermination from Sparta to Dafur* (2007), contains a chapter that brings both Rwanda and Cambodia together for a comparative analysis (539–69), in which Kiernan unearths the critical preconditions that gave rise to the genocides. Building from Kiernan's work, we can assert that genocidal events do not simply emerge out of thin air but result from a number of underlying social forces. Genocide is processional and is planned in advance (see Melvern 2004; Waller 2007). These forces are embedded in long-standing historical and economic factors. Geopolitical events also profoundly contribute to these preconditions.

There are **five preconditions** that allow us to compare Rwanda and Cambodia and explain why these events occurred. As will be shown below, these social forces led the perpetrators of genocide to plan and put it into practice. The first precondition in both Rwanda and Cambodia refers to what Kiernan (2007) calls the **cult of antiquity** a return to an idealistic ancient past. In both Rwanda and Cambodia, cults of antiquity persisted, whether real or imagined. Ancient kingdoms were reified in a highly idealized manner to represent the core essence of Khmer or Hutu identity and civilization (Kiernan, pp. 539–569). Pol Pot, the head of the Khmer Rouge, fantasized about Cambodia's past and blamed "polluting" elements and "enemies" associated with ethnic differences and Western culture for its decline. Rwandan Hutu strongman President Juvenal Habyarimana kept a historian, Ferdinand Nahimana, as one of his closest advisors. Nahimana received a doctorate in history from the University of Paris. His later work evolved into an elaborate reconstruction of the Hutu Kingdoms in central Africa. He was eventually convicted and imprisoned for crimes against humanity by the International Criminal Tribunal for Rwanda. These cults of antiquity, plus the revisiting and imagining of the past, played a foundational role in the genocides by identifying a pure civilization free from ethnic and cultural contaminants.

Agrarian ideals fleshed out the ideal type of person envisioned for the purified postgenocidal regime. The celebration and glorification of the traditional peasant in both Cambodia and Rwanda complemented the cult of antiquity. Fera of corrupting Western influences, along with mistrust of the urban inhabitants and environs, created an almost xenophobic hatred of anything outside of "pure agrarian types." Pol Pot's regime forcibly evacuated all the residents of Phnom Penh and other urban centers and subsequently assigned them to hard work as agricultural slave laborers. As Ung (2000) describes in her memoir, former city residents were classified as "new people" and were supervised by "base people"—traditional peasants who counted as the role models of this revolutionary nation-state. The everyday language of the perpetrators of these two genocidal regimes were couched in agrarian terms; "rooting out the weeds," "destroying the microbes," and "destroying the cockroaches" were all code for genocidal extermination of the undesirable "other" in both Rwanda and Cambodia.

Racial and ethnic hatred is the third precondition. Rwanda's colonial overseer, Belgium, issued "ethnic identity cards," which became a powerful way to cement and enforce divisions between the Hutu and Tutsi (Robbins 2011). Melvern (2004) shows that during the genocide, one's ethnic identity card became a matter of life or death. Economic competition between the Hutu (small farmers) and Tutsi (cattle herders) was further politically manipulated by Belgian colonialists, who in 1959 favored the Hutu majority, leading to the creation of a Tutsi diaspora, most notably in neighboring Uganda. The Tutsi later retaliated across these ethnic lines during the civil war that began in 1990 and was led by the Uganda-based, Tutsi-dominated Rwandan Patriotic Front (RPF). In Rwanda, a Tutsi could easily be stopped by a Hutu soldier and asked to produce their ethnic identity card. When the Tutsi produced the document, the Hutu soldier could easily harass the holder based on ethnic identity alone. In Cambodia, historical fears of being colonized by Vietnam gave rise to the Khmer Rouge state apparatus that purged even party members who were (falsely) accused of being "enemies" such as CIA, KGB, or Vietnamese spies and traitors. The notorious S-21 prison and associated "killing fields" outside of Phnom Penh were brutal institutions that Khmer Rouge leaders used to purify the party and eliminate "enemies" (Cruvellier 2014).

Irredentism refers to the desire to annex territory belonging to another ethnic group or nation-state. This claim on territory can be either real, a place where the annexing force once resided, or it can be imagined, cloaked in myth. In Rwanda, the Hutu Power groups desired the farmland occupied by Tutsi cattle herders and moderate Hutu farmers. A number of the leading perpetrators of the Rwandan genocide, militia members, and Hutu peasants seized land and cattle after the Tutsi owners fled or were executed. Pol Pot's Democratic Kampuchea sought territory where ethnic Khmer lived in Thailand along the southern part of Surin, Buriram, and Sri-Saket Provinces. Khmer-style Buddhist temples still dot the landscape. Likewise, the "Parrots Beak" section of Cambodia that juts into southern Vietnam and is occupied by ethnic Khmer and other affiliated groups was desired by the Khmer Rouge in the irredentist sense. The key point is that genocide also involves claims to land not occupied by the perpetrators. In the Rwandan case, a complicated series of contingent factors that led to the Great African War of 1996–2006 developed out of the RPF invasion of Eastern Congo to eradicate refugee remnants of the former Hutu army, militias, and ethnic Hutus. Proceeding from one success to another on the battlefield, a Central African coalition led by Rwanda's RPF overthrew the Congo dictator, Mobutu, who had presided over a nonfunctioning, collapsed state. The RPF then took advantage of the region's mineral wealth to fuel economic growth at home and further military expenditures in the Democratic Republic of Congo up to the present (Reyntjens 2009).

Global geopolitical events provide an overarching context for understanding the impetus for genocide. In Rwanda, the small country's proximity to mineral-rich Congo involved the jockeying for position by the French, who supported the Hutu government prior to the genocide of 1994, and German and Belgian colonialists, who exerted great effort to exploit central Africa but were stymied for decades due to the hostile environment and difficulty of travel. Robbins (2011) proposes that the collapse of world coffee prices in 1989 sparked factors that propelled the other preconditions into motion. The Rwandan economy was under austerity measures imposed by the

International Monetary Fund (IMF) and the World Bank, and the country was barely functioning at the time of the genocide. For instance, Rwandan police had no fuel for their vehicles, and wealthier people had to hire guards to protect private residences. France was looking to reassert Francophone influence in central Africa and acted as a strong supporter of the Hutu-dominated extremist government and military up to the 1994 genocide and beyond (Gourevitch, 1998; Prunier 1997). French military advisors trained some of the Hutu youth militia, the *Interamwhe*, who did the majority of the "work" (a euphemism used by the Hutu genocidaires themselves for killing) (Hatzfeld, 2005). Finally, the end of the Cold War led to the US withdrawal of support for its former ally, staunch anticommunist dictator Mobutu, and the corresponding collapse of the Congolese state. With US backing, the RPF was given the go ahead to replace Mobuto and establish themselves as one of the more powerful military forces in central Africa.

Pol Pot's Khmer Rouge regime was a direct result of the Cold War as played out in the Vietnam War theater. President Richard Nixon's decision to bomb the Ho Chi Minh Trail in western Cambodia created resentment among Cambodian peasants and served as a recruiting tool for the fledging Khmer Rouge movement. US efforts to prevent the fall of yet another domino in South-East Asia led to the corrupt and incompetent Lon Nol regime. When Lon Nol overthrew Prince Norodom Sihanouk in 1970, the Prince allied with the Khmer Rouge and was a decisive force in building up their ranks. The Khmer Rouge were able to defeat Lon Nol and begin "Year Zero" in April of 1975, which entailed the total reorganization of the country. Combined with the other preconditions, one could argue that these events made genocide almost inevitable.

Over two million people fell victim to genocide under the Khmer Rouge, and another one million Tutsi and moderate Hutu were murdered by the Hutu-led army, Presidential Guard, police, and militias in Rwanda (Melvern 2004). Distant as these events are now from the scrutinizing eye of media, the ongoing social impacts of these two genocides continue to resonate in more recent events, such as the Congo Civil War (see Prunier 2009) and Cambodia's ongoing efforts to recover. Rwanda's "army with a state" maintains very strict control over the population. While discussion of one's ethnicity is now a crime, inequality is growing more severe, especially among young people in rural areas (Sommers 2012). The recent economic growth touted in glowing terms by international aid agencies and diplomatic circles masks political, social, and economic hegemony by an urban Tutsi elite, notably returnees from Uganda (Longman 2017). Using the "genocide credit," the RPF runs an autocratic society both within the country and abroad in the eastern Congo region. The international community, who failed during the 1994 genocide, remains silent at present on the Rwandan government's war crimes abroad and human rights violations domestically (Longman 2017).

The majority of ex-Khmer Rouge were never brought to trial and currently live among the general population. Only three leaders have been sentenced to life imprisonment by the UN-sponsored international tribunal court. In contrast, a number of Hutu leaders have been convicted of genocide. One of the most poignant lessons of these two atrocities was the contemporary failure to call the events of 1994 in Rwanda and 1975–1979 in Cambodia "genocide." As Father Frances Pouchard states in the documentary *Scream Bloody Murder* (Amanpour 2012), "States prioritize short-term political gains over human rights." The two genocides were never called such because doing so could have necessitated military intervention, in compliance with the 1948 Geneva Convention (Robbins 2011). Hence in the Western media, "ancient tribal hatreds" and "interethnic violence" were common ways to spin and manufacture consent about an area of the world that held little strategic interest for Western powers, including the United States. Father Pouchard's prescient statement also applies to Cambodia, where the United States supported the Khmer Rouge as the legitimate representative of the country. This was due to the animosity between the United States and Vietnam. During their ten year occupation of Cambodia (1979–1989) Vietnam installed a pro-Vietnam government, and Vietnamese advisors served throughout the ministries. The Khmer Rouge held out along the remote mountainous western and northern Thai border regions until the late 1990s.

VISUAL PORTRAYALS OF THE GENOCIDE

Coming to terms with and developing a better understanding of the Cambodian and Rwandan genocide can also be greatly enhanced by some of the excellent documentaries and films listed below.

Cambodia

"Pol Pot: Secret Killer" (Nixon 2000). provides a biographical account of the Khmer Rouge leader. Pol Pot's ideology is carefully portrayed, and the documentary provides an incisive and gripping depiction of how "Year Zero" came into existence. You can watch the documentary at the following web link: https://www.youtube.com/watch?v=Bk_ezm5gVnc.

Scream Bloody Murder (Amanpour 2012) provides a succinct overview of the rise of the Khmer Rouge. The French Catholic Priest interviewed, Father Frances Pouchard, is especially insightful. You can access the film at this link: https://www.youtube.com/watch?v=GIw7uI_gVyM.

Rwanda

An excellent overview of the Rwandan Genocide (Crisis Watch Network 2012), undertaken by highly reputed documentarians from the Crisis Watch Network, can be found at this link: https://www.youtube.com/watch?v=u3DrvrrSgHI&t=4s.

The award-winning film *Hotel Rwanda (George 2004)* accurately depicts Rwandan genocide in highly realistic terms. You can find a short clip that illustrates the use of agrarian metaphors, the language of genocide, here: https://www.youtube.com/watch?v=6RW6tLBxxqg.

Genocide and mass killings raise fundamental questions concerning human nature that are difficult to rationalize or resolve. At the crux of the matter is the fact that genocide, ethnic cleansing, and ethnocide are perpetrated at present, which clearly demonstrates the paradox of what humans are and what they do. This paradox is further brought to light by Genocide Watch, a group that monitors global genocide. You can access their website at http://www.genocidewatch.org/.

Perhaps the best statement on genocide comes from David Chandler (1999) in his book on the Khmer Rouge secret prison, S-21:

> Explanations for S-21 are embedded in our capacities to order and obey each other and to bond with each other against strangers, to lose ourselves in groups, to yearn for perfection and approval, and to vent our anger and confusion, especially when we are encouraged so by people we respect, onto other, often helpless people. To find the source of the evil that was enacted at S-21 on a daily basis, we need to look no further than ourselves. (155)

Chandler's statement above and Kiernan's five preconditions have been encompassed by the path-breaking work of James Waller in *Becoming Evil: How Ordinary People Commit Genocide and Mass Murder* (2007). Figure 5.4 below summarizes Waller's model.

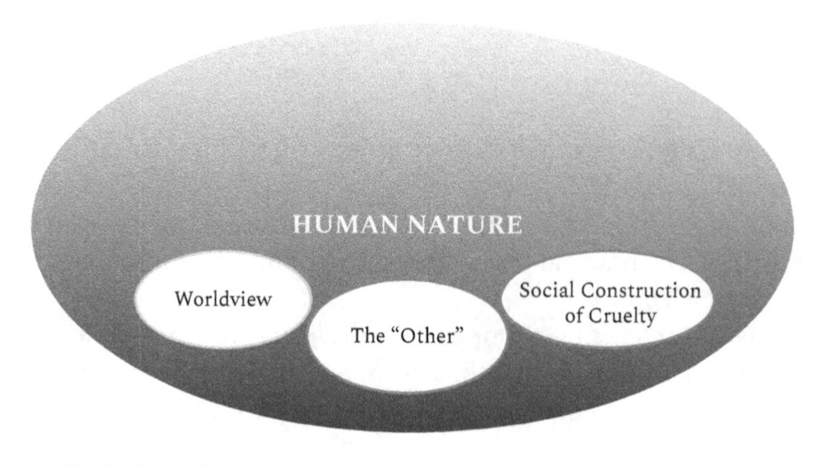

FIGURE 5.4 Waller's Model

Waller bases his theoretical model of "How Ordinary People Commit Genocide and Mass Murder" in human nature. The evolutionary psychology approach he advances argues that humans have adapted a number of primordial evolutionary traits to survive, procreate, cooperate, and compete, among others. We all embody these instincts or traits in everyday social interaction. The sum total of our human biological makeup contains metaphorically both a light and a dark side. We are, for instance, quite capable of violence, on the dark side, while we also exhibit altruistic behavior on the light side. Primordial human nature is the basis of our being, and these instincts or traits have ensured human survival for millions of years on the evolutionary continuum.

More proximate in the model above is our human nature-derived social life. Waller introduces three social arenas, exhibited in Figure 5.4 above: Worldview, the Other and the Social Construction of Cruelty. These arenas are proximate and are more or less evident in daily life. Our **worldview** consists of how we make sense of the world and our place in it. The dynamics of **otherness** evoke our outlook, attitudes, and relations between "us" and those people who we consider outside of our own personal organic ties to family, kin, community, and the nation-state, or "them". Lastly the **social construction of cruelty** is founded on "professional socialization, group identification, and binding factors of the group. In other words, an ordinary person *learns how to be cruel* and if not halted can be led to commit acts of "extraordinary evil," such as genocide and mass killing (Waller 2007).

Waller's evolutionary psychology-based model advances on the question of why "normal" people commit genocide and mass murder and amplifies the work of Kiernan (2007), Chandler (1999), and Hatzfeld (2005), among many others. Perpetrators of genocide and mass killings *are* ordinary people, like you and I, and research shows how mundane these individuals are, leading philosopher Hannah Arendt (1963) to coin the phrase "banality of evil." Combinations of the above sociohistorical forces, worldviews, the Other, and the social construction of cruelty precipitate and bring into social life opportunities, motives, and actions that result in "extraordinary evil" such as genocide and mass killings.

Given that the twentieth century was an era of genocide and mass killings, Waller's model greatly contributes to a better understanding of why ordinary people commit these acts of extraordinary evil. While most genocide scholars remain pessimistic that extraordinary evil will vanish from the human landscape during the twenty-first century, Waller (2007) does make note of some viable directions that could potentially lead to a halt of the monstrous proportions and scale of what has passed before us. First, various human rights and genocide watch groups bring troubled and remote areas to the attention of the world through early warning systems. In both Cambodia (1975–1979 and beyond) and Rwanda (1990 and beyond), there was very little world awareness until the genocides had already peaked. In both Cambodia and Rwanda, world attention subsided after the more spectacular and heart-wrenching stories and images passed. As Prunier (2009) notes, the Rwandan genocide was the catalyst for a continuing civil war in the neighboring Democratic Republic of Congo that remains unabated. Postgenocide Cambodia also fell from world attention after the Vietnamese occupation in 1979 (Brinkley, 2011). At present Cambodia shows signs of economic growth but this has come under an autocratic regime and widespread environmental degradation and human rights issues remain highly salient (Strangio 2014).

Genocide and mass killings overwhelm the human capacity for sane reasoning and international justice (Waller 2007). In the final analysis, the most promising mechanism remains the UN Security Council and International Courts. While the record of the UN is appalling in regard to stopping genocide, the permanent five security council members (the United States, France, Great Britain, China, and Russia) must be more consistent, committed, and unified and less obstructionist in addressing genocide and mass killings. This has clearly not been the case in the past or present, prohibiting closure from being reached on "how ordinary people commit genocide and mass murder."

CONCLUSION

In this chapter, we demonstrate that modernization is a complex process that involves multiple transformations in the economic, social, political, and cultural spheres. Hence, it requires systemic coordination and a comprehensive approach. As Smelser (1966) remarks,

> If too much speed is fostered in any one institutional sphere—for example, the economic—the society is likely to create an unbalanced pattern of growth, which is also a source of social unrest. It seems to me that the key problem in successful development is not to focus on a single criterion of growth, but rather to balance and measure development according to several different economic and social criteria. (121)

What the developed countries have accomplished certainly provides examples for developing countries to follow, but modernization cannot be achieved in developing countries simply by imitating the practices of the developed countries. Even though a number of factors that contribute to modernization have been identified by economists and other social scientists, be it physical capital, human capital, social capital, or the modern mindset, these factors cannot be simply copied as universal doctrines without fitting them into a country's unique history and cultural circumstances. There is by no means only one feasible path to development and modernization. What is best in the circumstances of one country may not be the best for another. The causes, consequences, and courses of modernization may vary widely from nation to nation. Inconsistencies and contradictories may not be exceptions but rather the norm in the real world. Therefore, for a particular country, where to draw the balance among various factors and how to utilize resources in the most efficient way may not be presented in any of the existing development guidebooks.

When it comes to explaining what caused the groundbreaking British industrial revolution, for example, the typical answers given are technological breakthroughs, such as the steam engine; laws that protected property rights; and migration of landless workers to the cities. Robert Allen, a professor of economic history at Oxford University, categorizes all these answers as on the supply side. He argues, however, that although these factors are certainly important, they are not sufficient for the great leap forward: "Property rights were arguably more secure in France; much of the science behind the steam engine took place in Italy and Germany; the Dutch were highly urbanized" (*The Economist* 2009). The overwhelming reason for the industrial revolution to occur in Britain in the eighteenth and early nineteenth centuries, he argues, is on the demand side—a particular combination of expensive labor and an inexpensive source of energy, coal, which is abundant in Britain. The high wages in the eighteenth century created high demand for consumer products, which made large-scale modern production profitable and sustainable. Meanwhile, cheap energy fuels the industrial engines moving forward: "Other countries were slow to follow suit not because they were stupid, sluggish or repressed, but because they did not have that particular combination" (*The Economist* 2009).

In another case, research has repeatedly shown the critical role of education in economic development. While the United States had become modernized by 1890 and launched the automobile revolution in the 1920s, less than 5 percent of its youth completed secondary schooling (Anderson 1966). The critical synergy between education and technology is crucial in this regard. In the nine decades between the 1870s and the 1960s, more than two-thirds of the growth in national income was attributed to technological innovation. Increase in capital and labor accounted for less than one-third (Wellisz 1966). However, for developing countries, pursuing the latest technology may not necessarily lead to the best economic outcome. What is abundant in most developing countries is labor. Automation brought by technology tends to produce either a small or no increase in employment, which is desperately needed in developing countries. Investment in new technology crowds out other low-cost opportunities that can create a larger number of jobs. And only a small number of local workers benefit from the exposure to modern technology. The introduction of a new technology without considering the conditions of the society in which it is applied is **transplantation**, not modernization. Transplantation, or blind copying, usually fails (Wellisz). Which approach works better is contingent upon a country's particular circumstances. As Weiner (1966) pointed out,

> societies differ so vastly that the priorities of one may not be those of another. In some societies, so few people may be motivated toward development that an elite may decide to emphasize education, communication, and other devices for restructuring motivations and attitudes on a large scale. In others, structural impediments may be so great that men with positive attitudes and motives are

> not given the opportunity to improve themselves or their society. In short, the skill of the governmental elite in grasping the nature of the problems in its own society and in skillfully choosing the most effective strategy for using its limited resources may be the paramount factor affecting development. (14)

The experiences of the world's recently established countries reflect these complexities. There is no one way to modernize, as each country is conditioned by its own environmental, historical, and social context. In some cases countries modernize, and in other cases these efforts go horribly awry, as we have demonstrated in this chapter with the cases of the Rwandan and Cambodian genocides.

REFERENCES

Amanpour, Christiane. *Scream Bloody Murder.* Aired November 8, 2012 on CNN. https://www.youtube.com/watch?v=GIw7uI_gVyM.

Anderson, C. Arnold. "The Modernization of Education." In *Modernization: The Dynamics of Growth*, edited by Myron Weiner, 68–80. New York: Basic Books, 1966.

Arendt, Hannah. *Eichmann in Jerusalem: A Report on the Banality of Evil.* New York: Viking Press, 1963.

Armer, J. Michael, and John Katsillis. "Modernization Theory." *Encyclopedia of Sociology*, vol. 3. 2001.

Asian Development Bank. "Water, Sanitation and Hygiene for a Healthy Asia and the Pacific." ABD's Take. February 7, 2014. http://www.adb.org/features/water-sanitation-and-hygiene-healthy-asia-and-pacific.

Atuoye, Kilian Nasung, Jenna Dixon, Andrea Rishworth, Sylvester Zakaria Galaa, Sheila A. Boamah, and Isaac Luginaah. "Can She Make It? Transportation Barriers to Accessing Maternal and Child Health Care Services in Rural Ghana." *BMC Health Services Research* 15, no. 333 (2015). DOI: 10.1186/s12913-015-1005-y.

Ayittey, George B.N. *Africa in Chaos: A Comparative History.* New York: St. Martins Press, 1999.

Beaubein, Jason "Nothing is Going Right in the World's Newest Nation." March 8, 2016. https://www.npr.org/templates/transcript/transcript.php?storyId=469502071

Black, Cyril E. "Change as a Condition of Modern Life." In *Modernization: The Dynamics of Growth*, edited by Myron Weiner, 17–27. New York: Basic Books, 1966.

Bloomberg Businessweek. 2015. "No Representation without Sanitation." November 18, 2015. https://www.bloomberg.com/news/articles/2015-11-18/no-representation-without-sanitation-india-s-toilet-politics

Brinkley, Joel. *Cambodia's Curse: The Modern History of a Troubled Land.* New York: Public Affairs, 2011.

Carr, Dara. "Improving the Health of the World's Poorest People." *Health Bulletin* 1 (2004): 1–34.

Chandler, David P. *Voices from S-21: Terror and History in Pol Pot's Secret Prison.* Chiang Mai, Thailand: Silkworm Books, 1999.

Crisis Watch Network. "Rwanda Genocide Documentary." CwnInternational, YouTube. March 13, 2012. https://www.youtube.com/watch?v=u3DrvrrSgHI&t=4s.

Cruvellier, Thierry. *The Master of Confessions: The Making of a Khmer Rouge Torturer.* New York: HarperCollins, 2014.

Eisenstadt, Shmuel N. *Modernization: Protest and Change.* Englewood Cliffs, NJ: Prentice Hall, 1966.

Fishbein, Robert. "Rural Infrastructure in Africa: Policy Directions." *Africa Region Working Paper Series*, Number 18. World Bank, 2001.

Genocide Watch. "Genocide Watch." The Alliance Against Genocide. http://GenocideWatch.com.

George, Terry. *Hotel Rwanda*. United Artists Lions Gate Films: MGM Distribution Co., 2004.

Giddens, Anthony. *Emile Durkheim: Selected Writings*. Cambridge, UK: Cambridge University Press, 1972.

Gourevitch, Philip. *We Wish to Inform You That Tomorrow We Will Be Killed With Our Families*. New York: Farrar, Straus and Giroux, 1998.

Graff, Corinne, and Winthrop, Rebecca. *Beyond Madrasas: Assessing the Links between Education and Militancy in Pakistan*. Washington, DC: Brookings Institution, 2010.

Hatzfeld, Jean. *Machete Season: The Killers in Rwanda Speak*. New York: Farrar, Straus and Giroux, 2005.

Inglehart, Ronald, and Wayne E. Baker. "Modernization, Cultural Change, and the Persistence of Traditional Values." *American Sociological Review* 65, no. 1 (February 2000): 19–51.

Inkeles, Alex. "The Modernization of Man." In *Modernization: The Dynamics of Growth*, edited by Myron Weiner, 138–50. New York: Basic Books, 1966.

Inkeles, Alex, and David H. Smith. *Becoming Modern: Individual Change in Six Developing Countries*. Cambridge, MA: Harvard University Press, 1974.

Kam, Christopher. "Four Lessons about Corruption from Victorian Britain." Paper presented at University of British Columbia, Vancouver, June 8–9, 2007.

Kaufmann, Daniel, Aart Kraay, and Massimo Mastruzzi. *Governance Matters VIII. Aggregate and Individual Governance Indicators, 1996–2008*. World Bank Policy Research Working Paper 4978. World Bank, 2009.

Kiernan, Ben. *Blood and Soil: A World History of Genocide and Extermination from Sparta to Darfur*. New Haven, CT: Yale University Press, 2007.

Landes, David. "Culture Makes Almost All the Difference." In *Culture Matters: How Values Shape Human Progress*, edited by Lawrence E. Harrison and Samuel P. Huntington, 2–13. New York: Basic Books, 2000.

Lerner, Daniel. *The Passing of Traditional Society: Modernizing the Middle East*. New York: Free Press, 1958.

Limão, Nuno, and Anthony J. Venables. "Infrastructure, Geographical Disadvantage, and Transport Costs." *World Bank Policy Research Working Paper* 2257. World Bank, 1999.

Lipset, Seymour M., and Gabriel S. Lenz. "Corruption, Culture, and Markets." In *Culture Matters: How Values Shape Human Progress*, edited by Lawrence E. Harrison and Samuel P. Huntington, 112–24. New York: Basic Books, 2000.

Longman, Timothy. *Memory and Justice in Post-Genocide Rwanda*. New York: Cambridge University Press, 2017.

Madariaga, Salvador de. *Democracy versus Liberty? The Faith of a Liberal Heretic*. London: Pall Mall Press, 1958.

McClelland, David C. "The Impulse to Modernization." In *Modernization: The Dynamics of Growth*, edited by Myron Weiner, 28–39. New York: Basic Books, 1966.

McGroarty, Patrick, and Joe Parkinson. "Mining Collapse Cripples Africa's Dreams of Prosperity." *Wall Street Journal*, March 4, 2016.

Melvern, Linda. *Conspiracy to Murder: The Rwandan Genocide*. London: Verso, 2004.

Morrison, John Alexander. *Alisar: A Unit of Land Occupance in the Kanak Su Basin of Central Anatolia*. Chicago: The University of Chicago Libraries, 1939.

Nagengast, Carole. "Violence, Terror, and the Crisis of the State." *Annual Review of Anthropology* 23 (1994): 109–36.

Nixon, Agnes. "Pol Pot: Secret Killer." *Biography*. January 20, 2000.

Onishi, Norimitsu. "Angola's Corruption Boom: Reconstruction Enriched the Politically Connected." *New York Times*. June 25, 2017 https://www.nytimes.com/2017/06/24/world/africa/angola-luanda-jose-eduardo-dos-santos.html.

Onishi, Norimitsu, and Jeffrey Moyo. "Trade on the Streets, and Off the Books, Keeps Zimbabwe Afloat." *New York Times*, March 4, 2017. https://www.nytimes.com/2017/03/04/world/africa/zimbabwe-economy-work-force.html.

Pettis, Michael. "The Four Stages of Chinese Growth." Carnegie Endowment for International Peace. June 18, 2014. http://carnegieendowment.org/chinafinancialmarkets/55947.

Pidd, Helen. 2012. "India Blackouts Leave 700 Million without Power." *The Guardian*. July 31, 2012. https://www.theguardian.com/world/2012/jul/31/india-blackout-electricity-power-cuts.

Population Reference Bureau. "The Urban-Rural Divide in Health and Development." Data Sheet. Washington, DC: Population Reference Bureau, 2015.

Potter, Robert B., Tony Binns, Jennifer A. Elliott, and David Smith. *Geographies of Development: An Introduction to Development Studies*. 3rd ed. New York: Routledge, 2013.

Prunier, Gérard. *The Rwanda Crisis: History of a Genocide*. New York: Columbia University Press, 1997.

———. From *Genocide to Continental War: The "Congolese" Conflict and the Crisis of Contemporary Africa*. London: Hurst and Company, 2009.

Putnam, Robert D. *Bowling Alone: The Collapse and Revival of American Community*. New York: Simon & Schuster, 2001.

Reyntjens, Filip. *The Great African War: Congo and Regional Geopolitics, 1996–2006*. New York: Cambridge University Press, 2009.

Rigg, Jonathan. *An Everyday Geography of the Global South*. New York: Routledge, 2007.

Robbins, Richard H. *Global Problems and the Culture of Capitalism*. 5th ed. Upper Saddle, NJ: Prentice Hall, 2011.

Rodney, Walter. *How Europe Underdeveloped Africa*. Washington, DC: Howard University Press, 1972.

Rosegrant, Mark W., Sarah A. Cline, Weibo Li, Timothy B. Sulser, and Rowena A. Valmonte-Santos. "Looking Ahead: Long-Term Prospects for Africa's Agricultural Development and Food Security." 2020 Discussion Paper No. 41. Washington, DC: International Food Policy Research Institute, 2005.

Rosenstein-Rodan, Paul N. "The Modernization of Industry." In *Modernization: The Dynamics of Growth*, edited by Myron Weiner, 270–80. New York: Basic Books, 1966.

Rostow, Walt Whitman. *The Stages of Economic Growth: A Non-Communist Manifesto*. Cambridge, UK: Cambridge University Press, 1960.

Sachs, Jeffrey D. "Stages of Economic Development." Speech at the Chinese Academy of Arts and Sciences, Beijing. June 19, 2004.

———. *The End of Poverty: Economic Possibilities for Our Time*. New York: Penguin Books, 2005.

Smelser, Neil J. "Modernization of Society and Culture." In *Modernization: The Dynamics of Growth*, edited by Myron Weiner, 110–21. New York: Basic Books, 1966.

Sommers, Marc. *Stuck: Rwandan Youth and the Struggle for Adulthood*. Athens, GA: University of Georgia Press, 2012.

Spengler, Joseph J. "Modernization of the Economy." In *Modernization: The Dynamics of Growth*, edited by Myron Weiner, 321–33. New York: Basic Books, 1966.

Staley, Eugene. "The Role of the State in Economic Development." In *Modernization: The Dynamics of Growth*, edited by Myron Weiner, 294–306. New York: Basic Books, 1966.

Strangio, Sebastian. *Hun Sens's Cambodia*. New Haven, CT: Yale University Press. 2014.

The Economist. "Much Worse to Come: The Ebola Crisis." October 16, 2014. https://www.economist.com/node/13688053.

Torero, Maximo, and Shyamal Chowdhury. *Increasing Access to Infrastructure for Africa's Rural Poor*. Washington, DC: International Food Policy Research Institute, 2005.

Ung, Loung. *First They Killed My Father: A Daughter of Cambodia Remembers*. New York: HarperCollins, 2000.

United Nations. *The Millennium Development Goals Report 2015*. New York: United Nations, 2015.

Waller, James. *Becoming Evil: How Ordinary People Commit Genocide and Mass Killing.* 2nd ed. New York: Oxford University Press, 2007.

Warrick, Joby. "This May Be the Biggest News Yet to Come out of the Paris Climate Meeting." *The Washington Post.* December 6, 2015. https://www.washingtonpost.com/news/energy-environment/wp/2015/12/04/this-may-be-the-biggest-news-yet-to-come-out-of-the-paris-climate-meeting/?utm_term=.0cb221755577

Weiner, Myron. "Introduction." In *Modernization: The Dynamics of Growth*, edited by Myron Weiner, 1–14. New York: Basic Books, 1966.

Wellisz, Stanislaw H. "Modernization of the Economy." In *Modernization: The Dynamics of Growth*, edited by Myron Weiner, 233–45. New York: Basic Books, 1966.

Whitton, Evan. 2007. "Kickback: Inside the Australian Wheat Board Scandal." *The Australian*, May 19.

Wood, Graeme. "What ISIS Really Wants." *The Atlantic.* March 2015. https://www.theatlantic.com/magazine/archive/2015/03/what-isis-really-wants/384980/.

World Bank. "Worldwide Governance Indicators." Data catalog. http://data.worldbank.org/data-catalog/worldwide-governance-indicators

Wriggins, Howard. "Modernization of Politics and Government." In *Modernization: The Dynamics of Growth*, edited by Myron Weiner, 181–91. New York: Basic Books, 1966.

Figure Credits

Fig. 5.1: Adapted from Ronald Inglehart and Wayne E. Baker, "Modernization, Cultural Change, and the Persistence of Traditional Values," American Sociological Review, vol. 65, no. 1, pp. 30. Copyright © 2000.

Fig. 5.2: Data Source: Inglehart and Baker, (2000).

CHAPTER SIX

Globalization

INTRODUCTION

In this chapter, we introduce the concept of globalization, its history, and how it became deeply entrenched in our everyday lives. We review what makes globalization possible—politically, technologically, and economically—shedding light on why globalization has become so powerful. We then discuss the far-reaching impacts globalization has had in both positive and negative terms. We feature reference to the impacts of globalization on a number of countries throughout the chapter. We then call attention to multipolar globalization, a new and recent restructuring of the global economic order. In the end, we discuss the implication of globalization on inequality.

WHAT IS GLOBALIZATION?

"Debating globalization is like debating whether autumn should follow summer," claimed former British Prime Minister Tony Blair. He further elaborated this point in a lecture on faith and globalization in 2008: "Old boundaries of culture, identity and even nationhood are falling. The 21st Century world is becoming ever more interdependent." He further describes "an era of globalization, of political interdependence, where the world is ever more swiftly opening up and the cliché about a global community becomes an economic, political and often social reality" (Blair 2008).

What is globalization? Unfortunately, there is no particular agreement among academics, politicians, and the business world about exactly how to define it. The following is a sample of definitions:

- "Globalization refers to the greater interconnectedness among the world's people" (Eitzen and Zinn 2009).
- An "unprecedented compression of time and space reflected in the tremendous intensification of social, political, economic, and cultural interconnectedness and interdependence on a global scale" (Steger 2002).
- "A transplanetary process or set of processes involving increasing liquidity and growing multidirectional flows of people, objects, places and information as well as the structures they encounter and create that are barriers to, or expedite, those flows" (Ritzer 2010).
- "The intensification of global interconnectedness, a process associated with the spread of capitalism as a production and market system" (Schech and Haggis 2000, 58).

Two major themes seem to stand out from the definitions above: the world is more intensely connected than ever before, and there are multiple flows of people, objects, and information that have had no earlier precedent. We define **globalization** as a set of recently intensified processes—economic, social, cultural, and others—by which the world is much more interconnected and interdependent.

Globalization is made manifest in a number of ways. The world is increasingly interconnected, which greatly broadens people's horizons, breaks geographical barriers, redraws the economic landscape, and refines social relations. Because of this, many local or national problems are now global problems. Examples include the 2008 recession, set off by subprime mortgages on Wall Street, climate change, pollution, drug and human trafficking, and terrorism. Globalization affects everyone; therefore, global problems require global solutions. To some, globalization embodies the ideals for mankind: freedom of choice, movement, and expression. Abandoning globalization

> to those violent forces hell-bent on keeping this world divided between the connected and disconnected is to admit that we no longer hold these truths to be self-evident: that all are created equal, and that all desire life, liberty, and a chance to pursue happiness. In short, we the people need to become we the planet. (Barnett 2004, 50)

Globalization has a long history; however, at present the concept displays an **intensification of interconnectedness** that is unprecedented. As this chapter demonstrates, the contemporary form of globalization has produced an array of differential impacts that cut across political, economic, and cultural boundaries. These impacts have fundamentally reoriented the organization of the world and how we relate to it.

GLOBALIZATION IN HISTORICAL CONTEXT

Globalization can be traced to the fifteenth century, marked by Portuguese caravels' sailing around the southern tip of Africa into the Indian Ocean in search of wealth from India and China. This event set in motion the Western "Age of Discovery and Conquest" (Prestowitz 2005). Others trace the origins of globalization to the European colonialization of Africa from 1870 to 1914 (Barnett 2004). In the distant past, there had been international trade across the globe, and the volume was quite high during some periods. Only a small number of countries, however, actively and freely participated in international trade. It is also accurate to state that some forms of global economic integration occurred after the Second World War. It was the end of the Cold War, however, that gave rise to contemporary globalization. During the Cold War, much of the world was largely divided around two superpowers: the capitalist West, led by the United States, and the communist/socialist East led by the Soviet Union; Third World countries largely remained detached from both camps. At this time, the world economy was far from being global. Three major events that occurred in the last two decades of the twentieth century paved the way for eventual formation of the global economy: (1) the economic reform of China; (2) the end of the Cold War in 1990; and (3) the transformation of India's economy.

In December 1978, under the new leadership of Deng Xiaoping, China announced economic reforms to participate in the world economy. Since then, China has gradually strayed from socialism and embraced the capitalist market economy. The idea that "getting rich is glorious" has taken root in Chinese minds. China quickly adopted an open-door trade policy to attract foreign investment and to lure foreign companies to set up plants in China. Along its east coast, a number of export-oriented **special economic zones** (**SEZs**) emerged that offered appealing benefits to outside investors, such as free land for factory sites, exemption from import duties, no income taxes for a certain number of years, and grants for labor training.

About a decade later, the fall of the Berlin Wall, in November 1989, ended decades of Cold War hostilities and heralded the collapse of the Soviet Union, which broke into 15 sovereign countries two years later. Virtually all of these countries, plus the Soviet Union's former satellite countries in Eastern Europe, have joined the capitalist world economy, some of which have become members of the European Union.

On the heels of these two dramatic events came a shift in India's economic policy. India had largely adhered to socialist policies since its independence in 1947, and its economy had been mostly insulated from the world up to the early 1990s. India's share of global trade had dropped from nearly 3 percent in 1938 under the British rule to 0.5 percent in 1980. The fall of the Soviet Union, which had been one of India's major trade partners, coupled with other economic woes, prompted India to seek economic policy change in the first decade of the twenty-first century. Prime Minister Manmohan Singh, who was in office between 2004 and 2014, and whose dissertation at Oxford was on free trade, pushed through remarkable measures, such as slashing tariffs, deregulating, and attracting foreign investment, that transformed India's economy and opened it up to the outside world. The joined forces of China, India, and the Eastern bloc brought "three billion new capitalists" into the world economy (Prestowitz 2005). Since then, history has turned a dramatic new page. Therefore, the era of contemporary globalization, in our view, starts with the confluence of the above three events: economic reform in China and India and the collapse of the Soviet Union.

HOW GLOBALIZED IS THE WORLD?

Globalization is defined as a multidimensional process, but it is undeniable that the intensification of **economic interconnectedness** is one of the most prominent aspects of the process. Many forces have pushed world economies to be interdependent, such as the removal of political barriers, improvement in transportation and communication, and the establishment of global supply chains. As world economies become more integrated, changes that occur in one country or region will inevitably create ripple effects across the world. No country seems to be insulated. For example, the 2008 financial crisis, fueled by subprime loans on Wall Street, stormed the entire global market, bringing the world economy to a halt and putting millions of workers out of jobs. Its impact can still be felt today in many parts of the world.

The impact on the global economy tends to originate from developed countries. The increased market integration and emerging economies of China and India, however, have brought more developing countries into the equation. The globalized world is changing, and an emerging restructuring of the world that we refer to as "multipolar globalization" is discussed later in this chapter. An International Monetary Fund (IMF) report issued in April 2016 found a growing connection between the developed and developing markets. While the performance of foreign markets contributed 50 percent to a particular nation's equity market in 1995, that figure has risen to 80 percent in 2015. When China's stock market dropped 7 percent on January 7, 2016, the panic spread to the United States, Japan, Australia, and South Korea. The Dow Jones Industrial Index slipped to its lowest level since August 2015. The *Wall Street Journal* commented, "twists and turns of the world's second largest economy [China] often appear to be more consequential on Wall Street than what is happening on America's Main Streets" (Mauldin 2016).

Another example of the global "ripple effect" occurred between 2011 and 2016, when 10,000 coal miners lost their jobs in West Virginia, down from a peak workforce of 22,000. Wyoming, another state with a large number of coal mining jobs, saw its unemployment rate rise to 4.7 percent in January 2016, up from 3.8 percent a year earlier. These particular cases underscore a larger picture of the entire coal industry struggling with high debt levels and low energy prices. Coal prices had fallen more than 60 percent between 2011 and 2016. The warm winter was partly to blame, but more importantly, the collapse of coal prices was in tandem with the world's slowing economy, including slowing steel production in China. Peabody Energy, the world's largest private coal company by volume, which operates 26 mines in the United States and Australia, was deeply in debt, by more than US$6 billion, in 2016 and was on the verge of bankruptcy (Miller 2016). About 15,000 British steel workers at the Port Talbot plant in South Wales were also at risk of losing their jobs in 2016 if new buyers could not be found for their products, since their major export market—China—was experiencing an economic slowdown (Mackintosh 2016).

People on the Move

In the era of contemporary globalization, more people are crossing national borders. In addition to a growing number of both legal and illegal immigrants, refugees, and temporary workers, the number of international tourists has grown at an extraordinary rate. Perhaps no example provides a better snapshot than tourism, one of the world's largest service industries. Only 50 million people travelled in 1950 (Potter et al. 2013). International tourist arrivals increased from 500 million in 1995 to 1.3 billion in 2015, and related direct income grew from US$500 billion to US$2.3 trillion during the same time period (Statista 2018). The profile of international tourism is changing as well, with high income countries accounting for 75 percent of the total tourist revenue. Middle and low income countries account for 25 percent of total tourist arrival and revenue. The revenue picture, however, is converging, as more tourists from middle and low income countries travel, or as countries promote economic development through tourism. Tourism is no longer limited between rich nations or from rich to poor. The growing middle class from developing countries has joined the ranks as well. Mainland Chinese tourists now represent 20–25 percent of all new arrivals to Thailand and Cambodia, surpassing those from the previously traditional North American and European points of departure. Bangkok, Thailand, leads the world in most international arrivals at 21 million international visitors, followed by London and Paris, with 20 and 18 million international arrivals, respectively (Millington 2016).

New variations in tourism are also being offered to increasingly affluent middle-class consumers from developed and developing countries (Pantelescu 2012). There is also a growing demand for specific types of niche tourism outside of the conventional business, packaged cruises, and leisure varieties. Eco-, gambling, sex, birth, culinary, bike, extreme, and medical tourism, along with many others, represent a sample of over 80 niche tourist markets. An extreme example is **thanatourism** or **dark tourism**, defined as visiting places associated with death, tragedy, or calamity (Hohenhaus, 2019). The 9/11 memorial in New York is an example of a dark tourism destination. In Cambodia, one of the world's poorest countries, thanatourism has become an integral part of the country's burgeoning tourist industry. In the capital city of Phnom Penh, approximately 250,000 tourists per annum visit the notorious Khmer Rouge prison, S-21 (Figure 6.1), and then take a short trip to Choeung Ek, the killing fields, located a few miles south of the prison.

FIGURE 6.1 The Former Khmer Rouge Prison, S-21, in Phnom Penh, Cambodia

In 1979, the Khmer Rouge regime was overthrown by a combined force of Vietnamese and former Khmer Rouge members who had defected. Pinched between the Thai border and the new Vietnamese-dominated government, the Khmer Rouge made the northern town of Anlong Veng their last stronghold. Until 1998, when the Cambodian military secured the area, the remnants of the Khmer Rouge held out and acted as a terrifying political and military force that hindered Cambodia's future prospects for peace and economic stability. With the collapse of the Khmer Rouge in 1998, Cambodia's autocratic government (led by a former Khmer Rouge, Hun Sen) has embraced globalization and embarked on an aggressive policy of patronage-oriented economic growth centered on reconstructing health and education services, agricultural development, light manufacturing, timber extraction, mining, and tourism.

The construction of an all-weather road from Siem Reap, home of the world-famous temple complex Angkor Wat, to Anlong Veng and the Thai border, has led some Cambodian officials to designate Anlong Veng as a tourist destination. Cambodian officials hope to capitalize on the nearby Dangrek Mountains and a number of former Khmer Rouge landmarks, including the grave of Pol Pot.

The Anlong Veng area already hosts a casino, restaurants, guest houses, and hotels to take advantage of the growing border trade with neighboring Thailand. Nhem En, a former Khmer Rouge photographer from S-21, has held numerous government positions in the province. He envisions the whole area as a tourist destination and has made plans to open a US$300,000 Khmer Rouge museum on the outskirts of the town (Cruvellier 2014). Along with other morbid tourist attractions, including various gravesites of Khmer Rouge leaders, such as Ta Mok and Son Sen, En entertains the idea of 1,000 tourists each month flowing into the province, capturing some of those who had visited Angkor Wat. As Cruvellier aptly summarizes, this display of thanatourism demonstrates that "today's Cambodia, for better or worse, is open for business" (177).

The increasing flow of people also poses a greater health risk to the world's population. The outbreak of Ebola in West Africa in 2014 sent waves across the world. The Ebola virus was first discovered in 1976. Over the past 40 years, there were already sporadic Ebola outbreaks across equatorial Africa. According to the United Nations (UN), Ebola infected about 2,400 people and took around 1,600 lives between 1976 and 2012 (United Nations 2015). These outbreaks did not make headlines around the world because they were confined to rural areas in some African countries. What gave the latest Ebola epidemic higher impact is that, in addition to being more severe and longer lasting, it quickly spread to urban centers in Guinea, Liberia, and Sierra Leone, where there is high population mobility, especially for international travel. A global epidemic was possible, and it is why Ebola was declared by the World Health Organization a public health emergency in late 2014. Dozens of deaths were later reported in a number of countries outside of Africa.

Not long after the outbreak of Ebola, world attention shifted to a new epidemic, the Zika virus, which may be linked to microcephaly, a birth defect in which babies are born with undersized brains and skulls. Since it was first confirmed in Brazil in May 2015, the Centers for Disease Control and Prevention has recorded more than 300 cases in the United States, and it has spread to more than 30 countries in Africa, Asia, and North and South America.

Increased Cultural Connectedness

What is more significant than the flow of people and tangible goods is the flow of information. A song, a picture, a video, or an event can go viral no matter where it occurs or is posted. Anything can be easily pushed in front of the world audience. Information, ideas, and emotions are shared instantly. More people may be able to tell who Nelson Mandela is than to name the mayor of their own city. You may not be able to point to South Korea on a map, but you can surely dance with "Gangnam Style." People outside the United States may have not heard of Cleveland, Ohio, but will acknowledge LeBron James. As we travel abroad, oftentimes we find the familiar in unfamiliar places: the Golden Arches, Levi jeans, hip-hop music, NBA games shown in bars, Starbucks at street corners, and people on their smart phones. In addition, the subjects that people talk about may sound familiar, too: refugees in Europe, oil prices, the latest Star Wars movie, and presidential politics in the United States. This is how closely connected we are. Though people may be thousands of miles apart, they can contact each other with just a click.

One possible outcome of such shared experiences may be the creation of a mixed global culture, in which unique cultures from different societies gradually fade and give way to a new, commonly shared culture, which is defined as **hybridization**. In this case, everything from everywhere is blended. National or local identity is lost in the process (Smith, Keri E. Iyall 2013). Some have concerns that globalization will eventually make the world more or less the same; others are worried that this homogenizing process is not random or balanced and that global culture is going to become more hybridized along the lines of Western culture. This is why some think that globalization is just a euphemism for **Americanization**—the spread of American products, business, images, and other tangible/intangible elements around the world—simply because the United States is so dominant on the world stage. There is plenty of evidence to point to this: iPhone, Facebook, Nike, NBA, NFL, and American music, shows, and movies. Even the French impose tariffs and quotas on movies and TV shows imported from America in fear of "cultural imperialism" (Steger 2009). In political scientist Benjamin R. Barber's (1995) terms, it is creating a "McWorld"—a homogeneous world economically and culturally dominated by America, symbolized by McDonalds. To Barber, commerce, entertainment, and culture are tied together. Exporting American products, athletic shoes, music, and fast food is indistinguishable from diffusing American culture. Nike captures market share "not by selling shoes but by cultivating trademark and brand loyalty that depends on lifestyle choices and the images associated with them ... the image and ideology of sports: health, victory, wealth, sex, money, energy." As claimed by Nike's executives, "We are not a shoe company, we are a sports company. ... We will simply export sports, the world's best economy" (Barber, 66).

However, not everyone agrees with such a concern. There are examples that counter the idea of Westernization or Americanization. One often cited phenomenon is **glocalization**, which is the practice of adapting global products or business models to local culture or circumstances. It is about bending the global standard to fit local uniqueness. Examples abound in this regard. Swiss food giant Nestlé is viewed as a master of adaptation. Its globally distributed products, such as coffee and chocolate, carry local flavors to cater to differing regional tastes. The company has been so successful in localizing their products that many consumers around the world think Nestlé is a local company (Bell and Shelman 2011).

David Bell, a marketing professor at the Wharton Business School at University of Pennsylvania, and his colleague presented a compelling case of glocalization based on KFC's success in China. Their central research question is: how do transnational corporations (TNCs) make their global products appeal to consumers in different markets? Since opening its first restaurant in Beijing in 1987, KFC has been expanding explosively in China, to 3,300 restaurants in 2011 and 5,000 in 2016. In the third quarter of 2010, KFC's revenue in China was more than US$1.1 billion, surpassing even that in the US market. What is its recipe for success? The major ingredient is "infusing a Western brand with Chinese characteristics" (Bell and Shelman 2011) KFC has had to adapt its US-designed business model to suit Chinese preferences. Instead of promoting KFC as simply a Western fast-food chain, franchises aim to make KFC a part of the local community. They realize that "an abundance of flavors and an inviting ambience would be necessary to win over consumers in great numbers" (Bell and Shelman).

KFC offers about 30 food items in the United States, but on Chinese menus there are about 50 items. In addition to fried chicken, french fries, and mashed potatoes, the menu also includes traditional Chinese food, such as fried dough sticks, egg tarts, soymilk drinks, and congee—a rice porridge that is common in Chinese restaurants for breakfast. Not only is the Chinese menu different from that of the United States, KFC has developed different menus within China to tailor to the tastes of specific regions. For example, they offer spicy dishes in Sichuan and Hunan, but not in Shanghai. In China, KFC has abandoned its emphasis on takeout. Like other Chinese restaurants, KFC offers more floor space to allow customers to dine in. KFC also makes efforts to accommodate multigenerational families to dine together. Since the extended menu also entails more complex food preparation and a bigger kitchen, as a result, a typical KFC outlet in China is about twice the size of that in the United States. In sum,

> Over time, KFC China has come to reflect China itself in some respects: It is large, growing, confident, and eager for variety and new experiences. ... Much of what the company has accomplished is the result of its homegrown strategy. ... If there is an overriding lesson to be drawn from KFC's experience in China, it is that when entering an emerging market, a multinational must decide whether it wants to garner quick extra sales or to establish a long-term presence. If it's there for the long haul, it should install local managers whose vision is to build an organization that will last. (Bell and Shelman)

WHAT MAKES GLOBALIZATION POSSIBLE?

As aforementioned, the era of contemporary globalization did not start until the early 1990s, with the fall of the Berlin Wall and the collapse of the Eastern bloc. The Berlin Wall not only physically divided Germany and Europe, it also stood as a divisor between two ideologies: communism and state-planned economies on one side, capitalism and free-market economies on the other. Furthermore, it was erected as a barrier to block the free flow of just about everything. When the wall fell, so did the communism/capitalism debate and the major divide that kept the world separate. In 1992, political scientist Francis Fukuyama published his influential book *The End of History and the Last Man,* and he announced: "What we may be witnessing is not just the end of the Cold War, or the passing of a particular period of post-war history, but the end of history as such: that is, the end point of mankind's ideological evolution and the universalization of Western liberal democracy as the final form of human government" (Fukuyama 1989, 1). With the collapse of the Cold War, people, goods, messages, opportunities, and investments started to flow on an unprecedented scale. Developing countries are joining the world economy; both China and India are exemplars. As billions more people embrace the global economy and express unbound ambitions, technological advances provide the vehicle to turn them into reality.

Technology That Connects the World

A striking feature of contemporary globalization has been technological development. In the following sections, we examine three critical areas of technological change: transport, the internet, and the extension of global supply chains. Much of the forging of new economic and social relations is augmented by the role that technology plays in intensifying the greater interconnectedness between people from different regions and cultures of the world.

Transport

Maritime goods shipping has been around for thousands of years, and for a long time it was risky, slow, and labor intensive. As a matter of fact, modern business insurance policies originated in the shipping industry in the late seventeenth century to insure cargos and ships. While it could take months to cross the ocean to get to a destination, it took at least as much time to load and unload goods, which were packed in different forms or in containers of different shapes, like barrels, bags, or wood crates. It took great planning and skills to load them to maximize the carrying capacity. Loading and unloading were largely done by human labor. As a result, shipping was slow and inefficient, which prohibited frequent and timely movement of large quantities of goods between distant places. In many cases, it was not worthwhile to trade internationally, when shipping could cost as much as 25 percent of the cost making the product (Levinson 2008).

The appearance of container ships in the mid-1950s changed everything. According to the World Shipping Council, although container-like boxes had been used in Britain and the United States occasionally since the end of the eighteenth century, it was Malcom P. McLean, a trucking entrepreneur from North Carolina, who put this idea into practice and revolutionized shipping. Truck trailers were transported through the entire process from trucks to ships and vice versa, with cargo inside untouched. This practice led to the birth of **intermodalism**, which "is a system that is based on the theory that efficiency will be vastly improved when the same container, with the same cargo, can be transported with minimum interruption via different transport modes from an initial place of receipt to a final delivery point many kilometers or miles away. That means the containers would move seamlessly between ships, trucks and trains" (World Shipping Council 2019). McLean found the shipping costs per ton of cargo dropped from US$5.83 for loose cargo on a standard ship to merely US$0.16 for container use (*The Economist* 2013). In 1961, the International Organization for Standardization set standard sizes of containers and gave birth to the two most commonly used containers today: the 20-foot and 40-foot lengths (see Figure 6.2).

FIGURE 6.2 Standardized Shipping Container Vessel

Standardized containers not only lowered freight costs but also saved time by allowing for quicker handling and less storage time in the process of transport from manufacturers to customers. As ships get bigger and can carry more containers, costs become even lower. A big container ship can carry as many as 15,000 containers, which can hold about 800 million bananas. Marc Levinson, a noted economist, gave a vivid example in his book, *The Box: How the Shipping Container Made the World Smaller and the World Economy Bigger* (2008):

> The result of all this activity is a nearly seamless system for shipping freight around the world. A 15-ton container of coffee makers can leave a factory in Malaysia, be loaded aboard a ship, and cover the 9,000 miles to Los Angeles in 16 days. A day later, the container is on a unit train to Chicago, where it is transferred immediately to a truck headed for Cincinnati. The 11,000-mile trip from the factory gate to the Ohio warehouse can take as little as 22 days, a rate of 500 miles per day, at a cost lower than that of a single first-class air ticket. (Levinson 2008, 7)

The Economist declared that, "although only a simple metal box, it has transformed global trade. In fact, new research suggests that the container has been more of a driver of globalization than all trade agreements in the past 50 years taken together." (2013).

For urgent deliveries, courier companies like FedEx, UPS, and DHL can virtually carry a package to your doorstep from anywhere within two days. Around 150 FedEx cargo planes land in the hub of Memphis every night after ten o'clock, when commercial flights in and out of Memphis end and FedEx time begins, until six o'clock in the morning. The planes may come from any of the more than 200 countries or territories in the six continents covered by FedEx. After the planes are unloaded, the goods are sorted by machines and workers right at the airport:

> Watching an assortment of packages course through myriad arterial conveyances is mind-boggling. When shipments arrive in the hub they are scanned and measured, identifying where a package is shipped from, how much it weighs, and where it's bound. Workers busily flip boxes label up, and place them on conveyors.
>
> Farther along, there's another conveyance, and a cascade of colored boxes of assorted shapes and sizes sliding off a tilt tray sorter—all triggered by a bar-code label scan. If you've ever seen an avalanche, and the detritus left in its wake, this is the distribution center equivalent. Workers pick through the debris that falls down the chute—Virginia Farms' flowers, blood packaged on dry ice, medicine packs, even boxes filled with live lobsters— and send them on their way. (O'Reilly 2011)

FedEx processes more than one million shipments every night like this, 365 days a year. For any company, a far-away, low-cost supplier still looks appealing when distance is greatly discounted.

The Internet

The Soviet Union's launch of the satellite Sputnik in 1957 sent shock waves around the world. As a response, the United States created the Advanced Research Projects

Agency (ARPA) to ensure US leadership in defense technology. To facilitate communications among research agencies, in 1972 ARPA created a network that links computers from 40 different locations. That was the preform of the internet. In 1989, Tim Berners-Lee at the European Center for High Energy Physics in Geneva developed the first browser, which he called the World Wide Web. It led to the later, improved browsers of Mosaic in 1993 and Netscape in 1994 and triggered an explosion of internet use. The number of websites bloomed from 3,000 in 1994 to over a million in 1997 (Prestowitz 2005). It is hard to exaggerate how much the internet itself has evolved since then in terms of business and our own lives.

Steve Case, the cofounder of AOL, asserts that the internet has evolved through three waves:

> The First Wave was about building the Internet. Companies such as AOL created the underlying infrastructure and brought America (and the rest of the world) online. This phase peaked around 2000, setting the stage for the Second Wave, which has been about building apps and services on top of the Internet. ... Second Wave startups have been centered on software: Build an app, do what you can to drive viral adoption, and then find a way to make money. ... Now the Third Wave has begun. Over the next decade and beyond, the Internet will rapidly become ubiquitous, integrated into our everyday lives, often in invisible ways. This will challenge industries such as health care, education, financial services, energy and transportation—which collectively represent more than half the U.S. economy. ... New startups are reimagining how we learn, eat, stay healthy and get around. This is only a start, as the Third Wave of the Internet gains strength. ... As more industries become "Uberized," an increasing share of employees will work multiple gigs. A full-time job with a single employer could become passé. (Case 2016).

The changing role of email is a good example of how fast communication technology is changing our lives. Email used to be thought of as revolutionary, a first-generation communication tool coming with the internet. To a large degree, it replaced traditional letters. Email made communication, for the first time, instantaneous and paperless. But how many young people nowadays use email? In his study of the so-called generation Z (born around and after 2000, the youngest generation at present), technology columnist Christopher Mims found that using email has become a rite of passage for teens and those in their early twenties, on par with the first kiss, first time behind the wheel, and first time registering to vote: "For them, email is about as much fun as applying to college or creating a résumé. ... Email is for communicating with old people, the digital equivalent of putting on a shirt and tie" (Mims 2016). Twitter, Instagram, MSN messenger, Facebook Messenger, and instantaneous texting apps on smart phones are popular instead.

The internet and related information and communication technologies have completely transformed the way people live and work. More fundamentally, they have expanded not only beyond national borders but also over the huge divide between developed and developing countries. Unlike previous waves of technological revolutions, which tended to be concentrated in a few rich countries, the current information technology revolution has reached distant areas as never before. The expanding networks, falling prices, and growing applications have benefited ever more and more people. According to the UN, internet users have grown from just over 6 percent of the world's population in 2000 to 43 percent in 2015. As a result, 3.2 billion people have access to the global network, thanks to rapid advances in fixed- and mobile-broadband technologies. The proportion of the world population covered by a mobile-cellular network grew from 58 percent in 2001 to 95 percent in 2015. There were over seven billion mobile-cellular subscriptions in 2015, a tenfold growth over 2000 (United Nations 2015).

Global Supply Chains

The removal of barriers to free market capitalism, emergence of container shipping and express air delivery, and development of the internet have combined to flatten the world. This makes it possible for a company to diversify its production and distribution. As a result, many companies have gone global, transforming themselves into **transnational corporations (TNCs)** and setting up supply chains around the globe. Places that are at the other end of the globe, like China and India, are no longer viewed as remote. Increasing volumes of manufacturing and service work are moved from North America and Europe to Asia and other places: "As global supply chains proliferate, organizations operating in one country will increasingly depend on organizations headquartered or operating within the boundaries of other countries to either supply material or market their products" (Stank, Burnette, and Dittman 2014).

A global supply chain stands in stark contrast to the model of the Ford River Rouge Complex, located in Dearborn, Michigan, built in the 1920s, and at that time the world's largest integrated factory. Henry Ford intended to build an automobile factory complex for total self-sufficiency by owning, operating, and coordinating all the resources needed to produce complete automobiles. It is an "ore to assembly," construction, with iron ore, coal, and limestone going in at one end of the plant and manufactured cars coming out at the other. The emergence of a global supply chain eclipsed this earlier model. Car parts no longer need to be produced locally. They can be **outsourced** to producers all over the world, where total costs are lower. Or the entire assembly line can be moved **offshore**. Nowadays, Ford Motor Company has over 1,000 suppliers worldwide and more than 60 car plants on six continents.

The production of the iPhone is yet another example. The iPhone is designed in the United States. Its supply chain, which supplies parts and components, spans the United States, Europe, and Asia, with suppliers from more than 30 countries. The sapphire glass for the display cover is produced by GT Advanced Technologies in Mesa, Arizona. Some of Apple's "A series chips" are provided by Samsung (aren't they competitors?), which has them manufactured in one of its plants in Austin, Texas. Its display panel is from LG (South Korea), its cameras from Sony, and its storage chips from Toshiba. All the parts are assembled in China. The finished products are shipped back to the United States and distributed to the US market and around the world.

Outsourcing and **offshoring** are two common global business strategies practiced by TNCs. **Outsourcing** means that instead of getting everything done in-house, as Ford did in the past, a company now has other companies contribute a portion of the total operation. It can be in the form of buying machine parts or delegating certain functions to outside contractors, such as advertising, IT support, office logistics, accounting, or reading X-rays (for doctors). As time goes by, functions or jobs outsourced get more complex and advanced. Morgan Stanley first moved its office operations to India, then started outsourcing more sophisticated functions as well, including analyzing financial statements, drafting business plans, and making investment recommendations. It is the same for Reuters, a well-known international news agency headquartered in London. The outsourcing of office operations was followed by shifting a large portion of its editorial staff to India. Many other companies are doing the same. Germany's SAP has set up software labs in India; Philips, a Dutch electronics company, has built up staff in China and India; Norwich Union, a British insurer, moved its office and customer services to India. Meanwhile, a number of French companies have moved their call centers to France's former colonies in Africa: Morocco, Mauritius, and Senegal (Prestowitz 2005). When the conditions of infrastructure, workforce, and other elements are well in place, TNCs will move the entire operation, such as a factory, to a foreign country, which is defined as **offshoring**. It is no longer news that many automobile, home appliance, and equipment factories are relocated from the United States to Mexico, China, and other countries. Production flows to the next place where the labor costs are lower.

Take the textile industry as an example. The textile industry migrated from early industrial powerhouse Britain to New England in the United States, then to the Carolinas, where labor was cheaper. The 1990s witnessed a new wave of industry exodus, heading to countries where labor cost was even lower, such as China, India, and Mexico. The apparel manufacturing industry lost more than 80 percent of its employees within two decades: from about 900,000 in 1990 to 150,000 in 2011. While there were 15,478 private business establishments in the apparel manufacturing industry in 2001, the number declined to 7,855 in 2010 (Bureau of Labor Statistics 2012).

Whether that of outsourcing or offshoring, the decisions are motivated by a total business-driven profit sense and allow companies to remain efficient and competitive in an increasingly competitive world. In 2016, the Eaton Corporation decided to shut down its factory in Berea, Ohio, that manufacturers quick-connect couplings for hydraulic lines. More than 100 workers lost their jobs. Eaton will buy the couplings from another manufacturer and ship them to its plant in Mexico to assemble them. The company issued a statement saying: "This decision is the result of an ongoing review of our manufacturing processes to ensure that Eaton is well-positioned for the future and that our businesses operate as efficiently as possible. ... This decision is not a reflection on Berea employees who have worked very hard over the years to meet our customers' needs" (Funk 2016).

MAKING A CASE FOR GLOBAL TRADE: COMPARATIVE ADVANTAGE

One of the major theories of international trade is the idea of **comparative advantage**, first put forward by English economist David Ricardo (1772–1823) in the early nineteenth century. Comparative advantage emphasizes specialization. Comparative advantage states that it is inefficient for a country to produce everything it needs. Instead, it should focus only on what it is best at, thereby creating an advantage over other countries. Comparative advantage is illustrated in a classic example of trade between England and Portugal, where only two commodities are produced: cloth and wine, respectively. Even when Portugal is efficient in producing both wine and cloth, Portugal should focus on what it is best at: winemaking. Likewise, England should only produce cloth. When all countries follow the same principle and find their particular niche in the world market, efficiency will be maximized and prices will be kept the lowest; everyone benefits.

According to the theory of comparative advantage, there is a world division of labor or specialization among countries. The industrialized, developed countries take the lead in product design, development of new technologies, new energy exploration, and high-end services in business, health, and education. As a result, unskilled or semiskilled jobs will fade away. Britain used to be the center of the industrial revolution. There is little heavy industry left today. Taking its place is finance, marketing, IT, high-tech engineering, and business development. As old jobs are disappearing, new jobs are created. For example, we are in the era of the internet. Information technology, ecommerce, and ebanking are booming. There are thousands of startups in Silicon Valley and other places, creating jobs in various new areas, many of which may have never been heard of. As cyber attacks become a new security concern for individuals, businesses, and government agencies, new businesses that address these challenges rise to the task. According to *The Economist* (August 1, 2015), in 2014, for the first time, Israel exported more cyber security products than weapons systems. Around US$6 billion of internet security software for home computers, businesses, and government organizations were sold to worldwide customers. The number of cyber security companies in Israel doubled from 2010 to 300 in 2015. The current generation of software can not only detect new strains of computer viruses but also predict where hackers may attack next, be it through mobile devices or the online cloud, and provide defenses against them (*The Economist* August 1, 2015).

Education is another advantage of developed countries. Most of the top-tier educational institutions are located in developed countries, which attract a growing number of students from developing countries. International students have become common on college campuses in the United States, Europe, and Australia. Based on statistics from the Institute of International Education, the total international student enrollment in the United States has grown from 560,000 in 2005–2006 to 970,000 in the 2014–2015 academic year. Of the top ten places of origin for these students, eight of them are developing countries, led by China, India, South Korea, and Saudi Arabia. Business management, engineering, mathematics, and computer sciences top the list of these students' fields of study. In the United States, not only are international students seen in the universities along the eastern or western coast, they have made their way to America's heartland. At Case Western Reserve University (CWRU) in Cleveland, Ohio, international students from more than 80 countries compose 20 percent of the student body. According to the local newspaper, the *Plain Dealer*, in 2013, "for the first time in memory, the top hometown of CWRU's freshman class is not Cleveland or Pittsburgh. It's Beijing. Shanghai ranks third" (Smith, Robert L. 2013). Since international students usually have limited access to financial aid, they typically pay the full cost, which is nearly US$60,000 a year at CWRU. College administrators in the United States make a strong effort to recruit these foreign tuition dollars.

In addition to attracting foreign students, education can also be literally exported to developing countries. There has been a quiet rush overseas by universities in the United States, such as New York University and the Massachusetts Institute of Technology (MIT), to set up partnerships by collaborating with other foreign universities. This partnership arrangement has also involved community colleges seeking to add new sources of revenue due to cuts or uncertain state funding. These US community colleges have set up campuses or programs abroad. The Rancho Santiago Community College District in California, which specializes in teaching drywall finishing, real estate finance, and infant development, helped two vocational schools take off in Saudi Arabia. To name a few, "The Lone Star College System, in the Houston area, is running a vocational school in Jakarta and conducting safety training for oil-and-gas workers in Malta. Nebraska's Central Community College helped launch an entrepreneurship program for Bahrain Polytechnic. Gateway Technical College in Kenosha, Wisconsin, has advised on automotive-diagnostic training programs in Morocco" (Korn 2016).

While rich countries focus on sectors requiring plenty of capital or cutting-edge technology and expertise, developing countries with a large and cheap labor force, according to the comparative advantage theory, are supposed to concentrate on labor-intensive industries. The offshoring of low-end, unskilled, or semiskilled manufacturing jobs to these areas reflects such a reality. In a global supply chain, developing countries are usually involved in assembly or other low-value components of the chain of production, with the more profitable parts of the operation, such as design and marketing, remaining in the West. According to a study published in 2010, Chinese workers contributed just 3.6 percent to the cost of an Apple iPhone, with chips imported from Japan (*The Economist* March 12, 2015a).

If the ubiquitous phrase "Made in China" suggests China's manufacturing strengths, "serviced in India" reveals India's eminent role in providing high-end services to the entire world, including software development, customer service, pharmaceutical production and research, accounting, medicine, and education, to name a few. To save on budgetary expenditures, the British National Health Service was considering sending blood samples to India for lab analysis, the results of which could be emailed back the next day. Nowadays in the United States, when you dial a 1-800-number, calling for customer service to book an air ticket or a hotel, fix your laptop, ask questions about a credit card or a product's warranty, or place a claim on car insurance, chances are that you will hear a "Steve" or "Michelle" answering your phone from India, halfway around the world. Not only do the representatives' name sound American, so do their accents. "Accent neutralization" classes are offered in call center training schools, where instructors are Americans who help young Indians overcome pronunciation pitfalls and make them sound like they are calling from Kansas or Ohio. In the so-called "shared economy," anyone can contribute as long as he or she has something to offer, be it a car ride or a vacation home or one's knowledge and expertise. And the latter is not limited by geography at all. When a high school student in Pennsylvania needs help with his geometry class, he can get a tutor online from India, whom he can talk to and who simultaneously shows him the solution on the screen.

There is constant competition in the global economy for virtually all products and services, from automobiles, housing, soft-drinks, and footwear to smart phones, wireless service, banking, and the new shared economy. Before Portuguese warships controlled the Straits of Hormuz on the Persian Gulf and Malacca Strait in South-East Asia in the sixteenth century, spices, silks and other goods from the East had to pass the Middle East, then travel through Venice and Genoa to Europe. Egypt kept the price of pepper high by limiting shipments to Venice. The direct trade with Asia completed by Portuguese ships after Portugal dominated the trading route on the Indian Ocean cut the pepper price in Lisbon by 80 percent, virtually destroying the Egyptian-Venetian trade overnight, which is viewed as "the first demonstration of the power of globalization" (Prestowitz 2005).

Protectionist policies, such as high tariffs on foreign goods, protect inefficient local industries at the expense of consumers. The United States adopted such policies in the nineteenth and early twentieth century to protect its young industries and increase government revenue. This practice was criticized by early free trade advocates:

> A century ago, remarkably enough, free trade was the populist position. In 1911, The Tariff in Our Times, a book by the muckraking journalist Ida Tarbell, argued that high tariff walls protected capitalists, not workers. Sheltered from competition from Europe, she wrote, oligopolies could get away with selling expensive, shoddy goods in the U.S. market. High tariffs on wool prevented tuberculosis patients from getting warm woolen clothes and blankets, she wrote. She condemned congressmen who voted repeatedly for high tariffs: "We have developed a politician who encourages the most dangerous kind of citizenship a democracy can know—the panicky, grasping, idealess kind." (Coy 2016)

More recently is an example in the ridesharing economy. Didi, a Beijing-based Chinese car-hailing company, recently teamed up with Lyft, an American company, to provide a ridesharing service in San Francisco. The goal of the coalition is to compete with Uber, their dominant competitor. The apps of Didi and Lyft are integrated so that Chinese customers of Didi can hail a ride in US cities. Didi users can open the app and choose Lyft cars on the screen. They will be charged the same amount as a local passenger, and the payment can be processed seamlessly. In case of communication barrier, the app provides instantaneous translation service that is contracted to a call center in China. The coalition may be further expanded to India and South-East Asia, where Uber is facing fierce competition. In response to this tactic, San Francisco-based Uber formed a Chinese affiliate, UberChina (MacMillan 2016). Such competition certainly brings customers more options and better services.

The Rise of China, India, and the Former Second World

As China, India, and the former Second World joined the global economy, they brought three billion new capitalists into the system. One question is: are there enough jobs for them? Or, at least, is there going to be a job left for "me"? Thomas Friedman expressed a similar concern for his daughter, who was a college student when he published his book *The World Is Flat*, but he was more convinced by the counterargument that globalization overall will benefit everyone in countries poor and rich. One myth he debunked is the so-called **lump of labor theory**, according to which there is a fixed amount of labor demand around the world; it is a zero-sum game. The lump of labor theory states that in the global labor market, China's or India's gain is automatically a loss of the United States. According to Friedman, this is simply not true. As the economy evolves, old jobs are gone and new jobs are created. More importantly, as a result of globalization, the rise of the developing world will only make the pie of global economy ever bigger, which will bring about more demand, more consumption, and *more* jobs.

In a book written by a few researchers in the Boston Consulting Group, it is predicted that there will be nearly one billion middle-class consumers in China and India by 2020. The consumer markets of China and India will triple over a decade and amount to US$10 trillion consumption annually (Silverstein et al. 2012). As Table 6.1 shows, the average income in China and India will nearly triple in one decade. While China's income will be absolutely higher, India's income will grow slightly faster, 180 percent versus 193 percent. More impressively, the total of consumer spending in these two countries will more than triple from US$3 trillion to nearly US$10 trillion. According to their survey of 24,000 consumers around the world, when asked, "How do you expect your discretionary spending to change over the next twelve months?" consumers from China and India gave the highest percentage of "Spend More" response, 36 percent and 19 percent, respectively, followed by Brazil (17 percent) and Russia (15 percent). In contrast, fewer consumers in developed countries chose this response: It was 11 percent for the United States, 8 percent for Europe as a whole, and 5 percent for Japan.

American companies that are directly involved in international trade are among the United States' most dynamic companies. As a result, workers from these companies earn 15–20 percent more than workers elsewhere in the country. Of the ten largest automobile markets in the world in 2011, three of them are in developing countries: China (first), Brazil (fourth), and India (sixth), and are expanding, while the markets in three developed countries on the list show signs of shrinkage (Japan, United Kingdom, and Italy). China overtook the United States to be the world's largest auto market in the world in 2009. In 2015, 24.6 million units were sold in China compared to 17.2 million units sold in the United States, the result of a surging demand from a rising middle class in China. General Motors (GM) is the top car seller in China and plans to roll out more than 60 new car models in China by 2020, with a focus on SUVs and minivans to meet the high demands of the growing Chinese consumer market. In light of China's often congested roads, GM will offer more automated features that, for example, can alert the driver of lane-drifting, detect blindspots, and

TABLE 6.1 *The Change of Average Annual Income and Total Spending in China and India (in US Dollars)*

	INCOME		CONSUMER SPENDING (IN TRILLIONS)		
	China	**India**	**China**	**India**	**Sum**
2010	$4,400	$1,500	$2.036T	$0.991T	$3.027T
2020	$12,300	$4,400	$6.187T	$3.584T	$9.771T
Growth	180%	193%	204%	262%	224%

Data source: Silverstein et al. 2012.

allow hands-free driving on the highway (Yu 2016). Ford Motors is also well positioned in its focus on the SUV sector of the Chinese market. Its SUV sales grew by about 40 percent in the first quarter of 2016. As China's middle class has grown to over 300 million people, consumption of goods and services increased almost 50 percent in two decades, from 1994 to 2014.

Trade and Peace

In his book *The World Is Flat*, Thomas Friedman puts forward two theories regarding how globalization prevents war and conflict. He noticed that "no two countries that both had McDonald's had ever fought a war against each other since each got its McDonald's" (Friedman 2007, 586). This led to his first theory, the Golden Arches Theory, which stipulates that the presence of McDonald's in a country results from the emergence of a middle class and rising living standards (true for most developing countries). The middle class is usually the steadying force against wars, due to their political tendencies or economic motives to protect their material interests. His second theory is called the Dell Theory, which works in the context of the global supply chain: "No two countries that are both part of a major global supply chain, like Dell's, will ever fight a war against each other" (586). The rationale is that such countries, if involved in war with others, would disrupt the supply chain and risk losing their spots in the chain. The stakes are simply so high that no country can afford it: "Governments whose countries are enmeshed in global supply chains will have to think three times, not just twice, about engaging in anything but a war of self-defense" (591).

It is no secret that there have been long-term tensions between China and Japan and competing maritime claims over the South China Sea among a number of countries. But the presence of a supply chain in this region, called "Factory Asia" by *The Economist* (March 12, 2015a), has successfully prompted these Asian countries "to put business ties above political disputes. Commerce has brought them closer together. ASEAN nations (those in South-East Asia) have a free-trade agreement with China. Japan, China and South Korea are negotiating a deal among themselves. There are also talks, still early, about a broader pact that would tie all countries in the region together, including India" (*The Economist* March 12, 2015a). In sum, as a country marches on the path of development, it needs energy to power its economy and infrastructure to support it. All these factors entail significant investment, which usually cannot be financed by the country itself. It has to rely on borrowing funds from international institutions and other countries. In this way, one nation's interest is intertwined with that of others. Engaging in conflict with other countries does not serve national interests.

To Thomas P. M. Barnett, a senior strategist and professor at the US Naval War College, the world's major rift is no longer between the East and West, representing opposing ideologies. Rather, it is between "the Core" and "the Gap," representing countries' membership in the globalized economy. While the **Core** refers to countries that have been integrated into the world economy, the **Gap** are those disconnected or left out of the process. To Barnett, the Core of globalization consists of North America, Europe, Japan, China, India, Australia, New Zealand, South Africa, Argentina, Brazil, and Chile—about two-thirds of the global population. The rest of the world falls in the Gap category. The causes for the disconnectedness of the Gap are multiple. It may be that a country is too impoverished to invest in, or that it does not have adequate rule sets or financial stability, or it is constantly disrupted by change of leadership or even wars. All these factors prompt investors to shy away from the Gap countries. Since 1950, there have been about US$7 trillion of foreign direct investment around the globe. As expected, the lion share of it goes to the Core: North America (24 percent), Europe (39 percent), and South and East Asia (21 percent). Of the 9 percent going to South America, most of it flows to Core members in the continent: Argentina, Brazil, and Chile. Africa and the Middle East attract only 2 percent each. In other words, the Gap, which accounts for one-third of the world population, gets by with one-twentieth of global long-term investment (Barnett 2004). The outcomes of being stuck in the Gap are poverty, short life expectancy, isolation, and desperation, which are the hotbed of rebellion and terror. Barnett sees the connection and urges action to bring connectivity to every corner of the world:

> To be disconnected in this world is to be kept isolated, deprived, repressed, and uneducated. ... For young men, it means being kept ignorant and bored and malleable. For the masses, being disconnected means a lack of choice and scarce access to ideas, capital, travel, entertainment, ... If disconnectedness is the real enemy, then the combatants we target in this war are those who promote it, enforce it, and terrorize those who seek to overcome it by reaching out to the larger world. Our strategic goals, therefore, are to extend connectivity in every way possible. (49)

The Rise of TNCs

The world's largest companies are moving on and moving ahead of governments and countries that they perceive to be inept and not suitable for fostering business. Indeed, the global emergence and dominance of **TNCs** is one of the most defining features of contemporary globalization (Potter et al. 2013). Most of the world's largest companies are TNCs. TNCs operate in multiple countries around the world. The TNC has unsettled the received definition of "global superpower," which was formerly reserved for nation-states. For example, the cash that Apple has on hand exceeds the GDPs of two-thirds of the world's countries. The ten biggest banks control almost 50 percent of assets under management worldwide. According to a report from Make Wealth History, which is based on data from the IMF, CIA, and Forbes, in 2012, 37 of the world's 100 largest economies were corporations. Table 6.2 shows the revenue of the top ten companies relative to nations in terms of GDP.

TABLE 6.2 *World's Top Ten Companies in 2012*

COMPANY	REVENUE (IN BILLION USD)	WORLD ECONOMIES RANKING	CLOSEST COUNTRY BELOW IT
WALMART	469	28	Austria
ROYAL DUTCH SHELL	467	29	Austria
EXXON MOBIL	421	30	Austria
CHINA SINOPEC	412	31	Austria
BP	371	35	Colombia
PETROCHINA	309	40	Malaysia
VOLKSWAGEN	254	47	Philippines
TOTAL S.A.	241	52	Pakistan
TOYOTA	232	54	Portugal
CHEVRON CORPORATION	225	55	Portugal

Data source: Williams 2014.

STATELESS CORPORATIONS

Globalization, for better or worse, has altered the national and international corporate landscape. The world is entering an era of business **denationalization**: companies design and structure their operations beyond traditional national borders, extending them to various locations of the global value chains: "The most powerful law is not that of sovereignty but that of supply and demand" (Khanna 2016). Companies are transformed to be stateless, or **metanational**, a term coined by some management scholars that refers to "a company that builds a new kind of competitive advantage by discovering, accessing, mobilizing, and leveraging knowledge from many locations around the world" (Doz, Santos, and Williamson 2001). With a global outreach, TNCs can efficiently tap into talents, intelligence, and special knowledge scattered around the world, as well as natural resources. The entire globe has become the source of their supply, and they no longer rely on input from a particular place, including the home country. TNCs like ExxonMobil, GE, IBM, and Visa may have management in one country, production in another, and logistics in a third. Decisions regarding locations are weighed on the basis of labor cost, abundance of resources, availability of local talent, and friendliness of regulations. As Patterson (2013) lamented,

> Sixty years later, where did the "America" in corporate America go? No longer committed to a particular place, people, country, or culture, our largest public companies have turned globalist while abdicating the responsibility they once

> assumed to America and its workers. … If stateless companies live by one rule, however, it's that there's always another place to go where profits are higher, oversight friendlier and opportunities more plentiful. This belief has helped nimble, mobile and smart corporations outgrow their original masters, including the world's reigning superpower. Seen in this light, metanationals disassociating from terrestrial restraints and harnessing the power of the cloud is anything but far-fetched.

The shift of manufacturing to Asia is a case in point. Japan emerged as a manufacturing power in the 1960s, followed by South Korea, Hong Kong, Taiwan, and Singapore (the Four Asian Tigers), in exporting electronics and consumer goods. Since its opening to the outside world in the 1980s, China has become a manufacturing hub thanks to its abundant and cheap labor. However, manufacturing wages in China have risen by an average of 12 percent a year since 2001. Although the average wage in China is still less than a quarter of that in America, China's labor cost is under pressure. As China's wages rise, TNCs start transferring their production to countries with cheaper labor. Much of this is passing to South-East Asia. In 2015, factory workers in China earned, on average, US$27.50 per day, compared with US$8.60 in Indonesia and US$6.70 in Vietnam (*The Economist* March 12, 2015a). While China's share in the export of shoes to America fell from 87 percent in 2009 to 79 percent in 2014, Vietnam's, Indonesia's, and Cambodia's shares went up (*The Economist* March 12, 2015b). Myanmar, another country in South-East Asia with much lower-cost labor, witnessed its clothing exports jump from US$700 million to US$1.7 billion between 2011 and 2014, as more companies, like H&M, moved their factories there from China. Samsung, Microsoft, and Toyota have also trimmed production in China and turned to places such as Myanmar and the Philippines (*The Economist* March 12, 2015a, b).

Many of the largest TNCs headquartered in the United States have revenues from overseas markets and hold trillions of dollars offshore, tax free, which are dubbed by some observers as "stateless income" (Khanna 2016). When such money is moved back to the United States, it is subject to income tax. To legally avoid it, one common practice is **tax inversion**, which according to the Congressional Research Service is "instances where U.S. firms reorganize their structure so that the 'parent' element of the group is a foreign corporation rather than a corporation chartered in the United States. The main objective of these transactions was tax savings and they involved little to no shift in actual economic activity. Bermuda and the Cayman Islands (countries with no corporate income tax) were the location of many of the newly created parent corporations" (Congressional Research Service 2019). Firms involved in tax inversion abound in the food, pharmaceutical, financial services, and manufacturing industries, among others.

The failed merge of Pfizer and Allergan is a much talked-about example. In November 2015, the two pharmaceutical companies agreed to merge in a record US$160 billion deal:

> The transaction is a complicated legal maneuver that technically lets Dublin-based Allergan buy its much larger New York-based partner. That will make it easier for the combined company to locate its tax address in Ireland, where corporate income is taxed at less than half the U.S. rate. If the new entity is able to establish itself abroad for a lower tax rate, a controversial process called an inversion, it will be the largest such move in history. (Koons and Cortez 2015)

COMPETITORS FROM NEARBY AND FAR AWAY

As a result of outsourcing and offshoring, contemporary globalization has met resistance and backlash in developed countries. In an international survey conducted by the Pew Research Center in 2014, half of Americans said trade destroys jobs, as did 49 percent in France and 59 percent in Italy. In contrast, the majority of people in developing countries, such as Bangladesh, Uganda, and Vietnam, held strong positive views toward trade (Coy 2016). Why? Because in this globalized economy, those living in poor countries see the hope that they now have a chance to get on the board and be part of the game.

The phrase "**the world is flat**" means the playing field is being leveled. Breakthroughs in information technology, including the processing power of computers, communication networks, and software development, have broken down physical barriers caused by distance and national borders, which in the past have kept millions, if not billions, of people from directly joining world competition. Nowadays, one does not need to get on an airplane from India or China to travel to California to get interviewed or to submit developed software. A picture of one's graduation can be instantaneously sent to the other end of the world, as can one's work or one's solution to a problem. Globalization has brought competitors from afar to the playing field everywhere. "Every young American today would be wise to think of himself or herself as competing against every young Chinese, Indian, and Brazilian," says Thomas Friedman (Friedman 2007, 278). In this flattened world, what matters may not be where one lives or one's citizenship but what one has to offer. One's talent, intellectual capacity, and other skills become more important than ever.

As author Clyde Prestowitz strolled around Bangalore, India's Silicon Valley, he heard young people in bars talking about software and what was going on in Silicon Valley, California. He found it amazing how much more these young people knew about the United States than did Americans themselves. Around 2000, Intel opened a research campus in Bangalore and hired 1,800 electrical engineers and computer scientists to develop next-generation microprocessors. It is true that the operating costs are a lot lower in India than in the United States, but the major reason is the talent that India provides: "Intel hires only the best. Because it can use more Ph.D. engineers than the U.S. supplies, the real driver here is the global search for the world's smartest, best-educated technologists" (Prestowitz 2005, 99).

Bill Gates once told Thomas Friedman about the changing relationship between geography and talent. He said, in the 1970s if one was given a choice of being a genius born in Bombay or Shanghai or being an average person in Poughkeepsie in New York, the latter would be the clear choice, because it was the place where the economy was thriving and had plenty of opportunities. Decades later, when the world is becoming more flat, that decision may change. What matters more in determining one's future is one's talent, which now trumps geography (Friedman 2007). And the competitors are many. A report released by the Organization for Economic Cooperation and Development (OECD) states that China is steadily increasing its investment in higher education, aiming to have 20 percent of its citizens—or 195 million people—obtain higher education degrees by 2020. "If this goal is realized, China will have a population of tertiary graduates that is roughly equal in size to the entire projected population of 25- to 64-year-olds in the United States in 2020," the report predicts (OECD 2012). It is a perplexing world to live in. To some, it feels full of hope and opportunities, and for others it is tough and stressful.

Smarter Machines

Outsourcing or offshoring is often singled out as the main culprit of job loss in developed countries. What is less visible is the role of technology. The machines we invent are running faster and smarter. It may not be such a remote possibility that someday they will outsmart their masters. Worse, they will take away lunch, too. More and more robots have been developed and tested to carry out blue-collar jobs. Atlas, a robot built by Boston Dynamics, was reported to be able to perform humanlike tasks such as opening doors and lifting and stacking boxes. A report released by the White House forecasts that most occupations that pay less than US$20 per hour, mainly those that require manual labor, are likely to be "automated into obsolescence":

> Human workers of all stripes pound the table claiming desperately that they're irreplaceable. Bus drivers. Bartenders. Financial advisers. Speechwriters. Firefighters. Umpires. Even doctors and surgeons. Meanwhile, corporations and investors are spending billions—at least $8.5 billion last year on AI (Artificial Intelligence), and $1.8 billion on robots—toward making all those jobs replaceable. Why? Because robots and computers don't need health care, pensions, vacation days or even salaries. ... Powerhouse consultancies like McKinsey & Co. forecast that 45 percent of today's workplace activities could be done by robots, AI or some other already demonstrated technology. Some professors argue that we could see 50 percent unemployment in 30 years. (Wright 2016)

Recently, there have been signs pointing to a new wave of "reshoring" manufacturing jobs back to the United States. The textile industry is creating more US jobs for the first time in decades. Rising wages in developing countries, especially China, are an often-cited reason. But that is only part of the story. The newly created manufacturing jobs in the United States are no longer those moving along the old assembly lines. Automatic systems, digital sensors, and robotics are the new faces on the factory floor. In 2012, the United States registered more exports of textile and apparel than three years earlier. The underlying force was the revival of the textile industry at home. Parkdale Mills in South Carolina is one example. Moving production from India back to the United States gives the company several advantages: lower transportation costs, quicker turnaround time, more certainty on quality control, and total elimination of customs duties. The major disadvantage is labor cost, which is US$17.00 per hour in the United States and US$3.50 in India. The magic power to overcome it is automation, which allows for employing far fewer workers:

> The mill here produces 2.5 million pounds of yarn a week with about 140 workers. In 1980, that production level would have required more than 2,000 people. ... Machines have replaced humans at almost every point in the production process. ... Only infrequently does a person interrupt the automation, mainly because certain tasks are still cheaper if performed by hand—like moving half-finished yarn between machines on forklifts. Beyond that, there is little that resembles the mills of just a few decades ago. (Clifford 2013)

Mr. Bayard Winthrop, the founder of Parkdale Mills, recapped such a strategy: "We've been able to be effective here because we invested in our manufacturing to the point that labor is not as big of an issue as far as total cost as it once was. It's allowed us to be able to compete more effectively with foreign countries that pay, you know, a fraction of what we pay in wages. We compete with them on technology and productivity" (Clifford 2013). This round of revival of manufacturing in the United States may not revive as many manufacturing jobs as one would like to see. Efficiency, or productivity, is the rule, which can be achieved by either foreign cheap labor or robots. Although the first victims seem to be blue-collar workers, white-collar professionals may be next: "Futurist Ray Kurzweil, who is also Google's director of engineering, says AI will equal human intelligence by 2029" (Wright 2016). An AI system developed by Google researchers has beaten a top human player at the game of Go, an ancient Eastern board game that involves great complexity and almost infinite possible moves. The human player, Lee Se-dol from South Korea, who holds multiple international championship titles, lost the five-round game by one to four in March 2016, which sent shock waves around the world. The computer relied on the so-called deep learning technique to train itself to learn. "Some technology experts who follow trends in artificial intelligence say it's only a matter of time before a well-designed algorithm wins a Pulitzer Prize for journalism," says Phillip Morris (2016), a columnist for the *Plain Dealer*. Computer systems have already been adopted in sports journalism by the Big 10 Network and Yahoo, although so far they have been limited to simpler, lower-level writing. The trend seems irreversible: "Few, if any, industries can escape the steady advance of technology. Sometimes, it seems that it's just a matter of time before machines march us all to the unemployment line" (Morris).

FADING NATIONS: THE DIMINISHED ROLE OF THE STATE

The state, led by the government, has many functions to perform that are essential to economic development. In the interim of economic growth in past centuries, Western governments have greatly expanded their functions by unifying national markets; building infrastructure needed for economic takeoff, including roads, railroads, and ports; providing public health care, control of diseases, formal education, and social welfare; and enforcing laws and contracts. In other words, the government's purpose is to remove obstacles that limit economic incentives and opportunities and, at the same time, to support institutions and structures that nurture them. It is a myth to assume that the best economic system is that run totally by the free market and private sector. Even in Great Britain, where originated the Industrial Revolution and modern capitalism, the government found it necessary to intervene to check abuses and problems when its modern economy came together in the nineteenth century and had introduced a welfare state by the mid-twentieth century (Staley 1966).

Although the economy of the United States is thought to be driven mainly by private enterprises, the role of the state in its development cannot be overlooked. Examples abound in US history. To aid the territorial expansion to the western frontier, Congress passed the Homestead Act in 1862, which granted ownership of lands to new settlers for free. It set in motion the continuing expansion of the United States during the nineteenth century. The US government also built or subsidized railways and canals and established educational institutions and agricultural experimental stations, which contributed to making the United States one of the most productive agricultural systems in the world (Staley 1966).

In recent decades, however, with the emergence of a global economy and the rise of TNCs, national governments worldwide have started to lose the capacity to handle their own business. The cloud of the European sovereign, debt crisis beginning in 2009, is still lingering; several member states of the Eurozone, such as Greece, Ireland, Portugal, Spain, and others to varying degrees, still have difficulty repaying or refinancing their national debt. The future of the euro or the even the European Union seems in doubt. In the developed world, most of the major economies are deep in debt. As of 2016, the Japanese national debt was equivalent to 228 percent of its GDP. The percentages were 98 percent for France, 91 percent for the UK, and 74 percent for the US, where the federal debt reached US$13.9 trillion. That is about US$43,000 per person. The

National Debt Clock displayed US$19 trillion, because it has included money borrowed from the Social Security Trust Fund. The debt keeps growing, although the annual deficit slowed to only US$405 billion in 2015, the lowest since 2008 (Grant 2016).

The state also retreats in the power struggle with TNCs. In the new era of a global economy, TNCs have a lot more leverage in deciding where to set up shop when they negotiate with national or local governments. It is a common practice for governments to offer various perks to attract investment, such as tax incentives and grants, which further contribute to the state's financial predicament. As a result, when the deficit is up, the coverage and quality of services that the state provides to its citizens are down. Years-old infrastructure fails to be updated. The fall of the Mississippi River bridge in Minneapolis, Minnesota, in 2007, and the water lead poisoning discovered in Flint, Michigan, in 2014, are just two examples that have caught world attention.

EMERGING MARKET ECONOMIES: CHINA, INDIA, BRAZIL, AND OTHERS

It is a fact that as more manufacturing and service jobs are shifted to developing countries, because local wages are only a fraction of what is paid in developed countries, workers involved in these sectors still make incomes substantially higher than the local average. Globalization has lifted millions out of poverty and improved the living standard of many in developing countries, including the most populous: China and India.

At its early stage of export, China was the world factory for low-value products, such as clothing, toys, simple tools, and steel. Gradually it moved up the production ladder, starting with the export of high-tech goods, such as machine tools and electronic components and equipment. Within three decades, Shenzhen, located in the Pearl River delta in the south of China, has transformed from a muddy coastal flat to a modern city of over ten million people. It is China's first special economic zone, which used to be home to hundreds of factories producing clothes, shoes, toys, and umbrellas. It is now "the world's largest manufacturer of electronics. It is a place that has dozens of high-tech accelerators (companies that help startups get off the ground), a plethora of hackerspaces, an array of giant, well-stocked electronics malls, over 2,000 design houses, 5,000 product integrators, and tens of thousands of electronics factories. ... *The Economist* called it the best place in the world for a hardware innovator to be" (Shepard 2016). "Every step along the way, from idea to just getting a proof of concept to getting a prototype, to getting manufacturing put together, to getting manufactured is in Shenzhen," said Mitch Altman, the founder of NoiseBridge, one of the first hackerspaces in the United States (quoted in Shepard).

In addition to thriving on software development and call centers, India has also become the world's largest generic drug producer, and its share of the global pharmaceutical and biotech market is rapidly expanding. India's service sector covers a wide range of operations: banking and finance, ecommerce, insurance, health care, and supply chain management. Satyam, an information service provider in Hyderabad, India, used to write computer programs for US companies. Now they have taken over the management of their clients' entire back offices and cut their costs by 70 percent. As mentioned earlier, Indian engineers and scientists in Bangalore are already involved in developing Intel's new processing chips. Bharat Biotech, an Indian pharmaceutical company whose founder received his degrees from the University of Wisconsin–Madison and University of Hawaii–Honolulu, developed a hepatitis B vaccine through a particular technology that makes it affordable for developing countries. The William and Melinda Gates Foundation also sponsored the company to develop a vaccine for malaria, which is one of the most common life threatening diseases in developing countries (Prestowitz 2005).

Although hit hard by the recent slowdown of the world economy, Brazil has become an economic powerhouse in South America, achieving success in many economic sectors, from soybean and other cash-crop cultivation to aircraft manufacturing and providing professional services. Coffee used to account for over half of its exports, but over the past three decades, that share has dropped to 2 percent. Meanwhile, manufactured goods now make up the majority of exports (Prestowitz 2005). According to the Office of the United States Trade Representative, aircraft was the second largest product category of import from Brazil to the United States in 2015, worth US$3 billion, after mineral fuels at US$4.5 billion. Other top categories included iron and steel (US$2.9 billion) and machinery (US$1.7 billion). The United States imported in total US$8.5 billion worth of services from Brazil in 2015, 368 percent greater than in 2005. The leading import services include professional and management services, maintenance and repair, and intellectual property sectors. Brazil's economy is projected to pass that of Germany by 2035 and is on track to be one of the five largest economies in the world, along with the United States, China, India, and the European Union.

Multipolar Globalization

In this era of contemporary globalization, many dynamic changes have affected world economic order and organization. Indeed, as this chapter has shown, the intensification of interconnectedness, whether in economic, political, cultural, or social terms, has permanently altered the way we go about our daily lives. Following the work of the notable development scholar Jan Nederveen Pieterse (2018), we can begin to anticipate a restructuring of the global economy, in which the dominant economic, political, and social relations between the Global North and Global South are receding into a rapidly emerging set of new East Asian–South and South-South constellations. The term used to define this restructuring of the global economic order is **multipolar globalization.** Recent economic trends and political events provide strong evidence for multipolar globalization. Historically, as Pieterse remarks, Asia had long been the dominant economic power in the world, up until the eighteenth century. The nineteenth and twentieth centuries saw the rise of the United States and Western Europe. The pendulum is now swinging back to Asia, notably fueled by the rise of China and India coupled with Japan and the four Asian Tigers (Singapore, Hong Kong, Taiwan, and South Korea).

The major event that signified the waning influence of the contemporary Global North was the 2008 global recession, first felt in the United States and then in Western Europe. A slowdown in export-oriented Asia was also noticeable, as these emerging economies were highly dependent on the Global North for export/import demand. Furthermore, oil producing countries were offset by a drop in the price of a barrel of oil coupled with the growth of oil shale fracking in the United States (Pieterse). In other words, a global recession with varying impacts became evident. One significant consequence was that Global North economies continued to stagnate, as recovery was slow. Despite stimulus efforts in the United States, unemployment rose, aggravating strong anti-immigrant sentiments in both the United States and Europe. The Western faith in free markets, deregulation, and government nonintervention in business have also had the effect of undermining the foundational core ideology of neoliberalism. Political and economic currents in the Global North have shifted to **protectionism**, growing social inequality, and institutional stagnation and deterioration. This outlook was met by Asian countries, especially China and, to a lesser extent, India, who have surged to the center stage of the global economy (Pieterse). China and India, along with Brazil, Russia, and South Africa, are aggressively repositioning their place in the world as emerging economies and global powers, replacing the previous two centuries of political and economic domination by the Global North.

Newly emerging economies, such as BRICS (Brazil, Russia, India, China, and South Africa), have begun to operate by their own rules and institutional formations that diverge from Global North hegemony, such as the Washington Consensus of the 1990s. In this regard, Pieterse anticipates significant global restructuring (199–204) whereby:

- Emerging economies will drive the world's economy; no longer will advanced economies from the Global North dominate global economic activity. Currently and well into the future, China and then India will dominate international trade (Pieterse). These changes mirror US withdrawal from international trade relations such as NAFTA and the failed Trans Pacific Partnership. The US withdrawal allows China and India room to develop regional trade relations and advance investment and domestic-demand-led growth, best evidenced by the unprecedented "One Belt One Road" initiative, which will be discussed in the next section.
- The rise of the Asian middle class has overtaken the Global North middle class, in terms of consumption and driving modern political and social policy reforms so that they serve middle-class interests. In very general terms, the middle class acts as a force for economic modernization and political stability. Generally, but not always, the middle class acts as consumers, modernizers, and prodemocracy and human rights advocates. At its core, however, the middle class fundamentally protects its newly acquired prosperity and, depending on the context, may

not necessarily embrace democracy or human rights. In China, for example, the newly minted urban middle class comprises 75 percent of the membership in the Chinese Communist Party (Pieterse, 163). Emerging economies produce a middle class, but if ruling elites are unaccountable or the number of middle class citizens is small or marginal (e.g., fewer middle class in proportion to the total population), then outcomes may vary tremendously in political choices and affiliation.

- East-South and South-South trade, investment, and loans are ignoring and/or bypassing Global North financial institutions, such as the World Bank and the IMF, through creation of new international and regional institutions such as the Asian Infrastructure and Investment Bank (China). The failure of the Trans Pacific Partnership allowed China in particular to establish trade relations and closer ties to other Asian and Latin American countries (Pieterse). The lynchpin in these new international relations is the "One Belt One Road" initiative by China, discussed in the next section. In broad terms:

> The rise of non-western economies is a deeply rooted historic shift that can survive any number of economic and political shocks. ... today's turmoil will not change the fact that emerging markets will grow faster than the developed world for decades to come. ... The rise of emerging economies during the past forty years has been propelled by lower labor costs, rising productivity, huge improvements in the communications and transport that connect them [China, India] to global markets. (Rachman 2014, quoted in Pieterse 2018, 200–201).

Along with these new institutional ties are political ones that promote stabilization in the region. That is not to say that Asia is without any serious social problems, such as environmental degradation, inequality, and human rights issues, but the economic foundation has been established to allow the dominance of Asia over a stagnant Global North as the driver of the world economy.

Despite the restructuring of the world economy, significant disparities are likely to remain entrenched throughout the world. Pieterse anticipates the following multipolar trends (199):

- Wages will remain depressed, and with a surfeit of workers available, corporations will continue sourcing the lowest cost labor possible. As mentioned earlier in this chapter, when the wage rate rose in China, corporations looked elsewhere in South-East Asia to source lower cost labor. The condition of low wages does not stimulate domestic purchasing power, hence economic development results in the middle-income trap (discussed in chapter 4).
- Migration, whether brought on by conflict, persecution, or the search for new economic opportunities, accentuates inequality, perhaps the most salient global problem of the twenty-first century. In addition, migration fuels populist

resentment, as evidenced in countries such as the United States and Great Britain. As the Global North closes borders, immigration bans, deportation, and surveillance of immigrant populations increase. Human trafficking and slave labor is existent in 167 countries as diverse as Cambodia, Haiti, India, Mauritania, Pakistan, Thailand, and the United States, among others. Upwards of 45 million people are estimated to be enslaved at present. The ethnic cleansing of an estimated 650,000 Rohingya Muslims from Myanmar is grounded on the assertion by the Buddhist Myanmar military government that they are "illegal immigrants," despite a centuries-old residence in the Rakhine state of western Myanmar. Caught between Pakistan and Myanmar, the unfolding Rohingya refugee crisis has led to widespread human rights violations.

- Globally, US hegemony is in decline, as are its various institutions on an international level. In the vacuum created by US withdrawal from the international stage, as implied in earlier sections of this chapter, China, and to a lesser extent, India are repositioning themselves as world economic powers. The next two sections provide a most compelling depiction of how this is so.

New Silk Roads

Figure 6.3 below displays a map of the most ambitious economic development project effort ever attempted, the **"One Belt One Road"** (**OBOR**) initiative announced by the Chinese government in 2013. OBOR is a massive US$1 trillion infrastructure plan that will link China via road, rail, and seaport to South-East Asia, Central and West Asia, and beyond, to points in Europe, Russia, West Africa, and the Persian Gulf (Osnos 2018; Pieterse 2018). OBOR investment is seven times greater than that

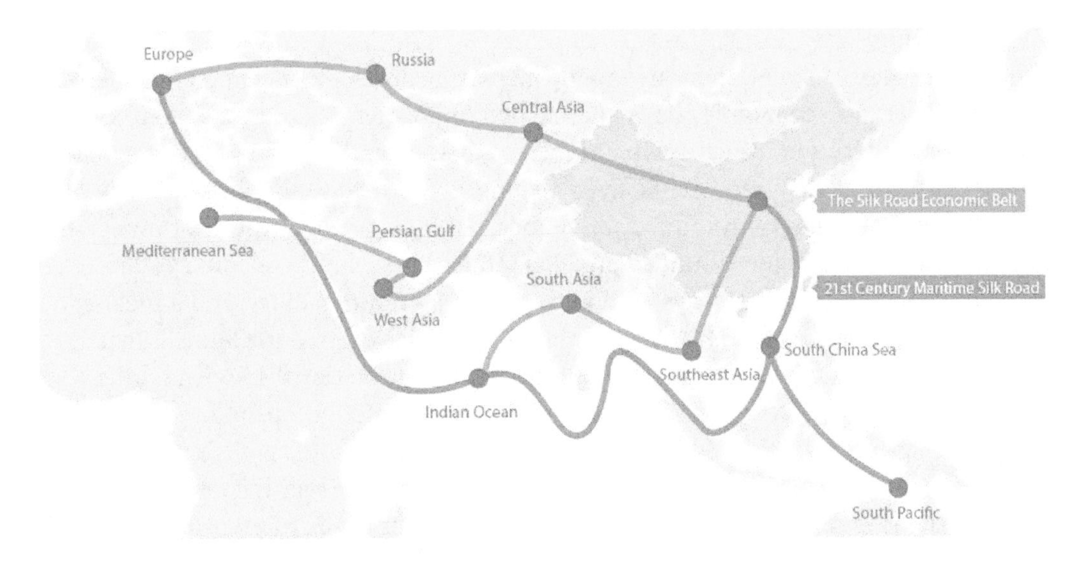

FIGURE 6.3 China's "One Belt One Road" Initiative

of the US-funded Marshall Plan for the reconstruction of Europe after the Second World War. The scale and scope of OBOR is unprecedented. Consider the following scenario, taken from the landlocked country of Laos:

> As the sun beat down on Chinese workers driving bulldozers, four huge tractor-trailers rolled into a storage area here in Vang Vieng [Laos], a difficult three hour drive over potholed roads from the capital, Vientiane. They each carried massive coils of steel wire. Half a mile away, a Chinese mixing plant with four bays glistened in the sun. Nearby, along a newly laid road, another Chinese factory was providing cement for tunnel construction. Nearly everything for the Laos project is made in China. At the peak of construction, there will be an estimated 100,000 Chinese workers. (Perlez and Huang 2017)

However, China confronts innumerable obstacles in this project, and OBOR faces numerous risks in the execution of several of its initiatives. For example, rail and road construction in South-East Asia pass through a number of long-contested territories in Myanmar, Thailand, and Laos. The upgrade of the rail system in Kenya falls under the aegis of a corrupt Kenyan authority. In the area of information technology, it must be pointed out that China is a nondemocratic, authoritarian state where privacy, fairness, and censorship are not citizen entitlements. Currently, China bans 11 of the most popular global websites, including Facebook, YouTube, Google, and Wikipedia, under cyber security policies. China has invested US$150 billion in developing artificial intelligence, whereas the US government spent US$1.2 billion over the same time period (Osnos 2018, 42–43). To what purposes this technology will be put to use poses a number of concerns for Chinese citizens and the rest of the world.

China in Africa

China and, to a lesser extent, India are rapidly increasing developmental activity in Africa. These two emerging economies have encroached on former US and European spheres of economic activity and influence. In Zambia, for instance, the world's largest uranium mine, the Husab facility, represents an investment of US$4.6 billion and is owned by China General Nuclear, with the Zambian government sharing 10-percent ownership (Larmer 2017). Other Chinese-funded projects in Zambia include a telemetry station, an artificial peninsula, new highways, a shopping mall, a granite factory, and a fuel depot. Uranium, timber, and, some say, endangered wildlife are exported to China (Larmer).

Zambia and the rest of Africa have had a long-term relationship with China that goes back to the Cold War years, when Chairman Mao Zedong promoted solidarity with the recently established African nations. At present, Zambia envisions that these investments, which are skewed to China's advantage, will raise national GDP by 5 percent from the Husab facility alone (Larmer). Uranium lies at the foundation of China's move to nuclear power and reducing its carbon emissions. The pace of nuclear power plant development in China will make it the world's top nuclear power, with plans for 110 reactors by 2030 (Larmer). Not all Zambians are thrilled, however, with the influx of Chinese workers and associated entrepreneurs who service the industrial and construction projects. In particular, the poaching of endangered wildlife that seems to "always end up in Chinese hands" has been a matter of conflict between Chinese firms and Zambian conservationists (Larmer). With the presence of between 10,000 and 100,000 Chinese nationals (the figures are disputed) in the country, it looks like Chinese presence in Zambia and the rest of Africa will continue, given the economic opportunities for Chinese workers to earn ten times their salary by working abroad.

Figure 6.4 illustrates Chinese investments in Africa since 2010. The figure shows that over half of these investments apply to securing energy sources. In these

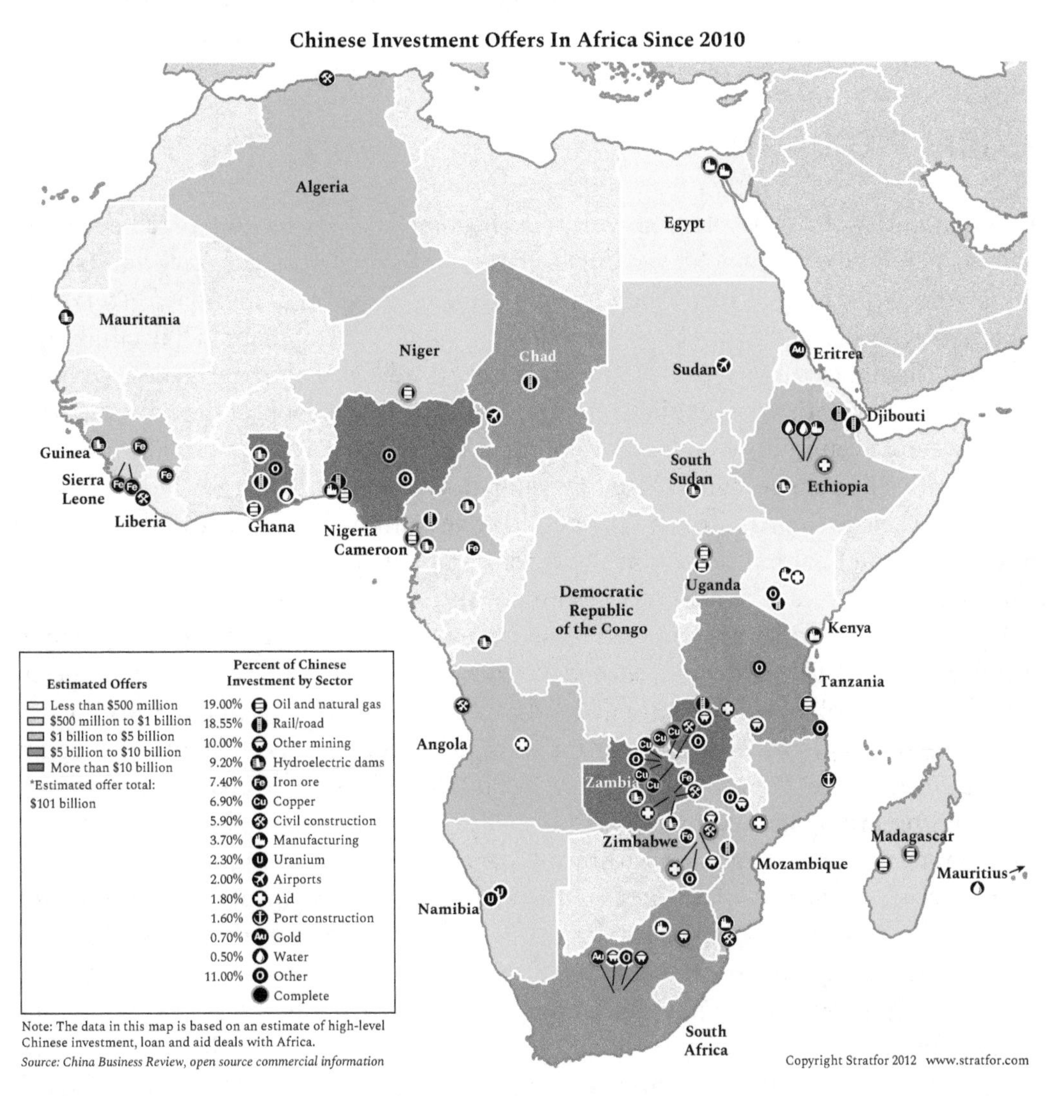

FIGURE 6.4 China's Investments in Africa

investment ventures, the Chinese government offers soft loans with few conditions, a "win-win" scenario, as pitched to African countries. Workers and materials are supplied almost exclusively by China. In this manner, China's foreign direct investment is expected to stimulate domestic demand as incomes rise through its growing and favorable trade relations with African nations. This opportunity for economic growth in Africa may hold some potential for increasing economic growth on the continent. At the same time, critics are skeptical and posit that the renewed interest China has taken in the continent is simply another form of Chinese imperialism. Nonetheless, China will soon lead the world in trade with Africa. The outcome of this long-term effort remains nebulous, however, in the restructured, multipolar, globalized world. China's new international status is expected to influence world economic organization in the immediate and distant future.

GLOBAL INEQUALITY

As the majority of the developing world has become part of the globalized economy and has made significant achievements in developing economic capacity and raising living standards, progress has been uneven across regions and countries. To Jeffery Sachs, an economist at Columbia University, economic development is like climbing a ladder, with higher rungs representing more advanced levels of material development and well-being. On this planet, there are roughly one billion people at the bottom, those who have not even set foot on the development ladder yet (Sachs 2005). These people are virtually all in the so-called **Least Developed Countries**, as introduced in chapter 1. Most of them are in Africa and Asia and have very limited income, simple means of production, and health problems and malnourishment. Their average income is only a quarter of the average of other developing countries, and the gap keeps widening.

While such disparities are relatively easier to make into media headlines, they tend to disguise a bigger and brighter picture of developing countries as a whole. Steven Radelet, an influential scholar in global human development, claimed (2015) that in the past two decades—contrary to widespread false images of pervasive poverty and famine, rampant disease and violence, extensive corruption, and failure—developing countries witnessed sweeping progress, marked by reduced poverty, growing income, better health outcomes, and less conflict and war within and between the developing countries.

In line with what we claim in this book, Radelet (2015) argued that the major progress for most developing countries did not occur until the early 1990s, although it started to emerge in a pocket of countries as early as the 1960s. In his analysis of 109 developing countries, which have complete data with populations over one million, he found that while there were previously only around 20 developing countries that registered moderate economic growth, the number has quickly expanded to 70 since the mid-1990s. One of the major drivers behind such a surge is globalization and the profound changes that go with it. The end of the Cold War removed geopolitical barriers for developing countries to participate in the global economy. Global supply chains have created millions of jobs in developing countries. The spread of new technologies, such as communication and the internet, provides opportunities for millions of talented young people to engage in modern sectors of the world economy. As investment, technologies, and information flow to developing countries, these countries' productivity goes up, and exports have increased five times over that of two decades ago (Radelet).

Michalopoulos and Ng (2013) showed a three-tier integration of developing countries into the global economy, in which some countries in East and South-East Asia, such as China, participated first, in the 1980s, and were followed by many other developing countries in all other regions, such as India, in the 1990s, then eventually joined by the least developed countries, which have shown an increase in their share of total world trade since 2000. The developing world as a whole saw its total merchandise exports balloon more than ten times, from about US$600 billion in 1980 to over US$6 trillion in 2010.

Such economic integration brings great benefits to people in the developing world. The number of people in extreme poverty (living on less than US$1.25 per day, as classified by the World Bank) fell from two billion in 1993 to just over one billion in 2011. There are more people in the developing world gaining access to clean water, sanitation, and electricity. The number of children in developing countries who receive vaccines increased tenfold, from 20 million in 1980 to 200 million in 2012, and the number of children who die from preventable causes, such as disease, war, and violence, has been cut from 13 million in 1990 to a little over six million by 2013. Meanwhile, life expectancy in the developing world has increased by six years (Radelet 2015).

Although there are still millions of people left behind and haunted by grave poverty and stagnation in some parts of the world, the majority of developing countries and the people living in them are on the path to progress and prosperity. There is no question that China and India, the two most populous countries in the world, play a critical role in reducing the percentage of population living in poverty in the developing world. China's portion of the population living in extreme poverty fell from 838 million in 1981, when it started to launch its economic reform, to 646 million by 1993 and declined further to 84 million by 2011. Its percentage dropped from 84 percent to 55 percent and 6 percent, respectively. India's number of people in extreme poverty decreased from 476 million in 2002 to 300 million in 2011. The decline in extreme poverty is also widespread, not only limited to these two giant countries. Impressive progress has been witnessed in Thailand, Indonesia, and Vietnam in South-East Asia; Brazil, Ecuador, and Guatemala in Latin America; and Bangladesh, Nepal, and Pakistan in South Asia. Even in Sub-Saharan Africa, the percentage of people living in extreme poverty decreased from 59 percent in 1999 to 47 percent in 2011 (Radelet).

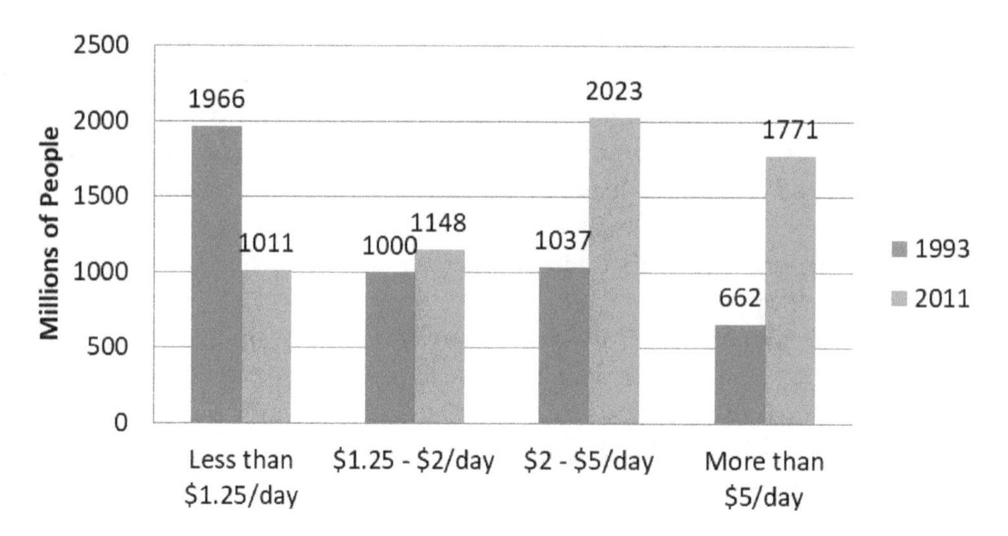

FIGURE 6.5 Distribution of the Number of People in Developing Countries in Consumption Brackets

This is a direct result of higher economic growth in more and more developing countries. While there were only 21 developing countries growing faster than 2 percent per year in GDP per capita between 1977 and 1994, such growth was achieved in 71 developing countries between 1995 and 2013, 17 of which were in Sub-Saharan Africa, such as Botswana, Ethiopia, and Uganda, and 30 of the 71 countries exceeded 4 percent per year (Radelet).

The following two charts, based on the Radelet's calculation from the World Bank database, show the shift in fortunes in developing countries between 1993 and 2011. Figure 6.5 shows the distribution of the number of people in developing countries in each consumption bracket. There was a clear leap in the two highest brackets: there were more than 1.7 billion people in developing countries living on more than US$5 per day in 2011, and more than 2 billion living on between US$2 and US$5 per day. Figure 6.6 clearly shows the shift of the share of each bracket during the same period of time. While in 1993 the majority of those living in developing countries, three out of six, were living on less than US$2 per day, the opposite was true in 2011, where three out of six were living on more than US$2 per day.

Between-Country Gap Narrowed

Since the 1990s, many developing countries' economies have grown faster than that of developed countries. Based on data from the World Bank, Radelet (2015) estimated that GDP per capita in all developing countries grew on average more than 70 percent between 1995 and 2013. During the recent global financial crisis, most developed countries registered negative economic growth in 2009, while developing countries' GDP grew by more than 3 percent in the same year. Because of the

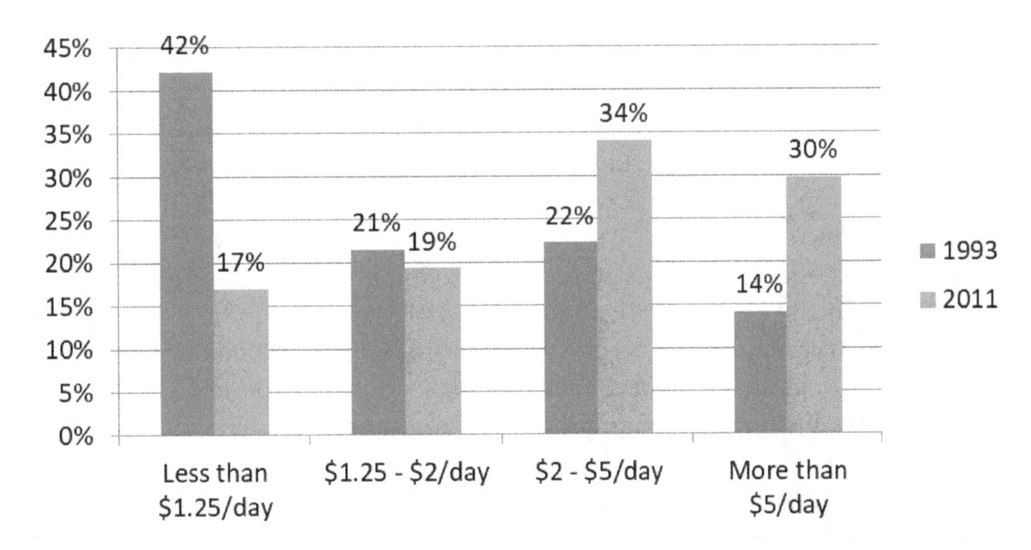

FIGURE 6.6 Percentage Distribution of People in Developing Countries in Consumption Brackets by Year

faster growth of developing countries, the income gap between the developing and developed countries has been narrowing in the past two decades. Radelet showed a convincing comparison: "In 1994 the average income in the world's 20 richest countries was more than eight times larger than the average in 109 developing countries; by 2011, the ratio had closed to around six" (71).

Bangladesh provides a key example of economic growth through its participation in the garment industry. Although there have been well-publicized anecdotes about hazardous sweatshop conditions and fire accidents in some garment factories' dorms that killed scores of local employees, Heath and Mobarak (2014) claimed that "the garment industry has likely played a key role in the remarkable progress Bangladesh has made in improving women's lives over the past 40 years." (27) The garment industry accounts for over 75 percent of the export earnings of Bangladesh, one of the low income countries of the world. The industry currently employs almost four million workers in Bangladesh, about 80 percent of whom are women, who have traditionally stayed at home. Since the work requires a certain level of literacy and numeracy, the garment industry lifts the education enrollment of girls. Heath and Mobarak found that garment workers have had more education, on average, than non-garment workers. The manufacturing growth also brings other changes for young women, such as a reduction in early marriage and declining fertility. The average number of births per woman has dropped from 5.9 in 1983 to 2.3 in 2009.

Within-Country Inequality: A Mixed Bag

In contrast, discussion on inequality often tends to be focused on that within a particular country. In many cases, the growing gulf between rich and poor tends to capture the public's attention, and it tends to be linked with globalization. This kind of perception is more evident in developed countries, in which the working and middle classes have suffered from income stagnation and relative decline since the late 1970s (Piketty 2014). As mentioned earlier in this chapter, globalization is more positively received in developing countries than in developed countries (Coy 2016).

Pieterse (2018) argues that with the rise of China and India, *global* inequality has decreased, but inequality *within* the advanced economies and emerging economies is increasing. Of the 75 developing countries with information on inequality that Radelet (2015) studied, inequality has deteriorated in less than a quarter of them. However, even in countries where inequality gets wider, such as China, incomes of the poor have been growing, and more and more people have escaped absolute poverty.

Robust statistical measures known as **Gini coefficients** are used by governments and multilateral aid agencies to assess a country's social inequality. Table 6.3 below quantifies the top ten countries in terms of inequality.

Other countries, such as the United States (ranked 39), China (52), Russia (51), Thailand (13), Rwanda (32), and Mexico (17) also exhibit high internal social inequality, but the Latin American region has the highest unequal distributions. In Brazil, the top 10 percent of the population accounts for 42 percent of the national income. In countries such as the United States, market fundamentalism has taken its toll in

TABLE 6.3 *Top Ten Countries with the Highest Level of Inequality*

COUNTRY	REGION	RANK	GNI PPP PER CAPITA	HDI WORLD RANK
NAMIBIA	Sub-Saharan Africa	1	$9,418	126
SOUTH AFRICA	Sub-Saharan Africa	2	$12,122	116
LESOTHO	Sub-Saharan Africa	3	$3,306	161
BOTSWANA	Sub-Saharan Africa	4	$16,646	106
SIERRA LEONE	Sub-Saharan Africa	5	$1,780	181
CENTRAL AFRICAN REPUBLIC	Sub-Saharan Africa	6	$581	187
HAITI	Caribbean	7	$1,669	163
COLOMBIA	Latin America	8	$12,040	97
BOLIVIA	Latin America	9	$5,760	119
HONDURAS	Latin America	10	$3,938	131

Data source: UN Development Program 2015; Lincoln 2011.

terms of unemployment, stagnant wages, outrageous CEO salaries, immigrant backlash, and the decline of bargaining power on the part of US workers (Pieterse 2018).

China's inequality gap lies between the urban and rural regions of the country, while the United States exhibits an inequality poverty profile similar to Romania (Pieterse, 88–89). Latin America as a region has some of the highest inequality ratios in the world. In many African countries, most notably South Africa, inequality ratios are extremely high, with a number of countries, such as Angola, exhibiting growing and polarizing patterns. The Middle East ranges from a low level on inequality in Yemen and Afghanistan, among the poorest countries, to a high level of inequality as is evident in Qatar. In the United Arab Emirates, a divide between citizens and migrant workers is very pronounced, with workers experiencing difficult work conditions, no organized labor power, and no citizenship rights.

In looking at the causes for increasing inequality within countries, Pieterse remarks, "Weak governance and weak institutions enable elite capture, which generates patches of wealth while leaving the economy as a whole behind and the majority in poverty" (94). Countries heavily reliant on mining and fossil fuels are particularly vulnerable. Strong, forward-looking institutions have been identified as the most important factor in fostering development (Pieterse). Underlying factors that weaken institutions are traceable to earlier feudal and colonial legacies that result in chronic intractable conditions of underdevelopment. In Latin America, South-East Asia, Pakistan, and the Philippines, politically elite families block equitable distribution of land and access to other resources, allowing for disproportionate accumulation of capital. New windfall wealth is then deployed into other economic ventures, thereby increasing monopolistic control and expansion of family wealth portfolios. Autocratic and often military governments inhibit any democratic impulse or representative civilian government. Thailand, Myanmar, the Philippines, and Cambodia are all currently run by either autocrats or the military. Cambodia, for example, has banned any major opposition political party. The Cambodian People's Party (CPP), run by former Khmer Rouge defector and one of the world's longest reigning prime ministers, Hun Sen, governs the country on a patron-client system, in which quid pro quo arrangements allow for the concentration of wealth and power within a ruling clique of business, government, and military officials (Brinkley 2011; Pieterse 2018; Strangio 2014).

Market fundamentalism, coupled with technological advancement, allows the vested elite numerous priority opportunities to create new wealth. As new production forces, such as telecommunications, emerge and become dominant, long-standing social relations will necessarily change. Some actors will be cast aside, while other actors have and will ascend into the ranks of global billionaires. Carlos Slim from Mexico and exiled former prime minister of Thailand Thaksin Shinawatra made fortunes by monopolizing new telecommunications technologies (Pieterse 2018).

CONCLUSION

Globalization, and its restructuring into multipolar globalization, can be characterized as a bricolage—a construction made up of many diverse moving parts, some complementary and others antagonistic, and whatever else is at hand. In this chapter, we have detailed the recent globalization era, its historical context, and its defining features. We defined the theory of comparative advantage, which serves as an overall modus operandi. We showed that some consequences of globalization, such as automation, shed further light on the rise of China, India, Brazil, and other emerging market economies. Finally, we suggested that a significant restructuring of the world economy, defined as multipolar globalization, is fast taking shape. Led by China, we presented the OBOR initiative, which envisions the world economy being centered in Asia, not the traditional Global North. We concluded the chapter with a brief discussion on global inequality, pointing out the different dynamics between and within countries.

REFERENCES

Barber, Benjamin R. *Jihad vs. McWorld: How Globalism and Tribalism Are Reshaping the World.* New York: Ballantine Books, 1995.

Barnett, Thomas, P. M. *The Pentagon's New Map: War and Peace in the Twenty-First Century.* New York: G. P. Putnam's Sons, 2004.

Bell, David, and Mary L. Shelman. "KFC's Radical Approach to China." *Harvard Business Review.* November 2011.

Blair, Tony. "Faith and Globalization." ABS-CBN News, July 01, 2008. https://news.abs-cbn.com/views-and-analysis/07/01/08/faith-and-globalization%E2%80%94tony-blair

Brinkley, Joel. *Cambodia's Curse: The Modern History of a Troubled Land.* New York: Public Affairs, 2011.

Bureau of Labor Statistics. Spotlight on Statistics: Fashion. June 2012. https://www.bls.gov/spotlight/2012/fashion/

Case, Steve. "The Next Wave in the Internet's Evolution." *Wall Street Journal*, April 4, 2016.

Clifford, Stephanie. "U.S. Textile Plants Return, With Floors Largely Empty of People." *New York Times.* September 19, 2013.

Congressional Research Service. "Corporate Expatriation, Inversions, and Mergers: Tax Issues." March, 2019. https://fas.org/sgp/crs/misc/R43568.pdf

Coy, Peter. "An Inconvenient Truth about Free Trade." *Bloomberg Businessweek.* April 4, 2016.

Cruvellier, Thierry. *The Master of Confessions: The Making of a Khmer Rouge Torturer.* New York: HarperCollins, 2014.

Doz, Yves L., Jose Santos, and Peter Williamson. *From Global to Metanational: How Companies Win in the Knowledge Economy.* Boston: Harvard Business Review Press, 2001.

Eitzen, D. Stanley, and Maxine Baca Zinn. "Globalization: An Introduction." In *Globalization: The Transformation of Social Worlds*, edited by D. Stanley Eitzen and Maxine Baca Zinn, 1–9. 2nd ed, Belmont, CA: Wadsworth Cengage Learning, 2009.

Friedman, Thomas L. *The World Is Flat.* New York: Picador, 2007.

Fukuyama, Francis. "The End of History?" *The National Interest.* Number 16, 1-18, Summer 1989.

Funk, John. "Eaton to Close Berea Plant, Lay Off 102, Outsource Jobs." *Plain Dealer*. February, 18, 2016.

Grant, James. "The United States of Insolvency." *Time*. April 25, 2016.

Heath, Rachel A., and Mushfiq Mobarak. "Manufacturing Growth and the Lives of Bangladeshi Women." *NBER Working Paper Series*. Cambridge, MA: Bureau Of Economic Research, 2014. http://www.nber.org/papers/w20383.

Hohenhaus, Peter. "Dark Tourism." http://www.dark-tourism.com/.

Khanna, Parag. "Corporations are More Powerful than Countries." Pittsburgh Post-Gazette. March 27, 2016.

Koons, Cynthia, and Michelle Cortez. "Pfizer and Allergan to Combine With Joint Value of $160 Billion." Bloomberg Businessweek, November 22, 2015.

Korn, Melissa. "Local Schools Rush Abroad." *Wall Street Journal*. April 12, 2016.

Larmer, Brook. "The Expansionists." *New York Times Magazine*. May 7, 2017.

Levine, Ruth. "Millions Saved: Proven Successes in Global Health." *CGD Brief* 3, no. 3 (2004): 1–7.

Levinson, Marc. *The Box: How the Shipping Container Made the World Smaller and the World Economy Bigger*. Princeton, NJ: Princeton University Press, 2008.

Lincoln, Kevin. "The 39 Most Unequal Countries in the World." *Business Insider*. October 6, 2011. https://www.businessinsider.com/most-unequal-countries-in-the-world-2011-10.

Mackintosh, James. "15,000 Layoffs? China's Bust Is the West's Suffering." *Wall Street Journal*. March 31, 2016.

MacMillan, Douglas. "Didi Kuaidi App Can Now Hail a Lyft Car in the U.S." *Wall Street Journal*. April, 12, 2016.

Mauldin, William. "IMF Warns of Emerging Market Risk to U.S. Stock Markets." *Wall Street Journal*. April 5, 2016.

Michalopoulos, Constantine, and Francis Ng. "Trends in Developing Country Trade 1980–2010." World Bank Policy Research Working Paper No. 6334. 2013. Available at SSRN: https://ssrn.com/abstract=2206182.

Miller, John W. "U.S. Coal Sector Faces Reckoning." *Wall Street Journal*. March 16, 2016.

Millington, Alison. "The 10 Most Visited Cities Around the World in 2016." *Independent*. December 20, 2016. http://www.independent.co.uk/travel/the-10-most-visited-cities-around-the-world-in-2016-a7487791.html.

Mims, Christopher. "For Generation Z, Email Has Become a Rite of Passage." *Wall Street Journal*. April 11, 2016.

Morris, Phillip. "Technology Will March On – and Over Those Who Can't Adapt." *The Plain Dealer*. April 24, 2016.

O'Reilly, Joseph. "On the Road: Midnight in Memphis." *Inbound Logistics*, January 15, 2011. https://www.inboundlogistics.com/cms/article/on-the-road-midnight-in-memphis/

Organization for Economic Cooperation and Development (OECD). "How Is the Global Talent Pool Changing?" *Education Indicators in Focus*. May 2012.

Osnos, Evan. "Making China Great Again." *The New Yorker*, 36–45. January 8, 2018.

Pantelescu, Andreea Marin. "Trends in International Tourism." *Cactus Tourism Journal* 3, no. 2 (2012): 231–35.

Patterson, Robert W. "'What's Good for America …'" *National Review*. July 1, 2013.

Perlez, Jane, and Yufan Huang. "Remaking Global Trade in China's Image." *New York Times*, May 14, 2017.

Pieterse, Jan Nederveen. *Multipolar Globalization: Emerging Economies and Development*. New York: Routledge, 2018.

Piketty, Thomas. *Capital in the Twenty-First Century*. Cambridge, MA: Harvard University Press, 2014.

Potter, Robert B., Tony Binns, Jennifer A. Elliott, and David Smith. *Geographies of Development: An Introduction to Development Studies*. 3rd ed. New York: Routledge, 2013.

Prestowitz, Clyde. *Three Billion New Capitalists: The Great Shift of Wealth and Power to the East.* New York: Basic Books, 2005.

Radelet, Steven. *The Great Surge: The Ascent of the Developing World.* New York: Simon & Schuster, 2015.

Ritzer, George. *Globalization: A Basic Text.* Malden, MA: Wiley-Blackwell, 2010.

Sachs, Jeffrey D. *The End of Poverty: Economic Possibilities for Our Time.* New York: Penguin Books, 2005.

Schech, Susanne, and Jane Haggis. *Culture and Development: A Critical Introduction.* Oxford: Blackwell, 2000.

Shepard, Wade. "Why The West's High-Tech Innovators Manufacture Their Dreams In China." *Forbes.* March 15, 2016.

Silverstein, Michael J., Abheek Singhi, Carol Liao, and David Michael. *The $10 Trillion Prize: Captivating the Newly Affluent in China and India.* Boston: Harvard Business Review Press, 2012.

Smith, Keri E. Iyall. "Globalizing Cultures." In *Sociology of Globalization*, edited by Keri E. Iyall Smith, 29–37. Philadelphia: Westview Press, 2013.

Smith, Robert L. "Cleveland's Economy May Get a Boost as International Students Flock to CWRU." *Plain Dealer.* September 7, 2013.

Staley, Eugene. "The Role of the State in Economic Development." In Myron Weiner (ed.), *Modernization: The Dynamics of Growth*, P294-306. New York: Basic Books, 1966.

Stank, Ted, Mike Burnette, and Paul Dittmann. *Global Supply Chains.* Game-Changers Series of University of Tennessee Supply Chain Management White Papers, 2014.

Statista. "International Tourist Arrivals Worldwide from 1995 to 2017, by Region (in Millions)." Travel, Tourism, and Hospitality. August 2018. https://www.statista.com/statistics/209349/forecast-number-of-international-tourist-arrivals-worldwide-by-region/.

Steger, Manfred B. *Globalization: The New Market Ideology.* Lanham, MD: Rowman & Littlefield, 2002.

Steger, Manfred B. "Global Culture: Sameness or Difference?" In *Globalization: The Transformation of Social Worlds*, edited by D. Stanley Eitzen and Maxine Baca Zinn, 147–50. 2nd ed. Belmont, CA: Wadsworth Cengage Learning, 2009.

Strangio, Sebastian. *Hun Sen's Cambodia.* New Haven, CT: Yale University Press, 2014.

The Economist. "The Humble Here." May 18, 2013. *The Economist.* "A Tightening Grip: The Future of Factory Asia." March 12, 2015a.

The Economist. "Made in China? Global Manufacturing." March 12, 2015b.

The Economist. "Cyber-boom or cyber-bubble?" August 1, 2015.

UN Development Program. "Statistical Annex." *Human Development Report 2015.* New York: United Nations, 2015. http://hdr.undp.org/sites/default/files/hdr_2015_statistical_annex.pdf.

United Nations. *The Millennium Development Goals Report 2015.* New York: United Nations, 2015.

Williams, Jeremy. "The Corporations Bigger than Nations." *The Earthbound Report.* February 3, 2014. https://makewealthhistory.org/2014/02/03/the-corporations-bigger-than-nations/.

World Shipping Council. "History of Containerization". May 31, 2019. http://www.worldshipping.org/about-the-industry/history-of-containerization

Wright, Bryan Dean. "Robots Are Coming for Your Job." *Los Angeles Times.* April 3, 2016.

Yu, Rose. "General Motors Gears Up in China Amid Shifting Demand." *Wall Street Journal*, March 21, 2016.

Figure Credits

Fig. 6.3: Source: http://w.chinagoabroad.com/en/knowledge/onebeltoneroad.

Fig. 6.4: Source: http://www.chinaafricarealstory.com/2016/02/chinese-mining-projects-in-africa-is-it.html.

CHAPTER SEVEN

Global Population Divide

INTRODUCTION

There is a divide between the developing and developed worlds in population, not only in size but in growth potential and age structure, as well. These different population profiles underscore different challenges faced by societies in the demand for social services, including public education, health care, labor force, and employment opportunities. In this chapter, we provide a brief description of the world population; its geographic distribution, history, and major transitions; and the prospect for growth in the future. We also introduce some basic concepts in demographic studies. Readers should bear in mind that the word "divide" is a simplification of the contrast between the developing and developed world. In reality, as discussed on other subjects in this book, the gap is not as clear-cut as it appears.

CURRENT POPULATION DIVIDE

The world population stood at 7.6 billion in 2018 (PRB 2018). Of the top five most populous countries—China (1.39 billion), India (1.37 billion), the United States (328 million), Indonesia (265 million), and Brazil (209 million)—four of them are developing countries, with the United States as the only exception. Worldwide, over six billion people live in the developing world, which accounts for five-sixths of the world population. Only 1.3 billion, or one-sixth of the world population, live in developed countries.

The map in Figure 7.1 shows the distribution of world population by country, proportional to the size of its population rather than the geographic territory. By this criterion, two stand out, China and India, the most populous countries on the planet. It is evident that most of the global population

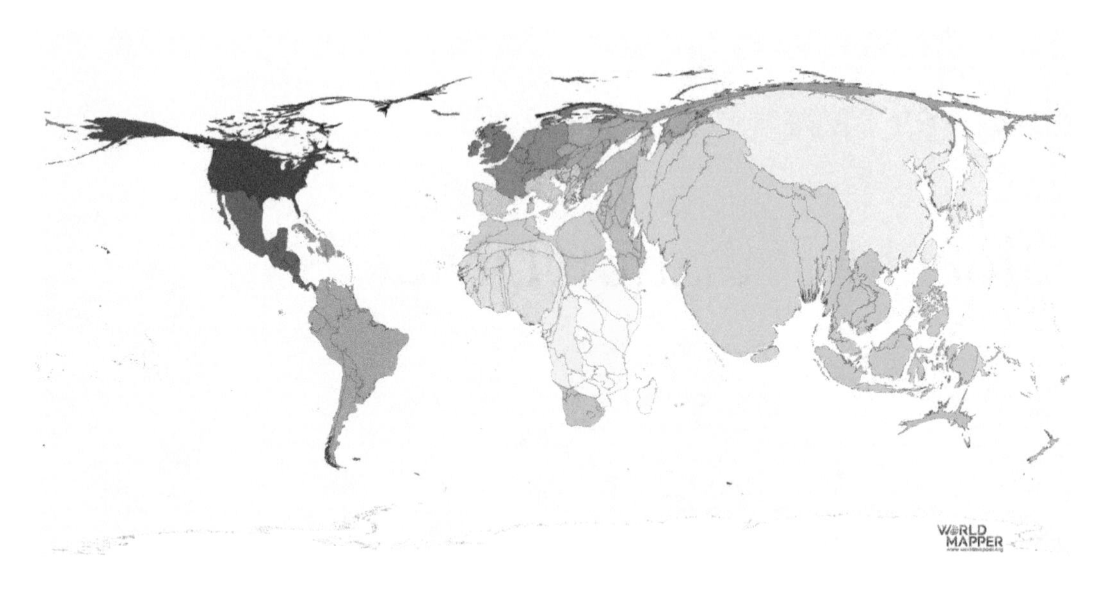

FIGURE 7.1 World Population Cartogram, 2018

resides in Asia (4.54 billion in 2018) and Africa (1.28 billion), followed by Europe (746 million). The rest of the developed world lives mainly in North America (357 million) (see Table 7.1).

Since most of the countries fall in the category of developing countries, it is not surprising to find that this is where the majority of the world population is. But the world population divide is more than merely the difference in population size. There are substantial differences in the pace of population growth, the age structure, and the population's overall well-being.

TABLE 7.1 ***World Population Distribution by Continent, 2018***

CONTINENT	POPULATION (IN MILLIONS)	% OF WORLD POPULATION
AFRICA	1,284	17%
ASIA	4,536	60%
EUROPE	746	10%
LATIN AMERICA AND CARIBBEAN	649	9%
NORTH AMERICA	365	5%
OCEANIA	41	<1%
TOTAL	7,621	100%

Data source: PRB 2018.

The Pace of Population Growth

Not only do developing countries have the largest share of the world's population, but their populations are also on a faster track of growth overall. Figure 7.2 shows discrepancies in the population growth rate worldwide. Europe, especially Eastern Europe, including Russia, has the lowest population growth rate, either no growth or decline. North America, Western Europe, and China are at the next lowest level, under 1 percent per year. Latin America and most other Asian countries are in the middle group, between 1 percent and 2 percent per year. Africa is the fastest growing continent, with many countries growing at 2 percent or more. In summary, it is fair to say that while the populations in the developed world either crawl at a minimal rate or have started stepping backward, the populations in many developing countries still witness substantial growth, and the gap between these two worlds will only continue to grow (we will discuss more below about future trends).

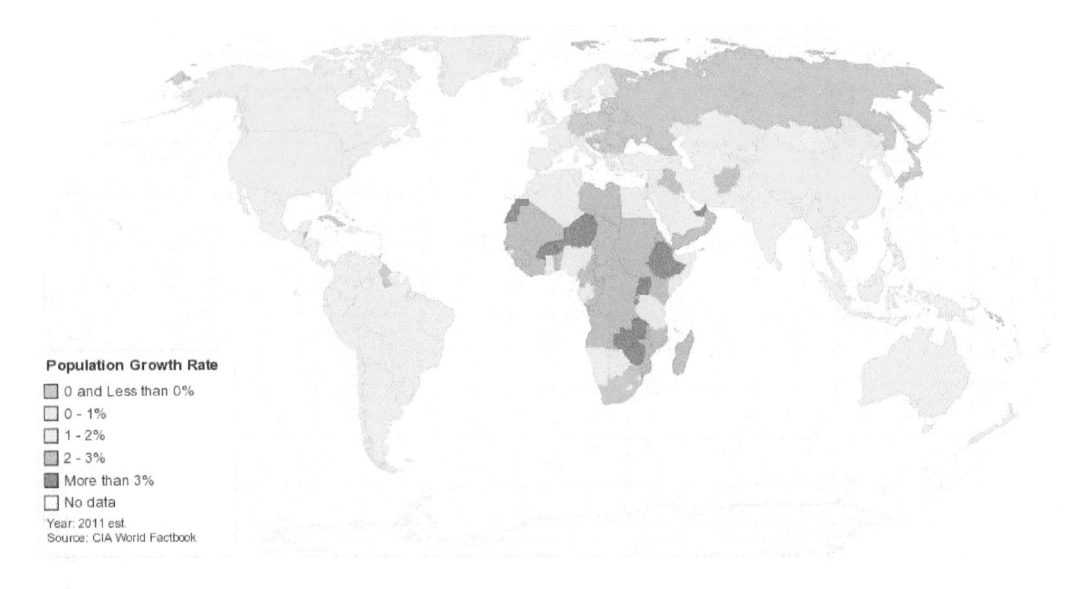

FIGURE 7.2 Population Growth Rate Worldwide

BOX 7.1 WHAT IS THE POPULATION GROWTH RATE?

The concept of growth rate applies to many arenas in both research and everyday lives. It refers to how fast an object increases or decreases (i.e., negative growth) over a specific time period, such as a year. It can be the growth rate of a country's GDP; the growth of one's bank savings, which is the interest rate; or the growth of prices of commodities on a year-to-year base, which is the rate of inflation. The growth rate is calculated by dividing the amount of growth, or change, either positive or negative, by the amount at the baseline (usually the amount from the previous year). When it comes to the population growth rate, it can be expressed in the following formula:

$$r = \frac{(\text{population in year } t+1) - (\text{population in year } t)}{\text{population in year } t} \times 100\%$$

Where *r* is the growth rate, the numerator is the difference in population size between year *t* and *t + 1* (*t* can be any integer). When *t* takes the value of 2013, *t + 1* will be 2014. The formula becomes

$$r = \frac{(\text{population in year 2014}) - (\text{population in year 2013})}{\text{population in year 2013}} \times 100\%$$

Here, we are calculating the population growth rate from 2013 to 2014. In practice, since the number of people varies even within each year, the population at midyear is usually adopted in the calculation. In the United States, for example, the midyear population was 316.2 million in 2013 and 317.7 million in 2014 (PRB 2014, 2013a). Therefore, the population growth rate for the United States from 2013 to 2014 will be:

$$r = \frac{317.7\text{m} - 316.2\text{m}}{316.2\text{m}} \times 100\% = 0.47\%$$

During the same period, Mexico's population grew from 117.6 million to 119.7 million. Can you calculate the growth rate for Mexico?

Age Structure and Population Pyramid

Different paces of population growth result in different shapes of population **age structure**, which is how a population is distributed across all age groups. The age structure is best illustrated by a **population pyramid**, a commonly applied graphic tool. It is composed of a series of horizontal bars that represent either the absolute volume or relative share of each age group of the entire population, from the youngest to the oldest group. A lot can be learned from a population pyramid. It shows where the majority of a population lies age-wise, what the growth potential is for the future, the impact of momentous events in the past, and socioeconomic implications for the society. There are typically three types of population pyramids, divided by their general shape: triangular, rectangular, and barrel shaped. Each shape represents a particular population profile that captures the major characteristics of a category of countries.

The **triangular-shaped** pyramid embodies an expanding population, in which there is a broad base at the bottom, with greater numbers of people in the younger age groups and increasingly fewer people in the older age groups. Such a population pyramid corresponds to high fertility and high mortality in a society. As younger cohorts enter reproductive ages, they themselves will produce more babies and keep the base growing even wider. Meanwhile, because of high mortality, people in older age groups steadily decline, with very few reaching very old ages. The triangular shape also applies to populations with high fertility but declining mortality, where the shrinkage of higher age groups is less substantial but there is still a substantially broad base at the bottom. In sum, a population pyramid with a triangular shape suggests an ever-expanding population (high growth potential), with youth being the majority. A case in point is Afghanistan, shown in Figure 7.3. Its population structure forms a nearly perfect triangle. The size of its younger age groups is almost always larger than that of its older ones. Both fertility and mortality are high. Women, on average, have 5.1 births in Afghanistan. Life expectancy is only 61 years. Almost half the population, 46 percent, is under age 15. Meanwhile, only 2 percent are above age 65.

In a **rectangular-shaped** pyramid, the sizes of all age groups become similar, especially at younger ages. It underscores slow or little growth as a result of both low fertility and low mortality. The average fertility tends to be around 2.1, which is the **replacement level**, or the number of children required to replace their parents (it is usually slightly higher than 2.0 when child mortality is taken into account). Because

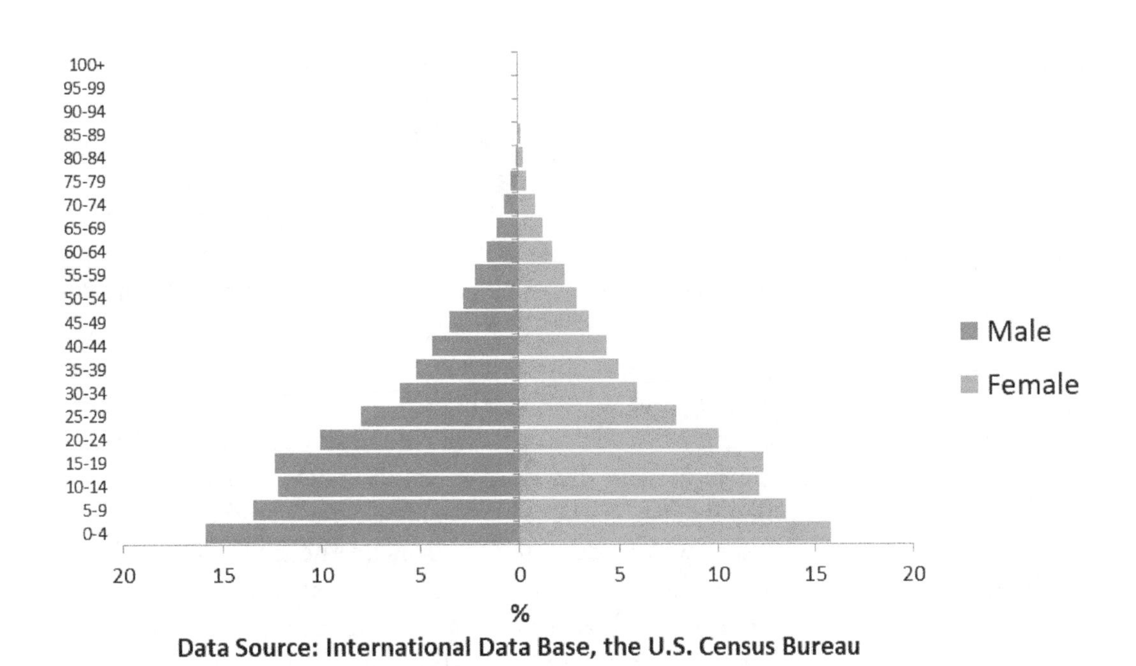

FIGURE 7.3 Population Pyramid of Afghanistan, 2015

FIGURE 7.4 Population Pyramid of Sri Lanka, 2015

of declined mortality, more people in the population can survive to older ages, stretching out the bars in the upper portion of the pyramid. Consequently, the share of the elderly population rises, which means that the population is aging. Sri Lanka is such an example, as shown in Figure 7.4. The age groups under 35 are more or less similar to each other, without apparent expansion, and the older age groups do not shrink as quickly as in Afghanistan. This is due to the decline in both fertility and mortality. Women, on average, have 2.1 births in Sri Lanka, right at the replacement level. The country's life expectancy is 74. The share of youth under age 15 is only 26 percent of the entire population, while 8 percent are over age 65.

Finally, a **barrel-shaped** pyramid, in which there is a reversed pyramid below middle age, suggests a slowing growth and projects steady population shrinkage in the long run. Populations exhibiting this shape are well below replacement-level fertility. This is accompanied by even higher shares of the elderly in the population. The total population has either witnessed a decline or is on the track of shrinkage. Germany is such an example, as shown in Figure 7.5. There is a steady decrease in the size of successively younger cohorts, those under age 50. German population registered a net 0.1 percent decrease in 2014 over 2013. Had it not been for immigration, it would have dropped 0.2 percent instead (PRB 2014). Both fertility and mortality are very low in Germany. The fertility is at 1.4, way below the replacement level. Life

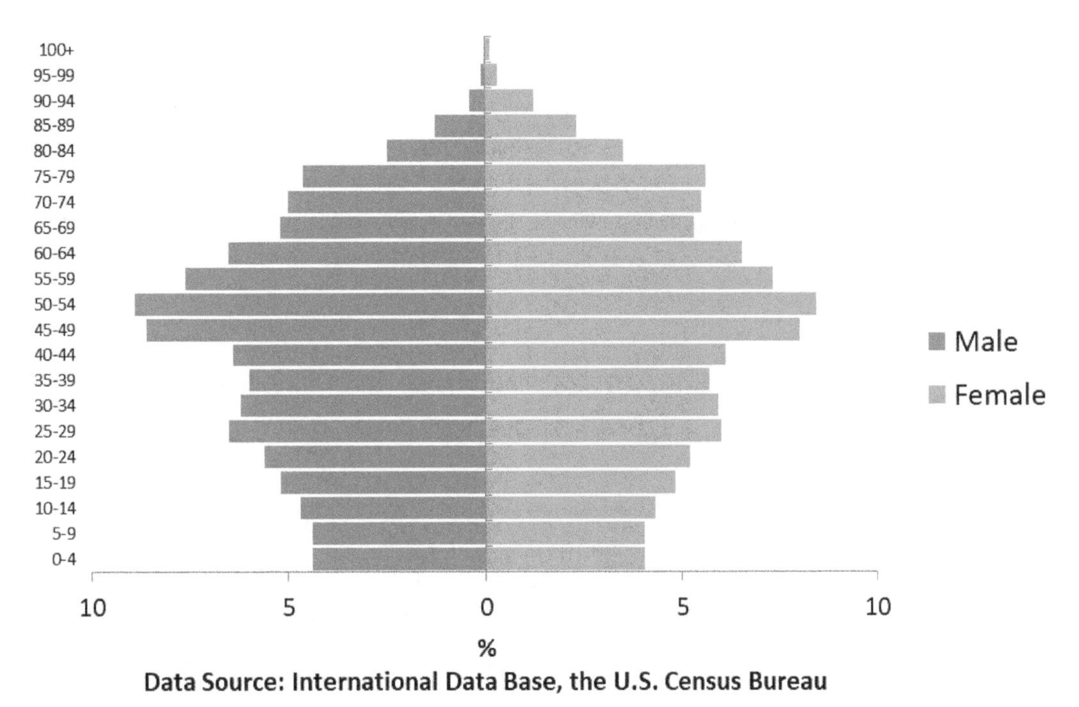

FIGURE 7.5 Population Pyramid of Germany, 2015

expectancy is 80 years. Only 13 percent of the German population is under age 15, but 21 percent are over age 65.

Generally speaking, many developing countries' populations take on the triangle shape, including most countries in Africa, some in Asia (like Afghanistan, India, Pakistan, and Yemen) and Latin America (like Bolivia and Guatemala). Most developed countries and some developing countries in Asia (like China and Thailand) and Latin America (like Brazil and Cuba) fall into the third category—the barrel shape—which means their populations have or will inevitably decline. The rest of the world is characterized by the rectangular shape, with slow or little growth.

BOX 7.2 THE CORRELATION BETWEEN FERTILITY AND MORTALITY

Worldwide, there is a strong correlation between fertility and mortality, which is usually measured by its inverse, life expectancy. Figure 7.6 is a scatter plot that shows **total fertility** *rate*—the average number of births given by women—and life expectancy. It is based on more than 170 countries and regions worldwide where data is available. The horizontal axis shows the average number of children per woman, while the vertical axis shows life expectancy. There seems to be a clear trend: countries with a higher level of fertility usually exhibit lower life expectancy. This provides empirical evidence for the discussion above about the three shapes of population pyramids. There are two points on the chart apparently away from the rest and below the trend line, representing two countries, Lesotho and Swaziland, both in Africa. These are called **outliers.** They share the same total fertility rate of 3.3, which, following the trend line, should be corresponding to a life expectancy of about 70 years. Instead, Lesotho has a life expectancy of only 44 years, and Swaziland's is 49 years. The main reason for this gap is that both countries suffer from the HIV/AIDS pandemic, which accounts for nearly half of all the deaths.

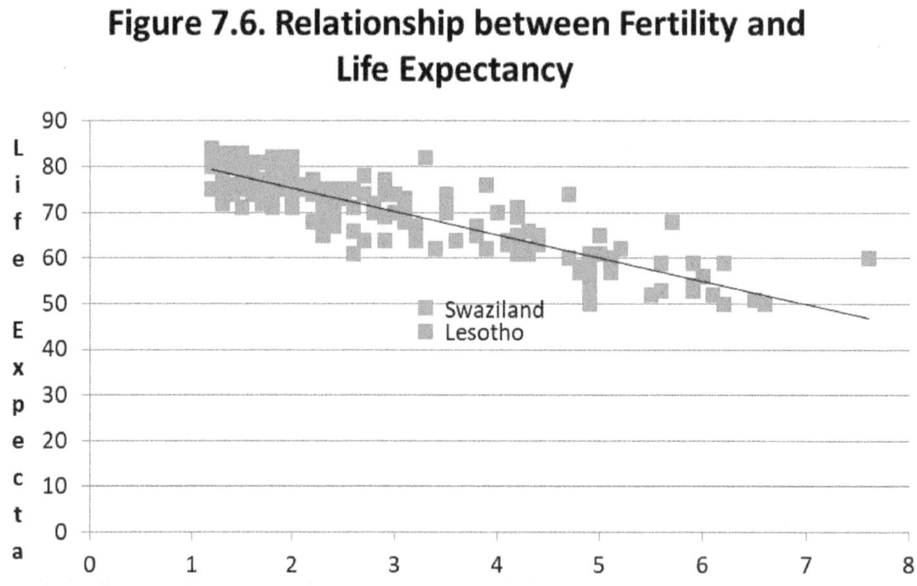

Figure 7.6. Relationship between Fertility and Life Expectancy

FIGURE 7.6 Relationship Between Fertility and Life Expectancy

POPULATION GROWTH AND WELL-BEING

Although there is disagreement about whether rapid population growth is a direct cause of many of the challenges faced by certain parts of the world, there seems to be some connection between the population divide described above and human well-being outcomes, including income, health, and education.

Figure 7.7 shows the relationship between gross domestic product (GDP) per capita and total fertility rates worldwide, which seems to show an "L" shape. Most of the high income countries, those with GDP per capita of US$20,000 or more, are concentrated at the lower end of the fertility spectrum, generally in a narrow band of less than two births per woman. Meanwhile, most of the countries with a total fertility rate of more than three have income less than US$10,000 per capita. The replacement level of fertility, about 2.1, seems to be the dividing point for income. If countries are divided into four categories by their fertility level, (1) less than 1.8, corresponding to the barrel-shaped population pyramid; (2) between 1.8 and 2.2, corresponding to the rectangular shape; (3) between 2.3 and 3.9, corresponding to a moderate triangle; and (4) equal to or greater than 4.0, a clear triangle, there is a strong correlation between the fertility level and average income of each category. The average income for the four groups is US$25,010, US$23,778, US$7,734, and US$2,417, respectively. Note that the average income for the first two groups is quite similar, but it drops off significantly for the other two groups. This is consistent with the 2.1 threshold claim mentioned earlier.

Of course, such a general trend is not without exceptions. Three outliers are marked in Figure 7.7: Equatorial Guinea, Gabon, and Israel. Equatorial Guinea and Gabon are two neighboring countries in Central Africa with relatively high fertility—5.1 for the former and 4.1 for the latter—but their average income is substantially above other countries with similar fertility levels: US$18,800 and US$14,926, respectively. In fact, they share a similar economic story. Both countries benefit from the discovery and exportation of oil and natural gas. For example, income in Gabon has surged since the discovery of offshore oil in the early 1970s (CIA 2015). In 2010, half of Gabon's GDP, about 70 percent of revenues, and nearly 90 percent of its exports were from oil production.

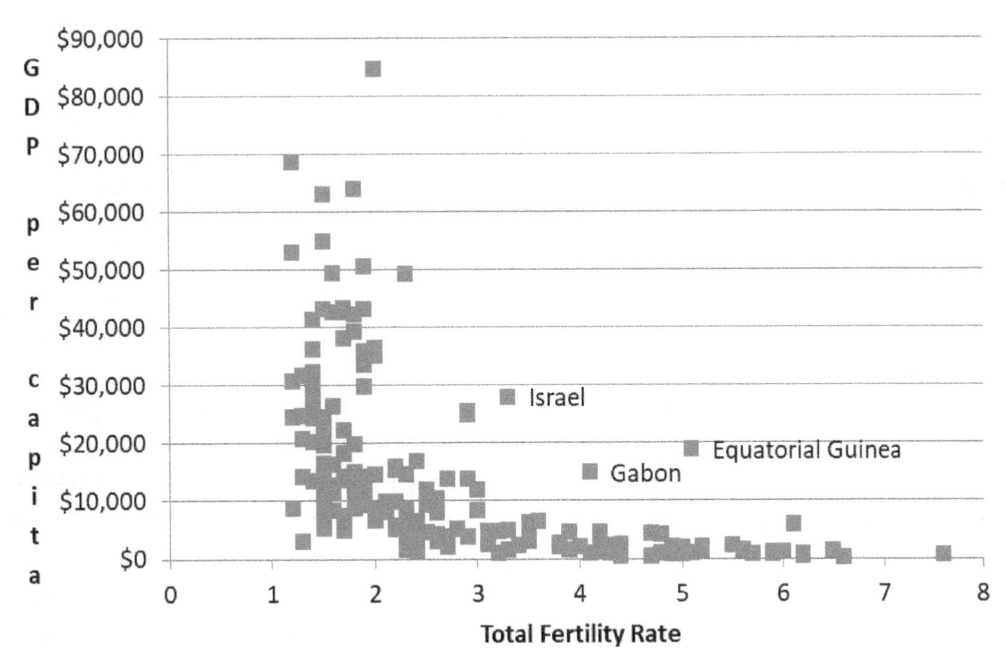

FIGURE 7.7 GDP Per Capita and Total Fertility Rate

As a high income country, with an average income of $28,070, Israel's fertility rate of 3.3 is unique. It reflects the complex cultural and religious composition of the population, which is composed of Jewish (75 percent), Arab (21 percent), and other non-Jewish (4 percent) citizens (DellaPergola, May, and Lynch 2014). About 10 percent of the Jewish population is *haredim,* a traditional group of Orthodox Jews who have high fertility rates, about 7 births per woman compared to 2.3 births for non-Orthodox Jewish women. In addition, the majority of the Arab population is Muslim, whose total fertility rate is around 3.5.

Notwithstanding these exceptions, the general message is that countries with lower levels of fertility, which in turn bring about lower population growth, enjoy higher average income.

Another benchmark of a population's well-being is **life expectancy**—the average number of years an individual in a population is expected to live as calculated at birth. In 2014, life expectancy for men and women in developed countries, where population growth was lower, was 76 and 82, respectively. It was 68 and 72, respectively, for their counterparts in developing countries, where population grew faster. Overall, there was about a ten-year difference (PRB 2015). Another important measure that reflects a country's health care quality is **infant mortality rate**—the number of deaths per 1,000 live births by the first birthday. The gap in infant mortality rate between the developed and developing world is even more striking. While on average, there were only five deaths for every 1,000 live births in developed countries in 2014, there were 40 deaths per 1,000 in developing countries in the same year. Along the wide spectrum, it was fewer than two for Iceland and Singapore on one end, but 109 for the Central African Republic on the other. As discussed in Box 7.2, there is a negative relationship between fertility and mortality. Thus, countries with higher levels of fertility and higher population growth tend to have higher levels of mortality and lower life expectancy.

Educational attainment is another important aspect of a population's well-being, or human capital. Figure 7.8 shows the relationship between female tertiary school enrollment ratio and the total fertility rate, where tertiary education refers to any postsecondary education, including universities and colleges, as well as vocational training. The tertiary enrollment ratio is the ratio of the number of students enrolled in tertiary education to the population in the postsecondary school age group (PRB 2013c). There is some similarity in the shape of this chart to that in Figure 7.7. It shows another L shape, though the dots are more spread out. There is an overall inverse relationship between a country's fertility and educational attainment: countries with higher fertility rates tend to have lower levels of education. In Niger, where women have on average 7.6 births, only 1 percent of women were enrolled in tertiary education. In Finland, however, where total fertility rate is 1.7, virtually all women of postsecondary school age have the opportunity to receive tertiary education. Again, the replacement fertility level seems to be a threshold. Countries where at least half

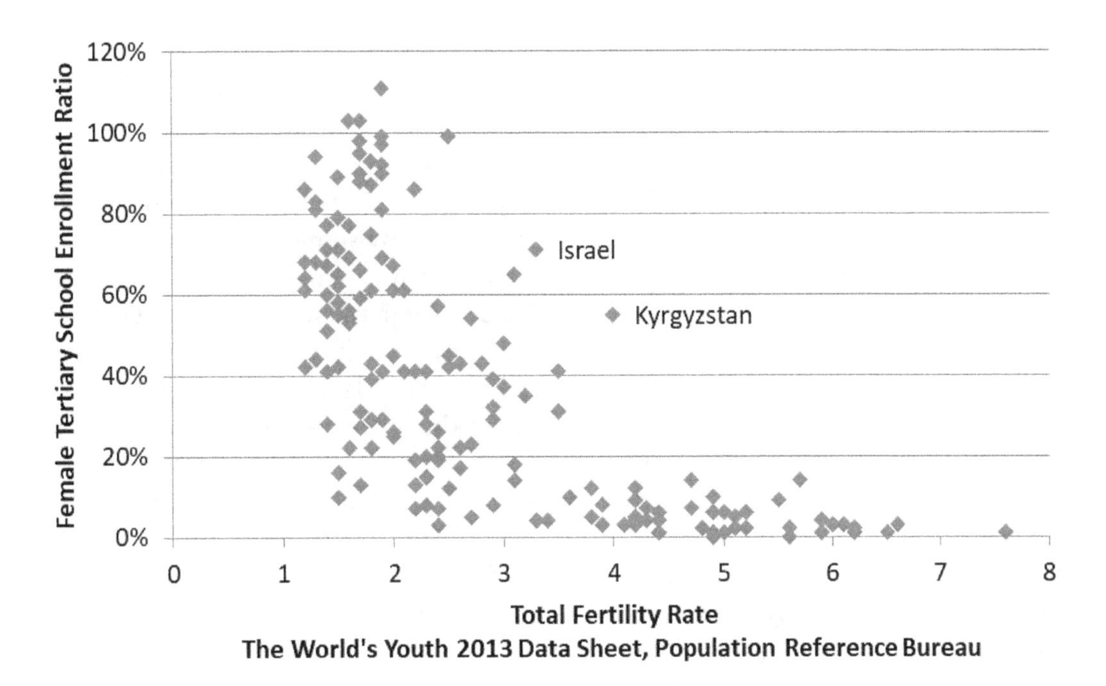

FIGURE 7.8 Female Tertiary School Enrollment Ratio and Total Fertility Rate

of its female population enrolled in tertiary education are lumped in a narrow band with fertility levels of less than 2.1.

Two exceptions are discussed here. The total fertility rate for Kyrgyzstan is 4.0, but its female tertiary school enrollment ratio is 55 percent, way above other countries with similar fertility levels. One possible explanation is that Kyrgyzstan, one of the Central Asian countries, used to be part of the former Soviet Union, where higher education was prevalent. Israel, with a total fertility rate of 3.3, also has a quite high female tertiary school enrollment ratio compared to other countries of similar fertility level. As discussed above, the explanation lies in its unique population composition.

THE HISTORY OF WORLD POPULATION GROWTH

The description above has provided, so far, a snapshot of contemporary discrepancies in world population. This section will present a historical overview of the evolution of the human population.

Some scholars argue that human beings have been around for at least 200,000 years, appearing first in Africa (Cann and Wilson 2003). One interesting question is: what trajectory has the human population followed to reach 7.6 billion as of 2018?

For most of human history, more than 90 percent of it, population growth was minimal, if indeed there was growth at all. The growth rate hovered around 0.01

percent or even less (Thomlinson 1975; Weinstein and Pillai 2001). In primitive hunting and gathering societies, human beings had to face harsh conditions, including that of both physical environment and human interaction, such as hunger, climate hazards, diseases, and wars, but they did so with very limited means to survive. The death rate was high, and for any tribe or society to survive, the family had to produce large numbers of children to compensate for the loss. By some demographers' estimates, the human population was around ten million at the time of the Agricultural Revolution 12,000 years ago, or around 8,000 BC, though the number could be much lower (Weeks 2008; Weinstein and Pillai 2001). The Agricultural Revolution brought about new ways of life: from nomads to settlers, people developed the capacity for more intensive use of the environment, such as grain cultivation and animal domestication, which in turn provided a more reliable food supply. The organization of settlements became more complex, and population started to grow more significantly. However, it was not until the Industrial Revolution, which started in Europe around the middle of the eighteenth century, that the population reached over seven hundred million and growth really started to take off. Some demographers used the year 1650, one century earlier, or the eve of Industrial Revolution, as the beginning of modern population growth (Weeks 2008; Yaukey and Anderson 2001). The world afterward, as popularly described, experienced a population explosion, with unprecedented growth, as shown in Figure 7.9.

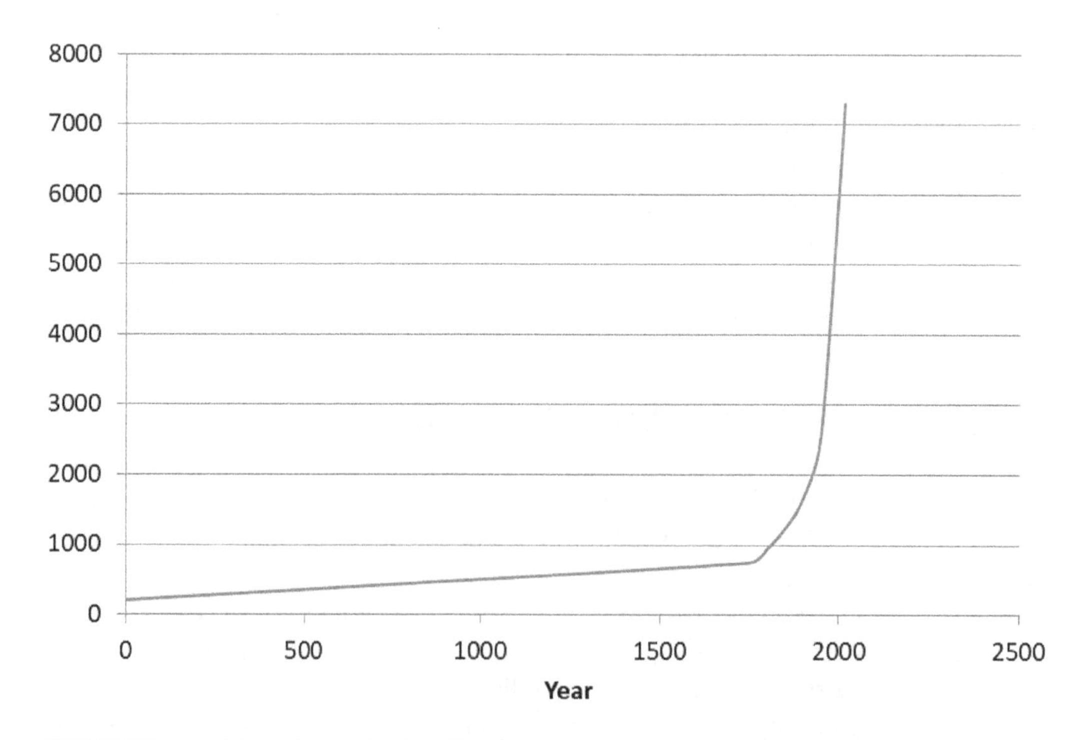

FIGURE 7.9 World Population Size (in Millions)

TABLE 7.2 ***Milestones in World Population Growth***

WORLD POPULATION (IN BILLIONS)	YEAR	NUMBER OF YEARS TAKEN TO REACH THEN-CURRENT BILLION
1	1804	at least 200,000
2	1927	123
3	1960	33
4	1974	14
5	1987	13
6	1999	12
7	2011	12

Data source: United Nations 2000; UNFPA 2011.

Table 7.2 shows the major milestones in the history of world population growth. Overall, the trend is clear: the time gap between the billion marks is getting narrower. It took thousands of years for human population to reach its first billion in 1804, since which it has been accelerating. Five of the seven billion marks occurred in the last century, and each of the last four were passed within a 15-year period. It explains why the line of world population growth in Figure 7.9 is almost horizontal before the year of 2000.

DEMOGRAPHIC TRANSITION AND THEORIES EXPLAINING FERTILITY DECLINE

The discussion above provides a brief overview of the history of world population change. The next question is: is there any pattern in the evolution of birth and death rates that individual societies follow? What are the underlying factors that shape population growth? As it turns out, most populations around the world do in large measure follow a generalized path, which is termed the **demographic transition**. There are four stages identified by demographers that depict the major profiles of population growth (Graff and Bremner 2014), which are shown in Figure 7.10 and Table 7.3.

Stage one is characterized by a high death rate, high birth rate, and low growth rate. Virtually all countries fell into this category until the eve of the Industrial Revolution. As discussed above, a high birth rate was necessary to compensate for the high death rate that resulted from humans' limited ability to meet environmental challenges. Life expectancy in Europe was estimated to be around 25 by 1750 (Maddison 1982).

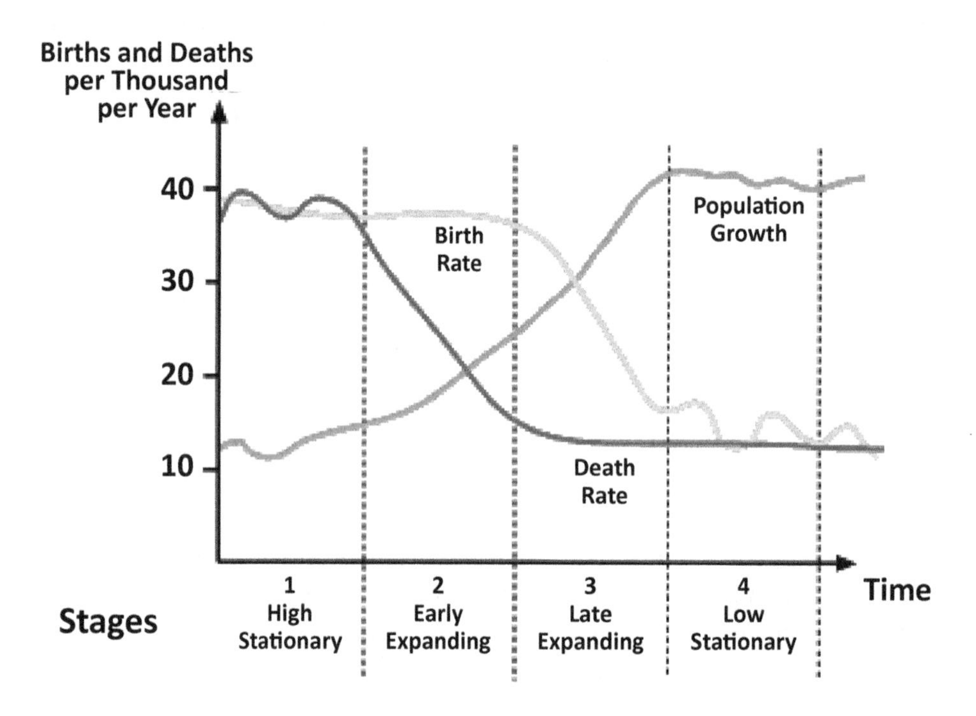

FIGURE 7.10 Demographic Transition Model

Stage two is marked by a substantial decline in mortality while fertility remains high. There forms a widening gap between the rates of birth and death, resulting in explosive population growth.

In stage three, following mortality decline, fertility starts to fall as well. The gap between births and deaths is narrowing. Although the size of the population still keeps expanding, it is at a much slower pace.

In stage four, fertility and mortality reach similar levels again, but this time both are at low levels. Population growth comes to a halt, and in some cases, turns to negative.

TABLE 7.3. *The Four Stages of Demographic Transition*

	BIRTH RATE	DEATH RATE	GROWTH RATE
STAGE 1	High	High	Low
STAGE 2	High	Falling	High
STAGE 3	Falling	Low	Moderate
STAGE 4	Low	Low	Low

Some scholars prefer a three-stage version of the theory, where stages two and three are combined (Weeks 2008).

Explaining Mortality Decline

But how to account for such transitions? What are the forces behind these changes? Modernization, or economic development, is viewed as the major contributor of falling mortality in stage two. The Industrial Revolution that originated in Europe in the eighteenth century brought sweeping changes to the West, which first entered the second stage of demographic transition, in which death rates started to fall though birth rates remained high. Significant growth in agricultural and industrial output in Western nations improved living standards, leading to better housing (reduction of crowding and better ventilation) and nutrition (less food shortage and malnutrition). The practice of personal hygiene and implementation of public health measures, such as access to clean water and the availability of sewer systems and garbage removal, also played crucial roles in improving population health. Later medical advances in immunization and antibiotics further reduced mortality, although their impact was not, as many thought, greater than the earlier overall improvement in living standards (Weinstein and Pillai 2001; Yaukey and Anderson 2001).

Life expectancy in developing countries in the 1930s was still only about 30 (Yaukey and Anderson 2001). They did not experience substantial mortality decline until the 1950s, after the Second World War. In addition to gradually improving living conditions, the diffusion of medical technology from the West and the available knowledge and practice of public health made important contributions. As a result, in comparison with developed countries, the decline in mortality in developing countries was markedly steeper. Within one or two decades, between 1950 and 1970, many developing countries achieved rapid mortality decline that had taken developed countries at least a century to accomplish (Stolnitz 1982). For example, Mexico's death rate in 1900 was higher than that of Sweden in the 1770s, but Mexico's death rate fell three times as fast as Sweden's had (PRB 2004a). Life expectancy in developing countries overall increased again from 41 years in 1950 to 69 in 2015 (PRB 2004a, 2015).

The discussion above provides some explanation for the initial mortality decline in stage two, which is more or less straightforward. But how to explain the following fertility decline in stage three? Why do couples start to limit their family size? This is a more complex process. The following provides a brief introduction to some of the theories on this subject.

Explaining Fertility Decline

Modernization theory, which explains the mortality decline in stage two, provides a general explanation for fertility decline as well (Weeks 2008). It is also referred to as **traditional demographic transition theory**. One direct cause of fertility decline, according to this theory, is the preceding decline of mortality, especially improvement in the survival of children. In the past, when mortality was high, giving a large number of births was a compensating strategy to ensure that a certain number of children would survive to adulthood (Notestein 1953). As a matter of fact, it is still a rationale prevalent in some developing countries today. The rising living standard, brought about by modern development, has greatly enhanced the survival chance of newborns, thus reducing the pressure for couples to have a high number of births. Modernization also creates a modern lifestyle and mindset. Consumerism gradually takes hold. Individualism and self-fulfillment are valued (Yaukey & Anderson 2001). Large families, associated with high demand in resources and time, become increasingly less desirable. In a rising economy, which opens up more opportunities, a desire for upward social mobility develops, as does a concern of losing out in the race. Kinsley Davis argued that when facing the possible negative consequences of large families, it is the fear of falling behind others, or relative deprivation, that motivates couples to limit their fertility (Davis 1963). The establishment of modern social institutions contributes to fertility decline as well. Public education, employment opportunities outside of homes provided by industrialization and specialization of the economy, public health care, and social safety nets have, to a large degree, substituted many of the functions assumed by families in the past, thus weakening the value of individual families and the benefits of having a large number of children. Improvement in women's status and education is another factor accompanied by modern development, which will be discussed in more detail later.

Modernization theory, presented above, is at the macro level. It is about how changes in socioeconomic structure and institutions impact individual reproductive behaviors. But it lacks an in-depth account of the process at the individual or household level. There are a number of economic theories developed in this regard at the micro level. Although they shed light on the issue of fertility decline from different angles, all these theories share a common thread: their focus is on how individual actors, from their own perspective, reach a decision of their desired family size. For this reason, they are lumped together here under a broader umbrella: **microeconomic theories**. Two specific theories are mentioned here. **Rational choice theory** assumes that as couples make decisions about their desired family size, they weigh the benefits against the costs of having any additional children (Weeks 2008). More children are desirable if they bring more net benefit to the parents. By the same token, fewer children will be wanted if childrearing becomes costly and outweighs the total benefit. When the total cost of raising a child to age 18 in the United States is nearly a quarter of a million dollars, including food, housing, child care, education, transportation, and other expenses (Lino 2014), parents are likely to think twice before adding another child. In a similar vein, **wealth flow theory** attributes smaller families to the reverse of the flow of wealth from children to parents (Caldwell 1982). In an agricultural society, in which family was the basic economic unit and manpower was a major source of production, more people meant more helping hands in the field, thus bringing more wealth to the family. Parents had the incentive to have as many children as they could. In the process of industrialization and urbanization, however, many young people moved from the countryside to cities and became employed in industrial sectors. As a result, parents left behind in the countryside had less direct control over their children's income. At the same time, the industrial economy required modern skills and knowledge through public education, which gradually become mandatory. These changes, among others, reduced the flow of wealth from children to parents and led to smaller families.

While these theories offer insights into fertility decline from an economic point of view at both macro and micro levels, **diffusion theory** approaches it from a more sociological perspective. Fertility behaviors may not be merely the outcome of individual rational calculations or of their economic circumstances or aspirations. They may be shaped by shifting norms and practices that are spread or diffused from one population to another at both local and national levels (Weinstein and Pillai 2001). The spreading pattern of family limitation suggests a diffusion process, which "refers to the process by which innovation spreads among regions, social groups, or individuals, often apparently independently of social and economic circumstances" (Bongaarts and Watkins 1996, 656). It spreads through social interaction within personal networks.

The popular portrait of Western families with small family sizes was credited as one of the most important factors leading to fertility declines in many contemporary developing countries. New attitudes and practices regarding fertility swept the developing world, including the introduction of modern means of fertility control, desires for consumer goods, higher career aspirations, and an awareness of alternative roles for women (Knodel and van de Walle 1979). The story of Brazilian soap operas is a case in point.

The total fertility rate for Brazil dropped from 6.3 in 1960 to 2.9 in 1991, but such a drastic change was not accompanied by rapid development in modern education. According to the Brazilian 2000 census, there were still about 40 percent of adults in urban areas, and more than 70 percent of adults in rural areas, with four or fewer years of schooling. Meanwhile, television ownership had increased from 8 percent of all households in 1970 to 81 percent in 1991. One study showed that watching television, especially soap operas, was a crucial factor in shifting individual preferences toward smaller families in Brazil (La Ferrara, Chong, and Duryea 2012). The soap operas shown on Rede Global, the leading national network in Brazil, attract high viewership, and some of the recurrent themes conveyed include consumption of luxurious goods, display of modern lifestyles, female pursuit of careers and pleasure, social mobility, and emphasis on individualism. An ideal family in these shows is portrayed as small, healthy, urban, and middle or upper middle class. Exposure to these values and ideas has played a crucial role in Brazil's fertility transition.

The theories introduced above are mainly focused on how individuals are impacted by various economic and social forces in setting a goal of limiting family size, though the diffusion theory touched upon the spread of modern contraceptive methods. When couples have a desired family size, there has to be an effective means to reach the goal. Modern contraceptive methods, such as condoms, hormonal pills, intrauterine devices, and sterilization techniques, have undoubtedly made remarkable contributions to fertility decline worldwide. In addition to providing contraceptive supplies and information, family planning programs also promote the idea of smaller and healthier families. In areas where fertility is near or below replacement level, including Europe, North America, Brazil, and China, more than 50 percent of married women age 15 to 49 use modern contraception (PRB 2013b). The use of family planning services increased from less than 10 percent of married women in the 1960s to about 60 percent in 2003, and up to 50 percent of the fertility decline in developing countries between the 1960s and 1990s can be attributed to family planning programs (PRB 2004a). For example, sustained fertility decline in Nigeria, the most populous country in Africa, was achieved through the rapidly increasing use of contraception for purposes of delaying the onset of childbearing and increasing the length of birth intervals. Contraceptives were provided by both government agencies and the private sector (Caldwell, Orubuloye, and Caldwell 1992). As aforementioned, family planning programs not only provide information and services but also promote messages that legitimate family planning practices. The legitimating function of a family planning program is of considerable importance in fertility transition (Knodel and van de Walle 1979).

Despite the dramatic increase in contraceptive use in the past few decades, however, more than 100 million women in developing countries, about one in six married women, who would prefer to avoid a pregnancy or postpone it are not using contraception (Ross and Winfrey 2002). This is referred to as an unmet need for family planning, which can lead to unintended pregnancies. In 2012, of the 213 million pregnancies worldwide, 40 percent of them, or 85 million pregnancies, were unintended. About 40 percent of the unintended pregnancies ended in an unintended birth, and another 40 percent ended in abortion (Sedgh, Singh, and Hussain 2014). Women who receive unsafe abortions to terminate unintended pregnancies usually cannot fulfill their responsibilities within the household, attend school, or make a living (Singh 2010). This poses risks for women, their children, and families. The causes of this unmet need are complex. Some women lack knowledge about contraceptive methods, some do not have access to them due to insufficient affordability or supply, some are concerned about the side effects, and some do not use them because of religious or cultural reasons (Ashford 2003).

In contrast, women who avoid unintended pregnancies enjoy better health with lower mortality for both mothers and children (Rutstein 2008). They have more time to participate in the labor force outside the home, increase their earning prospects, and help their families accumulate more wealth. Women who have access to family planning were also found to be empowered and more likely to be involved in household decision-making regarding nutrition and food security (Bremner, Patterson, and Yavinsky 2015).

In the end, it should be recognized that although family planning in developing countries in the past few decades has been a success story at large, the unmet need for family planning in some developing countries remains high. In a few dozen countries in Sub-Saharan Africa, Latin America, and Asia, such as Bolivia and Cambodia, more than 20 percent of married women's needs for family planning services are not met. In these countries, family planning services have not kept up with changes in fertility preferences (Kols 2008). Sources of obstacles are multiple. Increasing services becomes more difficult when infrastructure is underdeveloped, such as with insufficient health facilities and shortages of qualified providers. Service delivery systems are also disrupted by natural disasters or armed conflicts in some places. Finally, the success of family planning itself can be another negative factor. Since the program has been highly successful in many developing countries in bringing down the fertility level, international organizations or foundations have started to divert funding to other pressing issues, such as the alleviation of poverty and the AIDS pandemic.

The status of women, which can be measured by their educational attainment, labor force participation, and involvement in decision-making within the household, is of particular importance in fertility transition. In societies where women have little literacy or access to mass media, they may have little knowledge of reproductive health and the use of contraception to avoid unintended pregnancies.

Women in many parts of the world where unfair gender roles are imposed are deprived of equal rights and the opportunities enjoyed by their male counterparts. Women in the Middle East and North Africa, for example, are twice as likely to be illiterate as men. In Yemen, that gap is three times as large. Only 20 percent of women older than age 15 in this region are in the labor force (Roudi-Fahimi and Moghadam 2003). Such a gender gap could be attributed to the lower status of women in this region, which is affected by religion, family laws, and civil codes. For example, in some places, women need to have permission from a male relative for employment or travel, and they usually inherit a smaller share of family wealth.

In cultural settings where the female role is subordinate and where women are cut off from broader social networks, improving the status of women may be more conducive to fertility decline than either family planning programs alone or more general development efforts (Knodel and van de Walle 1979).

One prominent indicator of women's status, and an effective way to improve it, is public education, which has been consistently found to be conducive to fertility decline (Bremner, Patterson, and Yavinsky 2015). Educated women tend to fulfill their aspirations outside the home and contribute more to household income, which has a positive effect on child nutrition and the health of family members and, in turn, usually leads to smaller and healthier families (Roudi-Fahimi and Moghadam 2003).

Girls in Africa with secondary education are more likely to postpone marriage and use contraception (Caldwell, Orubuloye, and Caldwell 1992). According to the Demographic and Health Survey in Egypt in 2014, women who had a secondary or higher education had their first birth about three years later, on average, than women with no education. Among women age 40 to 49, those with no education had an average of 4.3 children, compared with 3.2 among those who had completed secondary education. The story of Indonesia also shows the robust link between girls' education and fertility (Graff and Bremner 2014). As the proportion of girls enrolled in secondary school rose from 21 percent in 1980 to more than 75 percent in 2014, the average number of children women had dropped from 4.1 to 2.6.

A study based on demographic and health surveys for nine Latin American countries particularly shed light on how women's education affects fertility outcomes (Castro, Juarez, and Juarez 1995). Women's educational attainment was found to serve first as a source of reproductive knowledge and cognitive skills. Girls learned the basic facts of human reproduction at school and obtained a better understanding of modern contraception. Schooling also increases women's exposure to mass media, which publicizes nontraditional lifestyles and smaller families, and serves as a resource that enhances their economic opportunities. Better educated women were found to have higher household incomes, to reside in urban areas, and to have a higher standard of living. Finally, it serves as a socialization channel that affects attitudes and aspirations. More educated women were less likely to take a fatalistic approach to life and more likely to command higher control over their reproduction. As a result, they tend to plan their family size and adopt more effective means to achieve their goals.

Improving women's status will also help overcome an additional cultural barrier to fertility decline—son preference—which is present in many developing countries. In such cultures, couples will keep giving birth until they have a certain number of sons. A study of six countries in Asia and Africa found that the number of pregnancies could have been reduced between 9 and 21 percent had there been no strong son preference (Arnold 1997).

GLOBAL DEMOGRAPHIC FUTURE: DIVIDE OR CONVERGENCE?

According to a recent projection made by the United Nations, world population will continue to grow, reaching 9.7 billion in 2050 and 11.2 billion in 2100 (United Nations 2015b). The UN projection is based on an assumed substantial fertility decline in medium to high fertility countries in the decades to come. The future of the world population largely hinges on how fertility will shape up. The world fertility rate currently stands at 2.5 children per woman. It is assumed to drop to 2.4 by 2030 and 2.0 by 2100. Any slower-than-projected declines will result in a higher global population than predicted.

The Demographic Divide

Over the next few decades, not only will population size become bigger, but its composition will also change (see Figures 7.11 and 7.12). As introduced at the beginning of this chapter, in 2015, Asia alone had the lion's share of world population—60 percent—which is not totally surprising, given the fact that it is where both China and India, the two most populous countries, are located. Africa takes a distant second place with 16 percent, followed by Europe, Latin America, North America, and

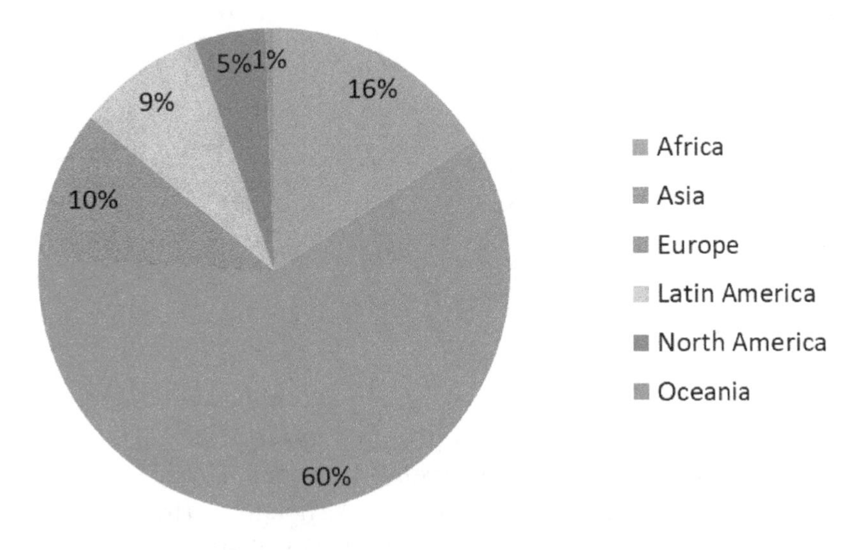

FIGURE 7.11 World Population Distribution in 2015

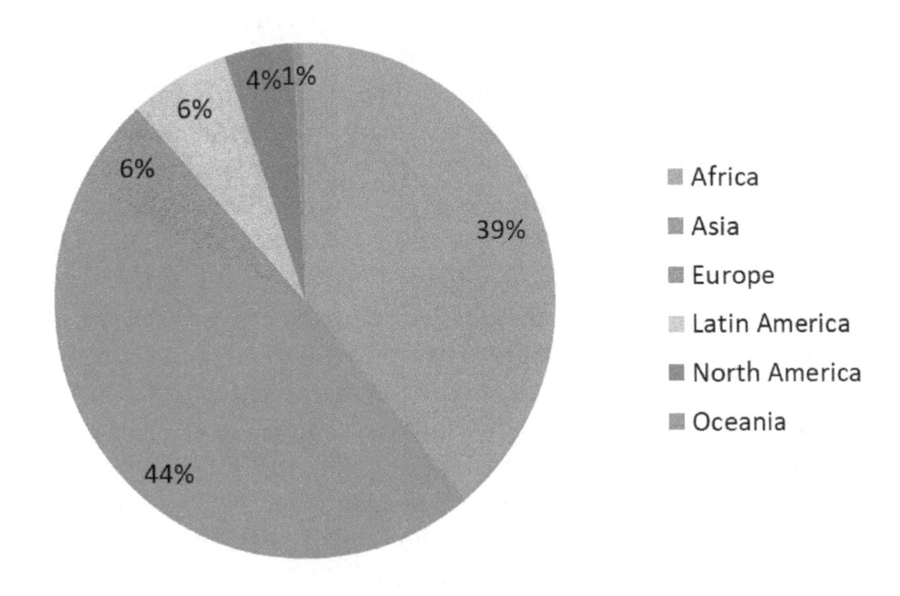

FIGURE 7.12 World Population Distribution in 2100

TABLE 7.4 *Population from 2015 to 2050 and 2100 (in Millions) and Relative Growth*

	2015	2050	2100	2015–2050 % GROWTH	2015–2100 % GROWTH
WORLD TOTAL	7,349	9,725	11,213	32%	53%
DEVELOPED COUNTRIES	1,135	1,197	1,217	5%	7%
EUROPE	738	707	646	-4%	-12%
NORTH AMERICA	358	433	500	21%	40%
OCEANIA	39	57	71	46%	82%
DEVELOPING COUNTRIES	6,213	8,539	9,997	37%	61%
AFRICA	1,186	2,478	4,387	109%	270%
ASIA	4,393	5,247	4,889	20%	11%
LATIN AMERICA	634	784	721	24%	14%

Data source: United Nations 2015b.

Oceania. By the end of this century, the biggest change will be the surge of Africa's population. Although it will still be in second place after Asia, the gap will be narrowed substantially to 39 percent versus 44 percent. The biggest decline will be in Europe, down from 10 percent to 6 percent. Although on the surface, Latin America and North America are both on the losing side as well, their stories are different. It is not because their populations are shrinking, like Europe. As analyzed in the following discussion, their populations will keep growing, just not as fast as Africa's.

As shown in Table 7.4 and Figures 7.13 and 7.14, population growth will unfold unevenly across the globe. For the purpose of comparison, developed countries refers to those in Europe, North America, and Oceania, where Australia and New Zealand together account for 70 percent of the continental population. Developing countries consist of Africa, Asia, and Latin America. Data show that world population will grow by about a third by 2050 and a half of current levels by 2100, respectively. There is a clear divide in the future population growth rates between developed and developing countries as a whole. The growth rates in developing countries in the same period of time are seven to eight times higher than those in developed countries (37 percent versus 5 percent, and 61 percent versus 7 percent, respectively). The gap is even more striking when viewed from a slightly different perspective. The size of the world's population will increase by 2.376 billion from 2015 to 2050, of which 97 percent will be from the developing world and only 3 percent from the developed world. The picture remains the same even on a longer horizon. The size of the world's population will increase by 3,864 million from 2015 to 2100. The share of contribution from developing and developed countries is 98 percent and 2 percent, respectively. Although

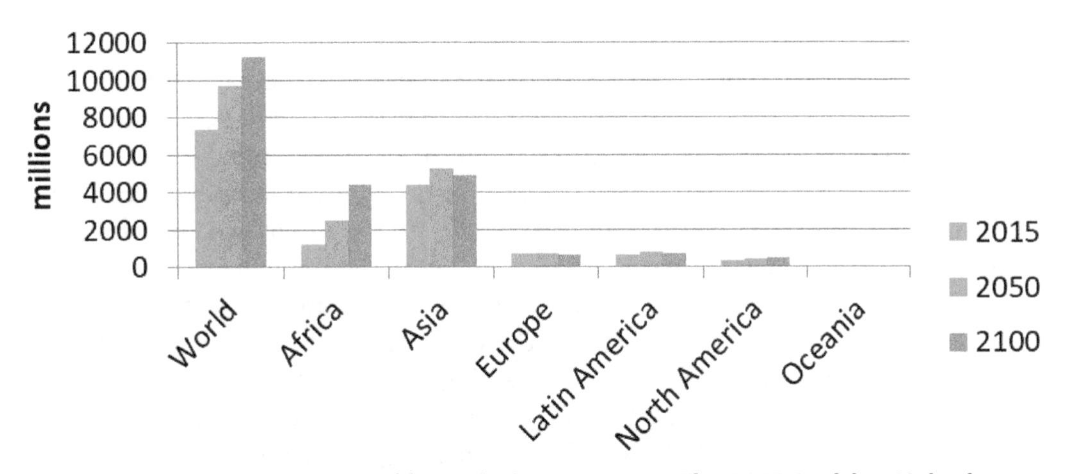

FIGURE 7.13 World Population Projection from 2015 to 2050, and 2100

it is tempting to claim that the future growth of the world's population is almost entirely from developing countries, the breakdown of each category by continent shows a more complex picture.

Africa is the fastest growing continent. More than half of global population growth between 2015 and 2050 is expected to occur in Africa. Between 2015 and 2050, 28

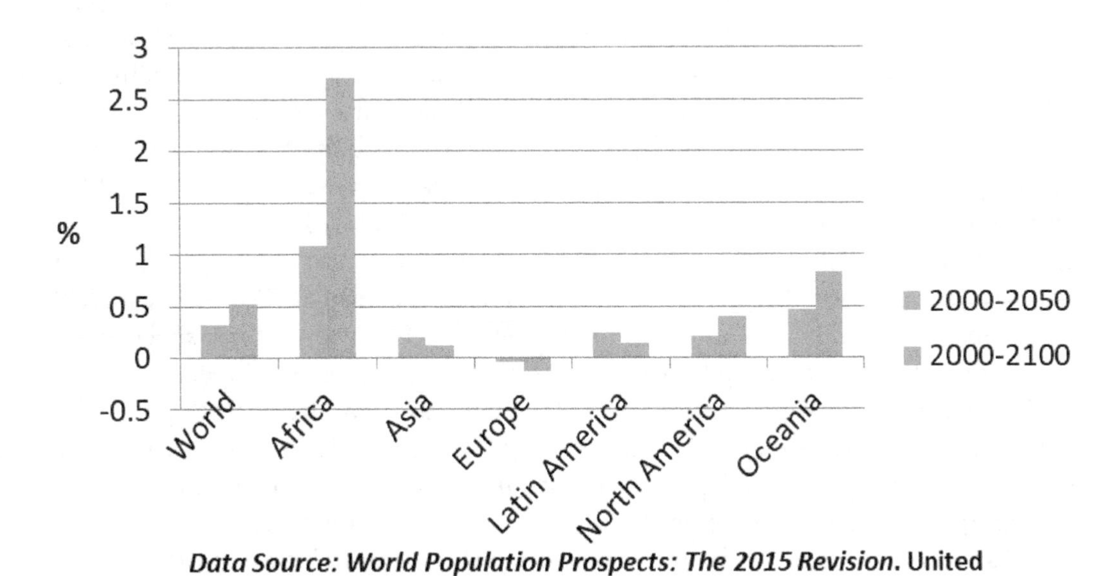

FIGURE 7.14 World Population Relative Growth from 2015 to 2050 and 2100

out of 50 African countries will see their populations more than double. By 2100, ten African countries' populations will increase at least five-fold. Nigeria, the most populated country in Africa, currently the seventh largest population in the world, will surpass the United States to become the third most populated country in the world by about 2050. One prominent feature of rapid-growing populations is their young age structure. In Africa, children under age 15 accounted for 41 percent of the population in 2015, much higher than the slower growing regions of Latin America and Asia, with 26 percent and 24 percent, respectively (United Nations 2015b). The society will face challenges of satisfying the basic needs of newcomers, providing sufficient education and health care, and creating enough job opportunities.

The second fastest growing continent is Oceania, where Australia resides. Because its population size is so small compared with other regions, its impact on world population is minimal. Surprisingly, it is North America, mainly the United States, that takes third place. (Although Latin America's population will grow faster than North America till 2050, 24 percent versus 21 percent. Over the longer term, by 2100, it will be outpaced by North America by a big margin, 14 percent versus 40 percent.) Note that Asia is the second largest contributor to future global population growth in terms of the number of people added, but not because of how fast its population grows (United Nations 2015b). As a matter of fact, its growth rates over the two periods of time are both below those of North America. This seeming contradiction is simply because of the much larger size of the Asian population to begin with. Latin America, Asia, and Europe take the last three places, and Europe, uniquely, is projected to have a shrinking population from now on. It is the only continent with negative population growth. Fertility in all European countries is below replacement level, with an average total fertility rate of 1.4. Ten countries in Europe (along with Japan in Asia) will see their populations decline by more than 15 percent by 2050. As a result, the European population is aging rapidly. Twenty-four percent of its population is already age 60 years or over, and that proportion is projected to reach 34 percent in 2050 and 35 percent in 2100 (United Nations 2015b). By 2050, in 24 European countries, the ratio of the number of working-age people between 20 and 64 to the number of people age 65 and over, known as the **Potential Support Ratio** (**PSR**), will be under 2 in Europe. This will have a profound impact on labor force conditions, social safety net programs, health care, and other aspects of the society as mentioned above.

The contrast between Europe and Africa suggests two opposing population dynamics: while the former, representing the developed world, is losing ground, the latter, representing the developing world, keeps swelling with momentum. But the demographic gap between the developed and developing countries is far from clear cut. Convergence starts to form as more developing countries are on the path of demographic transition and, at the same time, the populations of some developed countries, the United States in particular, are still substantially expanding.

The Demographic Convergence

Globally, life expectancy rose from 67 years between 2000 and 2005 to 70 years between 2010 and 2015 (United Nations 2015b). This improvement is shared virtually across the globe. More importantly, Africa, at the bottom of the chart, showed the most gain, with an increase of six years to a life expectancy of 60. Asia reached 72 years, and Latin America 75 years, compared to 77 years in Europe and Oceania and 79 years in North America. The gap between developed and developing countries is narrowing.

Developing countries have made strides in infant mortality as well, which is the probability of death before the first birthday, an important indicator of children's well-being and a society's socioeconomic development. According to the Population Reference Bureau, the global average fell from 56 per 1,000 live births in 2004 to 37 per 1,000 in 2015 (PRB 2004b, 2015). The gap between the developed and developing countries was reduced from seven versus 62 per 1,000 to six versus 45 per 1,000 during the same period. Africa, again, showed the largest reduction, from 90 to 59 per 1,000, followed by Asia, from 54 to 33 per 1,000. As this trend continues, the difference across regions will significantly diminish (United Nations 2015b).

Fertility has continued to decline in virtually all major areas of the world, including many developing countries. The number of countries with total fertility rates of 5 or more has dropped from 40 in 2000–2005 to 21 in 2010–2015. Among 126 countries with total fertility between 2.1 and 5, fertility has fallen in 108 of them. Eighty-three countries have reached below-replacement fertility level (2.1), accounting for 46 percent of the world's population. Of the nine largest populations with below-replacement fertility, five of them are developing countries: China, Brazil, Vietnam, Iran, and Thailand. Fertility decline has been roughly the same in Asia and Latin America over the same period, from 2.3 to 2.2. Africa experienced a decline as well, from 4.9 to 4.7, although its decline is much slower than that of other regions. The least developed countries are projected to undergo the steepest reduction in fertility, from 4.3 in 2015 to 3.5 by 2030 and 2.1 by 2100. Both North America and Europe have been below replacement level for some time, having a total fertility of 1.8 and 1.6, respectively, in 2010–2015.

As discussed earlier based on Figure 7.14, it is no longer true that all developing countries have higher population growth than developed countries. Although Africa is the fastest growing region, the next two regions are Oceania and North America, faster than Asia or Latin America. The three major English offshoot countries, the United States, Canada, and Australia, will see their populations swell by 40 percent, 39 percent, and 75 percent by 2100, respectively. Although this will mainly be fueled by immigration, fertility plays a role as well. The fertility rate of the United States has been hovering around replacement level, not as low as many European countries. Its total fertility rate was 1.9 in 2015, higher than China's rate of 1.7 (PRB 2015).

Population aging is not just a European phenomenon. It is occurring throughout the world. The proportion of people age 60 or over in North America will grow from 21 percent to 28 percent by 2050, and in Oceania from 16 percent to 23 percent. In the developing world, Asia and Latin America follow a similar path. Their shares of people age 60 or over will rise from 12 percent and 11 percent to 26 percent and 25 percent, respectively, in the same period. Africa, because of its substantially higher birth rate, ages at a much slower pace. The percentage of its population age 60 or over will increase from 5 percent in 2015 to 9 percent by 2050. Therefore, by 2050, all major regions of the world except Africa will have nearly a quarter or more of their populations age 60 or over. (United Nations 2015b).

Globally, the population of people age 60 or over is the fastest growing age group. In 2015, there were about 900 million people age 60 or over, or 12 percent of the world's population. It is projected to rise to 2.1 billion by 2050 and 3.2 billion by 2100. Bear in mind that of the 1.2 billion elderly population increase in the next 35 years between 2015 and 2050, two-thirds of the growth will be from Asia (United Nations 2015b).

Many developing countries see their population aging at a faster pace than rich, developed countries. It took France 114 years and the United States 69 years for people 65 or over to double from 7 percent of the population to 14 percent. But it will take Indonesia 22 years to undergo the same change (Chamie 2002). Such a dramatic aging process will bring developing countries a challenge unique in human history: getting old before getting rich (Longman 2004). For example, by 2050, China's population age 65 or over will swell to 330 million, or a quarter of its total population, a level that is on par with many developed countries. At the same time, however, China is still a developing country. Its GDP per capita was about US$13,000 in 2014, ranked in eighty-first place by the World Bank. China's pension reserve is relatively small, accounting for only 2 percent of China's GDP (*China News Network* 2012), compared to 83 percent in Norway, 25 percent in Japan, and 15 percent in the United States. As a result, the benefit is low, especially in the countryside (Huang 2013). How to support a growing elderly population with fewer youth and limited resources will be a challenge faced by many developing countries in the near future.

CONCLUSION

Generally speaking, developing countries, one after another, have embarked on the path of demographic transition, though the pace of change is vastly different between regions or countries. As a matter of fact, the pace of fertility decline in developing countries, on average, has been significantly more rapid than that in Europe decades earlier (Kirk 1971). While it took Britain 130 years to have its fertility rate drop from 5 to 2—1800 to 1930—it took South Korea just 20 years—1965 to 1985—to make the same transition. Iran's fertility dropped from 7 in 1984 to 1.9 in 2006, a reduction of five births in only 22 years (*The Economist* 2009).

The driving force of fertility decline could be a combination of an array of factors discussed in this chapter. Modernization, coupled with industrialization and urbanization, has brought sweeping changes to many developing societies, including improvement in the living standard, expansion of public education, employment opportunities in modern sectors, rise in the cost of raising children, and new aspirations for consumption and individual advancement. Like their counterparts in the developed world, many couples in developing countries make decisions regarding family size by comparing the benefits of raising children with the costs. In China, parents are expected to pay for their child's college tuition and living expenses in college and, after graduation, contribute to the purchase of their child's first car, first apartment, and wedding. These expenses together make parents keenly aware of the cost of raising a child. China in 2015 announced it was to abandon its one-child policy, which was held for 35 years, now allowing couples to have two children. But many young couples are not sure they want to take the chance, citing the expense and the pressures of raising children in a highly competitive society. In an era of globalized economy, along with the ease of communication and access to the Internet, diffusion of information and ideas gets unprecedentedly easier. More and more people in the developing world get to know the living standard and lifestyles in urban centers and abroad. Such exposure is likely to have an impact on individual aspirations, resetting of life priorities, and attitudes toward the size of families.

One of the major themes throughout this book is that the developing world is not homogenous. This applies to the subject of population growth, as well. While the demographic transition is already set in motion in Asia and Latin America, Africa still has a long way to go to get its population growth under control. The total fertility rate for the entire continent was 4.7 in 2015 (PRB 2015), more than double the replacement level of 2.1, at which the population will stabilize.

In addition, there is great diversity within each continent, as well. In Africa, for example, while 59 percent of married women in Southern Africa used modern contraceptive methods in 2013, it was only 18 percent in Western Africa, where in Guinea it was less than 6 percent (PRB 2013b). Similarly, in Asia the use of contraception varies. The share of married women using modern contraception was 54 percent in South Asia; Afghanistan had the lowest level at 21 percent in 2013. It was 81 percent in East Asia, where China registered the highest level of 84 percent (Population Reference Bureau 2013b).

In light of the spectrum in the level of development, of particular concern are the least developed countries, which fall far behind in the demographic transition. In these countries, fertility remains high. Limited resources are further pressed by high population growth, especially youth. The concentration of population growth in the poorest countries will make it harder for those governments to provide basic services, to expand education, to combat hunger and malnutrition, and to eradicate poverty (United Nations 2015a).

REFERENCES

Arnold, Fred. *DHS Comparative Studies 23: Gender Preferences for Children*. Calverton, MD: Macro International, 1997.

Ashford, Lori. "Unmet Need for Family Planning: Recent Trends and Their Implications for Programs." *Policy Brief.* Washington DC: Population Reference Bureau, February 2003.

Bongaarts, John, and Susan Cotts Watkins. "Social Interactions and Contemporary Fertility Transitions." *Population and Development Review* 22, no. 4 (December 1996): 639–82.

Caldwell, John C. *Theory of Fertility Decline (Population and Social Structure)*. London and New York: Academic Press, 1982.

Caldwell, John C., I. O. Orubuloye, and Pat Caldwell. "Fertility Decline in Africa: A New Type of Transition?" *Population and Development Review* 18, no. 2 (June 1992): 211–42.

Cann, Rebecca L., and Allan C. Wilson. "The Recent African Genesis of Humans." *Scientific American* 266, no. 4 (April 1992): 68–73.

Castro Martin, Teresa, and Fatima Juarez. "The Impact of Women's Education on Fertility In Latin America: Searching for Explanations." *International Perspectives on Sexual and Reproductive Health* 21, no. 2 (June 1995): 52–57, 80.

Chamie, Joseph. "As the World Ages." *Bloomberg*. April 3, 2012. http://www.bloomberg.com/bw/stories/2002-04-03/as-the-world-ages.

China News Network. "Dai Xianglong: China's pension reserve accounts for only 2% of GDP." Finance. December 17, 2012. http://finance.chinanews.com/cj/2012/12-17/4413841.shtml.

Central Intelligence Agency (CIA). "Africa: Gabon." *The World Factbook*. Accessed on May 28, 2019. https://www.cia.gov/library/publications/the-world-factbook/geos/gb.html.

Davis, Kingsley. "The Theory of Change and Response in Modern Demographic Theory." *Population Index* 29, no. 4 (October 1963): 345–66.

DellaPergola, Sergio, John F. May, and Allyson C. Lynch. *Israel's Demography Has a Unique History*. Washington, DC: Population Reference Bureau, 2014. http://www.prb.org/Publications/Articles/2014/israel-demography.aspx.

Graff, Maura, and Jason Bremner. *A Practical Guide to Population and Development*. Washington, DC: Population Reference Bureau, 2014.

Huang, Yanzhong. "Population Aging in China: A Mixed Blessing." *The Diplomat*. November 10, 2013. http://thediplomat.com/2013/11/population-aging-in-china-a-mixed-blessing/.

Kirk, Dudley. 1971. "A new demographic transition?" *Rapid Population Growth: Consequences and Policy Implications*. Research Papers (2013): 123–47.

Knodel, John, and Etienne van de Walle. "Lessons from the Past: Policy Implications of Historical Fertility Studies." *Population and Development Review* 5, no. 2 (June 1979): 217–45.

Kols, Adrienne. "Reducing Unmet Need for Family Planning: Evidence-Based Strategies and Approaches." *Outlook* 25, no. 1 (November 2008).

La Ferrara, Eliana, Alberto Chong, and Suzanne Duryea. "Soap Operas and Fertility: Evidence from Brazil." *American Economic Journal: Applied Economics* 4, no. 4 (October 2012): 1–31.

Lino, Mark. "Expenditures on Children by Families, 2013." US Department of Agriculture, Center for Nutrition Policy and Promotion. Miscellaneous Publication No. 1528-2013, 2014.

Longman, Phillip. *The Empty Cradle: How Falling Birthrates Threaten World Prosperity and What to Do About It*. New York: Basic Books, 2004.

Maddison, Angus. *Phases of Capitalist Development*. New York: Oxford University Press, 1982.

May, John F., Jean-Pierre Guengant, and Thomas R. Brooke. 2015. "Demographic Challenges of the Sahel." Population Reference Bureau. http://www.prb.org/Publications/Articles/2015/sahel-demographics.aspx.

Notestein, Frank. "Economic problems of population change." In *Proceedings of the Eighth International Conference of Agricultural Economists*, 13–31. London: Oxford University Press, 1953.

Patterson, Kristen P., Jason Bremner, and Rachel Yavinsky. "Building Resilience Through Family Planning: A Transformative Approach for Women, Families, and Communities." *Policy Brief.* Washington DC: Population Reference Bureau, 2015.

Population Reference Bureau (PRB). "Transitions in World Population." *Population Bulletin* 59, no. 1 (2004).

Population Reference Bureau (PRB). *2004 World Population Data Sheet.* Washington, DC: Population Reference Bureau, 2004b.

Population Reference Bureau (PRB). *2013 World Population Data Sheet.* Washington, DC: Population Reference Bureau, 2013.

Population Reference Bureau (PRB). *Family Planning Worldwide 2013 Data Sheet.* Washington, DC: Population Reference Bureau, 2013b.

Population Reference Bureau (PRB). *The World's Youth 2013 Data Sheet.* Washington, DC: Population Reference Bureau, 2013c.

Population Reference Bureau (PRB). *2014 World Population Data Sheet.* Washington, DC: Population Reference Bureau, 2014.

Population Reference Bureau (PRB). *2015 World Population Data Sheet.* Washington, DC: Population Reference Bureau, 2015.

Population Reference Bureau (PRB). *2018 World Population Data Sheet.* Washington, DC: Population Reference Bureau, 2018.

Ross, John A., and William L. Winfrey. "Unmet Need for Contraception in the Developing World and the Former Soviet Union: An Updated Estimate," *International Perspectives on Sexual and Reproductive Health* 28, no. 3 (September 2002):138–43.

Roudi-Fahimi, Farzaneh, and Valentine M. Moghadam. "Empowering Women, Developing Society: Female Education in the Middle East and North Africa." *Policy Brief.* Washington, DC: Population Reference Bureau, October 2003.

Rutstein, Shea O. "Further Evidence of the Effects of Preceding Birth Intervals on Neonatal, Infant, and Under-Five-Years Mortality and Nutritional Status in Developing Countries: Evidence from the Demographic and Health Surveys." *DHS Working Papers Series* 41. Calverton, MD: Macro International, 2008.

Sedgh, Gilda, Susheela Singh, and Rubina Hussain. 2014. "Intended and Unintended Pregnancies Worldwide in 2012 and Recent Trends." *Studies in Family Planning* 45, no. 3 (September 2014): 301–14.

Singh, Susheela. "Global Consequences of Unsafe Abortion." *Women's Health* 6, no. 6 (November 2010): 849–60.

Stolnitz, George J. "Mortality: Post-World War II Trends." In *International Encyclopedia of Population*, edited by John A. Ross. New York: The Free Press, 1982.

The Economist. "Falling Fertility: Demography, Growth and the Environment." October 29, 2009.

Thomlinson, Ralph. *Demographic Problems: Controversy over Population Control.* Encino, CA: Dickenson Publishing Company, 1975.

United Nations. *World Population Prospects: The 2000 Revision.* Department of Economic and Social Affairs, Population Division. New York: United Nations, 2000.

United Nations. *The Millennium Development Goals Report 2015.* New York: United Nations, 2015a.

United Nations. *World Population Prospects: The 2015 Revision, Key Findings and Advance Tables.* Working Paper No. ESA/P/WP.241. New York: United Nations, 2015b.

UN Population Fund (UNFPA). "Countdown to a World of Seven Billion People." Press release. September 12, 2011.

Weeks, John R. *Population: An Introduction to Concepts and Issues.* 10th ed. Belmont, CA: Thomson Higher Education, 2008.

Weinstein, Jay, and Vijayan K. Pillai. *Demography: The Science of Population.* Boston: Allyn and Bacon, 2001.

Yaukey, David, and Douglas L. Anderton. *Demography: The Study of Human Population.* 2nd ed. Prospect Heights, IL: Waveland Press, Inc., 2001.

Figure Credits

Fig. 7.1: Source: https://worldmapper.org/maps/population-year-2018/.

Fig. 7.2: Source: http://cdn3.chartsbin.com/chartimages/l_3385_150e6f59e87c3a99d7d1b94a1fb46e7b.

Fig. 7.11: Data Source: World Population Prospects: The 2015 Revision, United Nations.

Fig. 7.12: Data Source: World Population Prospects: The 2015 Revision, United Nations.

CHAPTER EIGHT

Environment and Culture

INTRODUCTION

The environment, or the **biosphere** (sum total of all life-sustaining ecosystems), provides humans with their sustenance. Our interaction with and outlook on the environment is greatly influenced by our **culture**—our worldview, consisting of values, beliefs, and the material objects that comprise the substance of our lives. Western capitalism is driven by an outlook that views the environment as a commodity that humans express **dominion** over, the idea that nature was put here for our use. In Western capitalism, there is a sharp division between nature and society. Not all cultural groups view themselves as having dominion over the natural world, but strong similarities prevail within those regions of the world that embody a capitalist framework.

In this chapter, we examine the relationship between the environment and the culture of capitalism. All too often, the environment is seen and experienced as an abstract, distant realm, removed from our everyday lives. We start with the reader assessing his or her own **ecological footprint**—an estimated total of the resources one uses to sustain one's current lifestyle. Through consumptive activities, such as daily transportation, housing, food, and services one makes use of, we can see that humans do in fact utilize more resources than the Earth can support.

In the first section, we provide a simple link that calculates the number of Earths required to support the world's population. Second, we draw attention to the most critical environmental issue of the twenty-first century—**climate change**. Climate change also overlaps a wide array of other global social and economic issues (Klein 2014). These issues include but are not limited to trade relations, (multipolar) globalization, development, migration, agriculture, the environmental movement, conflict, and the well-being of countless communities. Third, we examine **commodity chains**, the processes by which the natural world is transformed into the material objects that make up humans' everyday lives and, in part, capitalist culture. We use four commodity chain examples to illustrate the complexity and the enormous relevance that understanding commodity chains gives us on how to better manage the destructive impacts and consequences one's seemingly innocent lifestyle has on the environment. We start by examining the local and global food system, using the examples of beef, salmon, and shrimp (seafood consumption). Food production and consumption significantly contribute to climate change, and understanding of food systems is not well known to food consumers. We then look at electronics, with an emphasis on cell phones and other devices. Finally, we conclude this chapter by acknowledging the changes that seem to be on the horizon in terms of our relation to the environment and culture.

WHAT IS MY ECOLOGICAL FOOTPRINT?

The Earth Day Network Footprint Calculator begins our investigation into the impact that each person has on the planet. Please calculate your ecological footprint by following the link: https://www.footprintnetwork.org/resources/footprint-calculator/

In completing this short set of calculations, you may be surprised to see how many Earths it takes to support your seemingly modest lifestyle. In the United States, for example, it is impossible to fall under a three-Earth total. What may be considered a highly ecologically conscious lifestyle (e.g., no meat, locally sourced food, no car) will score in the three-planet range. In contrast, a poor peasant living in India will score less than one Earth through this assessment. However, this poor peasant is living in dire poverty.

When results are further examined we see that one's footprint can be broken down into the following source categories:

1. Services
2. Shelter
3. Mobility
4. Goods

The result of these activities leads to a quantifiable amount of carbon dioxide that is produced each year (see next section). As such, a precursory analysis of this data demonstrates that the mere fact of living in the United States (one of the highest consuming nations) will give rise to an unsustainable lifestyle. The calculator offers some suggestions that would reduce one's footprint, such as eating less meat and using public transportation or carpooling.

REDUCING ENERGY USE

At the same time, one's options are restricted in the United States. Here, culture and prosperity have grown around highly energy-intensive forms of transport, food production, and services. The average size of a US house, for example, has grown from 1,600 square feet to 2,700 square feet over the past 30 years (Christie 2014). Other countries, such as Denmark, Germany, Switzerland, and the UK, have somewhat lower footprints due to farsighted public policies implemented a number of decades ago (Klein 2014). The average home size in these countries is also significantly smaller than that of the United States (Yunghans 2011).

What becomes apparent in this brief exercise is that consumption levels are in great excess of what the biosphere can sustain. As the Earth Day Network Footprint Calculator recommends: "The largest reductions in Ecological Footprint can most commonly be achieved by reducing the total amount of materials consumed, rather than attempting to recycle them afterwards" (Earth Day Network, 2019).

In sum, the footprint exercise attempts to illustrate (1) our connection to the environment, and (2) our relationship with the environment. In a general sense, we understand this relationship through consumption, which rests on the capitalist exploitation of the environment. A key question in this regard is: **will global consumers be willing to reduce their consumption? Or will they have to be forced to do so?** The consequences of these actions lead into what may be the defining global environmental issue of the twenty-first century—climate change—which is discussed in the next section.

CLIMATE CHANGE

What is climate change? According to the Department of Ecology, State of Washington, United States:

> Climate is usually defined as the "average weather" in a place. It includes patterns of temperature, precipitation (rain or snow), humidity, wind and seasons. Climate patterns play a fundamental role in shaping natural ecosystems, and the human economies and cultures that depend on them. But the climate we've come to expect is not what it used to be, because the past is no longer a reliable predictor of the future. Our climate is rapidly changing with disruptive impacts, and that change is progressing faster than any seen in the last 2,000 years (Washington State Department of Ecology, 2019).

Assessing the fact that the climate is changing on a global level is done through the scientific analysis and reconstruction of relatively long-term weather pattern variations. Four facts emerge:

1. Based on available data over the past 100 years, the **Global Mean Temperature (GMT)** has risen by 0.85 degrees Celsius, with projected increases of 2.8–5.4 degrees Celsius over the next 80 years (Maslin 2014). The rise in temperature is due to the emission of **greenhouse gases (GHG)**, mainly carbon dioxide and methane, brought on mainly by the burning of fossil fuels such as coal, oil, and natural gases. These are the energy sources and go to the core of capitalist culture.
2. As a result of this relatively recent global warming, sea ice is melting (about 40 percent) and sea levels have increased by 20 centimeters (Maslin). Coastal and low-lying areas are at risk if sea levels continue to rise. In particular, island nations may become inundated and uninhabitable under these conditions.
3. The increased frequency of **extreme weather**, such as stronger hurricanes, droughts, flooding, and record-high temperatures, is yet another set of consequences traceable to climate change. More frequently occurring natural events, such as earthquakes and flooding, have been linked to climate patterns and responses to this crisis. It is important to balance these claims against the base observation that weather does indeed vary. However, weather extremes have increased in frequency, duration, and intensity.
4. The human-generated consequences of climate change could result in a dramatic reshaping of natural ecosystems and the human cultures that depend on them for their sustenance. For instance, farming systems in Africa would be unable to produce adequate food, and the extinction of a number of important animal species would be inevitable. At the same time, it has been shown that humans have adapted to climate extremes in both temperate and tropical weather climates. The rapidity of these changes, brought on by climate change, greatly constrains any sense of a secure transition to sustainable lifestyles, however (Maslin). Maslin further speaks of **tipping points**, instances when the climate changes in an unpredictable manner. These changes may be exponentially abrupt, muted, and nonlinear. Tipping points can also apply to humans in the manner that humans respond, often dramatically, to unforeseen weather events.

In sum, **global warming** has been detected and established by near-unanimous scientific consensus (Henson 2011; Klein 2014; Maslin 2014). Global warming is, however, only part of an overall climate change assessment. Beginning in earnest in the late 1980s, climate science has produced a tremendous number of credible studies, drawing from interdisciplinary backgrounds, that establish both the causes and consequences of this unprecedented global environmental issue. Coupled with the mainstreaming of climate change by governmental groups, international bodies, environmental groups, and media coverage, climate change forces us to "examine the whole basis of modern society" (Maslin 2014, xvii).

How Have Global Warming and Climate Change Occurred?

Global warming and climate change have their causes in **anthropogenic** (human) activities. Human activity, beginning in the industrial era and accelerating during the modernization period of world development, has led to the raising of the material standard of living, not only in the Global North but in many regions of the Global South. Yet this growth has not proceeded without consequences, as environmental degradation has gone hand-in-hand with modernization policies. Air, land, and water pollution have proved to be exceedingly difficult problems to address, because the costs for industrial pollution have been **externalized**. Hence, society bears the full consequences or costs of those processes (including waste and pollution) that provide higher standards of living. With increased environmental awareness and more robust scientific data and analysis, climate change has emerged as an environmental problem of global proportions.

On the biosphere side of climate change, the earth's atmosphere, including the ozone layer, insulates the warmth generated by the sun's energy in the form of light waves. Figure 8.1 below depicts the different spheres comprising the atmosphere.

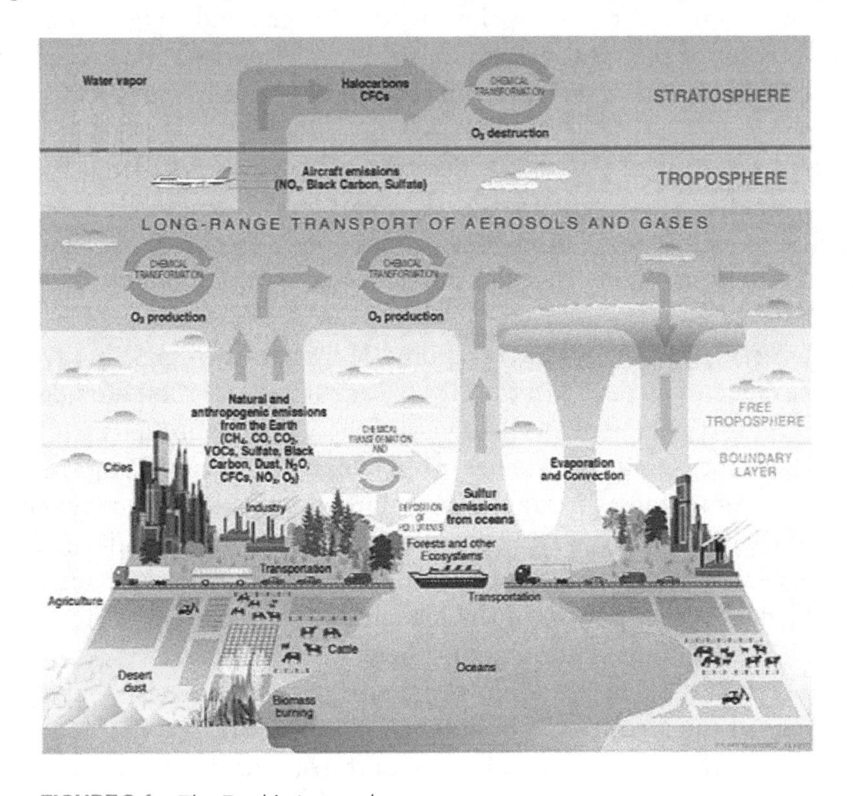

FIGURE 8.1 The Earth's Atmosphere

TABLE 8.1 *Atmospheric Gases (Vanessa Davis)*

EARTH'S ATMOSPHERE	PERCENTAGE	GHG?
Nitrogen	78.08%	No
Oxygen	20.95%	No
Water	0% to 4%	Yes
Argon	0.93%	No
Carbon Dioxide	0.039%	Yes
Neon	0.0018%	No
Helium	0.0005%	No
Methane	0.00017%	Yes
Hydrogen	0.00005%	No
Nitrous Oxide	0.00003%	Yes
Ozone	0.000004%	Yes

The atmosphere is composed primarily of nitrogen and oxygen, which together equal 99 percent of the total gas composition. As Table 8.1 illustrates, the GHGs **water**, **carbon dioxide**, **methane**, **nitrous oxide**, and **ozone** are found only in trace amounts.

GHGs retain some of the heat generated by the sun's radiation. Without these gases and atmospheric layers, the Earth would be inordinately cold and virtually uninhabitable. Specifically, it has been the increase in carbon dioxide levels, and to a lesser extent methane, that lies at the center of the global warming–climate change crisis.

As scientists have demonstrated, dramatic increases in mainly carbon dioxide levels correspond to increases in the GMT. For example, carbon dioxide levels measured atop Hawaii's Mauna Loa Observatory show that from 1960 up to the present, carbon dioxide measured in parts per million (ppm) increased from 312 to well over 400 ppm. The observatory, situated in the middle of the Pacific Ocean, acts as a global proxy, given that Hawaii is located far away from the major industrial and population centers where the majority of carbon emissions occur. Note that carbon dioxide is a natural component of the biosphere. Carbon dioxide, however, plays a dual role. It is part of the natural atmosphere, yet when the natural state is altered and more carbon dioxide is added to the atmosphere, as it has been during the industrial era, it can also act as a pollutant (Henson 2011). The GHG carbon dioxide insulates the earth, trapping more heat than the oceans, land, and atmosphere can stably absorb (Henson).

Sources of Carbon Dioxide Emissions

Henson estimates the source of human-generated GHGs (see Table 8.2). Complicating this list is the fact that countries like China will individually produce a different profile than that of the United States. Likewise, different regions of the world will display a different carbon emissions profile than others, such as Sub-Saharan Africa and Europe. This distinction is mentioned here because the differences between countries or regions play a critical role when international solutions are tabled in multilateral negotiation settings, such as the recent Conference of the Parties (COP21) meetings in Paris, France. Table 8.2 provides a general grouping of carbon emission sources.

As can be seen from the below list, sources of carbon emissions intersect with the lifestyle of virtually every human inhabitant of the world—recall the earlier exercise in calculating your ecological footprint at the beginning of this chapter. We can surmise, then, that global climate change is not an abstract, otherworldly matter but one of great significance that involves all humans on an intimate basis.

Some specific examples of high-emissions industries that provide energy are introduced below. This gives a better explanation of how using any sort of extractive energy can greatly impact one's ecological footprint.

Coal: Accounting for roughly 40 percent of all electricity generation, coal-fired power plants significantly contribute to global carbon emissions. Each plant has a lifespan of 60 years, and over 3,000 new plants are being proposed globally, with China among the world's leaders in developing new coal plants (Klein 2014). Natural gas powers some electricity plants and is seen as a "bridge fuel" to more renewable sources, such as solar and wind power. Countries such as Denmark and Germany have developed these renewable sources, with solar/wind accounting for 25 percent (in Germany) and 40 percent (in Denmark) of community and cooperative supplies of electricity. Future forecasts, given the already strong renewable energy policies in place, anticipate 95 percent renewable energy use in these countries by 2050 (Klein 2014). Yet this

TABLE 8.2 ***Carbon Emission Sources by Sector***

Sector	Share
Transportation (e.g., Road, Aviation, Rail, and Ship)	14%
Electricity and Heat (e.g., in Residential and Commercial Buildings)	25%
Industry (e.g., Manufacturing)	14%
Coal, Oil, and Gas Production	14%
Land Use (e.g., Deforestation)	18%
Agriculture (e.g., Energy Use, Soils, Livestock and Manure, Rice Cultivation)	14%
Waste (e.g., Landfills)	4%

Source: Adapted from Henson 2011, 41.

transition is not complete, and Germany, for instance, has recently seen its carbon emissions increase (though still remaining below 1990 levels) due to continued reliance on coal, which it also exports (Klein 2014). Finally, the United States' coal industry, while embattled, remains strong as both an export and electrical and manufacturing domestic energy source. Only 10 percent of US electrical energy is derived from renewable sources, with forecasts claiming this share can greatly increase by 2050 (EIA 2018).

Natural Gas: Forecasts and warnings about climate change have mobilized exploration for alternative sources of energy to fuel capitalist culture. It is very important to emphasize that our economy, culture, and way of life are inexorably wedded to fossil fuel consumption. Not only in the United States but in other countries of the world, fossil fuels drive economic growth and lead to an increased material standard of living for these populations. The question of whether this developmental pathway is sustainable over the short and long term remains at the center of global culture. With political and economic pressure cast on traditional energy sources such as petroleum and coal, the recent boom in natural gas production and consumption has led to some replacement of traditional energy sources in a wide array of human activities, such as electricity generation, heating, and transportation. The American Petroleum Institute (2019) summarizes the use of natural gas in our economy and how we obtain these essentials for our lives. Energy companies drill for natural gas. **Hydraulic fracking** is a major method to procure natural gas at present (see US Department of Energy, 2019). While assurances are plentiful that natural gas production is "clean" and has been practiced safely for many years, abundant evidence also exists that fracking may be environmentally damaging and threatening to human health. The British Broadcasting Corporation (*BBC News* 2018) illustrates the process of natural gas fracking, in which drilling into underground geological formations allows for the release of natural gas. In sum, natural gas production has been linked to increases in GHGs, problems with toxic wastewater disposal, and the increased frequency of tremors and earthquakes in Oklahoma, among other areas of the world (see OSEE, 2019; Philips 2015). Similar to other proposed transitions to so-called clean energy, or **energy bridges**, and alternatives to traditional petroleum, the direct effect on global warming and climate change remains unabated.

Oil Shale: Conventional oil and gas production make use of drilling into an oil or gas reservoir. Once the reservoir is tapped, the well is capped and pressure is then regulated to allow the oil to flow upward. As these reserves reach their limits, harder-to-extract oil is also found in great quantities but is mixed with shale deposits. Extraction of this cruder and "dirtier" oil requires more expensive mining and/or fracturing processes. The **boom and bust cycle** in fuel production is highly dependent on the price of crude oil derived from conventional drilling. Geopolitical conditions, especially in the Middle East, result in fluctuations in crude oil supply. When conventional supplies get tight and reserves are drawn down, oil shale extraction and production grow. The United States is a leading oil shale producer, and exploitation of accessible shale oil could almost double the known quantity of reserves in the world. Similar to tar sands (below), this source of energy comes with serious environmental costs and does nothing to address global warming, as the whole production and consumption process contributes to further global carbon emissions.

Tar Sands (Oil Sands): The link here provides a good overview of Alberta, Canada's tar sands, the largest industrial project in the world: https://www.youtube.com/watch?v=YkwoRivP17A (SustainableDevelopment 2011). Oil derived from the tar sands is an unconventional or "dirty" oil source. Although tar sands are more difficult to refine, rising oil prices and new technology have opened up the tar sands centered in Fort McMurray, Alberta (see Figure 8.2).

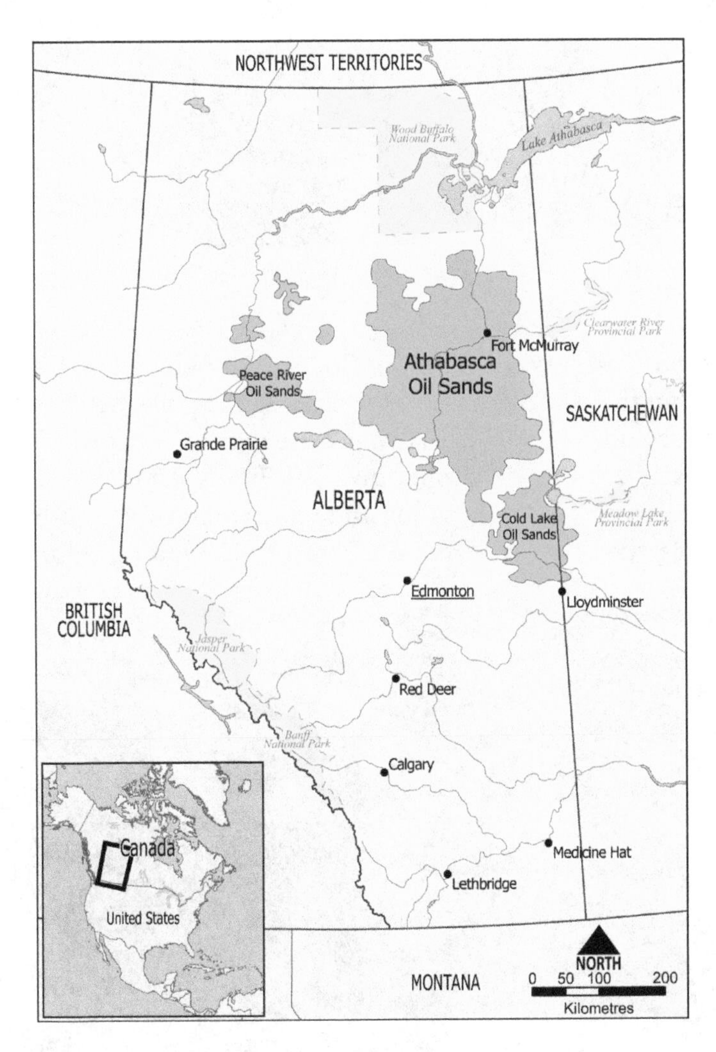

FIGURE 8.2 Alberta's Tar Sands Regions (Vanessa Davis)

These oil reserves appear relatively close to the surface and are found in the form of bituminous sands. Figure 8.3 below illustrates the "cold molasses" appearance of tar sands.

FIGURE 8.3 Tar Sands

Other tar sands reserves are found in Congo, Kazakhstan, Madagascar, Russia, and Venezuela, but these operations are not on an industrial scale like Alberta's. Since the oil-laden bituminous sands are relatively close to the surface, the boreal peat bogs, forests, and grasses are simply stripped away, as Figure 8.4 (below) illustrates.

The extracted raw bituminous sands undergo an extensive and highly dirty process of extracting the actual oil from the compound. Water used in this extraction

FIGURE 8.4 Before and After Tar Sands Extraction

process (called tailings) is collected in ponds near the mining sites. The pond water, highly toxic and carcinogenic, and has been known to leak into the nearby Athabasca River. A very recent development has been the extreme wildfires that led to the complete evacuation of the city of Fort McMurray, Alberta. Climate change may be the root cause of this unprecedented weather event (Lukacs 2016). The lifeline for tar sands oil and conventional petroleum products rests on the extensive pipeline grid that delivers oil to major markets in North America. Oil companies aggressively propose additional extensions and new lines that would deliver oil to the West Coast for export to Asia and the Gulf of Mexico for export to Europe. Former President Barack Obama's decision in 2015 to veto the Keystone XL pipeline was a major setback for the extremely profitable oil sector. Westward efforts to link pipelines with new deep water ports have also faced stiff opposition from environmental and Indigenous groups (Klein 2014). Figure 8.5 (below) shows the North American pipeline grid.

These pipelines are vulnerable to "normal accidents," and the tar sands oil is highly corrosive to the pipes. The chances of a break and leak in the lines are likely. In one high profile case, an Enbridge pipeline broke outside Marshall, Michigan, in 2010 and discharged 180,000 gallons of tar sands oil (piped from Alberta) into the nearby

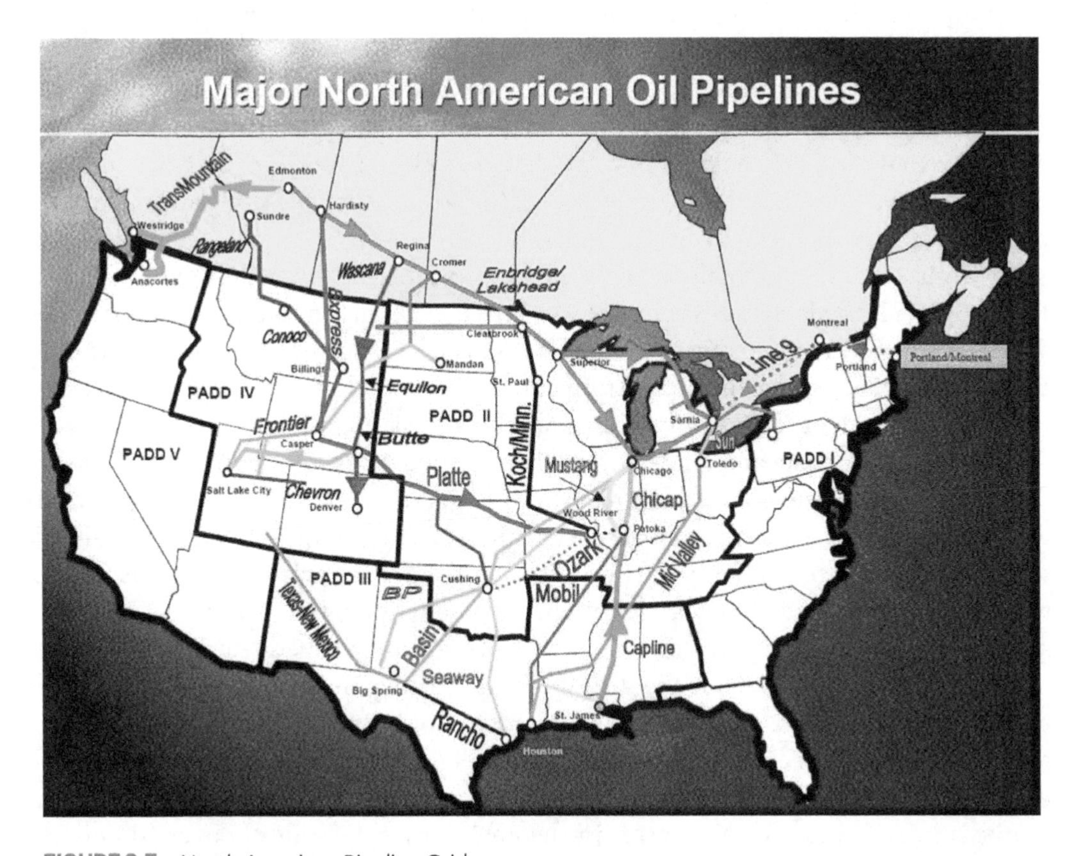

FIGURE 8.5 North American Pipeline Grid

Kalamazoo River. There were prolonged delays in discovering the spill, as company inspectors thought it was a "false alarm." Also, company employees ignored previous observations that this stretch of pipeline was seriously corroded. This spill represented the largest onshore oil disaster ever, and at this writing, remediation efforts are still underway, with cleanup costs surpassing over one billion dollars (Klein 2014).

As can be inferred from the sections above, we have entered into a "high risk" period in our quest for new sources of energy. While use of renewable sources (solar and wind) grows in countries such as Denmark and Germany, the United States lags far behind, with only 4 percent of its energy coming from these renewable sources. In the world oil market, instability in the Middle East, discord in the internal workings of the Organization of the Petroleum Exporting Countries (OPEC), and fluctuating prices per barrel of oil demonstrate that the industry tends to fluctuate in terms of supply and demand. When conventional oil prices surge, high-risk alternatives and environmentally degrading practices of extraction (e.g., natural gas, shale oil, and tar sands) come to the forefront, leading to "boom" periods. When prices fall in the conventional oil market, these high-risk and "dirty" forms of energy extraction go "bust." Irrespective of "booms" or "busts," the energy industry remains enormously profitable, thereby satisfying shareholders and executives who make decisions to continue tapping into established reserves in addition to endlessly exploring for new reserves (Klein 2014).

Nuclear Power: This source of energy provides about 10 percent of electrical power in the United States. Nuclear power plants are inordinately expensive to build and maintain (Hawken 2017). Nuclear power is relatively clean in terms of carbon emissions, but the risk of nuclear accidents and spread of highly radioactive uranium dampens the mass expansion of nuclear power. In the classic book *Normal Accidents*, Charles Perrow (1999) argues that our technological systems are so complex that failures are the norm. Perrow provides a detailed example of the Three Mile Island nuclear power disaster that occurred in Pennsylvania in 1979. Other disasters, such as the one in Chernobyl, Ukraine, in 1986, galvanized preexisting opposition to this source of energy. The 2011 Fukushima accident, caused by an earthquake and tsunami, has led to widespread environmental impacts and long-term health consequences for Japanese residents.

For the 438 nuclear power plants currently operating in 30 countries around the world, the disposal of highly radioactive uranium is a major unresolved issue. On-site storage of this waste at nuclear facilities is seen as a short-term solution. Disposal of nuclear waste at Nevada's Yucca Mountain, a sacred religious site for the Western Shoshone, mobilized significant citizen and political opposition. The site has had a number of start-ups and stoppages for the disposal of hazardous nuclear waste. Often, these hazardous waste disposal sites are located next to or within communities of color, a practice referred to as **environmental racism** (Bullard 2000; LaDuke 1999). At present, there are 67 proposed new plants in the planning and construction stage. China plans to invest heavily into nuclear power in the near future by building over 100 plants, making it the world's leader in this form of energy (Nuclear Energy Institute, 2019).

The next section addresses the question of what can be done about climate change. Different countries, classes, and other social groupings have dissimilar carbon emissions profiles. In addition, even if we were to halt all human-generated carbon emissions, the warming of the world would continue due to the century-long lifespan of carbon dioxide. Climate modelers tell us that this continued warming would equate to another half-degree Celsius (Henson 2011). With different actors exhibiting a diverse array of responses, we note that the matter of global climate change involves incredibly complex solutions, ones that go the core of one's way of life and place in the world.

How is Climate Changing?

Emergent and potentially even more drastic weather patterns and events are becoming more evident and common. If we begin by drawing connections between global warming and environmental effects, then the overall scope of global climate change becomes more apparent. Note that throughout this overview the interpretation of interaction between climate change and environmental effects must be balanced against weather variability and its impact. While the data that support these claims is not exacting, sufficient evidence is available from scientific bodies such as the Intergovernmental Panel on Climate Change (IPCC) to substantiate both evident and emerging environmental impacts. Some of the areas of scientific attention relate to the following:

- **Extreme Heat:** Heat waves are nothing new when it comes to seasonal weather. The duration and extremes of recent heat waves tell that our polluted population centers are having a much more difficult time coping with extended heat intervals (Henson 2011). During a heat wave, nighttime low temperatures with high humidity can become crippling, as the summer of 2003 demonstrated in Europe (Henson). Cities with little air conditioning and heat-absorbing buildings can lead to deaths, especially in young and older people. In another example, from 2010, a high number of Moscovites (1,200) who sought out beaches to escape a June extreme heat wave experienced disorientation due to the heat, coupled with excessive drinking, and drowned (Henson, 56). All in all, about 50,000 people died either directly or indirectly because of Europe's 2003 heat wave. Warning systems and various interventions (e.g., checking in on the elderly) have been some of the measures undertaken by governments in these afflicted areas.
- **Floods and Droughts:** While not precise, indications point to increased rainfall patterns in the Northern Hemisphere with expected drier conditions in the Southern Hemisphere. A key factor that clarifies the inconsistency in rainfall or snowfall is **precipitation intensity**. As Henson (68) remarks, when rain or snow occurs, the event is stronger in its duration leading to higher precipitation totals overall. Global warming tends to saturate humid climates while making drier areas even more arid, perpetuating drought. With the human interface, more rain and snow can lead to more extensive flooding, and deforestation,

among other human activities such as farming practices, can accelerate the severity of these weather events. Drought interfaces with human societies in two ways: hydrological and agricultural. Hydrological drought pertains to water for human consumption, such as levels in reservoirs used for these purposes. Agricultural drought refers to inadequate water supplies for crops. If a drought occurs during the critical phases of plant germination and growth, the whole crop may fail. It is clear that global warming and climate change play a role in all of these events. The exact effects of climate change in these instances, however, do appear to be variable across different regions of the world (Henson).

- **Melting Ice:** Figure 8.6 (below) shows the shrinking of the ice cap that once covered Greenland. Figure 8.6 is startling because we see over half of the ice sheet disappearing within a little over a decade. A similar set of observations can be made in the Arctic regions of the North Pole. With the shrinking of glaciers and ice caps, Arctic ecosystems and their human and animal inhabitants have been forced into habitat relocation and alterations in living environments. For example, polar bears (an estimated 20,000 to 25,000 currently exist) have less ice for hunting due to early springtime thaws. Grizzly bear populations' expanding

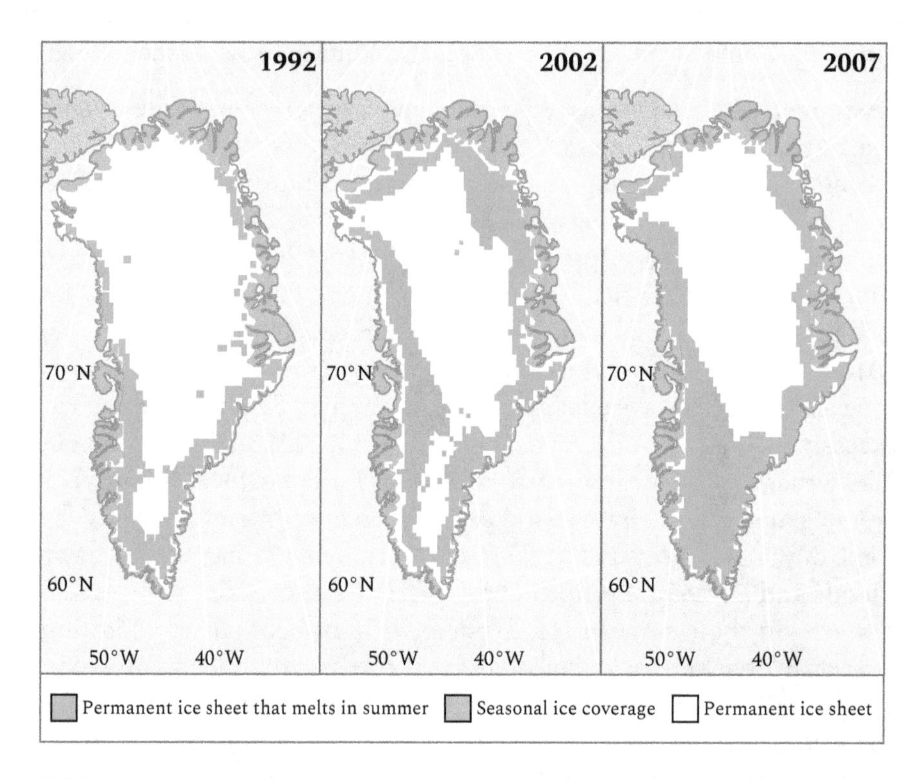

FIGURE 8.6 Greenland's Melting Ice Cap

northward led to a new species with the DNA genetic makeup of a hybrid polar-grizzly bear, known as "pizzly," discovered in 2006 (Henson, 89). With average polar bear cub live birth weights decreasing, polar bears may become extinct by the end of the century (Henson, 89). Likewise, arctic mammals such as seals, reindeer, and caribou, along with the Indigenous groups that depend upon them, are facing further stress due to the disruption of stable ice regions. While the effects are impossible to quantify exactly, high altitude temperate and tropical ice caps have also been decreasing in size over recent decades. The implications of these dramatic changes hold countless unforeseen consequences.

- **Oceans:** Covering over half the planet, oceans absorb the heat and carbon dioxide produced in the energy cycle. Among a plethora of plausible impacts of climate change, two stand out: rising ocean levels and acidification of seawater. While ascertaining the **median sea level (MSL)** of the world's oceans is difficult, the small island nations of Maldives and Tuvalu have experienced early warning signs of the effects of rising sea levels (Henson). Even though the islands are building expensive sea walls, preventing erosion, and creating landfills, scientists and government officials stress that these measures may not be enough to save the islands, which have a maximum height of three to six meters above sea level (Henson, 122). Both islands are exploring the option of relocating their citizens to safer areas, with worst-case forecasts anticipating a 2-foot rise by the end of the century. At present, tropical storms can inundate much of the land in these two remote places, as well.

  Other regions of the world are also at risk. The IPCC forecasts that a number of low-lying areas across the world, such as Bangladesh and even coastal Florida in the United States, could see rising sea levels by the end of the century, thus threatening these heavily populated communities (Henson). While difficult to predict due to current variability in global mean sea levels, **ocean acidification** (a measure of water's acidity) due to human-generated carbon has lowered the pH level of the oceans from a preindustrial 8.2 to a present 8.1, making the ocean more acidic. While a 0.1 decrease in pH doesn't seem significant, this slight change and the increasing acid content can negatively impact microscopic marine life, thereby altering the entire food chains built on them.
- **Storms:** Like with floods and droughts, described above, the causal connection between climate change and storms provides evidence that the intensity and frequency of storms, including hurricanes, is likely to increase (Maslin 2014). Areas that are subject to monsoon rains have been forecast to receive more intensive precipitation and subsequent flooding. Evidence also seems to indicate that tropical hurricanes are becoming more frequent and intense, although comprehensive data collection, monitoring, and analysis is still in its infancy (Henson 2011). On a global level, studies have shown that while the frequency of all hurricanes remained fairly constant, the frequency of category four and five storms has jumped by 50 percent

(Henson 2011). In sum, much more precision is still required to accurately assess these climate change matters. New methods and measurements are key here, and current estimations tend to be fragmented. Nonetheless, the issue has caught the attention of scientists and government officials.

- **Ecological Disruption, Extinction, and Human Crises:** Global warming is clearly impacting ecosystems in ominous ways. As mean temperatures increase, the canary in the coal mine analogy comes forth via temperature-dependent organisms such as frogs, butterflies, and small mammals. The interlinked nature of the ecologies of these organisms results in disruption of food chains and in a number of possible species extinctions (Henson 2011; Maslin 2014). A clarifying example that illuminates these issues refers to the increase in malaria regions of the world. As warming occurs, the range of malaria-carrying mosquitoes increases in both border and elevated regions. This disease then spreads to vulnerable populations. In the agricultural sector, widespread changes could negatively affect stable crops such as rice and other grains, thereby imperiling those populations that depend on these foods for their sustenance.

In sum, these emerging and forecasted impacts of climate change threaten human cultures. As temperatures rise from preindustrial levels to increases between 1–5 degrees Celsius, the list of potential impacts is indeed startling, as shown in Table 8.3.

TABLE 8.3 *Potential Impacts of Global Warming*

INCREASE (DEGREE CELSIUS)	POTENTIAL IMPACTS
1–2 degrees	- Significant impacts on polar, wetlands regions - Spread of infectious diseases - Increase in extreme weather events - Major impacts on ecosystems, e.g., coral reefs - Major impacts on agriculture, human health, and water resources - Significant extreme weather events
3–4 degrees	- Species extinction - Food and water security becomes evident - Forced evacuation and mass migration of affected populations - Signification human health crises - Extreme weather events are much more common
4–5 degrees	- 20% of world's population affected by flooding - 3 billion affected by water issues - Food failures, malnutrition, and starvation - Significant increase in human deaths brought on by malnutrition, starvation, disease, and extreme weather

Source: Adapted from Maslin 2014, 95–96; Vanessa Davis.

The above table is based on scientific studies that include current data assessments and analysis of a very extensive set of sources. Climate modeling is also a component of this projection. The IPCC is at the forefront in forecasting likely changes based on a plethora of studies from around the world in this regard. The IPCC, operating under the aegis of the United Nations, consists of 500 climate scientists from 120 countries, along with 2,000 peer reviewers of the periodic reports put out on climate change. The IPCC was awarded the 2008 Nobel Peace Prize (with Al Gore) for the work it has done (Maslin 2014).

ADDRESSING CLIMATE CHANGE

The above discussion on climate change addresses only the scientific side of the issue. We are at the interface between science and global politics with respect to what is being done to address climate change, as seen in Figure 8.7 (below).

The interface above can also guide us as to the varied responses to climate change. On one hand, various political and citizen groups deny the fact that climate change even exists. Although recently the "climate deniers" have more or less accepted the fact of climate change in general, they have turned to undermining the reliability of the data or stressing the negative impacts that addressing climate change will have on fossil fuel-run economies (Klein 2014). On the other end of the spectrum, groups that have prioritized the ominous realities of climate change propose solutions by advocating alternative sources of energy in the form of wind and solar power, as well

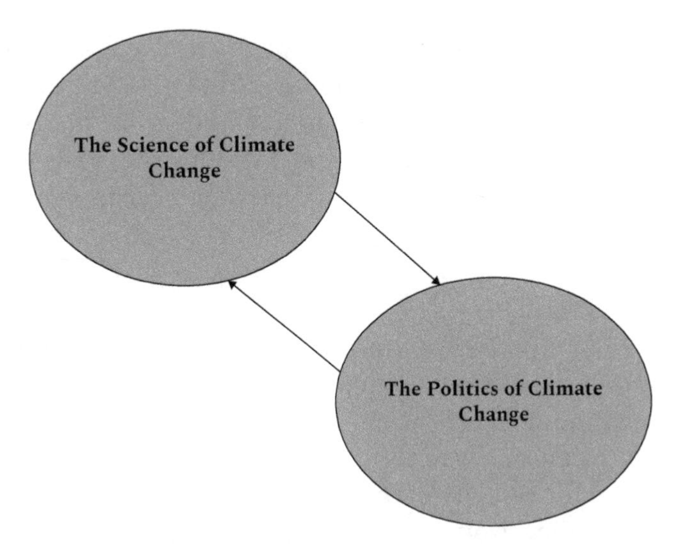

FIGURE 8.7 The Interface Between the Science and Politics of Climate Change (Vanessa Davis)

as for decreased carbon emissions consumption, which would necessitate a complete change in the way humans currently live (Klein 2014). In the middle are intergovernmental bodies, governments, and mainstream environmental groups, such as the Environmental Defense Fund (EDF), that have begun advancing market mechanisms in the form of cap and trade and offsetting to begin the process of lowering carbon emissions. It must also be noted that there are differences between industrial nations in the Global North, such as the United States, and industrializing nations, such as China, that further complicate matters. What follows is a very simplified outline of the efforts to address climate change. Figure 8.8 (below) sketches out a simplified set of positions that various politically oriented groups promote on climate change.

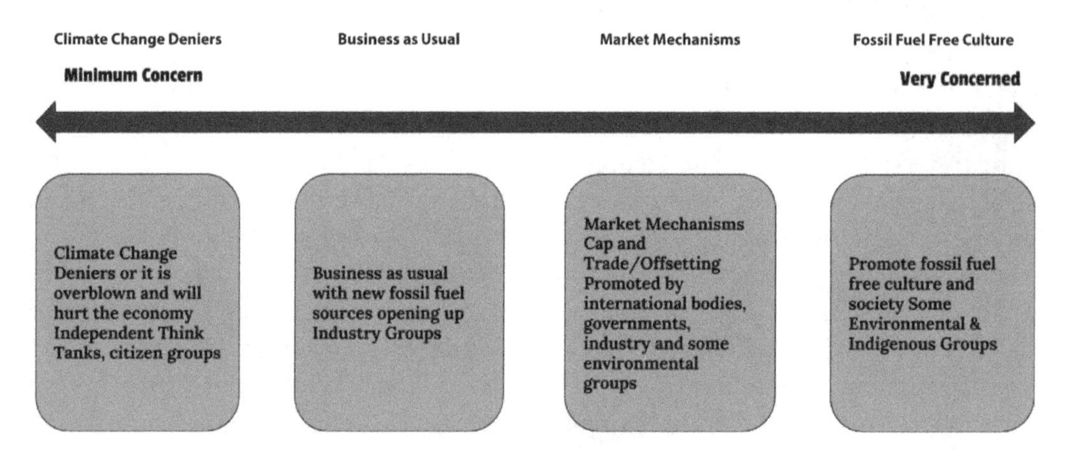

FIGURE 8.8 A Simplified Spectrum of Positions on Climate Change (Vanessa Davis)

Figure 8.8 illustrates a few of the diverse positions on climate change as advocated by a wide array of political actors. In her 2014 book *This Changes Everything: Capitalism vs. The Climate,* Naomi Klein provides a detailed account of the actors behind different views on climate change and groups the main views as follows: climate change denial, business as usual, and market mechanisms, such as cap and trade and offsetting.

Climate Change Denial

A well-organized and politically connected vocal minority, climate change deniers have moved more toward the center over recent years as the scientific data has become more robust, creditable, and convincing. In part, earlier media in the late 1980s to 1990s attempted to "balance" opposite points of view and indirectly gave these groups attention well beyond the veracity of their climate claims (Maslin 2014). A nonprofit research and public policy group, the Heartland Institute, stands at the forefront of minimizing action on climate change, arguing that address of climate change will negatively affect the economy (The Heartland Institute, 2019). Advocating free market worldviews, climate deniers see "warmists" (climate change proponents) as ushering in an era of state-regulated measures and greater restrictions on individual freedoms and liberties (Klein 2014).

In reviewing a series of revealing studies, Klein (2014) finds that climate deniers take issue with assertions of the severity of climate change despite the consensus stated by 97 percent of scientists trained in and researching the matter. Climate deniers are

> those with strong "hierarchical" and "individualistic" worldviews (marked by opposition to government assistance for the poor and minorities, strong support for industry, and the belief that we all get what we deserve),

while climate change supporters are

> *people with strong "egalitarian" and "communitarian" worldviews (marked by an inclination toward collective action and social justice, concern about inequality and suspicion of corporate power. (Klein 2014, 36)*

In short, there are **ideological** (worldview) positions at stake here that go beyond climate change. Importantly, this divide is not simply a matter of individual beliefs and attitudes, as climate deniers also form the support system for powerful political and economic interests who greatly benefit from delaying, distracting from, and even profiting from climate change in terms of initiating new insurance policies, investments and products (Klein 2014). Despite overwhelming scientific evidence on climate change, climate deniers are responding to the foreboding consequences that this matter brings to their outlook on who they are and how they see the world. This point was further made by McCright and Dunlap (2011) in a cleverly titled and highly researched article, "Cool Dudes: The Denial of Climate Change among Conservative White Males in the United States." Among their findings:

- "White males who report atypically low environmental risk perceptions are more conservative than other adults.
- Conservative white males in the general public would be more likely than other adults to embrace and defend the claims of conservative white male elites.
- Conservatives—and we would extend this to conservative white males—strongly display tendencies to justify and defend the current social and economic system. Conservatives dislike change and uncertainty and attempt to simplify complexity.
- The positive correlation between self-reported understanding of global warming and climate change denial among conservative white males is compelling evidence that climate change denial is a form of identity-protective cognition, reflecting a system-justifying tendency.
- Since the mid-1990s, organized climate change denial has diffused from the US to other Anglo nations with established think tanks that promote free-market

> conservatism and front groups promoting industry interests, most notably Great Britain, Canada, Australia and New Zealand" (McCright and Dunlap, 1171).

Thus, climate change denial is a matter of justifying one's worldview and not directly engaged with the facts of climate change itself.

Business as Usual

Any delay in undertaking meaningful measures to reduce global warming benefits the coal, oil, and gas industries and the elite who captain those industries. Other industries are envisioning ways to profit from the pending dislocations and disasters that forecasters are telling us will inevitably occur. For example, the insurance industry is exploring ways to prepare for climate disasters. Since these events are widespread and diverse, insurance premiums over a number of events could profitably cover one specific event (Klein 2014). The distractions put forth by climate deniers and the closely related fossil fuel industries act as **spin** (public relations efforts to give an often biased, favorable message on a particular media story, event, or action in order to persuade the public to agree with one's stance). A number of pundits, fossil fuel lobbyists, and public relations spokespersons spin views that climate change will be beneficial for advancing US geopolitical interests abroad. The reasoning is that since climate change will impact the globe, poorer countries will bear the majority of the climatic impacts in terms of flooding, storms, droughts, and other calamities. The United States, according to these spokespersons, can strengthen political and economic ties with other countries through infrastructure aid and relief efforts when climate-driven effects occur. In short, while acknowledging climate change as a matter of concern, the powerful fossil fuel industry detours around the matter and continues with record-setting profit maximization efforts while carbon emissions continue to grow (Klein 2014).

In sum, the fossil fuel industries have continued to pursue profit maximization even while recognizing climate change as a problem. The result is that little is being done and carbon emissions continue to increase. The promotion of "bridge fuels" to a sustainable and clean energy future have led to the highly controversial and carbon-emitting options introduced earlier, like natural gas **fracking** and the exploitation of **shale oil** and the **tar sands** in North America. Massive infrastructure developments involving railways, highways, deep water ports, and oil pipelines have been proposed, which will allow the United States to export coal, oil, and gas abroad. **Nuclear power** has also been proposed for energy revitalization.

Market Mechanisms: Carbon Cap and Trade and Offsetting

It should be clear that humans' production and consumption of fossil fuel energy has led to global warming and the emergence of troubling and cataclysmic weather patterns. As noted in the preceding sections, energy markets exhibit great flux and instability as to both supply and demand. At the same time, the energy sector remains highly profitable and aggressively ferrets out more marginal sources of energy with improved technology, regardless of whether it is oil shale, natural gas, or tar sands. The question of what the energy industries, government, and international bodies are doing to address carbon emissions brings forth an answer in terms of the mechanisms of **carbon trading** and **carbon offsetting** programs. We will explore whether these programs are effective in reducing carbon emissions.

What is Cap and Trade?

With carbon trading and offsetting schemes, we find international agencies, governments, industries, and some large "Big Green" environmental groups in a general consensus regarding the *theory*. The highly complex and intractable *practices* of these market mechanisms are much more variable and diffuse. To begin on a global level, the divide between the Global North and Global South is further exacerbated by the North's having a long industrial emissions history, while the South is seeking to industrialize in order to raise the standard of living. As a result, the South has placed pressure on the North to begin the processes of addressing climate change. The rapidly industrializing Global South nations (e.g., China) offer some resistance to implementing climate change policies because the fastest way to raise the material living standards is through traditional energy sources such as coal-fired power plants, oil, and associated manufacturing processes that make use of conventional fossil fuels. A matter of contention is whether Global South countries should be penalized for pursuing carbon-polluting industrial development. The Global South response has been to point to the industrialized Global North as the main source of carbon pollution while pursuing plans to industrialize along traditional development frameworks.

Cap and trade involves the creation of a market for carbon emissions (pollution). In theory, a number of free permits are given to companies, which set a limit on the amount of carbon emissions they can release into the environment. These caps, or pollution limits, are reduced each year, providing an incentive for polluting firms to innovate by reducing their emissions and investing in renewable energy sources. Companies are further allowed to trade these permits. If one company is under its carbon limit, it may sell its credits to another company who has exceeded its own carbon emissions limit. The Environmental Defense Fund (EDF) summarizes this market mechanism in the following link: https://www.edf.org/climate/how-cap-and-trade-works (EDF, 2019). EDF along with many energy businesses put enormous faith into a market for carbon pollution. By reducing the "cap" on a yearly basis, companies would be forced to innovate or risk going out of business.

Another related mechanism refers to **carbon offsets**. This type of market mechanism provides companies with the opportunity to compensate for their carbon emissions. For instance, recognizing that forests can act as "carbon sinks" (i.e., absorbing carbon dioxide) has led to the creation of the UN-REDD++ (United Nations–Reducing Emissions from Deforestation and Forest Degradation, with a + added to represent the additional goal of protecting local people and more recently another + added for safeguarding biodiversity). In theory, proponents envision this scheme as a win-win solution that both protects forests and reduces carbon emissions. UN-REDD++ was also championed at COP21 and seems to be gaining strong international momentum in addressing global warming (see UN-REDD++, 2019).

In short, a polluting entity establishes domain over a forest and can earn credits that count against emissions limits by maintaining that forest. As Maslin (2014, 132–33) remarks, the UN-REDD programs have often been poorly designed. They have failed to take into account that forest maintenance in one place may place pressure on other forest regions, a problem termed as "leakage." There are also a number of offset programs that are voluntary. At times, Indigenous forest dwellers have been displaced by these mechanisms.

The Nature Conservancy offers a program (see The Nature Conservancy, 2019) in which individuals donate to various forest projects managed by the Conservancy. Since forests are known to be carbon sinks, the Nature Conservancy, often in partnership with another agency, measures and monitors the carbon saved from these efforts, assuring donors that the funds are not wasted. The results from such initiatives require further scrutiny as to their effectiveness.

Criticisms of Carbon Cap and Trade and Carbon Offset Programs

Both cap and trade and offset mechanisms have been heavily criticized as to their effectiveness in reducing carbon emissions. In short, caps amount to free permits to pollute and can also be traded—a less polluting corporation can sell credits to another corporation that is exceeding their own limit. The market itself has been volatile, and the monitoring and management of pollution entails other costs that are usually passed on to the consumers of industries like electricity. Likewise, offset programs can be manipulated into windfalls for a polluting entity. The link below shows this in the case of commercial palm oil tree farms in Indonesia, which were substituted as offsets after removal of the original forest and its Indigenous inhabitants. In addition, a company may downsize plans to expand operations and receive offsets for this effort (see, Criticisms of Carbon Cap & Trade and Offset Mechanisms). At the same time, carbon dioxide levels have exceeded 400 ppm for the first time in recorded history, with 2015 being the warmest year on record (NASA 2016).

TOWARD A FOSSIL FUEL FREE CULTURE AND SOCIETY?

In sum, the first three positions illustrated in Figure 8.9 (below), climate deniers, business as usual, and the general consensus of market mechanisms involving cap and trade and offsets, have received criticism from those advocating a stronger direction that leads toward a fossil fuel free culture and society. These critics state that transition energy sources, such as natural gas and oil shale, along with the cap and trade and offset markets are "false solutions." Given that carbon dioxide stays in the atmosphere for a long time and the current measures exceed 400 ppm of carbon dioxide in the atmosphere, more drastic measures are needed to avert catastrophic climate change.

In this regard, some environmental groups, citizen organizations, and Indigenous groups have mobilized at the grassroots level (see chapter 9). These eclectic coalitions are more aggressively advocating renewable sources of energy, including wind and solar power development, and taking direct action in opposing industry efforts to expand current fossil fuel production methods (e.g., fracking, tar sands) and infrastructure (e.g., new coal plants and expanded pipelines). For example, a number of western Washington-based tribes, municipalities, and environmental groups are opposing seaport and pipeline expansion in the Pacific Northwest region (*Bellingham Herald* 2016).

Klein (2014) argues that a swelling mass movement is evident at the grassroots level and that Indigenous groups are critical to success in opposing the energy industry's relentless developmental expansion. This is due to the treaties that tribes have signed with the Canadian and US governments. These treaties provide a legal avenue to stop conventional fossil fuel energy expansion. Highway transport, deep water port development, and pipeline expansions have been blocked by court decisions in both the United States and Canada (Klein 2014). At present the movement has become even more far reaching, integrated and inclusive. The Climate Justice Alliance (2019) has advanced a community based action program that addresses not only climate change but overall citizen social and economic well being. Indeed politicians and other policy decision-makers are increasingly taking notice.

Finally, there are a plethora of new technologies that seek to reduce carbon emissions in the areas of energy, transport, buildings, cities, and materials such as lithium batteries (Hawken 2017). Some of these technologies have already arrived in the form of electric cars and LED lighting. Notably, solar, wind, and hydropower sources are replacing traditional reliance on coal for electricity generation. While there is a substantial ways to go in transitioning to renewable sources of energy and sustainability, the advancement of new energy sources is both widespread and promising. Will there be enough time to do so?

In sum, the question of a renewable energy future is at stake, and it can be surmised that international and even global consensus on aggressively reducing carbon emissions has not been effective in capping them. In 2018, carbon dioxide emissions reached record levels at 37 billion metric tons. With carbon emissions rising and carbon dioxide remaining in the atmosphere for long periods of time, radical deductions in these emissions will have to be achieved. It seems as though the consensus has been centered on market schemes and monetizing carbon pollution, which are both dubious methods for effectively addressing climate change. While highly lauded, COP21 has been seen as making only short-term gains on this most vital issue ("COP21 Paris Summit.", 2019). Fundamentally, to avoid reaching a 2-degrees-Celsius planetary increase, very steep cuts in conventional energy production and consumption will have to be adhered to and implemented in actual practice. Figure 8.9 (below) illustrates this point.

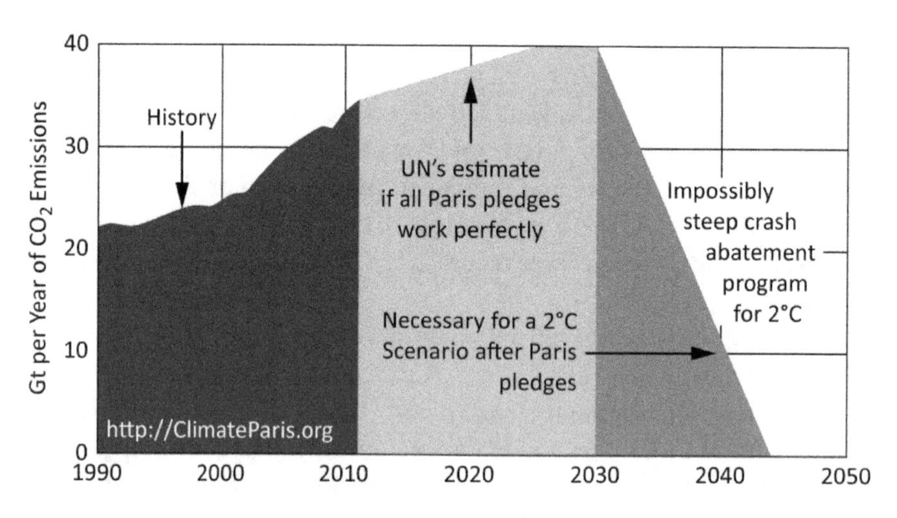

FIGURE 8.9 UN Pledges and Climate Realities Toward Harnessing Rising/Reducing Carbon Emissions

The question here is whether the global culture of capitalism has the ability to radically alter current fossil fuel energy-intensive production methods and lifestyles. The "false solutions" advocated by climate deniers, business as usual groups, and the financial interests that support market mechanisms weigh in on and point to "too little too late" outcomes. It is also highly questionable whether citizens and governments will voluntarily accept the consequences of climate change. Ironically, the costs for bringing efficient renewable energy such as solar and wind technology into competitive markets are rapidly decreasing. The only exception is the very high cost of nuclear power (Hawken 2017). Other identifiable efficiencies in water distribution (i.e., preventing leaks), electricity grid flexibility, hydropower, geothermal engineering, LED lighting, and tidal energy capture go along with new technologies such as "smart glass," insulation, and green rooftop redesign. The main question is whether there is the political will to bring these emerging technologies into concrete policy decisions and best practices for sustainable development.

Considerations Concerning Developed Versus Developing Countries

Climate change is anticipated to affect the most marginal populations and countries in an inverse manner. In other words, those Global South countries that did not contribute to climate change will be most impacted by it in terms of sheer survival. Extreme drought and flooding can destroy crops, thereby inducing severe food shortages in Sub-Saharan Africa and in low-lying rice-growing regions of Asia. Changing ecosystems can create animal and plant extinction, affecting those populations that depend on them for sustenance, such as in the Arctic regions of the world. Disease vectors such as malaria can expand as wet and warmer conditions become favorable for the mosquitos that harbor the virus. Rising sea levels have begun to create "climate refugees" from islands and low-lying areas along the world's coastlines.

Even in the developed Global North, taking into account marginal populations who are more impacted by extreme weather events, the matter of cost for extreme weather-related events is growing. In 2017, extreme weather and climate events cost US taxpayers an estimated US$306 billion. Three "once in a hundred years" hurricanes that hit Gulf of Mexico communities in 2017 accounted for US$265 billion in disaster relief (Reardon 2018). Other extreme weather events occurred in the Midwest, where severe hail, wind, and tornado-spawning thunderstorms accounted for US$5 billion dollars in disaster relief. The western US wildfires, notably in California, totaled US$18 billion. Even though climate change affects Global South countries most severely, it is clear that climate change affects everyone, especially the poor, regardless of their location.

A mixed divide exists between developed and developing countries in regard to carbon dioxide emissions, which have now reached a record 37 billion metric tons in 2018. Developed countries that industrialized earlier, such as the United States, Germany, Japan, and South Korea, or are rapidly industrializing, such as China, Russia, and India, emit the most carbon dioxide on a global scale (Global Carbon Project, 2019) and account for over 60 percent of all carbon dioxide emissions. Per capita carbon dioxide emissions from fuel combustion are highest in the United States and Canada at 15.5 metric tons per person. In contrast, China and India are relatively low, at 6.5 and 1.5 metric tons, respectively. Population size weighs in here, and with growing middle-class aspirations in these two countries, the per capita carbon dioxide emissions level is bound to rise (Union of Concerned Scientists, 2019).

The Case of China and Other Developing Countries

Developing countries advance the notion that long-industrialized, developed countries should bear the major responsibility for climate change mitigation. At the same time, the market demonstrates that pricing for renewable energy is becoming more and more competitive with conventional energy. Take China as an example. Currently, China is the world leader in carbon emissions. China is also the leading coal consumer in the world. The Chinese government prioritizes economic development as nonnegotiable to ensure political and social stability. At the same time, the Chinese government is well aware of air pollution in China's cities and rising ocean levels that can threaten coastal populations. Due to China's rapid industrialization, global carbon emissions peaked during the first decade of the twenty-first century, contributing to an unprecedented rise in the mean global temperature (see Figure 8.10). Since that time, political pressure has been focused on China, both domestically and internationally, to reduce carbon emissions. China has undertaken a broad approach in terms of developing renewable energy sources including nuclear, hydro, wind and solar energy sources. Recently, China has made plans to institute cap and trade as the main mechanism to address and reduce emissions from its power generation sector (Bradsher and Friedman 2017). The plan will be closely watched, despite poor performance of this method in the recent past in other parts of the world.

Finally, there has been a strong surge in renewable energy, especially when it comes to generating electricity. Twelve countries, led by Iceland, generate significant renewable energy from solar, wind, hydropower, and geothermal sources. Six of these countries can be classified as developing countries: China, Costa Rica, Kenya, Morocco, Nicaragua, and Uruguay. Kenya is developing geothermal sources for electricity generation. Uruguay has gone almost completely renewable in generating its electricity needs and did so in ten years. Costa Rica uses hydropower, wind, solar, and geothermal to attain high percentages of renewable electricity. China headquarters five of the largest solar module manufacturing plants, the leading lithium ion manufacturer (i.e., batteries), and the largest wind turbine manufacturer in the world (Click Energy 2017). In sum, China's efforts to reduce carbon dioxide emissions are diverse and entail a mix of traditional and renewable energy sources.

THE US FOOD SYSTEM, CARBON FOOTPRINTS, AND LOCAL AND GLOBAL VALUE CHAINS

As might be expected, carbon emissions emanate from the way we produce and consume our food. The carbon footprint from meat production alone accounts for 18 percent of total carbon emissions per year, and food system emissions could account for as much as a quarter of all human emissions. That is 12 percent from agricultural production, another 9 percent from farming-induced deforestation, and a further 3 percent from refrigeration and freight (Wilson, 2019).

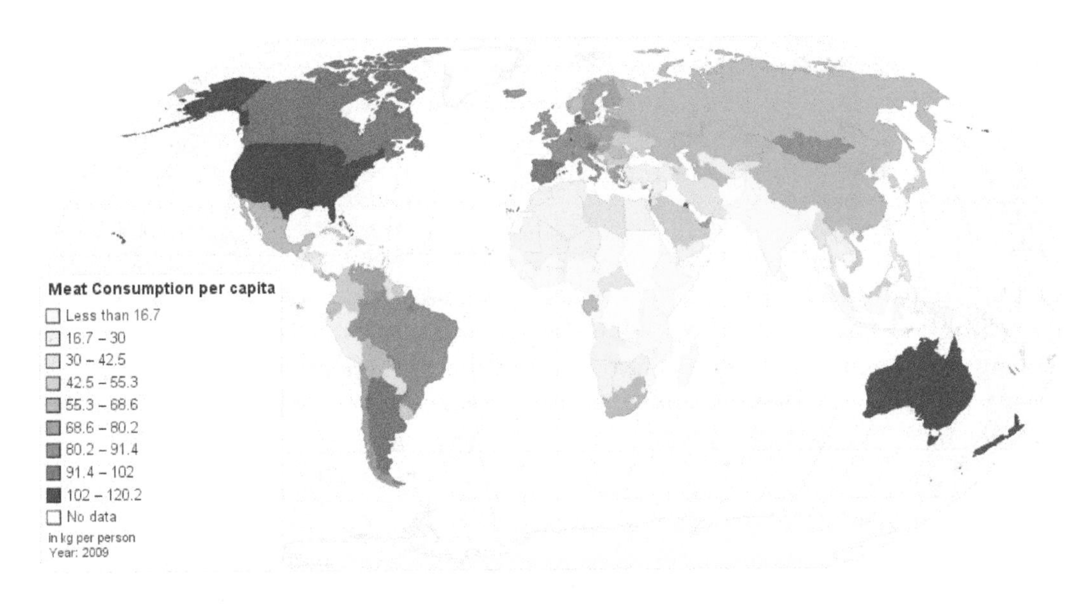

FIGURE 8.10 Global Meat Consumption Per Capita

As seen in Figure 8.10 (above), the United States and Australia are the world's leading meat consumers. The figure refers to red meats, meaning beef, pork, and lamb. Overall, the US diet is based on an inordinate amount of meat consumption. Table 8.4 below summarizes US meat consumption over the past 50 years:

TABLE 8.4 *U.S. Meat Consumption 1950–2000*

In 2000, Americans consumed an average 57 pounds more meat than they did annually in the 1950s, and a third fewer eggs

	Annual averages					
ITEM	1950–59	1960–69	1970–79	1980–89	1990–99	2000
	Pounds per capita, boneless-trimmed weight					
Total meats	138.2	161.7	177.2	182.2	189.0	195.2
Red meats	106.7	122.34	129.5	121.8	112.4	113.5
Beef	52.8	69.2	80.9	71.7	63.2	64.4
Pork	45.4	46.9	45.0	47.7	47.6	47.7
Veal and lamb	8.5	6.2	3.5	2.4	1.7	1.4
Poultry	20.5	28.7	35.2	46.2	61.9	66.5
Chicken	16.4	22.7	28.4	36.3	47.9	52.9
Turkey	4.1	6.0	6.8	9.9	13.9	13.6
Fish and shellfish	10.9	10.7	12.5	14.2	14.7	15.2
	Number per capita					
Eggs	374	320	285	257	236	250

Note: Totals may not add due to rounding.

Source: USDA's Economic Research Service.

A Short History of Beef

Meat consumption was once a luxury but has now turned into part of the average US diet. Robbins (2011, 192–202) provides a social history of beef in North America. Cattle were introduced into North America (Florida) in the 1500s. Early American colonialists were much more dependent on the production of pigs, due to their adaptability to forests, close confinement, and methods for procuring and saving the meat. Industrializing Britain looked for overseas sources of beef, and the US Great Plains was deemed an ideal place to introduce cattle for large-scale rearing on extensive parcels of land. At the time of the westward expansion, the grass prairies were occupied by Indigenous groups whose source of sustenance revolved around the American bison. In the late eighteenth century, the US government undertook a campaign to eliminate the bison and the Plains tribes that depended on them. Vast areas were turned into large cattle farms, where they destroyed the fragile native grasslands. "Fattening" facilities as early as the 1870s were further established for housing cattle prior to slaughter in the Midwest, where cattle were fed a high carbohydrate diet to produce the marbling of the meat then desired as the choice cut. Line production in Midwest slaughterhouses distributed beef throughout the United States and to other parts of the world. The cattle industry was also expanded in Latin America, where rainforests were cleared in Brazil, Costa Rica, and Mexico to make way for grass ranges. Finally, the rise of fast food hamburger outlets, coupled with the growth of automobile travel on the post–Second World War interstate system, allowed for the central prominence of beef in the current US diet.

Seafood Production

As Table 8.4 illustrates, seafood consumption is a relatively small part of total food consumption in the United States. Countries such as Japan and Maldives are among the world's highest seafood consumers (150 pounds/person/year and 300 pounds/person/year, respectively). In the United States, farmed shrimp (4 pounds per person) and salmon (2.3 pounds per person) are the most commonly consumed seafood items. Both shrimp and salmon are captured from the wild, but the majority of these species are raised by aquaculture (the controlled or farmed cultivation of aquatic organisms). Over 50 percent of globally consumed seafood is raised in aquaculture settings. Farmed salmon and shrimp have high carbon footprints, and due to the location of shrimp ponds in critical coastal areas, farmed shrimp have a particularly high carbon footprint (Stokstad 2012). Figure 8.11 (below) illustrates an industrial shrimp pond in Thailand. Note the aeration pumps due to high densities of shrimp per m^3.

Salmon are raised in protected estuarine coastal net pens. Figure 8.12 (below) shows one such facility off the coast of British Columbia. Each pen holds up to 50,000 adult fish.

FIGURE 8.11 Thai Shrimp Pond (Michael Skladany)

FIGURE 8.12 Salmon Net Pen Growing Facility

Although both shrimp and salmon are captured in the wild, over the last thirty 30 years, aquaculture of these species has been undertaken on an **industrial farm scale**. Globally, wild shrimp catches account for 3.6 million metric tons. Farmed shrimp from China, India, Indonesia, Thailand, and Vietnam account for about 75 percent of the 2.5 million metric tons cultivated annually. Shrimps farms in Brazil, Ecuador, and Mexico account for the other 25 percent. Along with its high carbon footprint, shrimp farming has been embroiled in longstanding environmentally deleterious impacts and human rights violations. (Philpott 2016). At the same time, shrimp remains the most valuable seafood commodity that is exchanged on the global market. While shrimp aquaculture can entail some serious risks due to disease, overall profitability has motivated a number of governments to create significant export industries. As

Asian and Latin American countries raise their income levels, a significant quantity of farmed shrimp also enters their domestic markets.

Like shrimp, wild salmon are mainly harvested from the Pacific Ocean through capture. The expansion of the wild salmon capture industry decimated the Atlantic salmon fisheries early on, and salmon aquaculture later proceeded up the West Coast of North America, ultimately centering on the massive wild salmon fisheries in Alaska. The destruction of prime spawning habitats due to dams and pollution has led to the establishment of hatcheries throughout the western North American coastline, concentrating in Alaska. In these hatcheries, young salmon are eventually released to live out their adult lives in the ocean, returning to home rivers to spawn and die. Wild salmon are important ecological **indicator species**, as they are essential to the environmental health of forest-laden coastal zones along the West Coast of North America (Skladany 2007).

Norway was the pioneer in adopting salmon to aquaculture (Skladany 2007). Raising salmon in coastal net pens proved to be a boon for this fledging industry in the 1980s. Favorable market conditions led Norwegian multinational corporations to establish joint ventures in British Columbia and Chile. Scotland, along with a few other countries, also has a significant salmon farming industry. Surprisingly, the majority of salmon encountered in the local super market are farmed. Atlantic salmon, the species of choice for global aquaculture farming, are native to the Atlantic Ocean but have been introduced to Pacific waters.

Similar to shrimp, salmon aquaculture has been embroiled in a number of longstanding environmental concerns. The recent approval of **GMO salmon** by the United States Food and Drug Administration (FDA) furthers these environmental concerns, because the farmed variety can compete for resources with wild salmon if they escape the net pens and can act as hosts for infectious diseases that are then passed on by nearby migrating wild salmon. Coastal fishers, including First Nations fishers in Canada, are opposed to industrial salmon farming. The salmon industry fights back with claims that environmental problems are being addressed through various **standards and certification processes**. These processes have been instituted to assure consumers, environmental groups, and local residents where the farms are located that the aquaculture practices are safe and the product is healthy. At the same time, the standards and certifying processes are often voluntary, enormously complicated, and can be extremely difficult to implement on a continuing basis.

In sum, globalization stimulated the industrial-scale farming of shrimp and salmon. The barriers to trade and investment domestically motivated entrepreneurial corporate organizations to establish industries in a variety of locations. Technological advancement in hatcheries, feed, and pond or cage management also provided further impetus. Global demand both at home and abroad stimulated expansion, and aquaculture now accounts for 50 percent of all seafood production. This fledging industry has not been without some serious environmental and human rights problems. Table 8.5 below lists some of the major concerns.

The issues exhibited in Table 8.5 have been ongoing for decades, and it remains to be seen whether or not environmentally sustainable standards can be rigorously and effectively put in place that monitor the daily operation of a given farm. Clearly, voluntary standards will not work. The question remains whether or not an authoritative and impartial regulatory agency can take on this task while keeping certification costs low. Many such schemes are merely spin and relatively meaningless. Recently, the EU and the United States have threatened a boycott of Thailand, the world's third leading exporter of seafood, due to slave labor on fishing boats and farms. In order to understand these charges, we will turn to a brief examination of the shrimp and salmon **commodity chains**.

TABLE 8.5 *Human and Environmental Concerns with Shrimp and Salmon Aquaculture (Vanessa Davis)*

CONCERN	SHRIMP AQUACULTURE	SALMON AQUACULTURE
Slave Labor	X	
Coastal Zone Pollution/Destruction	X	X
Escapees		X
GMO		X
Negative Impacts on Wild Capture Fisheries/Stock	X	X
Antibiotics	X	X
High Carbon Footprints	X	X
Diseases	X	X
Human Rights Violations	X	
Marine Mammal Predation		X

Shrimp and Salmon Commodity Chains

One major approach that is used to address environmental and human rights problems in the production of commodities is to examine the **commodity chain**. Each link in the chain from production to consumption is scrutinized to detect and correct environmental, health, and social problems that may result. Figure 8.13 (below) illustrates a very simplified commodity chain for the aquaculture of shrimp and salmon. By examining each step in the chain, transition points can be identified where problems may become apparent.

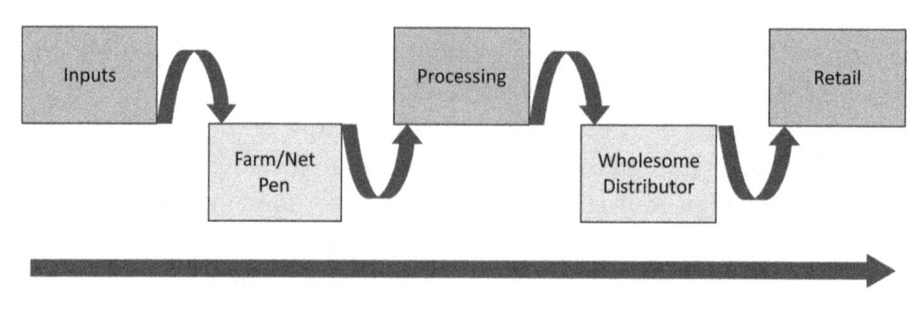

FIGURE 8.13 Simplified Shrimp/Salmon Commodity Chain (Vanessa Davis)

In Figure 8.13, we start with inputs, the components required to operate a pond- or ocean-based pen. These include seed from hatcheries, feed, chemicals, labor, and equipment. In shrimp farm production, commodity chain analysis has uncovered that in Thailand, the fishing boats that supply fish meal, the key component in the feed, use slave labor to harvest it from the sea (Hodal, Kelly, and Lawrence 2014). Critics have also charged that in both the salmon aquaculture and capture fishing industry the fish meal is harvested in a way that (1) destroys marine life and (2) is contaminated with harmful chemicals that ultimately end up in consumers' bodies. Fish meal is harvested in the ocean by trawlers. A trawler uses a fine mesh net and indiscriminately captures anything in its path, including economically important juvenile species, which is reduced to fish meal. In addition, this bycatch contains traces of harmful toxic substances that aggregate up through the food chain, ending in human consumption. A landmark study by Hites et al. (2004) demonstrated that farmed salmon contained more contaminants than wild salmon. This paper created shock waves in the farmed salmon industry and quickly generated spin that disputed the study (which was quite rigorous) and the almost instantaneous creation of "organic" farmed salmon.

As seen in Figures 8.12 and 8.13, shrimp farms and salmon net pen operations entail management and labor components. These facilities are guarded on a 24-four-hour basis due to the high value of the commodity. Shrimp farms in Thailand have been investigated for employing illegal immigrants, with attendant labor abuses in terms of working conditions, pay, and hours. Salmon net pens frequently rip, and Atlantic salmon are known to escape and subsequently compete with the wild Pacific stocks for food, habitat, and spawning areas. Given the great concentrations of fish per net pen, environmentalists and some scientists claim that these confined facilities can spread diseases and parasites, such as viruses and sea lice, putting wild salmon at risk when they pass by these crucial migratory routes on their way to spawning grounds. Salmon farm employees have also been known to eliminate predators, such as birds and seals, who feed on the confined salmon. The waste from net pens tends to aggregate on the ocean floor, smothering benthic sea life, and the widespread use of antibiotics in treating salmon diseases also enters into the ocean ecosystem. If this depiction isn't enough, the recent US FDA approval to bring GMO salmon into commercial production (in Panama) entails largely unforeseen environmental impacts that further complicate the salmon commodity chain (Morton, 2014).

Upon reaching desired market size, both shrimp and salmon are sent to processing facilities, where shrimp are deveined, peeled, and packed for transport and salmon are filleted, steaked, and packaged. Once again, Thailand's shrimp industry has been cast in an unfavorable light due to the use of slave labor at a few of these facilities (*Bangkok Post* 2015). The human rights violations exhibited in Thai shrimp farming have drawn warnings from both the United States and the European Union, who have threatened a boycott of Thai seafood. Thai officials have responded that they are correcting the problem.

Whether consumed domestically or exported, both shrimp and salmon are then sent to distribution centers, where they are further refined (e.g., packaged) and transported to the various retail centers where consumers make their purchases. At retail centers, these products are required to be labeled as to their country of origin and whether they are farmed or wild. At times, the labelling can become quite confusing, because some products can be mislabeled with, say, a common name such as "snapper" or "perch," or even "wild salmon," when the product is really farmed. In sum, the commodity chain illustrates how food is produced and how it arrives to the stores where consumers purchase these items. Commodity chains also illustrate how value is added during each particular step. Beef, shrimp, and salmon are produced on an industrial scale. Consumer and environmental groups, along with governmental officials, have applied pressure on these industrial food systems, with calls for safer, healthier, and more informative and sustainable ways to produce better food. The next section examines this new food movement.

INDUSTRIAL FOOD PRODUCTION AND THE TURN TO SUSTAINABLE LOCAL FOOD SYSTEMS

The vast majority of our food is produced in an industrial manner. Food production processes are dominated by agribusiness corporations that often exhibit **vertical integration** over the whole commodity chain. Vertical integration in poultry farming, for example, involves a corporation supplying a farmer with all inputs to produce large numbers of birds for market. Often times, the farmer is **contracted** by a company to undertake this production activity and shoulder the majority of risks associated with the labor-intensive activity of raising the birds. At each subsequent stage of the commodity chain, corporate processing, distribution, and in some cases, retailing can occur. Along each step in the commodity chain, the corporation adds value through packaging and advertising that makes the production and sale of these food commodities profitable. In order to make these industrial operations profitable, food production must be economically efficient, have centralized facilities, and produce food on a mass scale. My Science Academy has produced a video that illustrates how industrial food is produced (My Science Academy 2013).

Due to deleterious environmental effects, animal welfare concerns, and the questionable health impacts on our diet of industrial-produced food, a turn toward local and sustainable food production and consumption has taken root in the United States and throughout many other countries in the world. This movement focuses on healthier and more environmentally sound ways of providing consumers with a more nutritious and aesthetically satisfying experience. Farm to table restaurants, farmers' markets, celebrity chefs, non-GMO and organic food offerings, and "locally grown" selections in our supermarkets are all examples of the new turn toward sustainable food systems. Urban farms, Community Supported Agriculture (CSA), and community gardens are spreading rapidly and becoming much more prevalent in urban landscapes. In poorer urban neighborhoods, a number of new food initiatives are making efforts to offer local residents the opportunity to transform "food deserts" into locally grown food emporiums. For example, Rid-All Green Partnership in Cleveland, Ohio, has erected ten hoop houses on a vacated plot of land that was once an industrial site. Their motto, "Food is culture, culture is food," explains their mission to provide nutritionally affordable vegetables and fish to local community members and establish a relationship through education, community, and self-awareness (Rid-All Green Partnership, 2019).

At their far-reaching best, the new local food movements build social capital. **Social capital** refers to the integration of face-to-face connections between individuals and communities. Social capital strengthens networks between these actors and fosters trust and cooperation. Enhanced social capital networks allow us to resolve problems and collectively make decisions in a manner that benefits all. We can use this concept of social capital and apply it to how we eat in three ways (see Figures 8.14, 8.15, and 8.16).

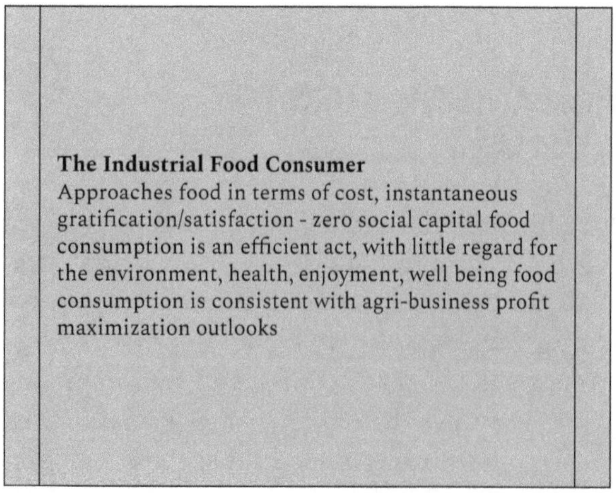

The Industrial Food Consumer
Approaches food in terms of cost, instantaneous gratification/satisfaction - zero social capital food consumption is an efficient act, with little regard for the environment, health, enjoyment, well being food consumption is consistent with agri-business profit maximization outlooks

FIGURE 8.14 Model 1: The Industrial Food Consumer and Social Capital (Vanessa Davis)

The three models illustrated above point to three different foodways, the way one approaches, consumes, and enjoys food. Those in the dominant, industrial model, (e.g., fast food and agribusiness commodities) do little to foster social capital and correspond with the environmental and human rights problems that were discussed earlier in the cases of shrimp and salmon aquaculture. The conscientious individual food consumer is mainly concerned with his or her own well-being but clearly recognizes the health and environmental consequences of his or her current food choices. Lastly, the social capital–oriented food consumer views food as a means to build community and understands the value of a sustainable lifestyle.

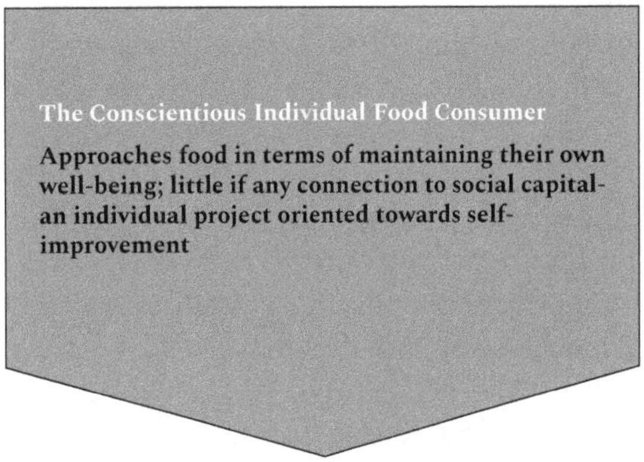

The Conscientious Individual Food Consumer

Approaches food in terms of maintaining their own well-being; little if any connection to social capital-an individual project oriented towards self-improvement

FIGURE 8.15 Model 2: The Conscientious Individual Food Consumer and Social Capital (Vanessa Davis)

Certifying Agricultural Production and Products

The global food system is undergoing tremendous changes. Local food systems have many advantages in this regard. Although the amount of locally sourced food most people eat is minuscule compared with the ever-present industrial food commonly available, one can know in some detail how a local item was produced. One can meet the farmer who grew the item, visit the farm, and invest a reliable sense of trust in such relationships. Because of this transition, the local food commodity chain is relatively short and transparent. In contrast, industrial food growers and retailers

FIGURE 8.16 Model 3: The Social Capital–Oriented Food Consumer (Vanessa Davis)

have implemented various certifications and standards schemes to ensure that the food commodities they grow and sell conform to environmental, health, and labor standards. Certifying that a given food commodity is environmentally sound is highly complex, as the methods involve constant monitoring, reporting, and reviewing. In some cases, corporations partner with "Big Green" environmental groups that lend corporations their "green" acquiescence.

One controversial, longstanding case is between Walmart and the Environmental Defense Fund (EDF). While the EDF publicly claims that they take no monies from their partners directly, the Walton Foundation (operated by the family who owns Walmart) has poured at least US$66 million into the EDF's coffers, thus allowing the EDF to emerge as one of the most powerful environmental groups in the world (Plambeck and Denend 2011). The Global Aquaculture Alliance, a worldwide fish farming advocacy group, has certified over 1,000 facilities worldwide with the label of "Best Management Practices" (Best Aquaculture Practices). These certification schemes, among many others, seek to establish credibility behind a given marketed food commodity in the World Wildlife Fund and the Global Aquaculture Alliance schemes (2019) and can give market credibility to a whole corporation, as in the EDF-Walmart partnership. In sum, these schemes vary but can be generally faulted because they are often voluntary in nature. These types of product differentiations are becoming more common and in the near future will probably be necessary for corporate survival. These partnerships are open to charges of "**greenwashing**," **spin**, and **distancing**, which keeps business operating as usual. Once again, the momentum shifts away from global certification of distanced and long-commodity chains to local sources.

CONFLICT MINERALS: COLTAN, CONGO, AND ELECTRONICS

Examining commodity chains not only applies to food production and consumption. The mining of minerals is a core and vital activity in the culture of capitalism. Mining is one of the most environmentally degrading processes. One group of mined products is **conflict minerals**. Conflict minerals refers to the industrial mining practice that

> has funded some of the world's most brutal conflicts for decades. Today, resources from conflict or high-risk areas, such as parts of Afghanistan, Colombia, the Democratic Republic of Congo (DRC), and Zimbabwe, can fund armed groups and fuel human rights abuses. These resources can enter global supply chains, ending up in our mobile phones, laptops, jewelry and other products. It is very difficult for consumers to know if their favorite products fund violence overseas. (Global Witness, 2019)

Conflict minerals, such as gold, tin, tungsten, cobalt, diamonds, and, for purposes here, **coltan**, are used in Western societies for a variety of essential electronic products (e.g., cellphones and computers). Gold and diamonds feature in jewelry. Cobalt is a major component of batteries for use in electric cars. Armed groups in Afghanistan, Colombia, Congo, and Zimbabwe control remote mining locations and sell the raw minerals in exchange for weapons, which are then used to arm militias who carry out war with the ruling nation-states and their neighbors. These remote areas in eastern Congo and elsewhere are beyond the effective control of the nation-state and international agencies such as the United Nations. The case of coltan is especially salient. In the video "Conflict Minerals, Rebels, and Child Soldiers in the Congo," a group of VICE journalists travels to the mining areas to record and interview the groups responsible for the mining and conflict. They note that, under pressure from human rights groups, the US Congress has passed legislation designed to ferret out these violent groups and remove them from the commodity chain (VICE 2012). The commodity chain for coltan is illustrated in Figure 8.17 (below), showing the long journey that coltan travels to make it into electronics.

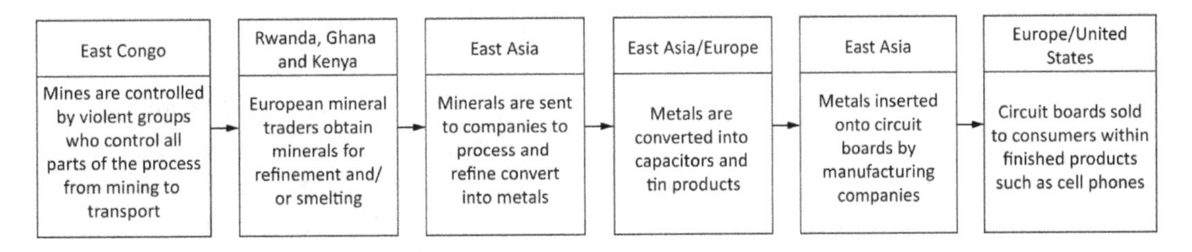

FIGURE 8.17 Coltan Commodity Chain (Vanessa Davis)

With 85 percent of the world's known coltan supplies found in the Eastern Congo region, armed groups maintain a longstanding and fierce presence in the region (see chapter 5). As we demonstrated in the examples of shrimp, salmon, and industrial food, standards and certification processes have been instituted as a means of addressing environmental and human rights problems. Likewise, corporate standards and certification processes have been instituted in the case of coltan to determine if it is "conflict free," to assuage consumer concerns. These processes are less than guaranteed, because the smelting of the mineral can consist of coltan from other parts of the world, making it difficult to determine the mineral's origin. In other words, sourcing coltan derived from varied locations undermines the efforts to precisely trace the origin of the mineral.

CONCLUSION

In this chapter, we have examined the environment and culture in terms of Western capitalist development. We note that the culture of capitalism is wedded to the use of fossil fuel energy that is at the basis for global warming and climate change. A review of climate change policies by industry, government, international agencies, and some environmental groups strongly indicates that too little is being done too late. The direction clearly points to continuing warming of Earth well into the future. In this context, a growing grassroots movement is advocating more fundamental change in values and culture. These environmental and Indigenous groups call for a complete break with the dependence on fossil fuels and a full-fledged transition to renewable energy sources.

We then examined our food system through a short history of beef and the current aquaculture of shrimp and salmon farming. We found that these food items contribute significantly to carbon emissions and environmental and human rights problems. The case was made that shifting to local as opposed to industrial food consumption can lessen these impacts. Lastly, we briefly examined conflict minerals through the case of coltan, a vital component in the electronics we use on a daily basis. Like in our food commodity examples, corporations have attempted to apply standards and certification processes to address the environmental and human rights abuses that occur in coltan's commodity chain. These standards and certification processes are less than precise.

Finally, we can surmise that the culture of capitalism is not sustainable as presently practiced throughout the world. The voices questioning what the alternatives will be can only become more vocal as various tipping points are reached. Whether or not humans can voluntarily reconstruct their values and culture is an agenda that will dominate the twenty-first century. If this does not happen, the forecast is dire. We started this chapter with an assessment of our ecological footprint. While modest, this exercise allows one to better come to grips with the imminently challenging obstacles confronting Earth's future survival.

So what can you do to help combat climate change and reduce your ecological footprint? There are many small steps that one can do on a personal level that make a big impact. Conick and Haley (2007) provide some ideas. One such suggestion is for communities to move toward better public transportation systems that make such transportation more practical for all citizens. While cars are convenient, participating in mass transit can drastically cut a community's dependence on oil. Additionally, airline travel is hugely consumptive of fossil fuel, so limiting flights is a smart way to cut emissions. Another idea that may seem small is to invest in energy-saving lighting and appliances that meet energy star standards. While this is a suggestion that seems very basic, just looking at your energy bills after diligent practice will be evidence enough that a positive change is occurring. On a similar note, remembering to turn off all lights and electronics when not in use also reduces one's energy footprint. Additionally, being aware of one's eating habits and becoming a more social capital-oriented food consumer is important. Reducing consumption of meat (especially beef, a large source of methane emissions) and making an effort to eat local food that relies less on oil-fueled transportation to get to grocery stores can make an impact. The EPA lists different ways you can save energy in all areas of your daily life in the following link: https://www.epa.gov/sustainability/how-can-i-help-sustainability.

REFERENCES

American Petroleum Institute. "Hydraulic Fracking," https://www.api.org/news-policy-and-issues/hydraulic-fracturing. 2019

Bangkok Post. "Shrimp Peeled by Slaves in Thailand." December 14, 2015. http://www.bangkokpost.com/archive/shrimp-peeled-by-slaves-in-thailand/794021.

BBC News. "What Is Fracking and Why Is It Controversial?" British Broadcasting Company. October 15, 2018. http://www.bbc.com/news/uk-14432401.

Bellingham Herald. "Lummis Join Tribes Opposing Massive Pipeline Expansion in Canada." January 22, 2016. http://www.bellinghamherald.com/news/local/article56084670.html.

Best Aquaculture Practices. "BAP Certification." http://bap.gaalliance.org/.

Bradsher, Keith, and Lisa Friedman. "China Unveils an Ambitious Plan to Curb Climate Change Emissions." *New York Times.* December 19, 2017. https://www.nytimes.com/2017/12/19/climate/china-carbon-market-climate-change-emissions.html.

Bullard, Robert D. *Dumping in Dixie: Race, Class, and Environmental Quality.* New York: Routledge, 2000.

Click Energy. "12 Countries Leading the Way in Renewable Energy." August 10, 2017. https://www.clickenergy.com.au/news-blog/12-countries-leading-the-way-in-renewable-energy.

Climate Justice Alliance. https://climatejusticealliance.org/about/. 2019

Conick, Cy, and Brendan Haley. "12-Step Program to Combat Climate Change." *Canadian Dimension* 41, no. 2 (2007): 39–41.

"COP21 Paris Summit." http://climateparis.org/.

Christie, Les. "American's Homes Are Bigger than Ever." *CNN Money.* June 5, 2014. http://money.cnn.com/2014/06/04/real_estate/american-home-size/.

Earth Day Network. Ecological Footprint Calculator. https://www.footprintnetwork.org/resources/footprint-calculator/.

Environmental Defense Fund (EDF). "How Cap and Trade Works." Climate. https://www.edf.org/climate/how-cap-and-trade-works.

Environmental Protection Agency (EPA). https://www.epa.gov/sustainability/how-can-i-help-sustainability, 2019.

Global Carbon Project. "CO2 Emissions." Global Carbon Atlas. http://www.globalcarbonatlas.org/en/CO2-emissions.

Global Witness. "Conflict Minerals." https://www.globalwitness.org/en/campaigns/conflict-minerals/.

Hawken, Paul (ed). *Drawdown: The Most Comprehensive Plan Ever Proposed to Reverse Global Warming.* New York: Penguin Books, 2017.

Henson, Robert. *The Rough Guide to Climate Change: The Symptoms, The Science, The Solutions.* London: Rough Guides Ltd, 2011.

Hites, Ronald A., Jeffrey A. Foran, David O. Carpenter, M. Coreen Hamilton, Barbara A. Knuth, and Steven J. Schwager. "Global Assessment of Organic Contaminants in Farmed Salmon." *Science* 303, no. 5655 (January 2004): 226–29.

Hodal, Kate, Chris Kelly, and Felicity Lawrence. "Revealed: Asian Slave Labor Producing Prawns for Supermarkets in US, UK." *The Guardian.* June 10, 2014. http://www.theguardian.com/global-development/2014/jun/10/supermarket-prawns-thailand-produced-slave-labour.

Klein, Naomi. *This Changes Everything: Capitalism vs. the Climate.* New York: Simon & Schuster Paperbacks, 2014.

LaDuke, Winona. *All Our Relations: Native Struggles for Land and Life.* Boston: South End Press, 1999.

Lukacs, Martin. "The Arsonists of Fort McMurray Have a Name." *The Guardian.* May 12, 2016. http://www.theguardian.com/environment/true-north/2016/may/12/the-arsonists-of-fort-mcmurray-have-a-name?CMP=share_btn_tw.

Maslin, Mark. *Climate Change: A Very Short Introduction.* Oxford: Oxford University Press, 2014.

McCright, Aaron M., and Riley E. Dunlap. "Cool Dudes: The Denial of Climate Change Among Conservative White Males in the United States." *Global Environmental Change* 21, no. 4 (October 2011): 1163–72.

Morton, Alexandra. "10 Reasons Not to Eat Farmed Salmon." https://alexandramorton.typepad.com/10_reasons_not_to_eat_far/. 2014

My Science Academy. "Without Saying a Word This 6 Minute Short Film Will Make You Speechless." August 19, 2013. http://myscienceacademy.org/2013/08/19/without-saying-a-word-this-6-minute-short-film-will-make-you-speechless/.

NASA. "Analyses Reveal Record-Shattering Global Warm Temperatures in 2015." Climate Change: News. January 19, 2016. http://climate.nasa.gov/news/2391/.

Nuclear Energy Institute. "Statistics." NEI.org. http://www.nei.org/Knowledge-Center/Nuclear-Statistics/World-Statistics.

Oklahoma State Office of the Secretary of Energy and Environment (OSEE). "Earthquakes in Oklahoma: What We Know." http://earthquakes.ok.gov/what-we-know/.

Perrow, Charles. *Normal Accidents: Living with High-Risk Technologies.* Princeton, NJ: Princeton University Press, 1999.

Philips, Matthew. "Oklahoma Earthquakes Are a National Security Threat." *Bloomberg.* October 23, 2015. http://www.bloomberg.com/news/articles/2015-10-23/oklahoma-earthquakes-are-a-national-security-threat.

Philpott, Tom. "As If Slavery Weren't Enough, 6 Other Reasons to Avoid Shrimp." *Mother Jones.* January 6, 2016. http://www.motherjones.com/tom-philpott/2016/01/six-reasons-think-hard-about-shrimp-craving.

Plambeck, Erica, and Lyn Denend. "The Greening of Walmart's Supply Chain ... Revisited." *Supply Chain Management Review* 15, no. 5 (September 2011): 16–23. https://www.gsb.stanford.edu/faculty-research/publications/greening-wal-marts-supply-chain-revisited.

Reardon, Kelly. "What Were the 16 Catastrophic Billion-Dollar Weather, Climate Events NOAA Reported in 2017?" Cleveland.com. January 2018. http://www.cleveland.com/weather/blog/index.ssf/2018/01/what_were_the_16_catastrophic.html#incart_river_home.

Rid-All Green Partnership. "Green Ghetto." http://www.greennghetto.org/.

Robbins, Richard H. *Global Problems in the Culture of Capitalism.* 5th ed. New York: Prentice Hall. 2011.

Skladany, Michael. "Social Life and Transformation in Salmon Fisheries and Aquaculture." In *The Fight Over Food: Producers, Consumers, and Activists Challenge the Global Food System*, edited by Wynne Wright and Gerad Middendorf, 117–200. University Park, PA: The Penn State University Press, 2007.

Stokstad, Erin. "The Carbon Footprint of a Shrimp Cocktail." *Science.* February 17, 2012. http://www.sciencemag.org/news/2012/02/carbon-footprint-shrimp-cocktail.

SustainableDevelopment. "Tar Sands Oil Extraction – The Dirty Truth." YouTube. Posted April 27, 2011. https://www.youtube.com/watch?v=YkwoRivP17A.

The Heartland Institute. "The Heartland Institute: Freedom Rising." https://www.heartland.org/.

The Nature Conservancy. "Frequently Asked Questions: Carbon Offset Program." Global Warming and Climate Change. http://www.nature.org/ourinitiatives/urgentissues/global-warming-climate-change/help/carbon-offset-program-frequently-asked-questions.

Union of Concerned Scientists. "Each Country's Share of CO2 Emissions." Science and Impacts. https://www.ucsusa.org/global-warming/science-and-impacts/science/each-countrys-share-of-co2.htmlns.xml.

UN-Reducing Emissions from Deforestation and Forest Degradation (UN-REDD++). http://www.unredd.net/index.php?option=com_content&view=article&id=2334:forest.

US Department of Energy. "Links for Students and Teachers." Overview of U.S. Gas and Oil Production, Office of Fossil Energy. http://www.fossil.energy.gov/education/energylessons/gas/gas_production.html.

US Energy Information Administration (EIA). "The United States Uses a Mix of Energy Sources." U.S. Energy Facts Explained. http://www.eia.gov/energyexplained/index.cfm?page=us_energy_home.

VICE. "Conflict Minerals, Rebels, and Child Soldiers in the Congo." YouTube. Posted May 22, 2012. https://www.youtube.com/watch?v=kYqrflGpTRE.

Washington State Department of Ecology. "About Climate Change." Air and Climate. http://www.ecy.wa.gov/climatechange/whatis.htm.

Wilson, Lindsay. The Carbon Foodprint of 5 Diets Compared." http://shrinkthatfootprint.com/food-carbon-footprint-diet/. 2019.

Yunghans, Regina. "Average Home Sizes Around the World." Apartment Therapy. July 20, 2011 http://www.apartmenttherapy.com/average-home-sizes-around-the-151738.

Figure Credits

Fig. 8.1: Illustrated by Philippe Rekacewicz, "The Earth's Atmosphere," https://www.whitehouse.gov/sites/default/files/microsites/ostp/ccspstratplan2003_all.pdf, pp. 30. Copyright in the Public Domain.

Fig. 8.2: Source: https://commons.wikimedia.org/wiki/File:Athabasca_Oil_Sands_map.png.

Fig. 8.3: Copyright © Depositphotos/curraheeshutter.

Fig. 8.4: Source: https://portlandrisingtide.org/campaigns/tar-sands-oil-exports/tar-sands-faq/.

Fig. 8.5: Source: https://www.unece.org/fileadmin/DAM/env/teia/water/pipeline/end_ve_van_egmond.pdf.

Fig. 8.6: Source: http://www.bssnews.net/newsDetails.php?cat=107&id=541359$date=2015-12-23&dateCurrent=2015-12-30.

Fig. 8.9: Source: http://climateparis.org/COP21.

Fig. 8.10: Source: http://chartsbin.com/view/12730.

Fig. 8.12: Copyright © Erik Christensen (CC BY-SA 3.0) at https://commons.wikimedia.org/wiki/File:Aquakultur-Vestmanna.jpg.

CHAPTER NINE

Global Social Change

INTRODUCTION

In this concluding chapter, we outline the dynamics of global social change. As part review, we outline the emerging loci of global social change, beginning with new alternative orientations to the top-down state-sanctioned development era (see chapters 1, 2, 4, and 5). Radical critics of development go further, calling attention to what they see as a postdevelopment era. Throughout this period, social movements have been ubiquitous and widespread and have covered a range of human concerns. We frame transnational social movements as systemic (originating from within the established institutional framework) and antisystemic (originating from outside the established system). Oftentimes, these two movements clash.

We hypothesize that there are three critical arenas that are fertile grounds for instigating new social movements: sustainability, gender inequality, and the pending trajectories of emerging middle classes. For each arena, we offer an overview and then follow up with concrete examples. For sustainability, we build on chapters 1 and 8 and detail some prominent organizational frames and positions taken by the **global climate justice movement**. Our discussion of gender inequality builds on chapters 2, 6, and 7 and is contextualized by an examination of **women in development** (**WID**). We illustrate systemic change in Rwanda regarding the ascension of women into previously male-dominated political, economic, and social roles and occupations. Building from chapter 6, we then examine the surge in creation of new **middle classes**. We note that there is no one universal middle class, as middle classes exhibit a wide array of political and social orientations. The growth of new middle classes in many parts of the world bears consideration for the direction of future social change. Lastly, we conclude with an invitation to the reader concerning our collective roles in these social change processes as development workers.

DEVELOPMENT TO ALTERNATIVE DEVELOPMENT TO POSTDEVELOPMENT?

Development is the guiding concept and point of reference throughout this book. We began with the notion that development, in the broadest sense, is defined as transformative change. In chapter 1, we qualified this definition by further contextualizing transformative change in economic, interventionist, and sustainable terms and forms. Chapter 2 was devoted to quantifying economic development under the Human Development Index and the United Nations (UN) Millennium Development Goals (MDG). We examined the MDGs of poverty and hunger and education and health over the period 2000–2015 and noted that significant gains have been made but found that Sub-Saharan Africa and South Asia lag behind other regions. Chapter 3 featured the origins of capitalism and the colonial era. Colonial relations greatly contributed to wealth accumulation in Europe and North America. In particular, the significance of slavery in this regard was highlighted. Chapter 4 examined early Cold War nation-state and economic development and used an illustrative example from Thailand. We concluded by noting that the adoption of the market economy has resulted in the middle-income trap for many developing countries. Chapter 5 explored modernization and the development pathway through the frame of modernization theory. We also remarked how this process can lead to state-sanctioned violence, as in the cases of Cambodia and Rwanda. Chapter 6 detailed the globalization era and ended with the emergence of multipolar globalization. China's efforts in terms of the "One Belt One Road" initiative provided an example of the new global constellation from East to South, encroaching on the previous Global North-South divide. We further noted that the classification of developed and developing countries is giving way to new schemes based on income levels and markets. Recently, one of the world's major institutions, the World Bank, has begun to reconsider the terms "developing" and "developed country." The World Bank is now reclassifying countries in terms of high, medium, and low income. Other classification schemes, such as the one used by the International Monetary Fund (IMF), have begun to label countries as advanced economies (AE) or emerging market economies (EME) (Khokar and Serajuddin 2015).

Alternative Development

The early era of development (1950–1985) was state-directed and can be characterized by a top-down approach. Objectives of embedding nationalism, political stabilization, and economic incorporation into the world capitalist system feature throughout this period. Experts, consultants, and national bureaucracies were the instigators of this policy and project-based processes. As the case of rural development in Thailand (chapter 4) demonstrated, the nation-state was able to more or less incorporate and consolidate urban and rural populations into relatively stable procapitalist configurations, thereby avoiding the communist threat. Overall, urban areas were favored, to the neglect of the countryside. Yet poverty persisted in both rural and urban areas, and few effective measures were undertaken to address and alleviate these conditions. Potter et al. (2013) remark that by the 1980s, official top-down development thinking reached a stalemate. As the neoliberal market-oriented paradigm surged forward and nation-states withdrew from economic management affairs, the alternative or bottom-up approach, often spurred and supplemented by a proliferation of **nongovernment organizations** (**NGOs**), led to a significant developmental reorientation. Potter et al. summarize what came to be defined as **alternative development** as the following;

- "A move towards redistributive mechanisms specifically targeting the poor,
- A focus on small-scale projects, often linked to urban or rural based community development programs,
- A focus on basic needs and human resource development,
- A re-focusing away from growth-oriented definitions of development, towards more broadly based human-oriented frameworks,
- A concern for local and community participation in the design and implementation of projects,
- An emphasis on self-reliance, reducing outside dependency and promoting sustainability" (118–19).

A more philosophical and intimate example is provided by Heim et al. (1986) in a classic statement that was at the core of Thai NGO training and development practice in the mid-1980s. For Thai NGO development workers, the alternative definition of development takes a cultural approach and begins with the realization that there is no one "correct" way of development. The Thai approach is based in Buddhist thought and practice and revolts against the seemingly anti-Buddhist values associated with Western materialism. As Heim et al. explains, the cultural approach "emphasizes ethnic and traditional practices and values" (43) This approach to life eschews attachment to "things," seeks to overcome desire and suffering, and attempts to live life righteously along the Noble Eightfold Path:

- "right understanding and right thought, which belong to the wisdom group,
- right speech, right action, and right livelihood, which belong to the virtue group,
- and right effort, right mindfulness, and right concentration, which belong to the concentration group" (Heim et al., 44).

Extending this set of principles, concepts, and practices into the field of development discourse, Heim et al. state:

> Development, which is defined as a step-by-step evolutionary process, influenced by exogenous circumstances combined with gradual endogenous unfolding, and which has the task of accelerating this process without undue haste, has to intervene in the confrontation between imperfect human beings and the world.

> It is the confrontation between imperfect human beings and an imperfect world. Both come together in a dialogue where human beings transform the world and undergo the effects of their transformation.
>
> This reciprocal process, which is a continuous confrontation, engenders continuous situational change.
>
> No situation is constant but rather changes permanently through various internal influences (confrontation between human beings and the world) and external influences (development projects, the environment, the food we eat ...) ... Adjustment to a changed situation does not suffice, as it implies an adaptation to something that belongs already in the past. (107–8)

The above "alternative definition" of development by Heim et al. is vastly different than theories such as modernization and state-led projects that were used in the cases of Accelerated Rural Development (ARD) and Rural Jobs Creation (RJC) (see chapter 4). In sum, the alternative definition of development begins from the inside and works toward a more holistic understanding of self and society through a mediated Buddhist interpretation, practice, and ethic. Likewise, Schumacher's popular *Small is Beautiful* (1973) approximates a number of similarities from a Western critique and standpoint. The point here is that "alternative development" is a way of life, a living philosophy that reaches out and extends beyond the scope of Western materialism, the cash economy, production, project planning, budgets, and logistics. Indeed Heim et al. (1986) are proposing a totally different means of development that instinctively appreciates and works with the total sense of human capability. The embodiment of this definition arrives in the concrete form and focuses on the key actor in these types of rural development endeavors, the **development worker**, which will be discussed in the concluding section of this chapter.

Postdevelopment?

Long on rhetoric and somewhat short on empirical evidence, a group of influential development scholars take a position "beyond development," articulating what they call **postdevelopmentalism**. A leading proponent of this critique is Arturo Escobar, and in his treatise *Encountering Development: The Making and the Unmaking of the Third World* (1995), he quotes Libia Grueso, Leyla Arroyo, and Carlos Rosero from the Organization of Black Communities of the Pacific Coast of Columbia:

> The government continues to bet on democracy and development; we respond by emphasizing cultural autonomy and the right to be who we are and have our own life project. To recognize the need to be different, to build an identity, are difficult tasks that demand persistent work among our communities, taking their very heterogeneity as a point of departure. However, the fact that we do not have worked out social and economic alternatives makes us vulnerable to the current onslaught of capital. This is one of one our most important political tasks at

> present: to advance in the formulation and implementation of alternative social and economic proposals. (cited in Escobar 1995, 212)

For critics like Escobar, modern development is a failure. Development in this view is a force of domination by Western powers that reproduces itself in Third World discourses. Escobar uses the example of Union Carbide's 1984 gas leak at their Bhopal, India, plant, in which over 5,000 people died and over 200,000 were affected. Escobar remarks that Union Carbide's corporate slogan, "Today something we do will touch your life" masks the hypocrisy, where the Bhopal leak acts as

> a reminder of the connection between the choices and power of some and the chances of others, a connection firmly established by the global economy with a deadly appearance of normalcy ... Bhopal is also a metaphor of development as a disaster of sorts which demands that the casualties be forgotten and dictates that a community that fails to develop is obsolescent. An entire structure of propaganda, erasure, and amnesia on Bhopal was orchestrated by science, government and corporations which allowed the language of compensation as the only expression of outrage and injustice. (214)

Thinkers like Escobar reject modern development and look to cultural autonomy and the building of authentic identities as an alternative to Western-imposed forces of social change. They vest much of this initiative in the mobilization of new social movements.

SOCIAL MOVEMENTS

Social movements are collective entities that work to bring about social change. The older social movements struggled to gain formal rights from the state, while more contemporary movements develop practices that challenge the power and dominant values held by the status quo (McMichael 2012). Our focus is on **transnational social movements** that occur in a global context. These formations tend to unfold in a series of stages, as exhibited in Table 9.1 (below):

TABLE 9.1 *The Formation of Transnational Movements*

STAGE	FORM	ACTIVITY
Beginning	Transnational Network	Information exchange
Intermediate	Transnational Advocacy	Campaigns and coordinated activity
Mature	Transnational Movement	Mobilization, seeking to bring about a desired outcome and long-lasting social change

Source: Adapted from Khagram, Riker, and Sikkink 2002, 9.

The ubiquity of electronic technologies has been one key element in fostering **transnational networks** that lead to global social movements. Citizens can now access and inform themselves on issues regarding local, national, and global problems. In this context, social media greatly facilitates network building and information exchange. In large measure, NGOs communicate with other parties by building normative counterframeworks, highlighting injustices and other political, social, environmental, and economic issues that negatively affect specific populations. As information concerning a particular issue expands and undergoes analysis, **campaigns** are formulated among the actors. **Transnational campaigns** require more formal communication and mapped out strategies to publicly address grievances and actions in order to bring about a desired social change. Campaigns are disruptive to the status quo, and at times those who uphold the status quo can mount a **countercampaign** to blunt the force of the initial NGO network and advocacy findings. A good example is the climate justice movement outlined in chapter 8. Fossil fuel free advocates, often citizen groups, environmental NGOs, and Indigenous groups, are countered by climate change deniers, fossil fuel industries, and, to an extent, environmental groups proposing market solutions. "Keep It in the Ground" is the slogan that sums up the campaigns for moving toward a fossil fuel free society. **Disinvestment campaigns** are another example, in which the fossil fuel free movement targets the individual stockholders of energy companies to persuade these investors to remove their holdings in a carbon polluting company and reinvest in clean energy (Klein 2014).

If the initial campaign strategies are successful and resonate with other groups and the wider public, campaigns can translate into long-term **transnational social movements**. Essential to these efforts to bring about long-term social change is funding that derives from the largesse of innumerable **foundations** devoted to environmental, economic, and social justice. Foundations can be large or relatively small and can be inordinately fickle, as their priorities can change rapidly depending on their reading of a social situation. Professional NGO groups are adept and politically skilled at attaining funding from these foundations. Not all information-sharing, campaign formulation, and movement generation are successful, however, as many efforts can fail. At the same time, a number of these movements have grown, as is evident in the remarkable "#Me Too" social media campaign in the United States. This campaign drew support from individuals and women's groups and quickly gained widespread traction, resulting in the outing and prosecution of a number of prominent men for sexual harassment and assault. It is highly likely that this movement will continue to reach far and wide due to the already existing feminist movement and, importantly, a formal legal structure that protects women's rights.

A final example of the above transnational social movements framework and process comes from the Indigenous Environmental Network (IEN). IEN, headquartered in Northern Minnesota, works on both a global and local level. For example, IEN attends, with other Indigenous delegates, the annual meetings of the UN Framework

Convention on Climate Change. IEN is also noted for their influential work on Indigenous human rights at the UN. At the local level, IEN's Regaining Food Sovereignty campaign

> explores the state of food systems in some Northern Minnesota Native communities; examining the relationship between history, health, tradition, culture and food. By reclaiming and revitalizing knowledge and practices around tradition, local and healthy foods, many communities and Tribal Nations are working toward a new model of community health and well-being for this and future generations. (IEN, 2019)

Other IEN campaigns involve stopping the use and cultivation of genetically engineered trees and the promotion of natural forest ecosystems. In each campaign, a strong traditional, cultural, and legal foundation provides the impetus for the long-term struggle to achieve desired outcomes. What is remarkable about IEN (and many other grassroots NGOs) is that they are able to undertake sustained campaigns and work toward holistic solutions over the long term with a small staff supported by modest foundation grants. Overall, there are many NGOs throughout the world that undertake this committed and dedicated work.

SYSTEMIC AND ANTISYSTEMIC CHANGE

In examining the location and origin of social change, we can identify two arenas: **systemic** and **antisystemic**. Systemic change originates from within the existing institutional structure of society. Antisystemic change originates from outside the system. Top-down systemic change can often be met by **resistance** from subordinate members of the public, whether subordinate status is on the basis of class, race, ethnicity, or gender. In the 1985 classic by James C. Scott, *Weapons of the Weak: Everyday Forms of Peasant Resistance,* the term resistance was defined as

> *any* act(s) by member(s) of a subordinate class that is or are *intended* either to mitigate or deny claims (for example, rents, taxes, prestige) made on that class by superordinate classes (for example, landlords, large farmers, the state) or to advance its own claims (for example, work, land, charity, respect) vis-à-vis those superordinate classes. (290)

Scott spent two years (1978–1980) living in the small Malaysian rice-growing village of Sedaka. He documented the coming of systemic Green Revolution rice-growing technology (chapter 4) and the forms of everyday resistance (e.g., gossip, sabotage of the combine harvesters, slowing down rice harvests) that the subordinate peasant class exhibited during this time of major systemic social change. As depicted in chapter 3, capitalism has a perpetual need to grow indefinitely, and poorer peasants were placed at a disadvantage by the wealthier farmers backed by the Malaysian state, who took advantage of the new technology (e.g., irrigation, land tenure, credit for fertilizer, insecticides, herbicides, high-quality seed). Poorer peasants resisted these tumultuous changes because they destroyed traditional social relations in the village.

In a similar example, rice farmers in Samlaut, Cambodia, were forced by the Prince Sihanouk regime to sell their rice crop to the government at lower prices than what they clandestinely obtained from sales to the Communist North Vietnamese (Chandler 1999). In 1967, fearing the loss of important government revenue, Prince Sihanouk sent armed representatives from his government to collect and buy the rice from angry farmers. Under then Prime Minister Lon Nol, government "action teams" were especially brutal in conducting rice sales in the Samlaut region. In April of 1967, Samlaut peasants attacked and killed two soldiers collecting rice and staged a **rebellion** denouncing the government (Becker 1986). In the aftermath, Lon Nol forces sought out communist agitators for retribution. Local militias were rewarded for bringing in the severed heads of "communists" and those responsible for the rebellion. Over 1,000 peasants died. Quietly, and concealed in the "Dragon's Tail" of the eastern jungle regions of the country, the nascent Khmer Rouge movement, fortified by the rebellion in Samlaut, made the decision to being waging armed **revolutionary war** against the US-backed Cambodian government (Chandler 1999). A five-year civil war (1970–1975) ensued and led to the eventual rise of the genocidal Pol Pot regime, as discussed in chapter 5.

The above examples illustrate the interplay between systemic and antisystemic change. The relationship between these two locations and origins of social change is represented visually in Figure 9.1 (below).

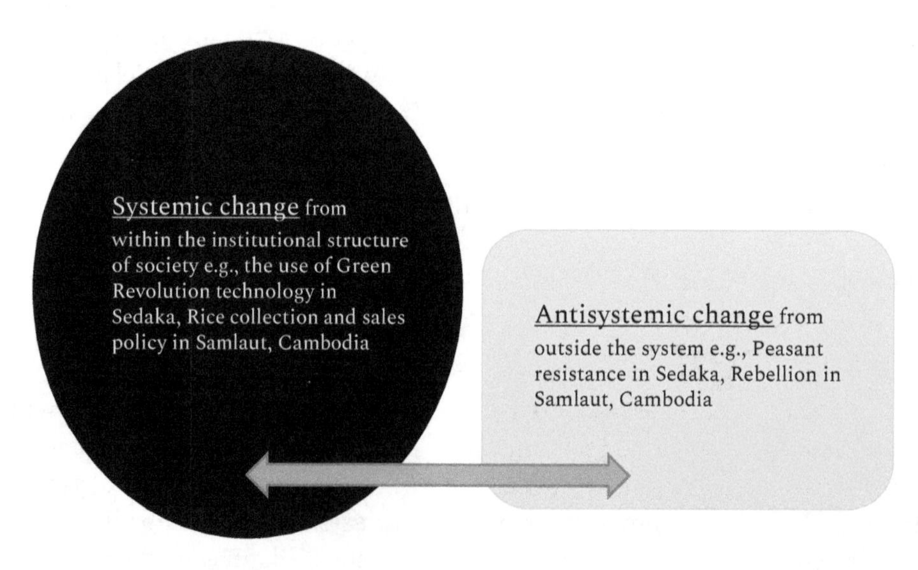

FIGURE 9.1 Systemic and Antisystemic Social Change

The above figure illustrates the relationship between systemic and antisystemic social change. In countless cases, the interaction between these two locations and origins of social change can also entail negotiations, cooptation, soft and hard political persuasion, countermovements, violence, imprisonment, and so on. In short, the locations and origins of social change are highly variable, heterogeneous, and multifaceted. In the next sections, we identify three loci—sustainability, social inequality, and the emerging middle class(es)—that will generate important forces for social change in the coming decades.

SUSTAINABILITY: CLIMATE CHANGE

In chapter 8 you were asked to calculate your ecological footprint. Inevitably, you found that your lifestyle was not sustainable because you consume more than the earth can support over the long term. Electricity use, automobiles, meat consumption, and living space were just a few factors that we all share that makes our lifestyles unsustainable. As chapter 2 illustrated, a number of world regions have experienced significant decreases in poverty and hunger, with Sub-Saharan Africa and South Asia lagging behind global averages. At the same time, continuing environmental degradation and growing inequality can substantially mitigate these gains and thwart the goal of sustainable development if left unaddressed (McMichael 2012).

Sustainable Development

The sustainability turn in development thinking arose out of the environmental movement and became part of global discourse with the establishment of the 1987 UN Brundtland Commission. The Commission declared that:

> Sustainable development is development that meets the needs of the present without compromising the ability of future generations to meet their own needs. It contains within it two key concepts:
>
> - the concept of "needs," in particular the essential needs of the world's poor, to which overriding priority should be given; and
> - the idea of limitations imposed by the state of technology and social organization on the environment's ability to meet present and future needs. (WCED 1987).

Since 1987, sustainable development has become much more prominent. A general consensus is that the world has reached its limit as to use of the planet's resources. The UN identifies 17 sustainable development goals (see WCED 1987). Five of these goals are directly related to sustainable ecosystems, with the other 12 goals overlapping. The five direct goals relate to (1) sustainable cities and communities, (2) responsible consumption and production, (3) life below water (e.g., oceans and freshwater),

(4) life on land (e.g., biodiversity, forests, and agriculture) and (5) mitigating the growing crisis of climate change. It is clear that implementing the "sustainability project" will require a vast reorientation of lifestyles that necessitates adaptation to living with less. As a coherent global stance, McMichael (2012) notes:

> The Sustainability Project is multifaceted and resembles a social tendency rather than a coordinated and/or coherent political-economic reality. It represents an emergent organizing principle in the complex world of development, whereby agencies, policies and movements are struggling to establish interrelated institutional frameworks and a multitude of practices that reduce or eliminate the so-called "externalities" of the market economy. (282)

Climate Change and Sustainability

In chapter 8, we noted that meaningful address of climate change was blocked by three factions; climate change deniers, conventional fossil fuel industries, and another faction that promotes market solutions. The market solutions faction consists of government, industry, and, surprisingly, some "Big Green" environmental groups. From the antisystemic standpoint, proposals emanating from these three factions are raked over as simply "false solutions." The most dramatic and far-reaching transnational movement for address of climate change comes from antisystemic groupings of citizens, some environmental groups, and especially Indigenous peoples.

Abundant evidence for the viability of a fossil fuel free society comes from Klein's *This Changes Everything: Capitalism vs. the Climate* (2014). Klein digs deeper and demonstrates how entrenched resistance to addressing climate change is centered on a clash not on the surface but with the three essential pillars of market fundamentalism:

> privatization of the public sphere, deregulation of the corporate sector, and lower corporate taxation, paid for with cuts to public spending ... very little ... has been written about how market fundamentalism has, from the very first moments, systematically sabotaged our collective response to climate change, a threat that came knocking just as this ideology was reaching its zenith. (19)

Klein marshals a plethora of evidence that clearly demonstrates that a fossil fuel free society is both possible and economically viable. From the examples of community-controlled renewable energy in Germany and Denmark and data that supports the claim that green energy will provide more long-term jobs, stimulating economic growth, Klein argues that this antisystemic transnational movement is up against some very, very vested and highly profitable interests (i.e., the conventional fossil fuel industry). At the grassroots level, Klein further dedicates a significant portion of her book to "Blockadia," the grassroots citizens, farmers, ranchers, and Indigenous groups who are mobilizing and blocking pipelines and highways transversed by trucks filled with tar sands shipments. Antisystemic movements have further blocked the construction of deep water ports in the Pacific Northwest where fossil fuels were destined for export.

Klein weaves together the different groups and strategies involved in this grassroots antisystemic movement and centers her most powerful arguments on the legal power that Indigenous groups have vis-à-vis the federal and state governments. In short, tribes have sent their best and brightest young people to law school, where they study the old treaties signed between a tribe and the federal government. This recovered legal standing provides a basis for legally challenging the extractive fossil fuel industries. But this is only half the battle. According to Klein;

> The reason why industry can get away with [extraction of fossil fuels] has little to do with what is legal and everything to do with raw political power: isolated and often impoverished Indigenous peoples generally lack the monetary resources and social clout to enforce their rights, and anyway, the police are controlled by the state. Moreover the costs of taking on multinational extractive companies in court are enormous. For instance in the landmark "Rainforest Chernobyl" case in which Ecuador's highest court ordered Chevron to pay $9.5 billion in damages, a company spokesperson famously said, "We're going to fight this until hell freezes over—and then we will fight it out on the ice." (And indeed, the fight drags on). (378)

Yet as evidence continues to mount for the coming calamity of an overheated Earth with dire social consequences (chapter 8), antisystemic network and advocacy organizations, such as the Climate Justice Alliance, forge ahead with a new vision of a fossil fuel free world. The Climate Justice Alliance states: "We envision a world:

- In which everyone lives a good life by being in a just and fair relationship with each other and within **healthy, interdependent ecosystems.**
- Based on a culture of sharing rather than hording; localized democracies rather than globalized exploitation; the Web of Life rather than the Chain of the Market. **Fairness, equity** and **ecological rootedness** are core values.
- That **celebrates and honors the beauty and diversity of life** and the rights of people to realize their **full potential** as creative beings." (CJA, emphasis added).

The Climate Justice Alliance works on **just transition**, the movement away from fossil fuels and towards a fossil fuel free society. At the international level, there has been a strong surge toward **earth jurisprudence**, which is a philosophical and legal view that endows Earth with the same values and legal rights as a person or a corporation. Known as the Rights of Nature, the position is stated as following:

> The terms Rights of Nature or Rights of Mother Earth are interchangeable, though Indigenous preference for the use of Mother Earth better describes our

> connection and relationship. Rights of Nature or Rights of Mother Earth seek to define equal legal rights for ecosystems to "exist, flourish, and regenerate their natural capacities." Recognizing these rights places obligations on humans to live within, not above, the natural world, of which we are only one part, and to protect and replenish the ecosystems upon which our mutual wellbeing depends. In essence, it is necessary to transform our human relationship with nature from property-based to a legal rights-bearing entity.
>
> We are pointing to the need for a wholly different framework that recognizes that Earth's living systems are not the enslaved property of humans. Just as it is wrong for men to consider women property or one race to consider another race as property, it is wrong for humans to see nature as property over which we have dominion. (Biggs, Goldtooth, and Lake 2017)

Mitigating the unknown and disastrous effects of climate change lies at the core of sustainability, because governmental and international actions have not been forthcoming in viable ways. As opportunities slip away and business as usual continues to dominate the global discourse, humans are placing our own lives, and those of future generations, into uncharted regions of risk and miasmic uncertainty.

INEQUALITY: GENDER AND WOMEN'S MOVEMENTS

Social inequality begs the question of how certain groups have fared with it. Hence, we will focus on global gender inequality, a major transnational social movement that offers extensive insights into social structures and the human condition. In chapter 2, we discussed secondary school enrollments by gender. Young girls in Sub-Saharan Africa and South Asia lag behind boys and behind other regions of the world. Only in developed countries is there 100 percent enrollment by gender in secondary education. Chapter 7 drew attention to the relationship between educational attainment and fertility transitions. Other related factors, such as family planning, labor force participation, household organization, family production, and reproduction are important variables in determining gender roles and statuses worldwide. Educational attainment is just one key to improving the status of women. At the same time, there are other structural obstacles that continually constrain women's struggle for equality. The global feminist movement and its manifestation in the development field are substantive arenas that illuminate both constraints and achievements.

Feminism

The feminist movement vastly precedes the lens and historical context of the modern development era. **Early feminism**, beginning as far back as the nineteenth century, involved gaining basic rights for women. **Second-wave feminism** in the 1970s was concerned with equality. This movement held different meanings for First and Third World women against diverse and nuanced differences in women's identity, orientation, and status among different societies (McMichael 2012). Below is an overview of how capitalism has historically undermined gender relations:

- As discussed in chapter 3, the transformation from common to private property denied most members of society access to and control over the means of production. Survival rested on obtaining wages and resulted in predominantly men's entry into the cash economy. In Sierra Leone, for example, Ishmael Beah, who wrote *A Long Way Gone: Memoirs of a Boy Soldier* (2007) lived with his stepmother while his biological father resided in a distant mining region of the country. Beah's stepmother relied on her husband's discretionary remittances to support the family. At one point, Beah's father informed him that he could no longer afford school fees.
- In chapter 3, we discussed how the market-based fur trade between Indigenous peoples such as the Iroquois and Cherokee with European fur traders brought both groups together into market relations and exchanges. Indigenous women, who had occupied central positions of authority in extended family and kin relations, were relegated to secondary status within the market-based cash economy. Thus, extended families declined and family structure became oriented toward the nuclear. Missionaries also contributed to the decline of women's autonomy and influence in Indigenous communities through the teachings related to the sanctity of the nuclear family.
- More recently, 1990s Structural Adjustment Programs (SAPs) enacted upon developing countries by multilateral agencies such as the IMF entailed significant national budget cuts that adversely affected women in the areas of education, social services, and health. In the 1990s, economic stagnation, unemployment, and divorce in the United States led to a condition known as the "feminization of poverty," in which single mothers with dependent children disproportionately bore the brunt of federal and state cuts in those social service and health areas that directly affected their and their children's social and economic well-being (Robbins 2011).

Women in Development (WID)

Women's inequality in development was officially recognized after the 1975 UN World Conference on Women (McMichael 2012). An immediate result from the conference was the **Women in Development (WID)** movement. The impulse was to extend women's involvement in the field of development and make them equals in the areas of employment, education, politics, and health. McMichael remarks that the impulse was to "institutionalize policy agendas committed to broad gender equality in a transformed concept of *human development*" (193, emphasis added). The early emphasis here pertained to remedies that inadvertently segregated women as a "special distinct topic," removed from general developmental discourse. Persistent feminist advocacy thus led to formulating alternative approaches under the **Gender and Development (GAD) initiative**. McMichael summarizes the overall WID/GAD feminist thread as "valuing equality in productive work; valuing the work of social reproduction; and reorienting social values from economism to humanism" (193). In 2000, the "Advocacy Guide to Women's World Demands," given during the World March of Women, declared:

> Neoliberalism and patriarchy feed off each other and reinforce each other in order to maintain the vast majority of women in a situation of cultural deprivation, social devaluation, economic marginalization, "invisibility" of their existence and labor, and the marketing and commercialization of their bodies. All these situations closely resemble apartheid (cited in McMichael, 193).

The feminist-inspired women's movement in development is a truly transnational one. Taking into account women's global diversity requires highly attuned cultural sensibilities and relativism. From Global North and Global South standpoints, different class, ethnic, religious, and sexual orientations can accentuate diversity, leading to cultural clashes and fragmentation (Robbins 2011). Nonetheless, the integrative process that underlies the recent set of feminist campaigns has broadly expanded from the earlier agenda-based orientation to an alternative relational orientation. New horizons include active women's participation in areas as diverse as the environment, human rights, employment, poverty, and fertility (see chapter 7).

We can surmise that overall, women's global struggle for equality has improved their standing but still faces obstacles from entrenched patriarchy. A brief assessment of the UN millennium development goal of gender equality recaps some of these gains and lingering obstacles:

> Goal 5: Achieve gender equality and empower all women and girls. While the world has achieved progress towards gender equality and women's empowerment under the Millennium Development Goals (including equal access to primary education between girls and boys), women and girls continue to suffer discrimination and violence in every part of the world. (United Nations)

Furthermore, the UN assesses specific goals met and areas that lag behind:

- About two-thirds of countries in the developing regions have achieved gender parity in primary education.
- In Southern Asia, only 74 girls were enrolled in primary school for every 100 boys in 1990. By 2012, the enrolment ratios were the same for girls as for boys.
- In Sub-Saharan Africa, Oceania, and Western Asia, girls still face barriers to entering both primary and secondary school.

- Women in Northern Africa hold less than one in five paid jobs in the nonagricultural sector. The proportion of women in paid employment outside the agriculture sector has increased from 35 percent in 1990 to 41 percent in 2015.
- In 46 countries, women now hold more than 30 percent of seats in national parliament in at least one chamber. (United Nations)

The UN also tabulates a **Gender Development Index**, similar to the Human Development Index. The aggregate data shows that women globally are living longer than men and have attained roughly the same educational levels. As we scroll down toward India (number 136), we observe, however, significant differences in mean years of schooling attained, coupled with low levels of primary education levels attained. Globally, there is a significant difference in GNI per capita PPP between men and women, regardless of country rank (Gender Development Index).

Other important measures are the number and percentages of women holding important political positions. Table 9.2 below shows the top ten countries and other countries noted in this volume where women hold relatively high level political positions:

TABLE 9.2 *Countries and Percentage of Women with High-Level Political Positions*

RANK	COUNTRY	WOMEN HOLDING POLITICAL POSITIONS %	GENDER DEVELOPMENT RANK
1	Rwanda	61%	159
2	Bolivia	53%	71
3	Cuba	49%	68
4	Nicaragua	46%	124
5	Sweden	44%	14
6	Mexico	43%	77
7	Finland	42%	23
7	Senegal	42%	162
9	South Africa	42%	119
10	Norway	41%	1
72	China	24%	90
93	Cambodia	20%	131
99	United States	19%	10
145	India	12%	131
181	Thailand	5%	87

Sources: Adapted from Inter-Parliamentary Union; UN Gender Development Index.

The above data shows women's political rise in representative governments. At the same time, differences remain in other measurable units when cross referenced with the Gender Development Index. For example, the United States ranks tenth on the GDI but has very low women's political representation. Rwanda ranks first in women's political representation but low on the GDI list. Hence, we need to examine the specific particulars and context that lie beneath the numbers for a given country.

Rwanda's case represents systemic change from the top down following the 1994 genocide and the ensuing turbulence that plagued the country (see chapter 5). Strongman Paul Kagame, the former Tutsi commander of the Rwandan Patriotic Front (RPF) and current President, has ruled the country since the genocide and allows for little dissent. With a postgenocide population that was estimated to be 60–70 percent women, Kagame mandated a 30-percent women's representation quota in parliament. In other formerly male-dominated occupational sectors of the country, Rwandan women work outside the household (previously unheard of), farm, and undertake other occupations, such as policing, that were once the providence of men alone. These gains by women, while impressive, are still met by entrenched patriarchy, similar to many other countries (Warner 2016).

At the same time, as Chugh (2013) reported for *The Guardian* on the high levels of domestic violence in the country:

> In spite of its impressive report card on female political empowerment, Rwanda is far from being a safe place for women. The country with a population of 11 million—52% of which is female—continues to have one of the highest incidences of gender-based and domestic violence in Africa. According to the United Nations Development Programme (UNDP), one in every three Rwandan women has experienced or continues to experience violence at the hands of her male relatives—mainly father and husband. Estimates released by Rwanda's Gender Desk in 2011 showed that up to 93% of the victims of physical and psychological abuse were women.
>
> "The problem of violence against women in Rwanda, as with many African countries, is rooted in the cultural beliefs and notions of masculinity reinforced through generations," says Peace Ruzage, CEO of Aspire Rwanda, a Kigali-based NGO providing free vocational skills to vulnerable women.

Likewise, as Brinkley (2011, 224–34) documents, widespread domestic and sexual violence in Cambodia is aggravated by widespread court and police corruption. A 2009 survey by the Cambodian Women's Affairs Ministry found the following:

- 70 percent of male and female respondents believed physical violence was "sometimes permissible," and
- 55 percent of female respondents stated that "they deserved to be beaten for questioning their husbands' spending or extramarital affairs."

Advances made by the global women's movement need to be tempered against remaining problems of harassment, abuse, and violence. In Cambodia, "acid or gasoline attacks," in which a woman is doused by her husband or another jealous rival with corrosive substances to permanently scar her, are widespread. The courts and laws are lax and/or corrupt when it comes to administering justice in these cases, and after a few sensational newspaper stories, they fade from view (Brinkley 2011). Importantly, however, we stress that violence against women is a global phenomenon and not only confined to the two example countries from above. In the United States and beyond, the burgeoning #MeToo movement is yet another clarion call for once again redressing long-standing critical gender-based concerns (see "Me Too", 2019). In sum, women's struggle for equality and humanity is ongoing and will remain so as new generations of women confront the embedded patriarchy of the modern world.

A QUESTION OF THE MIDDLE CLASS(ES)

Much of the content covered in this volume has focused on poverty and the poorer social classes. In chapters 2 through 6, we detailed the consequences of poverty. At the same time, both chapters 2 and 6 in particular provided strong evidence of rising incomes, global consumption convergence, and the post–Cold War entry of potentially three billion new consumers. These new entrants ascribe, more or less, to middle-class values, hopes, and aspirations. Entry into the middle class holds out an irresistible promise for a stable and financially secure economic life, education, leisure, meaningful work, material comfort, and so on. As a result of the global surge in incomes, upward mobility, and economic and employment opportunities (especially in Asia), we suggest that the middle class requires more concerted recognition as a locus of far-reaching social change in the coming future. A caveat is in order here. Globally, we cannot claim that there is one universal middle class (Pieterse 2018). Often historically categorized as the "vanguard" of liberal democracy and champions of human rights, environmental protection, justice, and progressive social change, the newly minted global middle classes will be increasingly difficult to lump into the one-size-fits-all historical model. At work are multifaceted class dynamics that respond to any number of ethnic, religious, populist, regional, economic, and social influences. These diverse influences produce variable middle-class orientations and outlooks (Pieterse 2018). Nonetheless, we argue that the middle class(es) will continue, as they have done in the past, to exert strong pressure on the direction and shape of society, whether this pressure is organized into a particular social movement or not. As such they are important social change agents, a fact that is accentuated in particular by the growing Asian middle class.

First, we must outline central tendencies that somewhat characterize the middle class(es). Above all, those in the middle class defend their privileges, wealth, and future prosperity. Governments realize this and tend to at least rhetorically cater to their needs and demands. The middle class demands accountability on the part of government because they pay taxes and expect quality services. How this all plays out reveals highly divergent outcomes. The relative size of the educated middle class is another important variable in shaping the direction of a country's economic development trajectory. According to the Asian Development Bank, members of a small middle class in a given emerging market country are

> generally extremely polarized, and find it difficult to reach consensus on economic issues; they are overly focused on the redistribution of resources between the elite and the impoverished masses, each of which alternates in controlling political power. Societies with a larger middle class are much less polarized and can more easily reach consensus on a broad range of issues and decisions relevant to economic development. (cited in Pieterse 2018, 157–58)

As Pieterse convincingly argues, the standard belief that the middle class equates with democracy and human rights simply doesn't apply in a wide variety of cases. Consider the following;

- During the Arab Spring of 2010, Egyptian media referred to the upstart Muslim Brotherhood as "terrorists," thereby casting itself on the side of the Egyptian military. As Pieterse observes, "Once this language [terrorists] was used it became inevitable that the military would intervene because now the protests had been framed in security terms. Thus, in effect, broadcast media—a key part of the middle class—had begun to call for military government. This is the moment of treason of the middle class. If democracy brings Islamism, better military rule than democracy" (160).
- In China, "a middle class without democracy" continues to support the Communist Party as long as income and living standards improve. Contrasted with conditional middle-class acquiescence to party rule, some of China's wealthiest families plan to emigrate within the next five years. As Pieterse puts it, "Preferred destinations are Hong Kong and Canada and key reasons are better education and employment opportunities for their children and environmental problems. If firms can go multinational, so can families if they have the means" (160).
- In Thailand, the urban-based middle class, known as the "Yellow Shirts," sided with the monarchy and military and viewed then Prime Minister Thaksin Shinawatra, who was elected on the basis of rural populist appeal, as corrupt. As Thaksin was forced into exile, his sister, Yingluck Shinawatra, won a landslide electoral victory on the same populist platform, which included a rice subsidy scheme. She was then forced out of power by a military coup and eventually left the country. As Pieterse summarizes, "if democracy unlocks the vote of the rural poor and comes with pro-poor policies, a significant segment (or a majority) of the middle class opts for military rule over democracy" (160).

On the side of radical extreme, we find that many of the founding members of some of the world's most militaristic and violent revolutionary movements come from solid and comfortable middle-class backgrounds. The Islamic State (ISIL) and its precursor, Al Qaeda, were both founded and led by middle-class intellectuals. The now-incarcerated Charles Taylor, head of the Liberian Revolutionary United Front and responsible for the war with neighboring Sierra Leone, received his undergraduate degree in the United States. In Rwanda, Ferdinand Nahimana, a close advisor to the genocidal leadership, received a doctorate in history from the University of Paris. Nahimana's reconstruction of a mythical Hutu past, coupled with his running of Hutu Power radio, greatly instigated and contributed to the 1994 genocide (see chapter 5). He was later convicted and sentenced to a 50-year prison sentence by the Rwanda International Criminal Tribunal for crimes against humanity. Lastly, the top leaders of the Khmer Rouge regime in Cambodia were educated in Paris in the 1950s. Other high-level cadre came from the Cambodian secondary and university teaching ranks. In sum, the middle-class past, present, and future is a dynamic instrumental vehicle for social change, whether examined as part of a social class or in terms of specific social movements. Indeed, as this section has elucidated, they warrant closer scrutiny as the harbingers of social change.

THE CITIZEN ACTIVIST AS DEVELOPMENT WORKER

In concluding this text, we extend an open invitation to the reader to reflect and examine their own life as to how they fit into this world of ours. We modestly suggest a model of the **citizen activist** as a potential development worker. Robbins (2011, 334), taking his impetus from noted development practitioner David C. Korten, argues that we need a new core culture, a new political center, and a new economic mainstream. Old strategies of creating countercultures, staging political protests, and designing economic alternatives fall short. Robbins calls for the emergence of the citizen activist, one who applies his or her particular expertise at the personal, household, community, national, and global levels. Perhaps a better way to phrase this is to "think globally and act locally; think locally and act globally."

Robbins aptly observes that the problems the world is experiencing are due to declines in political, social, and natural capital. Fueled by the doctrine of perpetual economic growth, **political capital**, our sense of civic virtue; **social capital**, the real and meaningful connections we have with other individuals based on the norms of reciprocity and trust; and **natural capital**, our relationship with the environment, are all being translated into **economic capital**. Economic capital consists of the assigning of monetary value to other forms of capital that were, at one time, nonmonetary. In other words, political, social, and natural capital are reduced to dollars and cents. The results have been disastrous. Voter apathy and lack of access to political decision-makers opens up space for lobbying by special interests, corporate meddling in political affairs, and the undue influence of money on political elections. The decline of what is known as civic virtue and active participation in public affairs, combined with slavish devotion to work, requiring two income earners per household, and the transfer of what was once based on reciprocity into profit-motivated behavior in health, education, food, and other services are all endemic to contemporary US life. The decline in natural capital was previously addressed in the unsustainable way US consumers live and the continued reliance on fossil fuels. Inaction on rethinking these "given values" gives rise to the coming specter of the climate change catastrophe.

To his credit, Robbins (2011) lists numerous everyday recommendations on how these deleterious effects can be reversed and restored by everyone. For Robbins (2011) our sense of what we value and the choices we make lie at the heart of the new culture, new political center, and new economic mainstream. To restore political capital, for instance, campaign financing reform is desperately needed. To restore social capital, one should shop locally and bank with local credit unions that have committed to communities. To restore natural capital, Robbins creatively recommends that living assets, such as the trees planted in our yards, should be considered as real assets, in contrast to virtual assets controlled by large international banks. While they may appear out of the ordinary, these recommendations can become everyday practices if our values and the choices we make line up with them.

Similar to Robbins, the UN offers a guide on what can be done to move toward a sustainable world. "The Lazy Person's Guide to Saving the World" (United Nations, 2019) is filled with simple, everyday actions that can instill in us the **practice of sustainability**. It is unrealistic to expect or confront people to make dramatic changes in their lives overnight. We do hope and expect that our readers, as educated persons, possess the knowledge to make informed and knowledgeable choices in their lives. In part, this is what is meant by **civic virtue**. Become virtuous!

What other recommendations do you envision that can restore political, economic, and social capital in your life?

Consider the following quote from Heim et al. (1986, 112) that defines the citizen activist as a development worker.

BOX 9.1

A good development worker has to be a rebel. The act of rebellion has its causes in one's personal existence. If one decides to rebel, it must be because one has decided that human society has some positive value. One tries to see things as they really are, without the concept of "given values". Values are developed and unfolded through one's own efforts and understanding, and through the cultivation of self-reliance.

> The rebel sees that all problems are contrary to satisfaction. This also includes the conflict between one's desires and the facts of life. One aims to solve the problems and conflicts, which are the reason for one's suffering. The burden to solve un-satisfactoriness is however, not shifted to an external agency. One gets on with the real task of developing one's inner forces and qualities. Values are deducted from the conditions of living. And as Life is a continuous process, values have to be accepted along with suffering which necessarily involves the limits of the possible.
>
> The rebel revolts.
>
> The nature of revolt can be the revolt of the poor against the rich, or the revolt against life itself. The first is concerned with equal rights for all, and the second is seeking deliverance which one must secure by themselves. Each individual is solely responsible for their own liberation. The cause of one's suffering is desire which keeps life going. It is a desire for clarity and unity against the suffering of life and death.

The development worker is an individual who has been stripped to their essential humanness and who questions the meaning of the world and one's place in it. The development worker occupies a crucial link in the phenomenon known as alternative development. Akin to the "existential individual," as evident in post-Second World War Western literature and philosophy, the development worker also draws complimentary parallels with Buddhism. The question that needs to be asked is, where will we find the conditions that permit practices that will allow the development worker to grow and flourish? How will the development worker resist the inroads made by the official "discourses of power" and the conflict-prone culture of national and global capitalism? In many respects, the acts of struggle best embodied in collective social action, covered in this concluding chapter, require close attention and serve as an individual and collective guide. Collective social movements provide the key nexus toward unlocking the dilemmas and paradoxes of modern life and development. We end with this idea of the citizen activist as development worker and its latent potential for improving our collective lives. Again, the matter rests on our conscience and values, expressed in the everyday choices we make, individually of course, but more importantly, collectively.

REFERENCES

Beah, Ishmael. *A Long Way Gone: Memoirs of a Boy Soldier.* New York: Sarah Crichton Books, 2007.

Becker, Elizabeth. *When the War Was Over: The Voices of Cambodia's Revolution and Its People.* New York: Simon & Schuster, 1986.

Biggs, Shannon, Tom B. K. Goldtooth, and Osprey Orielle Lake, eds. "Rights of Nature and Mother Earth: Rights-Based Law for Systemic Change." Oakland, CA: Movement Rights, 2017. http://www.ienearth.org/wp-content/uploads/2017/11/RONME-RightsBasedLaw-final-1.pdf.

Brinkley, Joel. *Cambodia's Curse: The Modern History of a Troubled Land.* New York: Public Affairs, 2011.

Chandler, David P. *Brother Number One: A Political Biography of Pol Pot.* Thailand, Burma, and Indochina edition. Chiang Mai, Thailand: Silkworm Books, 2000.

Chugh, Nishtha. "A Drive to Beat Rwanda's Gender-Based Violence." *The Guardian.* November 22, 2013. http//www.theguardian.com/global-development-professionals-network/2013/nov/22/rwanda-gender-based-violence.

Climate Justice Alliance. http://www.ourpowercampaign.org/. "ourcampaignpower.org" June, 2018

Escobar, Arturo. *Encountering Development: The Making and Unmaking of the Third World.* Princeton, NJ: Princeton University Press, 1995.

Heim, Franz G., Bantorn Ondam, Jitti Mongolnchaiarunya, and Akin Rabibhadana. *How to Develop the Small Farming Sector: The Case of Thailand.* Department of Community Development, Faculty of Social Administration. Bangkok: Thammasat University, 1986.

Inter-Parliamentary Union. "Women in National Parliaments." http://archive.ipu.org/wmn-e/classif.htm.

Khagram, Sanjeev, James V. Riker, and Kathryn Sikkink, eds. *Restructuring World Politics: Transnational Social Movements, Networks, and Norms.* Minneapolis, MN: University of Minnesota Press, 2002.

Khokar, Tariq, and Umar Serajuddin. "Should We Continue to Use the Term 'Developing World'?" World Bank: The Data Blog. November 16, 2015. https://blogs.worldbank.org/opendata/should-we-continue-use-term-developing-world.

Klein, Naomi. *This Changes Everything: Capitalism vs. the Climate.* New York: Simon & Schuster, 2014.

McMichael, Phillip. *Development and Social Change.* 5th ed. Thousand Oaks, CA: Sage Publications, 2012.

"Me Too." Me Too Movement. https://metoomvmt.org/.

Pieterse, Jan Nederveen. *Multipolar Globalization: Emerging Economies and Development.* New York: Routledge, 2018.

Potter, Robert B., Tony Binns, Jennifer A. Elliot, and David Smith. *Geographies of Development: An Introduction to Development Studies.* 3rd ed. New York: Routledge, 2013.

Robbins, Richard H. *Global Problems and the Culture of Capitalism.* 5th ed. Upper Saddle River, NJ: Prentice Hall, 2011.

Schumacher, E. F. *Small Is Beautiful: Economics as if People Mattered.* New York: Harper & Row Publishers, 1973.

Scott, James C. *Weapons of the Weak: Everyday Forms of Peasant Resistance.* New Haven, CT: Yale University Press, 1985.

Strangio, Sebastian. *Hun Sen's Cambodia.* New Haven, CT: Yale University Press, 2014.

The Indigenous Environmental Network (IEN). "Regaining Food Sovereignty: Neyaab Nimamoomin Mewinzha Gaa-inajigeyang." https://www.ienearth.org/regaining-food-sovereignty-neyaab-nimamoomin-mewinzha-gaa-inajigeyang/.

UN Development Program (UNDP). "Gender Development Index." Human Development Reports. http://hdr.undp.org/en/composite/GDI.

United Nations. "Goal 5: Achieve Gender Equality and Empower All Women and Girls." Sustainable Development Goals. http://www.un.org/sustainabledevelopment/gender-equality/.

United Nations. "The Lazy Person's Guide to Saving the World." Sustainable Development Goals. http://www.un.org/sustainabledevelopment/takeaction/.

Warner, Gregory. "It's The No. 1 Country For Women In Politics—But Not In Daily Life." National Public Radio (NPR) Goats and Soda Blog. July 29, 2016. https://www.npr.org/sections/goatsandsoda/2016/07/29/487360094/invisibilia-no-one-thought-this-all-womans-debate-team-could-crush-it.

World Commission on Environment and Development (WCED). "Report of the World Commission on Environment and Development: Our Common Future." Oxford: Oxford University Press, 1987. http://www.un-documents.net/our-common-future.pdf.

CPSIA information can be obtained
at www.ICGtesting.com
Printed in the USA
LVHW012248060819
626741LV00002B/9/P